THE WRITER'S RESOURCE: Readings for Composition

The Writer's Resource

READINGS FOR COMPOSITION

Third Edition

Susan Day
Illinois State University

Elizabeth McMahan
Illinois State University

McGraw-Hill, Inc.
New York St. Louis San Francisco Auckland Bogotá
Caracas Lisbon London Madrid Mexico Milan
Montreal New Delhi Paris San Juan Singapore
Sydney Tokyo Toronto

THE WRITER'S RESOURCE: Readings for Composition

4 5 6 7 8 9 0 DOC DOC 9 5 4 3 2

ISBN 0-07-016157-7

This book was set in Times Roman by Ruttle, Shaw & Wetherill, Inc.
The editors were Lesley Denton and David Dunham;
the production supervisor was Kathryn Porzio.
The cover was designed by Amy Becker.
R. R. Donnelley & Sons Company was printer and binder.

Library of Congress Cataloging-in-Publication Data

The Writer's resource: readings for composition / [edited by] Susan Day, Elizabeth McMahan.—3rd ed.
p. cm.
Includes index.
ISBN 0-07-016157-7
1. College readers. 2. English language—Rhetoric. I. Day, Susan. II. McMahan, Elizabeth.
PE1417.W674 1991
808'.0427—dc20 90-13285

ABOUT THE AUTHORS

SUSAN DAY has lived in Bloomington-Normal, Illinois, for over twenty years, attending Illinois State University as a student (B.S. in English Education, M.S. in English) and working there as a teacher since 1973. Nevertheless, Susie has managed to have an eventful and entertaining life, portions of which she will relate in surprising detail to complete strangers. With Elizabeth McMahan, she has co-authored three college texts for McGraw-Hill: *The Writer's Rhetoric and Handbook, The Writer's Handbook,* and *The Writer's Resource: Readings for Composition.* Because her presentations are practical, funny, and brief, Susie frequently appears as a speaker at professional conventions. If one could make a living as a conversationalist, she would; the occupation of writing helpful, amusing textbooks runs a close second.

ELIZABETH McMAHAN, professor of English at Illinois State University, grew up in College Station where her father taught physics at Texas A & M. Her B.A. and M.A. degrees in English are from the University of Houston; her Ph.D. (in American literature) is from the University of Oregon, where she enjoyed the benefits of an NDEA Fellowship. While still in graduate school, she wrote her first text, *A Crash Course in Composition,* now in its fourth edition, published by McGraw-Hill. Since then she has embraced the joys of collaborative writing with Susan Day. They have published the following texts with McGraw-Hill: *The Writer's Rhetoric and Handbook, The Writer's Handbook,* and *The Writer's Resource: Readings for Composition.*

In 1976 Dr. McMahan received the Illinois Arts Council Essay Award, and in 1990 she was selected to deliver the Arts and Sciences Lecture at Illinois State University. For five years she served as Director of Writing Programs.

To Jane Lee

CONTENTS

THEMATIC CONTENTS

CONSIDERING RACE

LIVING TODAY

PREFACE

This collection of readings, designed to help students improve their writing, has benefited from several years of classroom use. Writing classes from high school preparatory to community college to four-year university have given us valuable advice and gratifying encouragement in our efforts to provide essays and imaginative literature that will inspire students to write well. We have retained this format from the original edition:

Part 1, *The Writer's Design.* The selections, all serving specific rhetorical purposes, are intended as brief and interesting models for analysis.

Part 2, *The Reader's Resources.* Since any introductory course in composition should include discussion of the deliberate misuse of language, this section offers readings exposing the language of deception as well as providing examples of slanted writing and advertisements for in-class analysis.

Part 3, *Chapter 12, Using Sources.* This last section briefly covers the skills students need in order to compose fair and proficient essays using sources—summarizing, paraphrasing, integration of sources, documentation, and avoiding plagiarism.

Since sound organization is fundamental to good writing, all of the selections—essays, short stories, and poems—are arranged according to their major pattern of organization. Within each section the difficulty of the essays ranges from simple to challenging. The stories and poems provide further insights into organizational techniques and offer instructive examples of the skillful use of language. These imaginative works also serve to spark the process of invention and generate ideas for writing. Our primary purpose in including them, though, is to enrich the teaching of composition.

In this revision we have weeded out any selections that were outdated as well as any that students, colleagues, or reviewers found problematic for any reason. We have added pieces that are up to date and, we think, perfect for the classroom. The new essays are these: Robert Benchley's "Why I Am Pale," Langston Hughes's "Salvation," Sharon Begley's "The Stuff That Dreams Are Made Of," Marisa Bowe's "Black to Basics," Mary Kay Blakely's "I Do, I Do, I Do . . . ," David Denby's "Walk on the Mild Side," Andrew Potok's "Dash and Me," Bette Lee Sung's "Bicultural Conflict," Michael Green and Beverly Rainbolt's "He Doesn't Hit Me, But . . . ," Lerone Bennett, Jr.'s "The Ten Biggest Myths about the Black Family," Harry Middleton's "Trouble on the Wind," Susan J. Douglas's "Flex Appeal, Buns of Steel, and the Body in Question," Benjamin Spock's "Are You Giving Your Kids Too Much?" Clarence Page's "The Trouble with Legalizing Drugs," Joan Morgan's "The Pro-Rape Culture," Ellen Goodman's "We Do Not Need More Talk of War," Kurt Vonnegut, Jr.'s "What I'd Say If They Asked Me," Dan Wakefield's "Celebrating 'The Small Moments of Discovery,' " and James Hynes's, "And They Called It Yuppie Love. . . ." We have added one new story, Katharine Brush's "The Birthday Party," and these new poems: D. H. Lawrence's "Baby Running Barefoot," Ezra Pound's "In a Station of the Metro," and Edna St. Vincent Millay's "You Will Be Sorry."

Since the prereading exercises won approval from both students and teachers, we have added a number of new ones. These usually appear before pieces that have proven to be somewhat difficult for students. Prereading exercises enable students to develop an appropriate mind-set for reading a selection with understanding and enjoyment by evoking their own thoughts and feelings about the subject to be encountered. Often these activities provide additional writing practice as well.

The discussion questions following each reading—including the stories and poems—focus on rhetorical features. A brief biography of the author appears before each selection; following each reading are these study aids:

Vocabulary. Difficult words defined briefly in context.

Design and Meaning. Five or six discussion questions focusing on rhetorical analysis.

Similarity and Difference. One discussion question asking students to compare or contrast this reading with another in order to understand elements of style, diction, tone, meaning, etc.

Short Writing Ideas. Prewriting suggestion, process work, model imitation, etc.

Longer Writing Ideas. Essay topics for papers of 500 to 700 words.

Vocabulary Check. Matching, fill-in-the-blanks, sentence-completion, and word-power exercises.

The *Instructor's Manual* which accompanies this text provides practical suggestions for using these materials in the classroom.

We wish to thank the many people who have helped us put this book together, including our excellent editors at McGraw-Hill, Lesley Denton and David Dunham, and the following reviewers for the third edition: Michael Daly, Glendale College; Rebecca Imschweiler, Manatee Community College; Philip Pierpont, Vincennes University; Ruben Quintero, California State University, Los Angeles; Rene Viargues, California Maritime Academy; and Brenda Williams, Massasoit Community College.

As always, we have depended on the kindness of our dear friends David Lee and Dan LeSeure.

Susan Day
Elizabeth McMahan

TO THE STUDENT

We have chosen these readings primarily to provide you with helpful models of style and structure. At the same time, we have tried hard to select pieces that you will enjoy and find enlightening. The idea is to encourage in you a fondness for language and a sharp eye for technique, both of which will serve to make you a more skillful writer.

The selections include poetry and stories as well as essays, and the writing assignments sometimes ask you to do what might be called "creative writing." You may want to know why you should ponder a poem or describe a fantasy when the writing you will need to do in the working world consists of ordering parts from the Acme Showcase Company, reporting on water damage from burst pipes, or describing right-of-way specifications for a city street. Although these quite different kinds of writing appear to have little in common, the creative exercises will stretch your imagination and bolster your confidence. Any practice that helps you to realize fully your power over words will prove worthwhile. The ease of expression you develop during creative writing (when no rules apply) will carry over into anything you choose to write. Of course, every writer has times when the words stubbornly have minds of their own, kicking each other in the shins and refusing to stand nicely in line; but the more you think about and practice writing, the briefer these little rebellions will be.

Many students feel confident that they can understand an essay, but turn into quivering masses of uncertainty when given a poem to read. Don't let yourself be intimidated by the unusual word patterns of poets. If the meaning is unclear on first reading, go over it again—

aloud this time. Give yourself the pleasure of puzzling out the meaning. Assume an open, relaxed approach to the literary selections, and you will find that you can learn from them as much about rhetoric as you can from a comfortably paragraphed page of prose.

Your task will be made easier by the list of words and definitions following each reading. These definitions supply only the meaning of the word in the context of that selection. The words defined are those that may be new to you (like *interlocutor* or *vacuity*), those that carry a different meaning in the selection from the usual one (*exact* used as a verb, for example), and those that have changed meaning over time (*fancy* meaning "imagination," for instance).

Your most taxing work in using this text involves thinking. You will need to think critically in analyzing the selections, and you will have to think hard in planning and practicing your writing. But you should find, as you progress, that the line between work and pleasure grows steadily less distinct.

1

THE WRITER'S DESIGN

Description

YOU KNOW WHAT DESCRIPTIVE WRITING IS. It makes you smile or sigh; it causes shivers to run up your spine; it brings tears to your eyes; it makes you say to yourself, "Yes, that's just it. That's just what it's like."

Although you may seldom need to produce long passages of pure description except for your own personal satisfaction, good descriptive details are welcome in almost every kind of writing. Besides adding liveliness and interest to your work, clear description helps keep your readers from getting fogged in by abstractions and generalities.

But how is it done? What can you do with that limp paragraph you just wrote, lying there like yesterday's lunch? What you need to do is add images or create atmosphere. *Images* usually create mental pictures, but they can appeal imaginatively to emotions and to other senses besides sight. In "Auto Wreck," a poem you will read in this chapter, Karl Shapiro describes the flashing light of an ambulance this way: ". . . one ruby flare / Pulsing out red light like an artery." Surely that image prompts you to envision blood gushing from a wound, as well as crimson light streaming from a revolving flasher.

In adding small descriptive details you need to be especially sensitive to all the words you know that will convey thoughts and feelings. Choose the most specific one—precisely the right one. If you have written, "I felt terrible about what happened," you need to question yourself closely as you revise. Exactly how did you feel: humiliated, guilty, fearful, frustrated, sickened, or sad? Consult a thesaurus (a dictionary of synonyms) if you can't come up with the exact word. Consider always the many gradations and fine distinctions among feelings you may want to express. Were you restless, bored, exhausted, enervated, or brain dead? Impressed, surprised, shocked, astounded, or stunned? You don't need to add a slew of words to the page to achieve clear description. Just make sure the words you choose are the words you want.

We mentioned atmosphere as another component of descriptive writing. *Atmosphere,* which is quite similar to mood or tone, produces that foreboding feeling you get when reading Edgar Allan Poe's description of the house of Usher or that pleasant lift you get when reading Mark Twain's adventures as a river pilot. Atmosphere is often named as an emotion: a piece of writing can be depressing, cheerful, breathlessly exciting, hopeful, glum, humorous, expectant, anxious, nostalgic. Shapiro's image of the red light on the ambulance conveys an atmosphere of dread or danger partly because of its actual nature (a warning light) and partly because of its imaginative suggestion of spilled blood. The image has infinitely more impact than cold dishwater statements like, "An ambulance came up, flashing its red light," or even, "The flashing red light of the approaching ambulance gave me the creeps."

We have collected in this section a group of readings that contain strong images and detectable atmospheres. We hope that studying these selections and performing the activities following them will lead you to an understanding of how the readings achieve their effectiveness through descriptive techniques—precise word choice, clear images, and carefully selected details. Study these techniques; imitate them; adapt them to suit yourself, and your writing also can sparkle.

essays

Dereck Williamson

The Mudbacks

Besides producing humorous articles for popular magazines, Williamson, a journalist, also writes amusing "do-it-yourself" books. The following bit of nostalgia about bicycles in the good old days appeared in the *Saturday Review* in June of 1971.

I see by the local paper that the New Jersey town where I live will hold a bicycle safety check next week. The chief of police will inspect bikes at the municipal parking lot; checking "brakes, lights, sounding devices, reflectors, and general bike condition. Those bikes which are approved will be marked with a 1971 inspection sticker." [1]

I remember the bike I had when I was a kid. We didn't have bike inspections in those days, and it was a lucky thing. My bike would have flunked. Everybody's bike would have failed, mostly on "general bike condition." [2]

Many safety devices were missing. One kid had no handle bars. And take reflectors. None of the bikes had reflectors because the reflectors were fastened to the fenders, and the fenders got torn off early in the game. Nobody worried about fenders; you worried about spokes. It was very important to have enough spokes so that the wheel remained more or less round. Each of my bike wheels had thirty-six spokes, and I found by experience that I couldn't afford to lose more than twenty. When a wheel lost too many spokes it began to sag and it was difficult to ride the bike fast. [3]

The whole point was to ride the bike fast. You could tell a really fast bike rider by the streak of mud up his back. [4]

I don't recall any of the bikes having "sounding devices." Once in a while, a fancy bike came equipped with a "tank" mounted between the upper-frame bars. Inside the tank was an electric horn that made a thin beeping sound for about a day. Then the battery corroded, and the whole bike turned green. [5]

The most popular sounding device was the bike rider himself. He screamed when confronted by any obstacle, real or imaginary. Sometimes his voice changed in mid-scream, a terrible noise that could raise the mud on the back of your neck. [6]

There were three popular ways of stopping a bike—"coaster brake," "hand brake," and "hitting something." Less popular methods included accidentally sticking your foot in the front wheel or clamping hard on just the front hand brake, which made you do a tight little somersault over the handle bars. [7]

Another rather sloppy way to stop was to get your pantcuff caught between the front sprocket and the chain, causing a sudden shift of weight to starboard. You slowly fell off the bike and scraped along the ground. The bike, still attached to your leg, jarred around on top of you until an axle bolt stuck in your ear. [8]

Few bikes had built-in lights. For riding at night, you just stuck a flashlight in a metal bracket mounted on the handle bars. During the day, the bracket stuck up and lacerated your chest whenever you ran into something. [9]

A safety inspection also would have produced penalty points for loose seats and handle bars caused by stripped bolts or no bolts, missing pedal parts (just a spike stuck out), lack of air in the tires, or lack of tires to put air in. [10]

No bike would have had a prayer of passing a modern inspection. It's just as well. There was no place to put a sticker anyway. [11]

VOCABULARY

lacerate	to tear jaggedly
sprocket	a toothed wheel designed to fit into the links of a chain
starboard	the right-hand side, usually of a ship or airplane
style	way of using words to express thoughts

DESIGN AND MEANING

1. Does Williamson use an informal or a formal style? How can you tell? Why do you think he chose this style?
2. Williamson's essay is humorous because he exaggerates (see paragraph 5) and he uses unexpected phrasing ("There were three popular ways of stopping a bike—'coaster brake,' 'hand brake,' and 'hitting something.' "). Find more examples of exaggeration and unexpected phrasing. What other elements appeal to your sense of humor?

3. Compare the quotation from the newspaper in paragraph 1 with the content of the rest of the essay. What does the comparison reveal about how Williamson chose his material?
4. Is it your general impression that Williamson approves of modern bike inspections? What do you think his attitude is? Try to find parts of the essay that suggest his attitude.
5. Can you picture the mudbacks' bikes? What specific details appeal to you?

SIMILARITY AND DIFFERENCE

Read Mark Twain's "Boyhood Remembered," which follows, and comment on the difference in writing style between Twain and Williamson. Do the two pieces have anything in common?

SHORT WRITING IDEA

Make a list of phrases that describe an object you are especially fond of now or were fond of as a child. Try to list twenty-five phrases. Do not forget to appeal to senses other than sight.

LONGER WRITING IDEA

Using an informal style, write an essay that describes some element of your childhood that you see as quite different from its replacement for children of a younger generation. Some possibilities: dolls, bikes, grade school, books, cartoons, Halloween.

Mark Twain

Boyhood Remembered

In his day, Mark Twain (1835-1910) was celebrated worldwide as a novelist and humorist. He was also a master of descriptive and satirical writing. This selection is taken from his entertaining, but none too accurate, *Autobiography*.

I spent some parts of every year at the farm until I was twelve or thirteen years old. The life which I led there with my cousins was full of charm, and so is the memory of it yet. I can call back the solemn twilight and mystery of the deep woods, the earthy smells, the faint odors of the wild flowers, the sheen of rain-washed foliage, the rattling clatter of drops when the wind shook the trees, the far-off hammering of woodpeckers and the muffled drumming of wood pheasants in the remoteness of the forest, the snapshot glimpses of disturbed wild creatures scurrying through the grass—I can call it all back and make it as real as it ever was, and as blessed. I can call back the prairie, and its loneliness and peace, and a vast hawk hanging motionless in the sky, with his wings spread wide and the blue of the vault showing through the fringe of the end feathers. I can see the woods in their autumn dress, the oaks purple, the hickories washed with gold, the maples and the sumachs luminous with crimson fires, and I can hear the rustle made by the fallen leaves as we plowed through them. I can see the blue clusters of wild grapes hanging among the foliage of the saplings, and I remember the taste of them and the smell. I know how the wild blackberries looked, and how they tasted, and the same with the pawpaws, the hazelnuts, and the persimmons; and I can feel the thumping rain, upon my head, of hickory nuts and walnuts when we were out in the frosty dawn to scramble for them with the pigs, and the gusts of wind loosed them and sent them down. I know the stain of blackberries, and how pretty it is, and I know the stain of walnut hulls, and how little it minds soap and water, also what grudged experience it had of either of them. I know the taste of maple sap, and when to gather it, and how to arrange the troughs and the delivery tubes, and how to boil down the juice, and how to hook the sugar after it is made, also how much better hooked sugar tastes than any that is honestly come by, let bigots say what they will. I know how a prize watermelon looks when it is sunning its fat rotundity among pumpkin vines and "simblins"; I know how to tell when it is ripe without "plugging" it; I know how inviting it looks when it is cooling itself in a tub of water under the bed, waiting; I know how it looks when it lies on the table in the sheltered great floor space between house and kitchen, and the children gathered for the sacrifice and their mouths watering; I know the crackling sound it makes when the carving knife enters its end, and I can see the split fly along in front of the blade as the knife cleaves its way to the other end; I can see its halves fall apart and display the rich red meat and the black seeds, and the heart standing up, a luxury fit for the elect; I know how a boy looks behind a yard-long slice of that melon, and I know how he feels; for I have been there. I know the taste of the watermelon which has been honestly come by, and I know the taste of the watermelon which has been acquired by art. Both taste good but the experienced know which tastes best.

VOCABULARY

bigot	a narrow-minded, prejudiced person
elect	persons chosen by God for salvation and eternal life
foliage	the leaves of plants and trees
hook	to steal
luminous	full of light
plug	to cut a chunk from a melon to test its ripeness
rotundity	roundness
sumach	a kind of leafy plant with large, furry, red fruit
vault	an arched ceiling or roof

DESIGN AND MEANING

1. Find descriptive details that appeal to each of the five senses: smell, taste, sound, sight, touch.
2. Reread one part, marking repetitions of similar phrases ("I can call back," for example) and of similar grammatical patterns ("I know how a prize watermelon looks," "I know the crackling sound it makes," "I know how a boy looks"). Then listen to the piece as it is read aloud. What is the effect of the repetitions?
3. The average written sentence in English is twenty to twenty-five words long. Count the words in three of Twain's sentences: one

near the beginning, one near the middle, and one near the end. What is the effect of the unusual sentence length?

4. Looking at the end of the piece and considering what you know of the narrator as a boy, state which watermelon tastes best. How do you know?

SIMILARITY AND DIFFERENCE

"Another Copter," which appears later in Chapter 1, was written for publication in a newspaper. "The Mudbacks" was written for publication in a magazine. "Boyhood Remembered" is part of a book, Mark Twain's *Autobiography.* What comments can you make concerning the differences in descriptive writing among the three kinds of printed matter?

SHORT WRITING IDEA

Go to one of your favorite places (imaginatively or in reality) and make a list of details appealing to the senses of sound and smell. Then make the list into one or two long sentences of description.

LONGER WRITING IDEA

Pretend that you are writing your own autobiography. Describe a regular annual event that you attend or visit that you make, imitating Twain's style.

VOCABULARY CHECK

Using a dictionary, fill each blank with the appropriate variant of one of the vocabulary words above.

1. The moon was the ______ of the still, silvery landscape.
2. The kindergartners arranged orange and yellow shapes to make a ______ pattern for the fall bulletin board.
3. Prejudice against male nurses is a ______ attitude.
4. The little funeral director was red-faced and ______ in appearance, but quite spry.
5. The Puritans prayed for their ______ by God.

PREREADING EXERCISE

At the edge of our consciousness, our physical comfort and discomfort affect us all the time. Sometimes, these feelings are extreme enough to intrude into our thoughts and actions. Write a paragraph about a situation in which you feel physically very comfortable or very uncomfortable. Try to give details that will help your reader feel the experience.

Robert Benchley

Why I Am Pale

Robert Benchley (1889–1945) excelled at writing humorous essays. His tone is similar to James Thurber's. He wrote several collections with surprising titles like *My Ten Years in a Quandary* (1936). Talented also as a radio and movie star, he secured an Academy Award for his part in the film *How to Sleep.* He worked as an editor for *Life* magazine and served as *Harvard Lampoon's* president. His focus on the problems and trials of "the little man" won him a spot in the public heart. He is the father of Peter Benchley, author of *Jaws.*

One of the reasons (in case you give a darn) for that unreasonable pallor of mine in mid-Summer, is that I can seem to find no comfortable position in which to lie in the sun. A couple of minutes on my elbows, a couple of minutes on my back, and then the cramping sets in and I have to scramble to my feet. And you can't get very tanned in four minutes. [1]

I see other people, especially women (who must be made of rubber), taking books to the beach or up on the roof for a whole day of lolling about in the sun in various attitudes of relaxation, hardly moving from one position over a period of hours. I have even tried it myself. [2]

But after arranging myself in what I take, for the moment, to be a comfortable posture, with vast areas of my skin exposed to the actinic rays and the book in a shadow so that I do not blind myself, I find that my elbows are beginning to dig their way into the sand, or that they are acquiring "sheet-burns" from the mattress; that the small of my back is sinking in as far as my abdomen will allow, and that both knees are bending backward, with considerable tugging at the ligaments. [3]

This is obviously not the way for me to lie. So I roll over on my back, holding the book up in the air between my eyes and the sun. I am not even deluding myself by this maneuver. I know that it won't work for long. So, as soon as paralysis of the arms sets in, I drop the book on my chest (without having read more than three consecutive words), thinking that perhaps I may catch a little doze. [4]

But sun shining on closed eyelids (on *my* closed eyelids) soon induces large purple azaleas whirling against a yellow background, and the sand at the back of my neck starts crawling. (I can be stark [5] naked and still have something at the back of my neck for sand to get in under.) So it is a matter of perhaps a minute and a half before I am over on my stomach again with a grunt, this time with the sand in my lips.

[6] There are several positions in which I may arrange my arms, all of them wrong. Under my head, to keep the sand or mattress out of my mouth; down straight at my sides, or stretched out like a cross; no matter which, they soon develop unmistakable symptoms of arthritis and have to be shifted, also with grunting.

[7] Lying on one hip, with one elbow supporting the head, is no better, as both joints soon start swelling and aching, with every indication of becoming infected, and often I have to be assisted to my feet from this position.

[8] Once on my feet, I try to bask standing up in various postures, but this results only in a sunburn on the top of my forehead and the entire surface of my nose, with occasional painful blisters on the tops of my shoulders. So gradually, trying to look as if I were just ambling aimlessly about, I edge my way toward the clubhouse, where a good comfortable chair and a long, cooling drink soon put an end to all this monkey-business.

[9] I am afraid that I am more the pale type, and should definitely give up trying to look rugged.

VOCABULARY

actinic rays	light rays of short wavelengths that produce photochemical reactions
azaleas	big, bright flowers
pallor	unnatural paleness

DESIGN AND MEANING

1. What is Benchley's main purpose in this essay—to express himself, to inform the reader, to persuade the reader, or to entertain the reader? How did you decide on the main purpose?
2. What two senses are emphasized in this description? Find ten examples of images that appeal to these senses.
3. Who might enjoy reading this essay? Why?
4. What does Benchley reveal about himself in the closing? What does he imply about sunbathing?

SIMILARITY AND DIFFERENCE

Both "Why I Am Pale" and "The Mudbacks" derive part of their humor from descriptions of pain. How can you explain this anomaly?

SHORT WRITING IDEA

Write a one-sentence summary of "Why I Am Pale." Compare your summary with two other students' summaries and write a paragraph pointing out the differences you see.

LONGER WRITING IDEA

Though Benchley's tone in "Why I Am Pale" is light, underlying the essay is a hint of ridicule for the practice of sunbathing. Write a light essay describing some common practice that you find a bit ridiculous: for example, playing bridge, video games, or soccer; college beer-drinking contests; studying *The Wasteland.*

George Orwell

A Hanging

Born in India and educated in England, George Orwell (1903–1950), whose real name was Eric Blair, wrote novels and essays which have established him as perhaps the finest satirist of the twentieth century. "A Hanging" reflects his experience as a young man doing five years' service with the Imperial Police in Burma and is included in *Shooting an Elephant and Other Essays* (1945).

It was in Burma, a sodden morning of the rains. A sickly light, like yellow tinfoil, was slanting over the high walls into the jail yard. We were waiting outside the condemned cells, a row of sheds fronted with double bars, like small animal cages. Each cell measured about ten feet by ten and was quite bare within except for a plank bed and a pot of drinking water. In some of them brown silent men were squatting at the inner bars, with their blankets draped round them. These were the condemned men, due to be hanged within the next week or two. [1]

One prisoner had been brought out of his cell. He was a Hindu, a puny wisp of a man, with a shaven head and vague liquid eyes. He had a thick, sprouting moustache, absurdly too big for his body, rather like the moustache of a comic man on the films. Six tall Indian warders were guarding him and getting him ready for the gallows. Two of them stood by with rifles with fixed bayonets, while the others handcuffed him, passed a chain through his handcuffs and fixed it to their belts, and lashed his arms tight to his sides. They crowded very close about him, with their hands always on him in a careful, caressing grip, as though all the while feeling him to make sure he was there. It was like men handling a fish which is still alive and may jump back into the water. But he stood quite unresisting, yielding his arms limply to the ropes, as though he hardly noticed what was happening. [2]

Eight o'clock struck and a bugle call, desolately thin in the wet air, floated from the distant barracks. The superintendent of the jail, who was standing apart from the rest of us, moodily prodding the gravel with his stick, raised his head at the sound. He was an army doctor, with a grey toothbrush moustache and a gruff voice. "For God's sake hurry up, Francis," he said irritably. "The man ought to have been dead by this time. Aren't you ready yet?" [3]

Francis, the head jailer, a fat Dravidian in a white drill suit and gold spectacles, waved his black hand. "Yes sir, yes sir," he bubbled. "All iss satisfactorily prepared. The hangman iss waiting. We shall proceed." [4]

"Well, quick march, then. The prisoners can't get their breakfast till this job's over." [5]

We set out for the gallows. Two warders marched on either side of the prisoner, with their rifles at the slope; two others marched close against him, gripping him by arm and shoulder, as though at once pushing and supporting him. The rest of us, magistrates and the like, followed behind. Suddenly, when we had gone ten yards, the procession stopped short without any order or warning. A dreadful thing had happened—a dog, come goodness knows whence, had appeared in the yard. It came bounding among us with a loud volley of barks, and leapt round us wagging its whole body, wild with glee at finding so many human beings together. It was a large woolly dog, half Airedale, half pariah. For a moment it pranced round us, and then, before anyone could stop it, it had made a dash for the prisoner, and jumping up tried to lick his face. Everyone stood aghast, too taken aback even to grab at the dog. [6]

"Who let that bloody brute in here?" said the superintendent angrily. "Catch it, someone!" [7]

A warder, detached from the escort, charged clumsily after the dog, but it danced and gambolled just out of his reach, taking everything as part of the game. A young Eurasian jailer picked up a handful of gravel and tried to stone the dog away, but it dodged the stones and came after us again. Its yaps echoed from the jail walls. The prisoner, in the grasp of the two warders, looked on incuriously, as though this was another formality of the hanging. It was several minutes before someone managed to catch the dog. Then we put my handkerchief through its collar and moved off once more, with the dog still straining and whimpering. [8]

It was about forty yards to the gallows. I watched the bare brown back of the prisoner marching in front of me. He walked clumsily with his bound arms, but quite steadily, with that bobbing gait of the Indian who never straightens his knees. At each step his muscles slid neatly into place, the lock of hair on his scalp danced up and down, his feet printed themselves on the wet gravel. And once, in spite of the men who gripped him by each shoulder, he stepped slightly aside to avoid a puddle on the path. [9]

It is curious, but till that moment I had never realised what it means to destroy a healthy, conscious man. When I saw the prisoner step aside to avoid the puddle, I saw the mystery, the unspeakable wrongness, of cutting a life short when it is in full tide. This man was not dying, he was alive just as we were alive. All the organs [10] of his body were working—bowels digesting food, skin renewing itself, nails growing, tissues forming—all toiling away in solemn foolery. His nails would still be growing when he stood on the drop, when he was falling through the air with a tenth of a second to live. His eyes saw the yellow gravel and the grey walls, and his brain still remembered, foresaw, reasoned—reasoned even about puddles. He and we were a party of men walking together, seeing, hearing, feeling, understanding the same world; and in two minutes, with a sudden snap, one of us would be gone—one mind less, one world less.

The gallows stood in a small yard, separate from the main grounds of the prison, and overgrown with tall prickly weeds. It was a brick erection like three sides of a shed, with planking on top, and above that two beams and a crossbar with the rope dangling. The hangman, a greyhaired convict in the white uniform of the prison, was waiting beside his machine. He greeted us with a servile crouch as we entered. At a word from Francis the two warders, gripping the prisoner more closely than ever, half led, half pushed him to the gallows and helped him clumsily up the ladder. Then the hangman climbed up and fixed the rope around the prisoner's neck. [11]

We stood waiting, five yards away. The warders had formed in a rough circle round the gallows. And then, when the noose was fixed, the prisoner began crying out on his god. It was a high, reiterated cry of "Ram! Ram! Ram! Ram!", not urgent and fearful like a prayer or a cry for help, but steady, rhythmical, almost like the tolling of a bell. The dog answered the sound with a whine. The hangman, still standing on the gallows, produced a small cotton bag like a flour bag and drew it down over the prisoner's face. But the sound, muffled by the cloth, still persisted, over and over again: "Ram! Ram! Ram! Ram! Ram!" [12]

The hangman climbed down and stood ready, holding the lever. Minutes seemed to pass. The steady, muffled crying from the prisoner went on and on. "Ram! Ram! Ram!" never faltering for an instant. The superintendent, his head on his chest, was slowly poking the ground with his stick; perhaps he was counting the cries, allowing the prisoner a fixed number—fifty, perhaps, or a hundred. Everyone had changed colour. The Indians had gone grey like bad coffee, and one or two of the bayonets were wavering. We looked at the lashed, hooded man on the drop, and listened to his cries—each cry another second of life; the same thought was in all our minds: oh, kill him quickly, get it over, stop that abominable noise! [13]

Suddenly the superintendent made up his mind. Throwing up his head he made a swift motion with his stick. "Chalo!" he shouted almost fiercely. [14]

There was a clanking noise, and then dead silence. The prisoner had vanished, and the rope was twisting on itself. I let go of the dog, and it galloped immediately to the back of the gallows; but when it got there it stopped short, barked, and then retreated into a corner of the yard, where it stood among the weeds, looking timorously out at us. We went round the gallows to inspect the prisoner's body. He was dangling with his toes straight downwards, very slowly revolving, as dead as a stone. [15]

The superintendent reached out with his stick and poked the bare body; it oscillated, slightly. "*He's* all right," said the superintendent. He backed out from under the gallows, and blew out a deep breath. The moody look had gone out of his face quite suddenly. He glanced at his wristwatch. "Eight minutes past eight. Well, that's all for this morning, thank God." [16]

The warders unfixed bayonets and marched away. The dog, sobered and conscious of having misbehaved itself, slipped after them. We walked out of the gallows yard, past the condemned cells with their waiting prisoners, into the big central yard of the prison. The convicts, under the command of warders armed with lathis, were already receiving their breakfast. They squatted in long rows, each man holding a tin pannikin, while two warders with buckets marched round ladling out rice; it seemed quite a homely, jolly scene, after the hanging. An enormous relief had come upon us now that the job was done. One felt an impulse to sing, to break into a run, to snigger. All at once everyone began chattering gaily. [17]

The Eurasian boy walking beside me nodded toward the way we had come, with a knowing smile: "Do you know, sir, our friend (he meant the dead man), when he heard his appeal had been dismissed, he pissed on the floor of his cell. From fright.—Kindly take one of my cigarettes, sir. Do you not admire my new silver case, sir? From the boxwallah, two rupees eight annas. Classy European style." [18]

Several people laughed—at what, nobody seemed certain. [19]

Francis was walking by the superintendent, talking garrulously: "Well, sir, all hass passed off with the utmost satisfactoriness. It wass all finished—flick! like that. It iss not always so—oah, no! I have known cases where the doctor wass obliged to go beneath the gallows and pull the prisoner's legs to ensure decease. Most disagreeable!" [20]

"Wriggling about, eh? That's bad," said the superintendent. [21]

"Ach, sir, it iss worse when they become refractory! One man, I recall, clung to the bars of hiss cage when we went to take him out. You will scarcely credit, sir, that it took six warders to dislodge him, three pulling at each leg. We reasoned with him. 'My dear [22] fellow,' we said, 'think of all the pain and trouble you are causing to us!' But no, he would not listen! Ach, he wass very troublesome!"

I found that I was laughing quite loudly. Everyone was laughing. Even the superintendent grinned in a tolerant way. "You'd better all come out and have a drink," he said quite genially. "I've got a bottle of whisky in the car. We could do with it." [23]

We went through the big double gates of the prison, into the road. "Pulling at his legs!" exclaimed a Burmese magistrate suddenly, and burst into a loud chuckling. We all began laughing again. At that moment Francis's anecdote seemed extraordinarily funny. We all had a drink together, native and European alike, quite amicably. The dead man was a hundred yards away. [24]

VOCABULARY

amicably	in a friendly manner
Dravidian	a person of a mixed race in southern India and Burma
gambol	to skip or leap about in play
garrulous	talkative
incurious	not curious
oscillate	to swing back and forth
pariah	an outcast
refractory	stubborn
reiterate	to repeat
servile	like a slave
timorous	fearful

DESIGN AND MEANING

1. What descriptive words and details set a mood in paragraph 1? What is the mood?
2. Why is the dog's entrance (paragraph 6) called "a dreadful thing"? List the verbs in that paragraph. What general statement could you make about them?
3. Choose any paragraph in the essay that you consider a vivid description. Copy it; then underline words that appeal to the senses of sight, hearing, or touch.
4. What paragraph gives the main point of the essay? How does the puddle episode relate to it? How does the change of mood after the hanging support or detract from the main point?

SIMILARITY AND DIFFERENCE

List three elements that make Orwell's essay sound more formal than Williamson's.

SHORT WRITING IDEA

Choose one of the papers you have written. From one page, list all the verbs you used. Then substitute more vivid verbs for the lifeless ones like "is," "go," "are," "give," "went," "have."

LONGER WRITING IDEA

Describe a place that has a strong appeal (either positive or negative) to you. Include sensory details that will help reveal your feelings, but do not name the emotions themselves.

VOCABULARY CHECK

Make each of the following fragments into a reasonable sentence.

1. One's opinions can oscillate when
2. The philosophy professor reiterated that
3. Acting servile, Stan's wife
4. Our amicable agreement about washing dishes was
5. An incurious puppy

Tom Tiede

"Another Copter's Comin' In, Cap'n"

A war correspondent, sports columnist, and novelist, Tom Tiede (b. 1937) first gained national recognition through his syndicated human interest reports detailing the agony and the irony of the war in Vietnam.

BIEN HOA, VIET NAM—The men of the aid station sat, backs to tent poles and feet spread like 20 minutes to four. They slept, they scratched, they carved holes in the dirt with their heels. [1]

"It's quiet," said Capt. Buck Harper, M.D. "That's a bad sign." [2]

It was midday and the heat of it had cooked the breeze from the countryside. What air that did stir was putrid with farmyard manure left to sizzle in the sun. [3]

The cots were occupied by camp patients mostly; a sore foot, a headache, an upset stomach. But in one corner, a Vietnamese mother wept and smoothed the hair of her 4-year-old son. He and a playmate had stepped on an area mine. The pal died. The boy was left with hamburger on the inside of his legs. [4]

"How bad is the boy, captain?" somebody asked. [5]

"He'll live," was the reply. "Only he'll never father a family." [6]

The clatter of a helicopter interrupted . . . . [7]

"Cap'n" the radio man said, "rescue copter's coming in." [8]

"What's aboard?" [9]

"Litter cases." [10]

"Damn. I knew it was too quiet." [11]

Eyes squinted up. The bird had appeared from nowhere, as was its habit, and began to land. Its giant blades picked up dirt and debris and hurled it against the aid men who had turned tail to the force of the wind. [12]

The cargo doors flew open and small rivers of blood spilled on the ground to introduce the passengers. A man with a gaping hole in his face staggered out unassisted. Four others had to be carried. [13]

"You, hey, you," cried the copter pilot. "Get us some water buckets." [14]

"Water? Wha . . ." [15]

"We got an inch of blood on the floor of this thing. Swab it out. All hell's breaking loose in the hills. We gotta get right back." [16]

Hell was also breaking loose in the aid tent. [17]

"God help me," mumbled a man on a stretcher. [18]

Blood was everywhere. Men slipped on it. A jeep driver became ill. [19]

The man shot in the face sat bent over, a steady unbroken thread of red dripping from his mouth. Now and then he spat out a tooth or a chunk of flesh. Another man's leg jerked uncontrollably. One sergeant had no cot, so he sat on a stool and painstakingly counted the puncture holes in his mutilated legs. [20]

"Won't somebody get me some water?" a private pleaded. [21]

"You gotta wait, man," he was told. "You know you gotta wait." [22]

In combat, suffering is personal misery. One man's wound, regardless of degree, is invariably less than somebody else's. Aid men act not with courtesy or favor but with speed and proficiency. They must remain impersonal, professional. [23]

A shot of morphine, a wet rag, a hunk of gauze . . . . [24]

"Our job is to see they don't die," says Dr. Buck Harper, 173rd Airborne Brigade. "We haven't the time, the men nor the facilities to do much else. Sometimes we can't even stop the pain. [25]

"In as few minutes as possible, I've got to sort them out, decide the more serious, patch them up temporarily and then get them back to a larger hospital. Sometimes you can't get them all back at once. So I have to choose. And I have to choose right." [26]

The bleeding began to subside and the dull, quiet hurt set in. The private groaned and prayed. The sergeant quit counting his holes. [27]

"My feet," a man whispered. "I can't feel my feet." [28]

"They're there, boy," he was told. "Believe me, they're there." [29]

In the corner, the native woman still comforted her son. Two victims had fallen asleep. The man with the hole in his face stared down, impassively, into the pool of his own making. [30]

For a while it was quiet again. Then— [31]

"Cap'n," said the radio man. "Another rescue copter's comin' in." [32]

This is how it is in an aid tent at the edge of war. [33]

VOCABULARY

debris	rubble, litter, bits and pieces
image	a mental picture of something
impassive	not feeling or showing emotion
impersonal	not connected to any particular person

mutilated	damaged, injured
proficiency	skill
putrid	rotten and foul-smelling
subside	to become less intense
swab	to mop

DESIGN AND MEANING

1. After the intense descriptions of this place, the closing sentence, implying the purpose of the piece, seems understated and bare. Why do you think Tiede chose this closing? What were some alternatives to such understatement?
2. Point out several images in the piece. Some images, called "recurrent images," appear repeatedly in the piece of writing and tie it together. What is one recurrent image in Tiede's essay?
3. Tiede uses comparisons effectively in his writing: "feet spread like 20 minutes to four" (paragraph 1) and "small rivers of blood" (paragraph 13), for example. Find three more examples.
4. Write a list of the verbs in paragraph 13. What generalization can you make about them? Find at least five more examples of word choices that fit your generalization.
5. Why does the writer use dialog in this essay?

SIMILARITY AND DIFFERENCE

Name at least three elements that "Another Copter" shares with "The Death of the Ball Turret Gunner," which follows.

SHORT WRITING IDEA

Think of an intense experience you have had (a car accident, a war experience, an extreme disagreement). On paper, try to recreate descriptively only one minute (or less) of that experience. Then use a thesaurus and dictionary to revise your choice of words.

LONGER WRITING IDEA

"This is how it is where I work."

"This is how it is in the morning at my home."

"This is how it is in a high school restroom."

Using a sentence like one of the above for a closing line, write a descriptive essay. Choose a specific instance to describe, as Tiede does. Use dialog if possible.

VOCABULARY CHECK

Is the italicized word used correctly in each sentence? *Yes* or *no*?

1. The novel was *mutilated* by the fanatical censors.

2. The storm quickly *subsided* to its height of fury.

3. Sandy could not tell anything from Clyde's *impassive* expression.

4. *Debris* is an unlikable personality trait.

5. Sending Marla flowers was a romantic, *impersonal* gesture.

poetry

D. H. Lawrence

Baby Running Barefoot

Born in England, Lawrence (1885–1930) is probably best known for his sexually explicit novels such as *Lady Chatterly's Lover* (1928), *Women in Love* (1920), and *Sons and Lovers* (1913). These shocked both the general public and his peers, including T. S. Eliot. Lawrence also worked uninhibitedly with poetry and painting. He moved from country to country embracing a bohemian lifestyle, claiming that nothing was more depressing than returning to his hometown.

When the white feet of the baby beat across the grass
The little white feet nod like white flowers in a wind,
They poise and run like puffs of wind that pass
Over water where the weeds are thinned.

And the sight of their white playing in the grass [5]
Is winsome as a robin's song, so fluttering;
Or like two butterflies that settle on a glass
Cup for a moment, soft little wing-beats uttering.

And I wish that the baby would tack across here to me
Like a wind-shadow running on a pond, so she could stand [10]
With two little bare white feet upon my knee
And I could feel her feet in either hand

Cool as syringa buds in morning hours,
Or firm and silken as young peony flowers.

Ezra Pound

In a Station of the Metro

Born in Hailey, Idaho, Ezra Pound (1885–1972) left the United States at the age of 21 after being fired from the morally uptight Wabash College in Indiana for allegedly helping out a chorus girl in need. He wrote poetry in several languages, translated it, edited it, and encouraged new talent. He is regarded as the founder of the Imagist movement, which stressed simplicity, precision, and clarity, often ignoring traditional forms.

The apparition of these faces in the crowd;
Petals on a wet, black bough.

Karl Shapiro

Auto Wreck

Karl Shapiro (b. 1913) is a Pulitzer Prize-winning poet whose powerful imagery in "Auto Wreck" conveys the emotional as well as the physical scene.

Its quick soft silver bell beating, beating
And down the dark one ruby flare
Pulsing out red light like an artery,
The ambulance at top speed floating down
Past beacons and illuminated clocks [5]
Wings in a heavy curve, dips down,
And brakes speed, entering the crowd.
The doors leap open, emptying light;
Stretchers are laid out, the mangled lifted
And stowed into the little hospital. [10]
Then the bell, breaking the hush, tolls once,
And the ambulance with its terrible cargo
Rocking, slightly rocking, moves away,
As the doors, an afterthought, are closed.

We are deranged, walking among the cops [15]
Who sweep glass and are large and composed.
One is still making notes under the light.
One with a bucket douches ponds of blood
Into the street and gutter.
One hangs lanterns on the wrecks that cling, [20]
Empty husks of locusts, to iron poles.

Our throats were tight as tourniquets,
Our feet were bound with splints, but now
Like convalescents intimate and gauche,
We speak through sickly smiles and warn [25]
With the stubborn saw of common sense,
The grim joke and the banal resolution.
The traffic moves around with care,
But we remain, touching a wound
That opens to our richest horror. [30]

Already old, the question Who shall die?
Becomes unspoken Who is innocent?
For death in war is done by hands;
Suicide has cause and stillbirth, logic.
And cancer, simple as a flower, blooms. [35]
But this invites the occult mind,
Cancels our physics with a sneer,
And spatters all we knew of denouement
Across the expedient and wicked stones.

Randall Jarrell

The Death of the Ball Turret Gunner

Randall Jarrell (1914–1965), an influential poet and critic whose work is widely anthologized, was trained as a pilot in World War II. "The Death of the Ball Turret Gunner" was published in 1945.

From my mother's sleep I fell into the State,
And I hunched in its belly till my wet fur froze.
Six miles from earth, loosed from its dream of life,
I woke to black flak and the nightmare fighters.
When I died they washed me out of the turret with a hose. [5]

VOCABULARY

apparition	a ghostly appearance
ball turret	a transparent dome for a gunner on a bomber
banal	trite, hackneyed
composed	calm, self-possessed
denouement	the usual solution or clarification of a plot at the end of a drama
expedient	speedily effective means to an end
flak	the fire of antiaircraft guns
gauche	awkward, tactless
loosed	let loose
peony	a large, showy flower that grows on a shrub
poise	hover, balance
saw	an old saying, often repeated
syringa	fragrant, white flowers
tack	to follow a zigzag route
winsome	engaging or charming

DESIGN AND MEANING

1. List the words and phrases that appeal to the senses of sight and touch in "Baby Running Barefoot." What do all the comparisons in the poem have in common? Why are these comparisons appropriate to the description of the baby? What comparisons would be inappropriate?
2. If you ran across "In a Station of the Metro" in some other context than this, would you call it a poem? Why or why not? What does it have in common with other poems in this section? How does it differ?
3. Reread "Auto Wreck," paying attention to where the stanzas are divided. Can you see the logic behind these divisions?
4. The first stanza of "Auto Wreck" emphasizes light and movement. List the words and phrases that develop these visual images. What does the first stanza deemphasize?
5. In your opinion, what lines state the main point of Shapiro's poem? Does their placement seem appropriate to you? Does "In a Station of the Metro" have a main point? Does "Baby Running Barefoot"?
6. In "The Death of the Ball Turret Gunner," consider the paired concepts of dream and nightmare, sleep and waking, life and death. Can you see an unusual relationship among these concepts in the poem? For example, is death usually associated with sleep or waking?
7. Why is the word "State" capitalized in Jarrell's poem?
8. Why is the closing line shocking?

SHORT WRITING IDEAS

Describe an animal or a machine you know as though it were a person.

In the pattern of "In a Station of the Metro," think of an image for a crowd that you have observed, for example at a sports event, a concert, or a demonstration.

LONGER WRITING IDEA

Write a three-paragraph essay describing a crisis you have experienced or witnessed. In the first paragraph, emphasize light, movement, and sound. In the second paragraph, emphasize the actions of the people involved. In the third paragraph, emphasize your own emotional and intellectual reactions.

VOCABULARY CHECK

Fill in each blank with one of the vocabulary words.

1. The old ______ "It takes all kinds to make a world" is extremely irritating.
2. Clyde's ______ behavior at the party included asking Marla whether she would like to borrow his vacuum cleaner.
3. Sandy thought *Love Story* was sensitive and insightful, but Hubert considered it ______.
4. He especially objected to the tear-jerking ______ of the novel.
5. Marla found that depriving Clyde of liquor was the most ______ way to get rid of him.

Short Story

PREREADING EXERCISE ("EVE IN DARKNESS")

Choose one of these childhood memories, and write about it for fifteen minutes.

1. Children frequently mishear or misinterpret phrases their elders use in front of them. Do you remember a word or concept that you misunderstood as a child? Can you remember why you had an unclear or incorrect idea about it? Can you remember how you found out you were not right?
2. Describe a room in a friend or relative's house that held a special fascination for you as a child—because it was strange, scary, cozy, smelly, whatever. Try to remember exactly what it was like to you when you were small.

Reread what you wrote. Does your description reflect what you were like as a child? If so, can you still see the reflected qualities in yourself?

Short Story

Kaatje Hurlbut

Eve in Darkness

Hurlbut (b. 1921), a native New Yorker, is a writer fortified with considerable determination. She says, "I wrote four hours a day, five days a week, for ten years before I was published." She has since enjoyed acceptance in many literary and popular magazines. "Eve in Darkness" appeared first in *Mademoiselle* in 1957.

That little marble nude was so lovely. She was the loveliest thing I had ever seen. In a corner of my grandmother's dim, austere living room she stood on a pedestal like a small, bright ghost. [1]

I was about five when I used to stand and gaze up at her with admiration and delight. I thought that her toes and fingers were as beautiful as anything about her; they were long and narrow and expressive. She stood slightly bowed and the delicate slenderness of her emphasized the roundness of her little breasts, which were like the apple she held in her fingers. [2]

I wonder now who she was. I think she may have been Aphrodite and the apple was the golden prize, "for the fairest"—the fateful judgment of Paris. But Victoria, my cousin, who was older than I, said that she was Eve. And I believed her. [3]

We observed the quietness of that room, Eve and I, as though we were conspirators. I never talked to her or even whispered to her (as I did to the blackened bronze of Pallas Athene in the hall), but in the quietness I considered many things standing before her and she received my considerations with a faint, musing smile I found infinitely satisfying. [4]

Others came into the room and talked as though the quietness was nothing. Molly, the Irishwoman who cleaned, bustled about with a dustcloth, muttering and sighing. Victoria even shouted there. Only my grandmother did not shatter the quietness because she had the kind of voice that only brushed against it. Callers were the worst for, sitting with teacups and smelling of strange scents, [5] they threatened never to leave but to sit forever and say in old continuous voices, "We really must go now" and "My dear, promise you will come soon" and "Where have I put my gloves?"

[6] But leave they did. And after the teacups had been removed and the carpet sweeper run over the crumbs I would go back to the room alone and stand before Eve to consider, often as not, the reason for one of the callers wearing a velvet band around her wrinkled old throat. My cousin Victoria said that it was because her throat had been cut by a maniac and she wore the velvet band to hide the terrible scar. I suspected that this was not the truth. But it was interesting to consider. Eve smiled. It might have been true.

[7] Eve smiled because of the things she knew. She knew that I had handled the snuffboxes I had been forbidden to touch; some of them were silver but some were enamel with radiant miniatures painted on the lids and when I looked closely at the faces the eyes gazed back at me, bold and bright. Eve knew that at four-thirty I went to the front window to stick out my tongue at the wolfish paperboy, to whom I had been told to be very kind because he was so much less fortunate than I. She knew that I was deathly afraid of the ragman, who drove over from the East Side now and then, bawling, "I cash old cloths." You couldn't really tell what he was saying but that was what he was supposed to be saying. Victoria told me that he took little girls when he could get them and smothered them under the mound of dirty rags and papers piled high on his rickety old cart. I laughed at Victoria and hoped she didn't know how afraid I was. But Eve knew.

[8] Sometimes I only considered Eve herself because of her loveliness. When the room was dim she gleamed in the shadowy corner; but when the sun came into the room in the morning she dazzled until she seemed to be made of light pressed into hardness. And the cleanness of her was cleaner than anything I could think of: cleaner than my grandmother's kid gloves; cleaner than witch hazel on a white handkerchief.

[9] As I stood before Eve one afternoon Victoria came up behind me so silently I did not hear her.

[10] "What are *you* doing?" she asked suddenly.

[11] I jumped and turned to find her smiling a wide, fixed smile, with her eyes fully open and glassy.

[12] "Nothing," I said, and an instinctive flash of guilt died away, for it was true: I was doing nothing. But she continued to stare at me and smile fixedly until I lowered my eyes and started to move away.

[13] "Wait."

[14] "What?"

"Do you know what that is?" she asked slyly and touched the apple Eve held in her fingers. [15]

"An apple." [16]

"No," she said, smiling more intensely. "That," she thrust her face close to mine and almost whispered, "that is the forbidden fruit." She enunciated each syllable slowly and somehow dreadfully. [17]

"What kind of fruit?" I asked, backing away. [18]

She stopped smiling and looked steadily at me, her eyes growing wider and wider. And then with a kind of hushed violence, as when she would tell me about the murders in the Rue Morgue and about an insane man who howled and swung a club in a nearby alley on moonless nights, she told me about the Garden of Eden; and about the tree and the serpent; and about the man, Adam, and the woman, Eve. [19]

"And the forbidden fruit," she said at last in a harsh flat whisper, "is *sin!*" [20]

"Sin." She whispered the word again and gazed balefully at the little marble statue of Eve. I followed her gaze with dread, knowing all at once that sin was not any kind of fruit but something else: something that filled me with alarm and grief because I loved Eve. And as I stared she only looked past me with her blind marble eyes and smiled. [21]

I suppose that it was the first time in my life that I experienced sorrow. For I remember the strangeness of what I felt: regret and helplessness and a deeper love. [22]

"Sin." [23]

My mind tried to enhance the word and find its meaning, for it belonged to Eve now. But I could not grasp it. So I said the word to myself and listened to it. [24]

"Sin." [25]

It was beautiful. It was a word like "rain" and "sleep": lovely but of sorrowful loveliness. "Sin": it was lovely and sorrowful and it belonged to Eve. [26]

Victoria, who had been watching me, asked with a sudden, writhing delight: "Do you know what sin is?" [27]

"No," I said, wishing fiercely that she would go away. [28]

"And I won't tell you," she said slyly. "You're much too little to know." [29]

For a time after that I was so preoccupied with the vague sorrow that surrounded Eve that I went to the room only out of a reluctant sense of duty. I felt that I might somehow console her. And there she would be, holding the apple in her delicate fingers, smiling. And I wondered how she could be smiling with sorrow all around her. I looked long at her, until her smile almost hypnotized me, and all at once it occurred to me that she did not know about Sin. Poor [30] little Eve. She didn't even know that Sin was all around her, belonging to her. She was only white and beautiful and smiling.

But as Christmas drew near I went to her again as I had gone before: out of need. I went to consider the curious and wonderful things I had seen in the German toy store over on Amsterdam Avenue. There was the old German himself, fat and gentle and sad. My grandmother had told me people had stopped going to his store during the First World War because the Americans and the Germans were enemies. And I hoped earnestly that he did not think I was his enemy. Eve smiled. She knew that I wasn't. And she smiled about the bold colors of the toys trimmed in gold; and about the ugly laughing faces of the carved wooden dolls, too real for dolls' faces but more like the faces of dried shrunken people, as Victoria said they were. [31]

Someone who had made the grand tour had brought home, along with the laces and lava carvings and watercolor scenes of Cairo, an exquisitely small manger in which the Infant Christ lay wrapped in swaddling clothes. His arms were flung out bravely and his palms were open. He was always taken from the box at Christmastime and placed on a low table where I might play with him if I did not take him from the table. But he was so small and beautiful and brave-looking that I could not bring myself to play with him as I would a toy. Overcome with enchantment one afternoon, I took him up and carried him across the room to Eve. I held him up before her blind marble eyes and she smiled. It was a tremendous relief to have her smile at him. [32]

I looked regretfully at the apple and turned away from her. I held the baby Christ close to my lips and whispered the lovely sorrowful word to him. [33]

"Sin." [34]

But little and brave as ever, with his arms flung out and his palms open, he seemed not to have heard me. [35]

That night I wandered aimlessly down to the basement where the kitchen was and when I approached the kitchen door in the darkness of the hall I bumped into Victoria, who was standing at the closed door listening to the hum of voices that came from inside the kitchen. [36]

She grabbed me and quickly clamped her hand over my mouth. [37]

"Go," she whispered fiercely. "Go back." [38]

But I was frightened and clung to her helplessly. Still holding her hand over my mouth, she led me back down the hall and up the dark stairs, stumbling into the hall above. By that time I was crying and she tried to quiet me still whispering fiercely. [39]

"Listen," she hissed, "if you won't tell you saw me there I'll tell you something *horrible*." [40]

"I won't tell," I said to her palm. I hadn't thought of telling; I was too frightened. [41]

"Do you know who that was in the kitchen? It was Molly." [42]

Molly, I remembered, was to come that night: my grandmother had put crisp new bills in an envelope and had said Molly was coming for her Christmas present. [43]

"Molly," said Victoria, "was crying. A horrible thing has happened. Her daughter—" she stared at me with wide frightening eyes that I wanted to turn from but couldn't, "—her daughter *sinned!*" [44]

"What do you mean?" I asked in alarm, thinking of Eve. I was afraid I was going to cry again and I clenched my fists and doubled up my toes so that I wouldn't. [45]

"She had a baby!" She looked hard at me, fierce and accusing. I backed away from her. [46]

"You won't tell you saw me there?" [47]

"How did she sin?" I asked, thinking of the brave baby and Eve gleaming in the dark corner smiling at him. [48]

"She had a baby, I told you," she replied impatiently. And then, as she looked at me, an expression of evasive cunning crept into her eyes. "King David sinned also." [49]

"King David in the Bible?" I asked. [50]

"Yes. Now promise you won't tell you saw me." [51]

"I promise," I said. [52]

I tried to remember something about King David, but all I could think of was the beginning of a poem: "King David and King Solomon led merry, merry lives." [53]

He sounded happy and grand like Old King Cole was-a-merry-old-soul. I tried to imagine how the sadness of Sin belonged to him: I wondered if he held an apple, like Eve; I didn't think he could have a baby, like Molly's daughter. [54]

I thought about Sin when I lay in bed that night sniffing the lavender scent of the sheets. I whispered the word to myself, carefully separating it from other words and considering all that I knew about it: Eve held Sin in her slender fingers and looked past it with blind marble eyes. Molly's daughter sinned (I wondered if she was as beautiful as Eve); she sinned and had a baby: a little brave baby with his arms flung out and his palms open. Sin. Why, it was hardly sorrowful at all. [55]

When my grandmother came in to say good night I sat up to kiss the fragrant velvet cheek and whispered privately: "What did King David do?" [56]

"What did King David do? King David played his harp!" she answered gaily, and it sounded like the beginning of a song. [57]

King David played his harp! He sinned and played his harp! Lovely, lovely Sin: he played his harp! [58]

Slowly at first, and then swiftly, the remains of the vague sorrow spiraled out of sight and rejoicing came up in its place. [59]

Over and over again I beheld them, bright in the darkness on a hidden merry-go-round, swinging past me, friendly and gay: King David holding aloft his harp; Molly's daughter's little baby with his arms flung out so bravely; and brightest of all came Eve with her apple, smiling and shining with Sin. [60]

VOCABULARY

Aphrodite and Paris	Aphrodite, the goddess of love, beauty, and laughter, won a golden apple from Paris and helped him win Helen of Sparta, leading to the downfall of Troy.
austere	plain; lacking luxuries
Pallas Athene	goddess of wisdom, skills, warfare

DESIGN AND MEANING

1. How is the "persona" (the "I" who narrated the story) different from the writer herself? Does the story make any direct reference to this difference?
2. Point out words that appeal to the senses of sight, touch, and smell in paragraph 8.
3. The narrator never makes any generalizations about Victoria. What general statements could you make from the descriptive details presented? How do Victoria's concept of evil and the narrator's concept (shown in paragraph 7, for instance) differ? Why is the difference between the girls important to the story?
4. Find as many phrases as you can in the story that describe a character's tone of voice.
5. Why does the child never understand what sin is?

SIMILARITY AND DIFFERENCE

In "Boyhood Remembered" (Chapter 1), Mark Twain also looks through his childhood eyes. What are some differences and similarities between the Twain child and the Hurlbut child? What conditions could account for the contrasts?

SHORT WRITING IDEA

Looking back over the last few days, consider the various tones of voice you have spoken in and heard. Using a thesaurus, write descriptive phrases to depict these tones.

LONGER WRITING IDEA

Describe a situation in your childhood in which you came to a mistaken conclusion about something because of the way it was explained (or not explained) to you. Tell how you later discovered you were wrong.

Narration

> And when Laurie went out to go to work Monday morning—no, it must've been Tuesday, she has Monday off—and looked in the back seat, there were all the presents—quit it, Amy, Mommy's talking—all the presents she'd given him, just dumped in a heap. Want some more tea? This is that new orange kind. Anyway, she felt terrible, so . . .

A NARRATIVE IS A STORY, and luckily, people have a knack for following oral narratives, which are usually delivered in a fragmented, disorderly way. When writers use narrative, though, they have much more control: their stories need not be punctuated with spilled juice and ringing telephones and decisions about whether it happened Monday or Tuesday. Writers have time to think and to revise, so we expect more from a written narrative.

First, we expect that the writer has weeded out insignificant details, has consciously chosen which parts of the story to emphasize, and has decided where to begin and end. While you are willing to forgive a kitchen-table narrator for starting too early or too late in the story, you want a written narrative to begin where you can pick up enough background to understand what is going on and to end with a sense of closure.

Second, we expect a conscious order to the written story. The most obvious order is, of course, straight through from beginning to end. We do not anticipate that the writer will forget an important incident and have to put it in later, out of its chronological order, although that happens all the time in oral narration. When we do find a written narrative jumping around in seeming disorder, we assume that the writer wants it that way and we look for a reason other than absentmindedness.

We have these rather strict expectations for one reason: we view the writer as having a clear purpose—a main point—in mind. That main point rules what goes in, when, and in what words. A disorderly narrative, for example, may be meant to show the disorder in the narrator's mind—and remember, in fiction the narrator and the writer are not necessarily the same person. You can believe a story from the point of view of an eight-year-old without believing for a minute that it was written by an eight-year-old. The pretended narrator of a story is called its *persona;* thus, Huck Finn is Mark Twain's persona in *Adventures of Huckleberry Finn;* Holden Caulfield is J. D. Salinger's persona in *Catcher in the Rye;* and in this chapter, the mother is Tillie Olsen's persona in "I Stand Here Ironing." But the "I" who narrates "Getting 'Em Ready for Darrell" is actually Larry L. King, and the first-person narrator of "An Absence of Windows" really is Richard Selzer.

You see narrative in its pure form whenever you read fiction. And informal essays, like the ones included in this chapter, often consist entirely of narrative. You are also quite likely to find narrative passages in many kinds of expository writing. A brief narrative can spark the readers' interest in your introduction; it can provide convincing anecdotal evidence in your body paragraphs; it can add the validity of actual experience to your conclusion. An essay in which you attempt to persuade college students not to procrastinate will probably include a story of your own grim experiences with procrastination, and in that story you should marshall all the narrative skills you are about to practice as you go through the writing suggestions in this chapter.

Narrative ties ideas to real, sensory, day-to-day experience; it binds the abstract to the concrete. That is why narration gives all kinds of writing greater clarity, increased meaning, and additional interest. Do not hesitate to amuse or inform your readers with a lively, relevant story, no matter what kind of essay you are composing. The one exception to that bit of advice would be when you are engaged in extremely formal, scholarly writing. But most of the writing you do in this course and in everyday life will not be that formal, and brief anecdotes will be welcome.

You will find in the following narrative readings that a writer rarely gives you a direct statement of the main point—not at the beginning or at the end—but you can tell what it is anyway. The purpose of narrative writing varies from illustrating a general principle (racism in "Incident") to serving as an argument (against nuclear warfare in "I Thought My Last Hour Had Come"). Sometimes the purpose of a narrative is just to amuse or delight you. And, as we just mentioned, often a short narrative occurs within a different mode of exposition, where it provides one form of support for the thesis or serves to enliven the introduction or conclusion.

The best thing about narrative writing is that, in all likelihood, you will be quite successful at it yourself. After all, you have been telling stories ever since you were able to string two sentences together. As you study the selections in this chapter, pay attention to the way the professionals do it. Notice how they catch your interest at the outset, how they select only the most pertinent details, how they achieve immediacy with dialog, how they convey emotion through description, and how they get their point across without ever stating it. Try in your own writing to imitate all of those sterling qualities.

essays

PREREADING EXERCISE

In both big and small ways, we sometimes conform to others' hopes and expectations against our true feelings. Discuss one such experience from your own life.

essays

Langston Hughes

Salvation

Born in Joplin, Missouri, and schooled at Pennsylvania's Lincoln University, Langston Hughes (1902–1967) wrote often about the problems of blacks in the U.S. in his newspaper columns, poetry, and books. He was a war correspondent during the Spanish Civil War. His legacy will no doubt center on his poetry, which ignored the standard conventions and forms and played with the rhythms of jazz and folk music. He wrote four collections of short stories and seven novels.

I was saved from sin when I was going on thirteen. But not really saved. It happened like this. There was a big revival at my Auntie Reed's church. Every night for weeks there had been much preaching, singing, praying, and shouting, and some very hardened sinners had been brought to Christ, and the membership of the church had grown by leaps and bounds. Then just before the revival ended, they held a special meeting for children, "to bring the young lambs to the fold." My aunt spoke of it for days ahead. That night I was escorted to the front row and placed on the mourners' bench with all the other young sinners, who had not yet been brought to Jesus. [1]

My aunt told me that when you were saved you saw a light, and something happened to you inside! And Jesus came into your life! And God was with you from then on! She said you could see and hear and feel Jesus in your soul. I believed her. I had heard a great many old people say the same thing and it seemed to me they ought to know. So I sat there calmly in the hot, crowded church, waiting for Jesus to come to me. [2]

The preacher preached a wonderful rhythmical sermon, all moans and shouts and lonely cries and dire pictures of hell, and then he sang a song about the ninety and nine safe in the fold, but one little lamb was left out in the cold. Then he said: "Won't you come? Won't you come to Jesus? Young lambs, won't you come?" [3]

And he held out his arms to all of us young sinners there on the mourners' bench. And the little girls cried. And some of them jumped up and went to Jesus right away. But most of us just sat there.

A great many old people came and knelt around us and prayed, old women with jet-black faces and braided hair, old men with workgnarled hands. And the church sang a song about the lower lights are burning, some poor sinners to be saved. And the whole building rocked with prayer and song. [4]

Still I kept waiting to *see* Jesus. [5]

Finally all the young people had gone to the altar and were saved, but one boy and me. He was a rounder's son named Westley. Westley and I were surrounded by sisters and deacons praying. It was very hot in the church, and getting late now. Finally Westley said to me in a whisper: "God damn! I'm tired o' sitting here. Let's get up and be saved." So he got up and was saved. [6]

Then I was left all alone on the mourners' bench. My aunt came and knelt at my knees and cried, while prayers and song swirled all around me in the little church. The whole congregation prayed for me alone, in a mighty wail of moans and voices. And I kept waiting serenely for Jesus, waiting, waiting—but he didn't come. I wanted to see him, but nothing happened to me. Nothing! I wanted something to happen to me, but nothing happened. [7]

I heard the songs and the minister saying: "Why don't you come? My dear child, why don't you come to Jesus? Jesus is waiting for you. He wants you. Why don't you come? Sister Reed, what is this child's name?" [8]

"Langston," my aunt sobbed. [9]

"Langston, why don't you come? Why don't you come and be saved? Oh, Lamb of God! Why don't you come?" [10]

Now it was really getting late. I began to be ashamed of myself, holding everything up so long. I began to wonder what God thought about Westley, who certainly hadn't seen Jesus either, but who was now sitting proudly on the platform, swinging his knickerbockered legs and grinning down at me, surrounded by deacons and old women on their knees praying. God had not struck Westley dead for taking his name in vain or for lying in the temple. So I decided that maybe to save further trouble, I'd better lie, too, and say that Jesus had come, and get up and be saved. [11]

So I got up. [12]

Suddenly the whole room broke into a sea of shouting, as they saw me rise. Waves of rejoicing swept the place. Women leaped in the air. My aunt threw her arms around me. The minister took me by the hand and led me to the platform. [13]

When things quieted down, in a hushed silence, punctuated by [14] a few ecstatic "Amens," all the new young lambs were blessed in the name of God. Then joyous singing filled the room.

[15] That night, for the last time in my life but one—for I was a big boy twelve years old—I cried. I cried, in bed alone, and couldn't stop. I buried my head under the quilts, but my aunt heard me. She woke up and told my uncle I was crying because the Holy Ghost had come into my life, and because I had seen Jesus. But I was really crying because I couldn't bear to tell her that I had lied, that I had deceived everybody in the church, that I hadn't seen Jesus, and that now I didn't believe there was a Jesus any more, since he didn't come to help me.

VOCABULARY

rounder a good-for-nothing

DESIGN AND MEANING

1. How does the style of this narrative reflect the child's point of view? How does it reflect the grown author's point of view?
2. What makes the event Hughes describes easy to visualize, almost as though it were on a movie screen?
3. Why does young Langston finally stand up to get saved? Why does he later cry about it? Was he really "saved" in any sense?
4. In reading this essay, do you get the idea that Hughes is criticizing religion? What else may he be criticizing here?

SIMILARITY AND DIFFERENCE

"Salvation," "The Mudbacks" (Chapter 1), and "Boyhood Remembered" (Chapter 1) all involve adult writers reflecting on their childhoods. Do all of the writers have purposes other than self-expression? What might they be?

SHORT WRITING IDEA

Most of us can point to an event that changed our lives. Some of these events are clearly significant, like the death of a parent, and some are less obvious, like reading a particular book. Describe an event that changed your life.

LONGER WRITING IDEA

Expand on the discussion or description you used in either the Pre-reading Exercise or the Short Writing Idea. Use vivid details and sentence variety as Hughes does.

PREREADING EXERCISE ("ARETHA HAS THE BEST MAN")

When our sisters, brothers, and close friends become romantically involved, we're likely to consider their chosen partner not quite good enough for them. We may like the partner and understand the attraction, but we wish we could make a few changes. Write a one-page essay about a time when you experienced this feeling about the partner of a person close to you. Or, as an alternative, write about a time when you were involved in a relationship that your friends or relatives didn't think was quite good enough for you.

Jane Howard

Aretha Has the Best Man

Howard (b. 1935) is an editor and journalist whose books analyze segments of American society. Her technique involves transcribing interviews with people all over the country to present a balanced viewpoint. The following selection is taken from her best-seller *Families* (1978).

"Aretha has the best man of any of my girls," Cora said. "Oh, she and he have their troubles, but he's special—he's a career Navy officer—and so was she. She's not only an artist and a writer and in college, but she was one of the first women and first blacks to work on the newspaper on her base. She's bright, Aretha. She's got quite a future. When you get to Philadelphia, you ought to drop by to see her and her children." [1]

A couple of months later, I did. [2]

Aretha Taylor White and her children live in a third-floor walkup apartment in a dismal reconverted row house in south central Philadelphia. She wouldn't let me into the kitchen. "I've got so many dirty dishes piled up in there, I wouldn't let *anyone* see," she told me. "I can't *wait* till Traci learns to wash dishes." Traci, her six-year-old, and Augie, who was four, stared at me for a few minutes while Aretha made instant coffee. I looked around at her artwork. A number of her paintings and carvings were on display, but what struck me most were the pictures, every four feet or so, of Mel, the children's father. [3]

There was Mel in enlarged black-and-white snapshots, Mel in tinted formal portraits, Mel in his full-dress Navy uniform, Mel in a bathing suit, Mel with and without his mustache and glasses. The man in a painting of Aretha's called "Pregnant Woman and How She Got That Way" looked pretty much like Mel, too. [4]

"Good-looking man," I told her when she returned with my coffee and an ale she had poured for herself. [5]

"I almost forget how he looks," she said. "Here it is Thursday morning, and he said he'd be home Monday night. He's been in Florida for three weeks taking a special race-relations training course the Navy sent him to. 'Take the bus home,' I told him when he called last week. 'The bus'll get you from Pensacola to Philly in thirty-four hours.' I know; I checked. But no. [6]

"No, Mel said he could save money by getting a ride back here with a buddy from the course. Driving would be cheaper—it wasn't as if we had cash to spare. But cheap or no cheap, next time he goes somewhere I'm going along, and so are the kids. Never mind missing school: I'm smart, and so are they; I can teach them myself. Their daddy's smart too, which is why you might think it would occur to him to call up to tell me just *how* much later he's going to be. [7]

"Of course I did tell him the phone might be disconnected, because we don't always pay the bills when we're supposed to, and some of those bills have been high lately. But even so, wouldn't you think he could pull off the road to find a Western Union, and at least send a wire? Couldn't he at least tell me when to expect him? [8]

"Of course, for all I know he could be dead. Maybe I ought to be afraid. Maybe his family knows and they're not telling me. You never *saw* anything more depressing than the place where they live, near some bakery outside of Denver. Six of his thirteen brothers and sisters live at home there, and you ought to see the way they twist him to get him to do what they want. One of his sisters even conned him into buying her a forty-dollar plastic chinaware set. How do you like *that,* with these kids here needing shoes the way they do?" [9]

Traci asked for a piece of candy "You eat *all* the candy that was here yesterday?" Aretha asked. "Must have been a hundred pieces. Oh all right, you can split this piece of licorice." For herself she poured another glass of ale, then showed me a poem she had written to Mel called "Silk Sheets and Wine." She liked to write, she told me, especially when it was raining, or when the television was on. She was going to write a novel someday, and its title would be *A Nigger Is a Bitch.* [10]

"That's the title Daddy suggested. We used to talk about things like that a lot. He wanted me to keep on in college till I got my Ph.D. Maybe I will. Maybe I'll go back in the Navy and do more editorial work. Want to see the papers I edited?" Sure I did, so she went to get them. While I read them she kept staring at the wall behind me. [11]

"No," she decided, "Mel's not dead. I'd *feel* it if he were. He's on his way here, and I know where, too. This isn't the first trick he's pulled in the seven years we've been together. Once he left at four in the afternoon, saying he was going to wash his car, and you know when he came home? Seven in the morning, that's when. [12]

" 'I met some of the fellows,' he told me, 'and we decided to wash our cars together.' [13]

" 'Oh?' I said. 'Until *seven?* In the *morning?*' [14]

" 'Well,' he told me, 'we found an after-hours club.' [15]

"Next time that happened, I was waiting for him with a .32. That's when he decided maybe we ought to move someplace where it'd be easier to find babysitters, so we could get out *together*. So we moved here, but it turns out the other people around here aren't what you'd call the babysitting type. So for a while what we'd do is all four of us go places together, even the kids, to places like the zoo." [16]

"That gives me an idea," I told her. "Let's get out of here." It was too bright a day to sit indoors, and I was getting nervous myself, watching that phone not ring. [17]

"Go away, bumblebee, get away from my kid," says Aretha. We came in my rented car to Fairmount Park, a twenty-minute drive from the phone in South Philadelphia. Waiting for our lunch we look out over the Schuylkill at sculls. Traci is afraid of the bee that hovers over our table, but Aretha hugs and comforts her. [18]

"I love my mother," Traci tells me, "and someday I'll find a place where there are no bumblebees, and go pick her some flowers." [19]

"That's sweet, baby," Aretha said. "You know what *I'm* going to do? I think I'll have some flowers sent to Mommy. At Daddy's funeral I kept thinking: All these flowers and he can't smell a damn one. Lord have mercy." [20]

She has big ideas, Aretha. She would like to open a nightclub "with out-of-sight prices" called the Club Gazelle, with an island in the middle of the dance floor where a mother gazelle and her baby could graze, with soft jazz and "music for *couples* to dance to." I'd like to take an ocean voyage sometime, and ride naked on a horse in San Francisco, and go on the Johnny Carson show, and tell Sammy Davis, Junior, what an Oreo I think he is. [21]

"There's not really too much left for me to do. I've already sung before two thousand people at a state church convocation in Gary, and you know what I did then? I fell off the stage. People thought I must have been touched by the Spirit, until they heard me say, 'Oh, shit!' I figured that was as good a time as any to quit the choir. [22]

"If I don't stay on in college I'll go back in the WAVES. I joined in the first place because I was the baddest thing that ever hit Gary, Indiana; I grew up a smartass kid and I knew I needed to learn to do what I was told to without any lip. Mommy didn't think I could accept that kind of regimentation, and for a while she was right; boot camp was the worst ever. It wasn't as bad as the Marines, though. A girlfriend of mine joined the marines and they'd tell her, 'I don't want to hear a lip smacking or a cunt clacking, all I want to hear is feet cracking!' That girl had sand flea bites all over her legs, because she couldn't scratch or swat while standing at attention. [23]

"In the Navy I worked for a while in the machine shop. It was a terrible job; I'd have to work both shifts with no overtime. That's when I started drinking; I'd bring cough syrup to work and after a while it'd take me more than a fifth to get bombed. If my husband saw me drinking malt ale he'd be pissed off; it has more alcohol in it than beer." [24]

We are back in the apartment now. Still no Mel. The phone hasn't been disconnected; when we pick it up we get a dial tone. Aretha puts a record on the phonograph—it is the "1812 Overture"—and conducts it at the dining room table, with a pair of chopsticks. "Mommy tells me I ought to be flattered to be Number One with Mel," she said, "but I want to be the *only* one. Or else. In fact, I'd be in Mommy's house in Gary right now, only Mommy wouldn't want me. She says I've got too much going for me to leave Mel. Besides, Mel wouldn't even let me go there for a visit while he was in Florida. [25]

"He's probably figured that if I got with my sisters, I'd run in the streets and meet men. My sister Augustina ran a little wild, sometimes. Poor Gussie, I worry about her, she can't find her identity. She was Daddy's favorite, and she never even knew it. They were so alike in so many ways, little quirks they had in common. I hate to see her screwed up, because that's an intelligent girl there. Every now and then I get a card from Gussy and that means she wants to talk, so I call her." Augustina, I have noticed, is the only Taylor daughter who doesn't look busy and stylish. Her sisters hurry in and out of the house in fashionable costumes, with much on their minds; she usually sits staring into space, wearing a bathrobe. Once I asked her what was wrong, and she said her navel hurt. [26]

"Maybe if I went home I *would* go a little wild for a while," Aretha is saying. "Mel knows that as long as I stay here in Philly, I'm Miss Goody Two-Shoes. Well, he's going to find out that this is my last pair of that kind of shoes. Anyway, he should talk. He told me he wasn't married, when we met, because he knew I didn't date married men—I'd learned from experience that married men mean trouble. [27]

"I believed him, and forgot all about Thighbone and Reno and all the other men in my life, and wrote home that I'd finally found a dude I wanted to spend the rest of my life with. And not till I ordered the invitations—not till Mommy had bought an airplane ticket from Chicago (Daddy couldn't come because there was only enough money for one of them to make the trip)—not until I'd gone and got a *dress* to get married in did I find out, by checking with Personnel, that Mel never really did get a divorce from the woman he'd been married to before, in Japan. [28]

"And you know what a *thing* I've got against Japanese women? They won't let men wash their own *anything*—they've got to wash it for them." Aretha takes me to her closet to show me the wedding gown she never has worn. It hangs among Mel's suits to remind him. "See how pretty it is, with the jacket and train? This brocade cost five dollars a yard, but brocade's my favorite material, and you just watch and see if I don't wear this dress someday after all. That's what I got it for, and that's what I'm going to do with it. [29]

"I'm going to marry *Mel* in it, too. Nobody else. I'm not fickle. If I were fickle I'd take up with some dudes from my class; I have chances. But I'll wait. Meanwhile, when people ask how long we've been married, I'll just keep on saying, 'Long enough.' It's none of anybody's business. [30]

"Maybe what we ought to do is fight more. Mommy and Daddy really fought, but all we do is argue. Maybe arguing isn't enough. I could fight if I had to. I can shoot an ant pissing on cotton. I'm a good rifle shot; my daddy used to take me hunting. My mother's got a beautiful double-barrel shotgun. My own next gun's going to be either a .357 Magnum or else a nine-millimeter with hollow-point bullets, the kind that sound like a cannon and explode inside like shrapnel. [31]

"Melvin knows all about the hurts I've had in my life, and every now and then I tell him, 'I'll kill you, darling, I'll blow you away,' but I wouldn't really do that. I'd sooner castrate him, call an ambulance, and get him to the hospital. Must be the Scorpio in me coming out. The time to get to a man is when he's asleep, and you know what? Sometimes that motherfucker falls asleep while I'm *talking* to him! [32]

"One night when he fell asleep I got really pissed. I walked out carrying the tool I used for my woodcarvings. On the street a strange man said, 'Don't you know what can happen, lady, if you come out here alone at night?' I showed him the carving tool. He just said, 'Look, I'll be honest with you; I'm trying to get me a stable. Any time you want work, give me a call.' But that's not the kind of work I want to do. What I want to do is pour hot grits on Mel's feet, so I could incapacitate his running power and his ass would be *mine*. Or throw hot noddles on him in the shower so he'll look like a puzzle." [33]

Darkness falls. The phone still sits silent. "Let's go get something to eat," I suggest. Aretha leads us to Gino's, a franchised hamburger place. As we wait for our order, a sleek car pulls up outside, and Aretha surveys its driver. Luckily he can't hear what she says to him: "Oh, blood, you look so *tacky*, running around in that big Cadillac—you probably haven't even paid the rent." [34]

Back home the phone still has a dial tone. Its silence screams. [35]

The children yawn, but Aretha doesn't put them to bed. "They're all the company I have," she says, "so I let them stay up longer than they ought to."

"Do birds go to sleep?" asks Augie, as he squirms on her lap. [36]

"Yes, boy, just like people." [37]

"When?" [38]

"When they get hungry." Later she tells me how hungry she has been, on occasion, herself. "When Mel and I first lived together, there was a week when all we had to eat was popcorn, and it made him so sad he'd go into the other room and cry. [39]

"You know what my idea of soul food is? Never mind neck bones and greens; my idea of soul food is lobster thermidor." [40]

The phone rings. At last. She lets it ring four times before she picks it up. [41]

"Oh. Hi, Mommy." [42]

DESIGN AND MEANING

1. As Aretha speaks, her character and Mel's are revealed. List three words that you think describe each of them. What anecdotes led you to choose those words?
2. Aretha's monolog sounds true to life, as though you were sitting there listening to her talk. Point out some elements that make her speech seem realistic.
3. Why is the phone call at the end of the selection an appropriate closing?
4. Aretha's mother says that Aretha's "got quite a future." Do you agree or disagree? What led you to your opinion?
5. Who do you think would be a good audience for this selection? Are there some people who would not like it? Why?

SIMILARITY AND DIFFERENCE

Both "Aretha" and "I Thought My Last Hour Had Come" (Chapter 2) are basically monologs. Point out some differences in the speaking style of the two narrators.

SHORT WRITING IDEA

Imitating Aretha's speaking style, write a paragraph in which she gives her daughter Traci some advice.

LONGER WRITING IDEA

Ask a friend to talk informally for five minutes about a sweetheart or best friend. Tape-record this talk. Transcribe the tape as exactly as you can. Then edit the transcript as though you were going to publish it in a book like Howard's. What kinds of editing are necessary?

Larry L. King

Getting 'Em Ready for Darrell

A native Texan and proud of it, King writes humorous satirical articles for national publications. The "Darrell" mentioned in the title is Darrell Royal, for many years the celebrated coach of the Texas University football team. This essay, which first appeared in 1970, is included in a collection of King's work entitled *The Old Man and Lesser Mortals* (1974).

The day was miserably cold and wet for mid-October, the wind cutting down from the north with a keen blade. A ghostly mist blew in about midnight. By daylight the Texas desert air knew a coastal chill, clammy and bone-numbing. Soon Midland's flat paved streets flowed like shallow rivers. [1]

Seventh and eighth graders of the city's three junior high schools on awakening may have groaned into the weather's wet face, but they pulled on their football jerseys in compliance with a tradition requiring them to set themselves apart as gladiators each Thursday, which is Game Day. They would wear the jerseys in their classrooms. [2]

Three hundred strong, ranging in age from twelve to fourteen years, they comprised the dozen junior high football teams—four to a school, two to a grade—that play blood-and-thunder eight-game schedules with provisions for the more successful to play through to a city championship. Each team practices from two to two and one-half hours per day, except on game days; no homework is assigned to football players the night before a game. [3]

A blond twelve-year-old named Bradley, who weighed all of 107 pounds and limped on a swollen left knee, was having a more modest thought than of the city championship. "Maybe we can score on a wet field," he said. "We haven't done so good on a dry one." His team, the San Jacinto Seventh Grade Blues, had not known the dignity or solace of a touchdown in four previous outings. Their frustrated coach, a chunky, red-faced young man only recently out of college, had promised to run two laps around the football field for each touchdown his Blues scored against the unbeaten Trinity Orange. This prospect made Bradley grin. "You gonna play on that [4] bad knee?" Bradley's visiting father asked. "I played on it last week," he shrugged.

There were perhaps a dozen shivering spectators behind each bench—mostly parents—when the Blues kicked off to Trinity at 3:30 p.m. Bradley, who had started all four previous games, was chagrined to find himself benched. "Maybe the coach is protecting your knee," his father suggested. [5]

But Bradley believed he had been benched because he had missed two practice sessions that week, due to the death of his grandfather. [6]

Trinity marched through the Blues for four consecutive first downs, most of the damage done by a ponderous fullback who, though slow, had enough strength and size to run over the smaller defensive kids. Even so, his performance did not satisfy his coach. "Come on, Don," he shouted from the Orange sideline. "Duck that shoulder and *go!* You're just falling forward out there!" [7]

Meanwhile, the Blues' coach exhorted his collapsing defense: "Get mean out there! Come on, pop 'em! Bobby Joe, dammit, I'm gonna come out there and *kick* you if you let that ole fat boy run over you again!" Bobby Joe, who may have weighed all of a hundred pounds, sneaked a timid glance at the sideline. "You look like a *girl,* Bobby Joe," a man in boots and a western hat shouted through his cupped hands. "I'm his father," he said to a glaring visitor, as if that mitigated the circumstance. [8]

Trinity fumbled five yards away from a certain touchdown, losing the ball. The Blues jumped and yelled in celebration, while over on the Trinity side the Orange coach tore his rain-wet hair and shouted toward the sullen heavens. "Start runnin', coach," a skinny Blue said, picking up his helmet. "We're gonna score." "Way to *talk,* Donny!" an assistant coach said, slapping the youngster's rump as he ran on the field. [9]

But scoreless San Jacinto could not move the ball. Backs, attempting double and multiple handoffs, ran into each other and fell. Orange linemen poured through to overwhelm the quarterback before he could pass. "We gonna have us some blocking practice at half time if you guys don't knock somebody down," the Blue coach screamed. As if in defiance, the Blue line next permitted several Orange linemen to roar through and block a punt near their own goal line. "Blocking practice at the half!" the Blue coach screamed, his face contorted. "I mean it, now. You dadgummed guys didn't touch a man!" The Orange in four plays plunged for a touchdown, then ran in the two-point conversion for an 8–0 lead. [10]

"I told you guys to get in a goal-line defense, Mike!" the Blue [11] coach raved. "Dammit, *always* get in a goal-line defense inside the ten."

"I thought we was *in* a goal-line defense," Mike alibied, his teeth chattering in the cold. He turned to a teammate: "Gene, wasn't we in a goal-line defense?" Gene was bent over, his head between his legs, arms hugging his ribs. "Somebody kicked me in the belly," he answered. The Blue coach missed this drama. He was up at the fifty-yard line, shooing off a concerned mother attempting to wrap the substitutes in blankets she had brought from a station wagon. "They won't be cold if they'll *hit* somebody," the coach shouted. [12]

"Same ole thing," Bradley muttered from the bench as his team prepared to receive the kickoff. He had been inserted into the game long enough to know the indignity of having the touchdown scored over his left tackle position. "I had 'em," he said, "but then I slipped in the mud." Nobody said anything, for Bradley had clearly been driven out of the play like a dump truck. [13]

Midway in the second quarter Bradley redeemed himself, fighting off two blockers to dump a ball carrier who had gotten outside the defensive end. He ended up at the bottom of a considerable pile and rose dragging his right foot, hopping back into position while grimacing at the sidelines as if in hope of relief. The coach did not see him, however, for he was busying chastising the offending end: "Paul, dammit, don't give him the outside! Protect your territory!" "Bobby Joe," his father yelled, "*crack* somebody out there. You just standin' around." Bradley played the remainder of the half, limping more on the injured ankle than on the swollen knee. Rain was coming down in windblown and near-freezing torrents when the young teams ran to their respective buses for half-time inspirations. [14]

Four or five fathers shivered near the fifty-yard line, asses turned to the wind, smoking and talking of the 41–9 crusher applied to Oklahoma by the University of Texas. "They sure looked good," one of them said. "I think ole Darrell Royal's got his best team." [15]

A mother in red slacks, her coat collar turned up and her nose red, approached the men. "I think it's just terrible to play those little fellers in weather like this," she said. The men chuckled indulgently. "Well," one of them said. "we got to git 'em ready for Darrell." The men laughed. [16]

A balding portly man in a mackinaw puffed up. "How's Jerry doing?" he inquired. "Well," one of the men hedged, "none of our boys lookin' *too* good. Especially on offense." "I went to see my other boy play the first half," the newcomer said. "His bunch was ahead 19–0. They looked great. 'Course, they're eighth graders." [17]

When the teams returned on the field the newcomer grabbed [18] his son, a thick-legged little back. "Jerry," he said, "son, you got to get tough. Leland's lookin' tough. His team's ahead 19–0."

"We got to *hurt* some people," a stubby little towhead with the complexion of a small girl said. "We got to *kill* us some people." The men laughed. [19]

Bradley, soaking wet like all his teammates, was dispirited. What had the coach said to the Blues at half time? "He said we're better than they are and that we can beat 'em." The disapproving mother had returned with her blankets. Having wrapped up the bench warmers, she approached Bradley, who shrugged warmth off with a grunt: "I'm starting." An assistant coach, moving in to confiscate the coddling blankets, thought better of it when the mother stood her ground. "Damnfool *men,*" she muttered, glaring. [20]

The Blues drove sixty yards in the third period, their best-sustained drive of the season, inspiring their coach to whoop and holler like a delegate to the Democratic National Convention. "Way to *go,* Jerry!" the portly father shouted on play after play as he ran up and down. "Get outta them blankets!" the assistant coach yelled at the bench warmers as soon as the corrupting mother had fled to her station wagon. "If you don't think about being cold you won't *be* cold." Ten yards short of a touchdown three Blue backs collided behind the line in attempting a tricky double reverse, fumbling the ball and losing it in the process. The coach threw his red baseball cap in the mud and stomped it some. [21]

"Coach," the visiting father said, "don't you think your offense is pretty complicated for a bunch of kids? I mean, why not have simple plays they can execute?" [22]

The harassed coach cast a suspicious glance at the visitor. "We teach 'em the same basic system they'll need in high school," he snapped, turning away. [23]

Trinity's Orange picked up a couple of first downs and then fumbled the ball back. The Blues, trembling in a new opportunity, came to the line of scrimmage a man short of the required eleven. The coach grabbed Bradley and thrust him into the game at right guard. Four plays later, failing to pick up a first down, the Blue offense trooped off the field. Water ran down their young faces. Two little girls in short cheerleaders' skirts gave them soggy rah-rahs from beneath a tent of blankets, their voices thin and self-conscious. [24]

"Coach," Bradley said, "I don't know the plays for guard." [25]

"You *don't*? Well, why not? Didn't you read the playbook?" [26]

"Yeah, but you never *played* me at guard before. I'm a tackle." [27]

"Oh," the coach said. "Well . . . Bobby *Joe*, dern you, *hit* somebody!" [28]

"Way to *go*, Jerry!" the portly father shouted, breathing heavily as he kept pace with the action, jogging up and down the sideline. He turned to a bystander, puffing and beaming: "Jerry's not the ballplayer Leland is. 'Course, Leland's an eighth grader." [29]

The visiting father touched the wet arm of his downcast son. "Bradley," he said, "you're standing up on defense before you charge. That gives the blocking linemen a better angle on you. Go in low. If your first charge is forward instead of up, you'll have so much power the laws of physics will guarantee your penetration." [30]

"*Wow*!" one of the teenybopper cheerleaders said. "The laws of physics! Outta sight!" Her legs were blue in the cold. [31]

"Way to go, Jerry!" [32]

On his next defensive opportunity, Bradley charged in low and powerfully, his penetration carrying him so deep into the Orange backfield that he overran the ball carrier—who immediately shot through the vacated territory for a twenty-yard gain. Bradley stood back at the fifty-yard line, hands on hips, shaking his head in disgust and staring coldly at the visiting father, who suddenly studied his shoes. [33]

San Jacinto's scoreless Blues got off a final fourth-quarter drive, aided by two unnecessary roughness penalties against the Orange. "Coach," one of the bench warmers sang out, "they're playing dirty." [34]

"Let 'em play dirty," Jerry's father responded. "We'll take that fifteen yards every *time*, baby." [35]

But balls were dropped and young feet slid in the mud, and in the end the Blue drive ended ignominiously. San Jacinto's Blues were fighting off another Orange advance when the game ended. They lost again, 0–8; their coach was safe from running laps. [36]

"We gonna work in the blocking pits next week," he promised his young charges as they ran through the rain to their bus. [37]

Bradley, showered and dressed in street clothes, limped slowly to his visiting father's car. His right shoe was unlaced because of the swollen ankle; by nightfall it would show dark blue around the shinbone with bright red welts running along the heel base. [38]

"I'm sorry I didn't do better," Bradley said. "I got confused. You yelled one thing at me and the coach yelled another. *You* said charge hard and *he* said just stay there and plug up the hole." [39]

"Well," the visiting father said lamely, "I'm sorry I yelled anything at you." There had been too much yelling. "Can't you get heat treatment for that ankle? Or at least some supporting tape?" [40]

"Naw," Bradley said. "They don't give us those things until high school." [41]

They drove along in the rain, the windows steaming over. They passed Robert E. Lee High School, where a squad of perhaps sixty [42] young men drilled in the rain, padless, tuning up for their Friday-night game against Abilene. Thousands would drive the two hundred miles east, some of them drunk or drinking. Probably at least one would hit another car or a telephone pole.

"I may not play in high school," Bradley blurted. "I may not even play next year. The eighth-grade coach came scouting around last week, and he asked me some questions and I told him I might not even *play* next year." His blond hair was wet; his creamy young face was red. He looked angry and haggard and somehow old. [43]

"Way to *go,* Bradley," his visiting father said. [44]

AFTERWORD

A love-hate relationship with football may rest deep in the family genes. My son came to me shortly after "Getting 'Em Ready for Darrell" had appeared in the *Texas Observer* to indicate—with a bit of bashful toe digging—that he might try football for one more year. Why? "Well," he said with an abashed grin, "I kinda liked the publicity." He was on the verge of quitting a second time when the article was reprinted in *Chris Schenkel's Football Sportscene*—inspiring him to consider himself a national, rather than a regional, celebrity. He now has given up the game, however, and is in a private school where competitive sports are limited to swimming, sailing, and soccer. "I just got tired of football," he said recently. "Hell, I played seven years." Bradley King is fifteen. [45]

VOCABULARY

chagrin	embarrassment and annoyance
chastise	to punish or scold
coddle	to treat tenderly
compliance	giving in to a request or wish
contorted	violently distorted
dispirited	dejected, in low spirits
exhort	to urge earnestly
grimace	to twist the face, expressing pain, contempt, or disgust
ignominious	shameful, dishonorable
mitigate	to make less severe; to improve
ponderous	heavy and bulky
portly	large and heavy; stout
solace	comfort; a consolation

DESIGN AND MEANING

1. The visiting father is King himself, but he always writes "he" instead of "I" in this selection. Why do you think he avoids the first person?
2. King frequently quotes the men watching and coaching the game. What do the quoted comments have in common?
3. Summarize the various tactics the men use to get the boys to play well.
4. This essay has an implied thesis (main point). What is it?

SIMILARITY AND DIFFERENCE

Neither of the essays included so far in this section on narration—"Aretha" and "Getting 'Em Ready"—has a directly stated main point. Why do you think this is so?

SHORT WRITING IDEA

Copy the first paragraph of King's essay. Using that passage as a pattern, write a description of some extreme weather in your town.

LONGER WRITING IDEA

Almost all of us have felt at some time as though we were pushed into doing something we were not entirely sure we wanted. Narrate your experience of being pushed by friends, relatives, or others.

VOCABULARY CHECK

Complete each sentence in a brief and reasonable way.

1. The hearty dinner was not much solace for having
2. Clyde exhorted Marla to
3. Marla chastised Clyde for being
4. The crew felt ignominious when
5. The dispirited committee decided
6. Clyde tried to mitigate his insult by
7. With a great deal of chagrin, he

Robert Guillain

"I Thought My Last Hour Had Come . . ."

Robert Guillain (b. 1908), a French journalist who writes about the far east, has published a book called *I Saw Tokyo Burning* which describes through eyewitness accounts the devastation of Japan by the Allies at the close of World War II. The following selection, which presents Mrs. Futaba Kitayama's description of the atomic explosion at Hiroshima as told to Guillain, was translated from the French by William R. Byron and appeared in the *Atlantic* in August of 1980.

"It was in Hiroshima, that morning of August 6. I had joined a team of women who, like me, worked as volunteers in cutting firepaths against incendiary raids by demolishing whole rows of houses. My husband, because of a raid alert the previous night, had stayed at the *Chunichi (Central Japan Journal),* where he worked. [1]

"Our group had passed the Tsurumi bridge, Indian-file, when there was an alert; an enemy plane appeared all alone, very high over our heads. Its silver wings shone brightly in the sun. A woman exclaimed, 'Oh, look—a parachute!' I turned toward where she was pointing, and just at that moment a shattering flash filled the whole sky. [2]

"Was it the flash that came first, or the sound of the explosion, tearing up my insides? I don't remember. I was thrown to the ground, pinned to the earth, and immediately the world began to collapse around me, on my head, my shoulders. I couldn't see anything. It was completely dark. I thought my last hour had come. I thought of my three children, who had been evacuated to the country to be safe from the raids. I couldn't move; debris kept falling, beams and tiles piled up on top of me. [3]

"Finally I did manage to crawl free. There was a terrible smell in the air. Thinking the bomb that hit us might have been a yellow phosphorus incendiary like those that had fallen on so many other cities, I rubbed my nose and mouth hard with a *tenugui* (a kind of towel) I had at my waist. To my horror, I found that the skin of my face had come off in the towel. Oh! The skin on my hands, on my arms, came off too. From elbow to fingertips, all the skin on my [4] right arm had come loose and was hanging grotesquely. The skin on my left hand fell off too, the five fingers, like a glove.

"I found myself sitting on the ground, prostrate. Gradually I registered that all my companions had disappeared. What had happened to them? A frantic panic gripped me, I wanted to run, but where? Around me was just debris, wooden framing, beams and roofing tiles; there wasn't a single landmark left. [5]

"And what had happened to the sky, so blue a moment ago? Now it was as black as night. Everything seemed vague and fuzzy. It was as though a cloud covered my eyes and I wondered if I had lost my senses. I finally saw the Tsurumi bridge and I ran headlong toward it, jumping over the piles of rubble. What I saw under the bridge then horrified me. [6]

"People by the hundreds were flailing in the river. I couldn't tell if they were men or women; they were all in the same state: their faces were puffy and ashen, their hair tangled, they held their hands raised and, groaning with pain, threw themselves into the water. I had a violent impulse to do so myself, because of the pain burning through my whole body. But I can't swim and I held back. [7]

"Past the bridge, I looked back to see that the whole Hachobori district had suddenly caught fire, to my surprise, because I thought only the district I was in had been bombed. As I ran, I shouted my children's names. Where was I going? I have no idea, but I can still see the scenes of horror I glimpsed here and there on my way. [8]

"A mother, her face and shoulders covered with blood, tried frantically to run into a burning house. A man held her back and she screamed, 'Let me go! Let me go! My son is burning in there!' She was like a mad demon. Under the Kojin bridge, which had half collapsed and had lost its heavy, reinforced-concrete parapets, I saw a lot of bodies floating in the water like dead dogs, almost naked, with their clothes in shreds. At the river's edge, near the bank, a woman lay on her back with her breasts ripped off, bathed in blood. How could such a frightful thing have happened? I thought of the scenes of the Buddhist hell my grandmother had described to me when I was little. [9]

"I must have wandered for at least two hours before finding myself on the Eastern military parade ground. My burns were hurting me, but the pain was different from an ordinary burn. It was a dull pain that seemed somehow to come from outside my body. A kind of yellow pus oozed from my hands, and I thought that my face must also be horrible to see. [10]

"Around me on the parade ground were a number of grade-school and secondary-school children, boys and girls, writhing in spasms of agony. Like me, they were members of the anti-air raid volunteer corps. I heard them crying 'Mama! Mama!' as though [11] they'd gone crazy. They were so burned and bloody that looking at them was insupportable. I forced myself to do so just the same, and I cried out in rage. 'Why? Why these children?' But there was no one to rage at and I could do nothing but watch them die, one after the other, vainly calling for their mothers.

"After lying almost unconscious for a long time on the parade ground, I started walking again. As far as I could see with my failing sight, everything was in flames, as far as the Hiroshima station and the Atago district. It seemed to me that my face was hardening little by little. I cautiously touched my hands to my cheeks. My face felt as though it had doubled in size. I could see less and less clearly. Was I going blind, then? After so much hardship, was I going to die? I kept on walking anyway and I reached a suburban area. [12]

"In that district, farther removed from the center, I found my elder sister alive, with only slight injuries to the head and feet. She didn't recognize me at first, then she burst into tears. In a handcart, she wheeled me nearly three miles to the first-aid center at Yaga. It was night when we arrived. I later learned there was a pile of corpses and countless injured there. I spent two nights there, unconscious; my sister told me that in my delirium I kept repeating, 'My children! Take me to my children!' [13]

"On August 8, I was carried on a stretcher to a train and transported to the home of relatives in the village of Kasumi. The village doctor said my case was hopeless. My children, recalled from their evacuation refuge, rushed to my side. I could no longer see them; I could recognize them only by smelling their good odor. On August 11, my husband joined us. The children wept with joy as they embraced him. [14]

"Our happiness soon ended. My husband, who bore no trace of injury, died suddenly three days later, vomiting blood. We had been married sixteen years and now, because I was at the brink of death myself, I couldn't even rest his head as I should have on the pillow of the dead. [15]

"I said to myself, 'My poor children, because of you I don't have the right to die!' And finally, by a miracle, I survived after I had again and again been given up for lost. [16]

"My sight returned fairly quickly, and after twenty days I could dimly see my children's features. The burns on my face and hands did not heal so rapidly, and the wounds remained pulpy, like rotten tomatoes. It wasn't until December that I could walk again. When my bandages were removed in January, I knew that my face and hands would always be deformed. My left ear was half its original size. A streak of cheloma, a dark brown swelling as wide as my hand, runs from the side of my head across my mouth to my throat. [17]

My right hand is striped with a cheloma two inches wide from the wrist to the little finger. The five fingers on my left hand are now fused at the base . . . ."

VOCABULARY

incendiary	designed to cause fires
parapet	a low wall or railing
prostrate	in a state of physical exhaustion or weakness
insupportable	unbearable

DESIGN AND MEANING

1. How would you describe the atmosphere of the woman's narrative? What elements contribute to that atmosphere?
2. Guillain transcribed the woman's story, which she told to him out loud. Choose four or five consecutive paragraphs and see if you can justify Guillain's choice of paragraph division.
3. Notice the frequency of questions asked in the narrative. What is their effect on the reader?
4. If you were presented with this essay and a well-reasoned argument against nuclear warfare, which would you find more convincing? Why?

SIMILARITY AND DIFFERENCE

Note some similarities in style between Guillain's essay and Tillie Olsen's "I Stand Here Ironing" at the end of this chapter.

SHORT WRITING IDEA

Pretending that you are the interviewer, write a closing paragraph for this essay, in which you condemn nuclear warfare.

LONGER WRITING IDEA

Write a narrative whose purpose is to persuade the reader to take a certain stance on a controversial issue.

Richard Selzer

An Absence of Windows

A professor of surgery at Yale Medical School, Selzer (b. 1928) also writes short stories and essays which portray with sympathy but without sentimentality the dramatic, sometimes agonizing, experiences of a practicing surgeon.

Not long ago, operating rooms had windows. It was a boon and a blessing in spite of the occasional fly that managed to strain through the screens and threaten our very sterility. For the adventurous insect drawn to such a ravishing spectacle, a quick swat and, Presto! The door to the next world sprang open. But for us who battled on, there was the benediction of the sky, the applause and reproach of thunder. A Divine consultation crackled in on the lightning! And at night, in Emergency, there was the pomp, the longevity of the stars to deflate a surgeon's ego. It did no patient a disservice to have Heaven looking over his doctor's shoulder. I very much fear that, having bricked up our windows, we have lost more than the breeze; we have severed a celestial connection. [1]

Part of my surgical training was spent in a rural hospital in eastern Connecticut. The building was situated on the slope of a modest hill. Behind it, cows grazed in a pasture. The operating theater occupied the fourth, the ultimate floor, wherefrom huge windows looked down upon the scene. To glance up from our work and see the lovely cattle about theirs, calmed the frenzy of the most temperamental of prima donnas. Intuition tells me that our patients had fewer wound infections and made speedier recoveries than those operated upon in the airless sealed boxes where now we strive. Certainly the surgeons were of a gentler stripe. [2]

I have spent too much time in these windowless rooms. Some part of me would avoid them if I could. Still, even here, in these bloody closets, sparks fly up from the dry husks of the human body. Most go unnoticed, burn out in an instant. But now and then, they coalesce into a fire which is an inflammation of the mind of him who watches. [3]

Not in large cities is it likely to happen, but in towns the size of ours, that an undertaker will come to preside over the funeral of a close friend; a policeman will capture a burglar only to find that [4] the miscreant is the uncle of his brother's wife. Say that a fire breaks out. The fire truck rushes to the scene; it proves to be the very house where one of the firemen was born, and the luckless man is now called on to complete, axe and hose, the destruction of his natal place. Hardly a civic landmark, you say, but for him who gulped first air within those walls, it is a hard destiny. So it is with a hospital, which is itself a community. Its citizens—orderlies, maids, nurses, x-ray technicians, doctors, a hundred others.

A man whom I knew has died. He was the hospital mailman. It was I that presided over his death. A week ago I performed an exploratory operation upon him for acute surgical abdomen. That is the name given to an illness that is unknown, and for which there is no time to make a diagnosis with tests of the blood and urine, x-rays. I saw him writhing in pain, rolling from side to side, his knees drawn up, his breaths coming in short little draughts. The belly I lay the flat of my hand upon was hot to the touch. The slightest pressure of my fingers caused him to cry out—a great primitive howl of vowel and diphthong. This kind of pain owns no consonants. Only later, when the pain settles in, long and solid, only then does it grow a spine to sharpen the glottals and dentals a man can grip with his teeth, his throat. Fiercely then, to hide it from his wife, his children, for the pain shames him. [5]

In the emergency room, fluid is given into the mailman's veins. Bags of blood are sent for, and poured in. Oxygen is piped into his nostrils, and a plastic tube is let down into his stomach. This, for suction. A dark tarry yield slides into a jar on the wall. In another moment, a second tube has sprouted from his penis, carrying away his urine. Such is the costume of acute surgical abdomen. In an hour, I know that nothing has helped him. At his wrist, a mouse skitters, stops, then darts away. His salty lips insist upon still more oxygen. His blood pressure, they say, is falling. I place the earpieces of my stethoscope, this ever-asking Y, in my ears. Always, I am comforted a bit by this ungainly little hose. It is my oldest, my dearest friend. More, it is my lucky charm. I place the disc upon the tense mounding blue-tinted belly, gently, so as not to shock the viscera into commotion (those vowels!), and I listen for a long time. I hear nothing. The bowel sleeps. It plays possum in the presence of the catastrophe that engulfs it. We must go to the operating room. There must be an exploration. I tell this to the mailman. Narcotized, he nods and takes my fingers in his own, pressing. Thus has he given me all of his trust. [6]

A woman speaks to me. [7]

"Do your best for him, Doctor. Please." [8]

My best? An anger rises toward her for the charge she has given. Still, I cover her hand with mine. [9]

"Yes," I say, "my best." [10]

An underground tunnel separates the buildings of our hospital. I accompany the stretcher that carries the mailman through that tunnel, cursing for the thousandth time the demonic architect that placed the emergency room in one building, and the operating room in the other. [11]

Each tiny ridge in the cement floor is a rut from which rise and echo still more vowels of pain, new sounds that I have never heard before. Pain invents its own language. With this tongue, we others are not conversant. Never mind, we shall know it in our time. [12]

We lift the mailman from the stretcher to the operating table. The anesthetist is ready with still another tube. [13]

"Go to sleep, Pete," I say into his ear, my lips so close it is almost a kiss. "When you wake up, it will all be over, all behind you." [14]

I should not have spoken his name aloud! No good will come of it. The syllable has peeled from me something, a skin that I need. In a minute, the chest of the mailman is studded with electrodes. From his mouth a snorkel leads to tanks of gas. Each of these tanks is painted a different color. One is bright green. That is for oxygen. They group behind the anesthetist, hissing. I have never come to this place without seeing that dreadful headless choir of gas tanks. [15]

Now red paint tracks across the bulging flanks of the mailman. It is a harbinger of the blood to come. [16]

"May we go ahead?" I ask the anesthetist. [17]

"Yes," he says. And I pull the scalpel across the framed skin, skirting the navel. There are arteries and veins to be clamped, cut, tied, and cauterized, fat and fascia to divide. The details of work engage a man, hold his terror at bay. Beneath us now, the peritoneum. A slit, and we are in. Hot fluid spouts through the small opening I have made. It is gray, with flecks of black. Pancreatitis! We all speak the word at once. We have seen it many times before. It is an old enemy. I open the peritoneum its full length. My fingers swim into the purse of the belly, against the tide of the issuing fluid. The pancreas is swollen, necrotic, a dead fish that has gotten tossed in, and now lies spoiling across the upper abdomen. I withdraw my hand. [18]

"Feel," I invite the others. They do, and murmur against the disease. But they do not say anything that I have not heard many times. Unlike the mailman, who was rendered eloquent in its presence, we others are reduced to the commonplace at the touch of such stuff. [19]

We suction away the fluid that has escaped from the sick pancreas. It is rich in enzymes. If these enzymes remain free in the abdomen, they will digest the tissues there, the other organs. It is the pancreas alone that can contain them safely. This mailman and [20] his pancreas—careful neighbors for fifty-two years until the night the one turned rampant and set fire to the house of the other. The digestion of tissues has already begun. Soap has formed here and there, from the compounding of the liberated calcium and the fat. It would be good to place a tube (still another tube) into the common bile duct, to siphon away the bile that is a stimulant to the pancreas. At least that. We try, but we cannot even see the approach to that duct, so swollen is the pancreas about it. And so we mop and suck and scour the floors and walls of this ruined place. Even as we do, the gutters run with new streams of the fluid. We lay in rubber drains and lead them to the outside. It is all that is left to us to do.

"Zero chromic on a Lukens," I say, and the nurse hands me the suture for closure. [21]

I must not say too much at the operating table. There are new medical students here. I must take care what sparks I let fly toward such inflammable matter. [22]

The mailman awakens in the recovery room. I speak his magic name once more. [23]

"Pete." Again, "Pete," I call. [24]

He sees me, gropes for my hand. [25]

"What happens now?" he asks me. [26]

"In a day or two, the pain will let up," I say. "You will get better." [27]

"Was there any . . .?" [28]

"No," I say, knowing. "There was no cancer. You are clean as a whistle." [29]

"Thank God," he whispers, and then, "Thank *you,* Doctor." [30]

It took him a week to die in fever and pallor and pain. [31]

It is the morning of the autopsy. It has been scheduled for eleven o'clock. Together, the students and I return from our coffee. I walk slowly. I do not want to arrive until the postmortem examination is well under way. It is twenty minutes past eleven when we enter the morgue. I pick the mailman out at once from the others. Damn! They have not even started. Anger swells in me, at being forced to face the *whole* patient again. [32]

It isn't fair! Dismantled, he would at least be at some remove . . . a tube of flesh. But look! There is an aftertaste of life in him. In his fallen mouth a single canine tooth, perfectly embedded, gleams, a badge of better days. [33]

The pathologist is a young resident who was once a student of mine. A tall lanky fellow with a bushy red beard. He wears the green pajamas of his trade. He pulls on rubber gloves, and turns to greet me. [34]

"I've been waiting for you," he smiles. "Now we can start." [35]

He steps to the table and picks up the large knife with which he will lay open the body from neck to pubis. All at once, he pauses, and, reaching with his left hand, he closes the lids of the mailman's eyes. When he removes his hand, one lid comes unstuck and slowly rises. Once more, he reaches up to press it down. This time it stays. The gesture stuns me. My heart is pounding, my head trembling. I think that the students are watching me. Perhaps my own heart has become visible, beating beneath this white laboratory coat. [36]

The pathologist raises his knife. [37]

"Wait," I say. "Do you always do that? Close the eyes?" [38]

He is embarrassed. He smiles faintly. His face is beautiful, soft. [39]

"No," he says, and shakes his head. "But just then, I remembered that he brought the mail each morning . . . how his blue eyes used to twinkle." [40]

Now he lifts the knife, and, like a vandal looting a gallery, carves open the body. [41]

To work in windowless rooms is to live in a jungle where you cannot see the sky. Because there is no sky to see, there is no grand vision of God. Instead, there are the numberless fragmented spirits that lurk behind leaves, beneath streams. The one is no better than the other, no worse. Still, a man is entitled to the temple of his preference. Mine lies out on a prairie, wondering up at Heaven. Or in a many windowed operating room where, just outside the panes of glass, cows graze, and the stars shine down upon my carpentry. [42]

VOCABULARY

boon — advantage
coalesce — to combine
dental — sound made with the teeth and tongue
diphthong — a blended vowel sound, like "oy" in "boy"
glottal — sound made in the throat
narcotized — numb, sedated
necrotic — dead
pancreatitis — infection of the pancreas

DESIGN AND MEANING

1. The most subtle element of this essay is the relationship between the frame story (paragraphs 1–3 and 42) and the narrative sandwiched within it. What do you think the relationship is? If we look

at the piece as a recording of Selzer's thought process, what could it be about the windowless operating rooms that reminds him of the story of the mailman?

2. A stimulating narrative always contains one or more conflicts. Selzer's essay does not involve conflict between characters, but a conflict within himself. What two roles does he find conflicting? Why (in paragraphs 14–15) does he exclaim, "I should not have spoken his name aloud!" Why does he lie to the patient? Why does he want to be late for the autopsy?
3. A narrative can never include every incident that happened. A writer selects what to leave out, where to begin, and at what point to end. Why is the incident with the pathologist reported in this narrative?
4. Selzer's writing is marked by the use of short sentences (as in the opening of paragraph 5), direct dialog, and vivid comparisons. Point out where some of these features occur. Imagine the narrative without these features. What would it lack? Try rewriting a section without one of these features.

SIMILARITY AND DIFFERENCE

Selzer's essay has many similarities to Orwell's "A Hanging" (Chapter 1). What are a few of them? Look in particular at the role and character of the narrator.

SHORT WRITING IDEA

In paragraph 18, Selzer writes, "The details of work engage a man, hold his terror at bay." Write a paragraph explaining this sentence, using your own experience to develop the idea.

LONGER WRITING IDEA

Situations arise in which we realize that two of our roles are in conflict: Can we be a daughter and a friend to our mothers? Can a student be a pal to a teacher? Can a boyfriend or girlfriend act as both supporter and critic? Can you be a team or clique member and an individualist? Tell the story of one such situation you have been in, and analyze your response to it.

poetry

Countee Cullen

Incident

Cullen (1903–1946), a poet of the Harlem Renaissance of the twenties and thirties, also wrote a novel and several plays. As early as 1927, he edited an anthology of black poetry.

Once riding in old Baltimore,
    Heart-filled, head-filled with glee,
I saw a Baltimorean
    Keep looking straight at me.

Now I was eight and very small, [5]
    And he was no whit bigger,
And so I smiled, but he poked out
    His tongue and called me, "Nigger."

I saw the whole of Baltimore
    From May until December: [10]
Of all the things that happened there
    That's all that I remember.

Robert Frost

"Out, Out—"

Perhaps America's favorite modern poet, Frost (1874–1963) combined fine craftsmanship and restrained emotion in writing about simple, down-to-earth experiences.

The buzz saw snarled and rattled in the yard
And made dust and dropped stove-length sticks of wood,
Sweet-scented stuff when the breeze drew across it.
And from there those that lifted eyes could count
Five mountain ranges one behind the other [5]
Under the sunset far into Vermont.
And the saw snarled and rattled, snarled and rattled,
As it ran light, or had to bear a load.
And nothing happened: day was all but done.
Call it a day, I wish they might have said [10]
To please the boy by giving him the half hour
That a boy counts so much when saved from work.
His sister stood beside them in her apron
To tell them 'Supper.' At the word, the saw,
As if to prove saws knew what supper meant, [15]
Leaped out at the boy's hand, or seemed to leap—,
He must have given the hand. However it was,
Neither refused the meeting. But the hand!
The boy's first outcry was a rueful laugh,
As he swung toward them holding up the hand [20]
Half in appeal, but half as if to keep
The life from spilling. Then the boy saw all—
Since he was old enough to know, big boy
Doing a man's work, though a child at heart—
He saw all spoiled. 'Don't let him cut my hand off— [25]
The doctor, when he comes. Don't let him, sister!'
So. But the hand was gone already.
The doctor put him in the dark of ether.
He lay and puffed his lips out with his breath.
And then—the watcher at his pulse took fright. [30]
No one believed. They listened at his heart.
Little—less—nothing!—and that ended it.
No more to build on there. And they, since they
Were not the one dead, turned to their affairs.

DESIGN AND MEANING

1. What is the unstated main point of "Incident"? What lines suggest the main point most strongly?
2. "Incident" has great simplicity of rhyme, rhythm, and word choice. Why do you think Cullen chose this simplicity?
3. What are the two senses most strongly appealed to in the imagery of "Out, Out—"? Point out some examples of the sensory details.
4. How does Frost give the saw a human character? What kind of character is it?
5. What attitude toward life is expressed in "Out, Out—"? Explain its relationship to the origin of the title, this passage from *Macbeth:*

   Out, out, brief candle!
   Life's but a walking shadow, a poor player,
   That struts and frets his hour upon the stage
   And then is heard no more. It is a tale
   Told by an idiot, full of sound and fury,
   Signifying nothing.

   V.v. 23–28

6. What attitude toward humanity is suggested in "Out, Out—"? What is the major evidence for your answer?

SIMILARITY AND DIFFERENCE

Read "Departmental" in Chapter 5. What similarities and differences can you see between the two Frost poems?

SHORT WRITING IDEA

Take part of one of the narratives you have written and try dividing it into lines of poetry. Revise lines if you wish. (You may benefit from looking up a definition of "blank verse.")

LONGER WRITING IDEA

Narrate the story of an incident that introduced you to a side of life or humanity you had not confronted before (altruism, poverty, wealth, racism, violence).

Short Story

Katharine Brush

Birthday Party

An American writer, Katharine Ingham Brush (1900–1952) wrote *Young Man of Manhattan* (1930), *Red-Headed Woman* (1931), *The Boy from Maine* (1942), and many short stories.

They were a couple in their late thirties, and they looked unmistakably married. They sat on the banquette opposite us in a little narrow restaurant, having dinner. The man had a round, self-satisfied face, with glasses on it; the woman was fadingly pretty, in a big hat. There was nothing conspicuous about them, nothing particularly noticeable, until the end of their meal, when it suddenly became obvious that this was an Occasion—in fact, the husband's birthday, and the wife had planned a little surprise for him. [1]

It arrived, in the form of a small but glossy birthday cake, with one pink candle burning in the center. The headwaiter brought it in and placed it before the husband, and meanwhile the violin-and-piano orchestra played "Happy Birthday to You" and the wife beamed with shy pride over her little surprise, and such few people as there were in the restaurant tried to help out with a pattering of applause. It became clear at once that help was needed, because the husband was not pleased. Instead he was hotly embarrassed, and indignant at his wife for embarrassing him. [2]

You looked at him and you saw this and you thought, "Oh, now, don't *be* like that!" But he was like that, and as soon as the little cake had been deposited on the table, and the orchestra had finished the birthday piece, and the general attention had shifted from the man and the woman, I saw him say something to her under his breath—some punishing thing, quick and curt and unkind. I couldn't bear to look at the woman then, so I stared at my plate and waited for quite a long time. Not long enough, though. She was still crying when I finally glanced over there again. Crying quietly and heartbrokenly and hopelessly, all to herself, under the gay big brim of her best hat. [3]

VOCABULARY

banquette an upholstered bench along a wall

DESIGN AND MEANING

1. Katharine Brush's story, only about 300 words long, is a triumph of conciseness. What do we know about the husband at the end of the first paragraph? About the wife? How are those character details reinforced in the final two paragraphs?
2. With whom do your sympathies lie? How does point of view in the narrative function in directing your response?
3. Why do you think Brush included the details about the woman's hat in the first and last paragraphs?
4. What does Brush mean in the first sentence when she says the couple "looked unmistakably married"? Do you think this incident would have happened if the couple had been merely dating, instead of married? Explain.
5. In the final sentence Brush describes the wife as "*Crying quietly and heartbrokenly and hopelessly.*" She could have written that phrase this way: "*Crying quietly, heartbrokenly, and hopelessly.*" Which version do you find more effective? Can you tell why?

SIMILARITY AND DIFFERENCE

What is the major difference in the first-person point of view in Katharine Brush's "Birthday Party" and in Jane Howard's "Aretha Has the Best Man"?

SHORT WRITING IDEA

Rewrite "Birthday Party" from the husband's point of view. Do not make your version any longer than Brush's. Try to be as careful in choosing your details as she is. Make every word count.

LONGER WRITING IDEA

Describe a surprise that you planned for someone (or that someone planned for you) and tell how it turned out. In order to make this piece of writing effective, you'll need to use plenty of concrete details and select them carefully. Consider your purpose and your audience. Are you writing simply to entertain your readers? Or are you, like Brush, writing a narrative to make a point without stating it?

Tillie Olsen

I Stand Here Ironing

Drawing on her own experience as a working mother, Olsen (b. 1913) has recently produced an important book entitled *Silences,* examining the reasons why many women fail to write. In 1961 she won the O'Henry Award, followed by numerous grants and fellowships for creative writing. "I Stand Here Ironing" appears in her collection *Tell Me a Riddle* (1961).

I stand here ironing, and what you asked me moves tormented back and forth with the iron. [1]

"I wish you would manage the time to come in and talk with me about your daughter. I'm sure you can help me understand her. She's a youngster who needs help and whom I'm deeply interested in helping." [2]

"Who needs help?" Even if I came what good would it do? You think because I am her mother I have a key, or that in some way you could use me as a key? She has lived for nineteen years. There is all that life that has happened outside of me, beyond me. [3]

And when is there time to remember, to sift, to weigh, to estimate, to total? I will start and there will be an interruption and I will have to gather it all together again. Or I will become engulfed with all I did or did not do, with what should have been and what cannot be helped. [4]

She was a beautiful baby. The first and only one of our five that was beautiful at birth. You do not guess how new and uneasy her tenancy in her now-loveliness. You did not know her all those years she was thought homely, or see her poring over her baby pictures, making me tell her over and over how beautiful she had been—and would be, I would tell her—and was now, to the seeing eye. But the seeing eyes were few or nonexistent. Including mine. [5]

I nursed her. They feel that's important nowadays. I nursed all the children, but with her, with all the fierce rigidity of first motherhood, I did like the books said. Though her cries battered me to trembling and my breasts ached with swollenness, I waited till the clock decreed. [6]

Why do I put that first? I do not even know if it matters, or if it explains anything. [7]

She was a beautiful baby. She blew shining bubbles of sound. She loved motion, loved light, loved color and music and textures. [8]

She would lie on the floor in her blue overalls patting the surface so hard in ecstasy her hands and feet would blur. She was a miracle to me, but when she was eight months old I had to leave her daytimes with the woman downstairs to whom she was no miracle at all, for I worked or looked for work and for Emily's father, who "could no longer endure" (he wrote in his good-by note) "sharing want with us."

I was nineteen. It was the pre-relief, pre-WPA world of the depression. I would start running as soon as I got off the streetcar, running up the stairs, the place smelling sour, and awake or asleep to startle awake, when she saw me she would break into a clogged weeping that could not be comforted, a weeping I can yet hear. [9]

After a while I found a job hashing at night so I could be with her days, and it was better. But it came to where I had to bring her to his family and leave her. [10]

It took a long time to raise the money for her fare back. Then she got chicken pox and I had to wait longer. When she finally came, I hardly knew her, walking quick and nervous like her father, looking like her father, thin, and dressed in a shoddy red that yellowed her skin and glared at the pock marks. All the baby loveliness gone. [11]

She was two. Old enough for nursery school they said, and I did not know then what I know now—the fatigue of the long day, and the lacerations of group life in the kinds of nurseries that are only parking places for children. [12]

Except that it would have made no difference if I had known. It was the only place there was. It was the only way we could be together, the only way I could hold a job. [13]

And even without knowing, I knew. I knew the teacher that was evil because all these years it has curdled into my memory, the little boy hunched in the corner, her rasp, "why aren't you outside, because Alvin hits you? that's no reason, go out, scaredy." I knew Emily hated it even if she did not clutch and implore "don't go Mommy" like the other children, mornings. [14]

She always had a reason why we should stay home. Momma, you look sick. Momma, I feel sick. Momma, the teachers aren't there today, they're sick. Momma there was a fire there last night. Momma it's a holiday today, no school, they told me. [15]

But never a direct protest, never rebellion. I think of our others in their three-, four-year-oldness—the explosions, the tempers, the denunciations, the demands—and I feel suddenly ill. I stop the ironing. What in me demanded that goodness in her? And what was the cost, the cost to her of such goodness? [16]

The old man living in the back once said in his gentle way: "You should smile at Emily more when you look at her." What *was* [17] in my face when I looked at her? I loved her. There were all the acts of love.

It was only with the others I remembered what he said, so that it was the face of joy, and not of care or tightness or worry I turned to them—too late for Emily. She does not smile easily, let alone almost always as her brothers and sisters do. Her face is closed and somber, but when she wants, how fluid. You must have seen it in her pantomimes, you spoke of her rare gift for comedy on the stage that rouses a laughter out of the audience so dear they applaud and applaud and do not want to let her go. [18]

Where does it come from, that comedy? There was none of it in her when she came back to me that second time, after I had had to send her away again. She had a new daddy now to learn to love, and I think perhaps it was a better time. Except when we left her alone nights, telling ourselves she was old enough. [19]

"Can't you go some other time Mommy, like tomorrow?" she would ask. "Will it be just a little while you'll be gone? Do you promise?" [20]

The time we came back, the front door open, the clock on the floor in the hall. She rigid awake. "It wasn't just a little while. I didn't cry. I called you three times, just three times, and then I ran downstairs to open the door so you could come faster. The clock talked loud, I threw it away, it scared me when it talked." [21]

She said the clock talked loud that night I went to the hospital to have Susan. She was delirious with the fever that comes before red measles, but she was fully conscious all the week I was gone and the week after we were home when she could not come near the new baby or me. [22]

She did not get well. She stayed skeleton thin, not wanting to eat, and night after night she had nightmares. She would call for me, and I would sleepily call back, "you're all right, darling, go to sleep, it's just a dream," and if she still called, in a sterner voice, "now go to sleep Emily, there's nothing to hurt you." Twice, only twice, when I had to get up for Susan anyway, I went in to sit with her. [23]

Now when it is too late (as if she would let me hold and comfort her like I do the others) I get up and go to her at her moan or restless stirring. "Are you awake? Can I get you anything?" And the answer is always the same: "No, I'm all right, go back to sleep Mother." [24]

They persuaded me at the clinic to send her away to a convalescent home in the country where "she can have the kind of food and care you can't manage for her, and you'll be free to concentrate on the new baby." They still send children to that place. I see pictures on the society page of sleek young women planning affairs [25] to raise money for it, or dancing at the affairs, or decorating Easter eggs or filling Christmas stockings for children.

[26] They never have a picture of the children so I do not know if they still wear those gigantic red bows and the ravaged looks on the every other Sunday when parents can come to visit "unless otherwise notified"—as we were notified the first six weeks.

[27] Oh it is a handsome place, green lawns and tall trees and fluted flower beds. High up on the balconies of each cottage the children stand, the girls in their red bows and white dresses, the boys in white suits and giant red ties. The parents stand below shrieking up to be heard and the children shriek down to be heard, and between them the invisible wall "Not To Be Contaminated by Parental Germs or Physical Affection."

[28] There was a tiny girl who always stood hand in hand with Emily. Her parents never came. One visit she was gone. "They moved her to Rose Cottage," Emily shouted in explanation. "They don't like you to love anybody here."

[29] She wrote once a week, the labored writing of a seven-year-old. "I am fine. How is the baby. If I write my leter nicly I will have a star. Love." There was never a star. We wrote every other day, letters she could never hold or keep but only hear read—once. "We simply do not have room for children to keep any personal possessions," they patiently explained when we pieced one Sunday's shrieking together to plead how much it would mean to Emily to keep her letters and cards.

[30] Each visit she looked frailer. "She isn't eating," they told us.

[31] (They had runny eggs for breakfast or mush with lumps, Emily said later, I'd hold it in my mouth and not swallow. Nothing ever tasted good, just when they had chicken.)

[32] It took us eight months to get her released home, and only the fact that she gained back so little of her seven lost pounds convinced the social worker.

[33] I used to try to hold and love her after she came back, but her body would stay stiff, and after a while she'd push away. She ate little. Food sickened her, and I think much of life too. Oh she had physical lightness and brightness, twinkling by on skates, bouncing like a ball up and down up and down over the jump rope, skimming over the hill; but these were momentary.

[34] She fretted about her appearance, thin and dark and foreign-looking at a time when every little girl was supposed to look or thought she should look a chubby blond replica of Shirley Temple. The doorbell sometimes rang for her, but no one seemed to come and play in the house or be a best friend. Maybe because we moved so much.

[35] There was a boy she loved painfully through two school semes-

ters. Months later she told me how she had taken pennies from my purse to buy him candy. "Licorice was his favorite and I bought him some every day, but he still liked Jennifer better'n me. Why Mommy why?" The kind of question for which there is no answer.

School was a worry to her. She was not glib or quick in a world where glibness and quickness were easily confused with ability to learn. To her over-worked and exasperated teachers she was an over-conscientious "slow learner" who kept trying to catch up and was absent entirely too often. [36]

I let her be absent, though sometimes the illness was imaginary. How different from my now-strictness about attendance with the others. I wasn't working. We had a new baby, I was home anyhow. Sometimes, after Susan grew old enough, I would keep her home from school, too, to have them all together. [37]

Mostly Emily had asthma, and her breathing, harsh and labored, would fill the house with a curiously tranquil sound. I would bring the two old dresser mirrors and her boxes of collections to her bed. She would select beads and single earrings, bottle tops and shells, dried flowers and pebbles, old postcards and scraps, all sorts of oddments; then she and Susan would play Kingdom, setting up landscapes and furniture, peopling them with action. [38]

Those were the only times of peaceful companionship between her and Susan. I have edged away from it, that poisonous feeling between them, that terrible balancing of hurts and needs I had to do between the two, and did so badly, those earlier years. [39]

Oh there are conflicts between the others too, each one human, needing, demanding, hurting, taking—but only between Emily and Susan, no, Emily toward Susan that corroding resentment. It seems so obvious on the surface, yet it is not obvious. Susan, the second child, Susan, golden and curly haired and chubby, quick and articulate and assured, everything in appearance and manner Emily was not; Susan, not able to resist Emily's precious things, losing or sometimes clumsily breaking them; Susan telling jokes and riddles to company for applause while Emily sat silent (to say to me later: that was *my* riddle, Mother, I told it to Susan); Susan, who for all the five years' difference in age was just a year behind Emily in developing physically. [40]

I am glad for that slow physical development that widened the difference between her and her contemporaries, though she suffered over it. She was too vulnerable for that terrible world of youthful competition, of preening and parading, of constant measuring of yourself against every other, of envy: "If I had that copper hair," or "If I had that skin . . . ." She tormented herself enough about not looking like the others, there was enough to the unsureness, the [41] having to be conscious of words before you speak, the constant caring—what are they thinking of me? what kind of an impression am I making—without having it all magnified unendurably by the merciless physical drives.

Ronnie is calling. He is wet and I change him. It is rare there is such a cry now. That time of motherhood is almost behind me when the ear is not one's own but must always be racked and listening for the child cry, the child call. We sit for a while and I hold him, looking out over the city spread in charcoal with its soft aisles of light. "*Shoogily,*" he breathes and curls closer. I carry him back to bed, asleep. *Shoogily.* A funny word, a family word, inherited from Emily, invented by her to say: *comfort.* [42]

In this and other ways she leaves her seal, I say aloud. And startle at my saying it. What do I mean? What did I start to gather together, to try and make coherent? I was at the terrible, growing years. War years. I do not remember them well. I was working again, there were four smaller ones now, there was no time for her. She had to help be a mother, and housekeeper, and shopper. She had to set her seal. Mornings of crisis and near hysteria trying to get lunches packed, hair combed, coats and shoes found, everyone to school or Child Care on time, the baby ready for transportation. And always the paper scribbled on by a smaller one, the book looked at by Susan then mislaid, the homework not done. Running out to that huge school where she was one, she was lost, she was a drop; suffering over her unpreparedness, stammering and unsure in her classes. [43]

There was so little left at night after the kids were bedded down. She would struggle over her books, always eating (it was in those years she developed her enormous appetite that is legendary in our family) and I would be ironing, or preparing food for the next day, or writing V-mail to Bill, or tending the baby. Sometimes, to make me laugh, or out of her despair, she would imitate happenings or types at school. [44]

I think I said once: "Why don't you do something like this in the school amateur show?" One morning she phoned me at work, hardly understandable through the weeping: "Mother, I did it. I won, I won; they gave me first prize; they clapped and clapped and wouldn't let me go." [45]

Now suddenly she was Somebody, and as imprisoned in her difference as she had been in her anonymity. [46]

She began to be asked to perform at other high schools, even in colleges, then at city and state-wide affairs. The first one we went to, I only recognized her that first moment when thin, shy, she almost drowned herself into the curtains. Then: Was this Emily? [47]

the control, the command, the convulsing and deadly clowning, the spell, then the roaring, stamping audience, unwilling to let this rare and precious laughter out of their lives.

[48] Afterwards: You ought to do something about her with a gift like that—but without money or knowing how, what does one do? We have left it all to her, and the gift has as often eddied inside, clogged and clotted, as been used and growing.

[49] She is coming. She runs up the stairs two at a time with her light graceful step, and I know she is happy tonight. Whatever it was that occasioned your call did not happen today.

[50] "Aren't you ever going to finish the ironing, Mother? Whistler painted his mother in a rocker. I'd have to paint mine standing over an ironing board." This is one of the communicative nights and she tells me everything and nothing as she fixes herself a plate of food out of the icebox.

[51] She is so lovely. Why did you want me to come in at all? Why were you concerned? She will find her way.

[52] She starts up the stairs to bed. "Don't get *me* up with the rest in the morning." "But I thought you were having midterms." "Oh, those," she comes back in and says quite lightly, "in a couple of years when we'll all be atom-dead they won't matter a bit."

[53] She has said it before. She *believes* it. But because I have been dredging the past, and all that compounds a human being is so heavy and meaningful to me, I cannot endure it tonight.

[54] I will never total it all. I will never come in to say: "She was a child seldom smiled at. Her father left me before she was a year old. I had to work away from her her first six years when there was work, or I sent her home and to his relatives. There were years she had care she hated. She was dark and thin and foreign-looking in a world where the prestige went to blondness and curly hair and dimples, she was slow where glibness was prized. She was a child of anxious, not proud, love. We were poor and could not afford for her the soil of easy growth. I was a young mother, I was a distracted mother. There were the other children pushing up, demanding. Her younger sister seemed all that she was not. There were years she did not want me to touch her. She kept too much in herself, her life was such she had to keep too much in herself. My wisdom came too late. She has much to her and probably little will come of it. She is a child of her age, of depression, or war, of fear.

[55] Let her be. So all that is in her will not bloom—but in how many does it? There is still enough left to live by. Only help her to know—help make it so there is cause for her to know—that she is more than this dress on the ironing board, helpless before the iron.

DESIGN AND MEANING

1. Whom is the narrator speaking to? How do you know?
2. What are the conflicts in the story? Are any of them resolved?
3. Ironing is mentioned in the title and repeated in the story. Do you think that the act of ironing stands for more than itself? What could it stand for?
4. How did the closing summary of Emily's upbringing affect you?
5. Do you feel a positive or negative view of life in the story? What elements support your feeling?

SIMILARITY AND DIFFERENCE

How is Aretha in "Aretha Has the Best Man" like the mother in Olsen's story? How is she like the daughter?

SHORT WRITING IDEA

Reread the second-to-last paragraph in the story. See if you can write a paragraph summarizing the major familial, social, and historical factors that formed your personality.

LONGER WRITING IDEA

"I Stand Here Ironing" is called an "interior monolog" because only one person speaks and does not address anyone else out loud; the story is a series of thoughts. See if you can write an interior monolog, with yourself as narrator, about some problem or decision. First you will have to practice listening to yourself think.

Illustration and Example

A COMPOSITION TEACHER we know tells his students that a typical expository paragraph is half a page long when typed double-spaced on 8½-by-11-inch paper. The bluntness of such a directive may seem quaint, but sometimes it comes in handy to have things oversimplified a bit. This same instructor advises his students that if they can't think what to say next in a paragraph, they should write the words, "For example," and if they can't come up with an example, something's wrong with what they've written so far.

That piece of advice is a gem, and we wish more writers would use examples to explain their ideas. You have no doubt slogged through a paragraph of abstract generalizations and struggled to grasp the meaning but found yourself baffled. Consider, for instance, the following paragraph which aims to explain one of the many distinctions between formal and informal English:

> Standard English adds the *-ly* [to adjectives] and uses the resulting adverbs rather freely as to position. But very informal—and not necessarily substandard—English does not favor *-ly* adverbs before the verb or verb phrase. It favors the other position (after) or some adverb not ending in *-ly*.

Got it? Probably not—because we sneakily took out the examples. Now, try the same passage as it appears in Dwight Bollinger's *Aspects of Language* (1968)—with examples:

> Standard English adds the *-ly* [to adjectives] and uses the resulting adverbs rather freely as to position: *They left rapidly, They rapidly left*. But very informal—not necessarily substandard—English does

> not favor *-ly* adverbs before the verb or verb phrase. It prefers the other position (after) or some adverb not ending in *-ly:* instead of *He grew steadily worse, I promptly told him,* and *She's constantly complaining;* it will say *He grew worse and worse, I told him right there,* and *She's all the time complaining.*

The passage doesn't seem nearly as murky when you have examples, does it?

Another valuable use of examples, a close cousin of the one illustrated above, is to clarify a concept. This next passage proves conclusively that no one would ever understand linguistics without examples:

> In an elaborated [communication] code, the speaker and listener are acting parts in which they must improvise. Their standing with each other is such that neither can take much for granted about the other. Intentions and purposes have to be brought into the open and defined. What the speaker will say is hard to predict, because it is not about commonplaces but about something more or less unique, related less to some forseeable role and more to him as an individual. He is wearing not a comic nor a tragic mask but his own face, and that is harder to put into words. An example would be that of a man told to do something by his boss and having to explain why it is impossible for him to comply.
>
> —Bolinger, *Aspects of Language* (1968).

We found that definition fairly fuzzy until the end of the paragraph, where the concrete example gave us the flash of recognition we needed to understand the whole concept. In fact, we think that perhaps if the writer had worked the example in after the first sentence, we would not have been puzzled at all.

Even if you are not writing about something difficult or abstract, you still need examples to prove your point—to support your idea as well as to add verve and interest. If you say, "Sue is a dreadful cook," you are likely to follow it up with, "To the potluck supper last month, she brought overcooked, mushy macaroni in a mudlike, yellow-gray sauce of brewer's yeast and cheese. Someone tactfully asked her about the unusual flavor, and she proudly answered that she'd spiced it with cinnamon, cloves, and a dash of garlic. She's so inept that she called ten different people to invite them over for lasagna last Friday, and every single person had other plans." The examples clarify exactly what you mean by "a dreadful cook"—she isn't just someone who goes heavy on the oat bran once in a while. Specific examples also give your general claim validity; few people are going to argue that the muddy casserole sounds appetizing. So, examples explain, clarify, and support your points.

All good writing includes examples and illustrations. Most people use those terms interchangeably; those who do not usually consider an illustration to be longer and more narrative in form. We have chosen some selections that rely heavily on examples for their development. Study them to see how the professionals do it. And, to improve your own writing, do not forget our exemplary colleague's advice.

essays

James Thurber

What a Lovely Generalization!

Thurber (1894–1961) has long been admired for his humorously ironic essays, short stories, and cartoons, most of which were published in the *New Yorker.*

I have collected, in my time, derringers, snowstorm paperweights, and china and porcelain dogs, and perhaps I should explain what happened to these old collections before I go on to my newest hobby, which is the true subject of this monograph. My derringer collection may be regarded as having been discontinued, since I collected only two, the second and last item as long ago as 1935. There were originally seventeen snowstorm paperweights, but only four or five are left. This kind of collection is known to the expert as a "diminished collection," and it is not considered cricket to list it in your *Who's Who* biography. The snowstorm paperweight suffers from its easy appeal to the eye and the hand. House guests like to play with paperweights and to slip them into their luggage while packing up to leave. As for my china and porcelain dogs, I disposed of that collection some two years ago. I had decided that the collection of actual objects, of any kind, was too much of a strain, and I determined to devote myself, instead, to the impalpable and the intangible. [1]

Nothing in my new collection can be broken or stolen or juggled or thrown at cats. What I collect now is a certain kind of Broad Generalization, or Sweeping Statement. You will see what I mean when I bring out some of my rare and cherished pieces. All you need to start a collection of generalizations like mine is an attentive ear. Listen in particular to women, whose average generalization is from three to five times as broad as a man's. Generalizations, male or female, may be true ("Women don't sleep very well"), untrue [2]

("There are no pianos in Japan"), half true ("People would rather drink than go to the theater"), debatable ("Architects have the wrong idea"), libelous ("Doctors don't know what they're doing"), ridiculous ("You never see foreigners fishing"), fascinating but undemonstrable ("People who break into houses don't drink wine"), or idiosyncratic ("Peach ice cream is never as good as you think it's going to be").

[3] "There are no pianos in Japan" was the first item in my collection. I picked it up at a reception while discussing an old movie called "The Battle," or "Thunder in the East," which starred Charles Boyer, Merle Oberon, and John Loder, some twenty years ago. In one scene, Boyer, as a Japanese naval captain, comes upon Miss Oberon, as his wife, Matsuko, playing an Old Japanese air on the piano for the entertainment of Loder, a British naval officer with a dimple, who has forgotten more about fire control, range finding, marksmanship, and lovemaking than the Japanese commander is ever going to know. "Matsuko," says the latter, "Why do you play that silly little song? It may be tedious for our fran." Their fran, John Loder, says, "No, it is, as a matter of—" But I don't know why I have to go into the whole plot. The lady with whom I was discussing the movie, at the reception, said that the detail about Matsuko and the piano was absurd, since "there are no pianos in Japan." It seems that this lady was an authority on the musical setup in Japan because her great-uncle had married a singsong girl in Tokyo in 1912.

[4] Now, I might have accepted the declarations that there are no saxophones in Bessarabia, no banjo-mandolins in Mozambique, no double bases in Zanzibar, no jew's-harps in Rhodesia, no zithers in Madagascar, and no dulcimers in Milwaukee, but I could not believe that Japan, made out in the movie as a great imitator of Western culture, would not have any pianos. Some months after the reception, I picked up an old copy of the *Saturday Evening Post* and, in an article on Japan, read that there were, before the war, some fifteen thousand pianos in Japan. It just happened to say that, right there in the article.

[5] You may wonder where I heard some of the other Sweeping Statements I have mentioned above. Well, the one about peach ice cream was contributed to my collection by a fifteen-year-old girl. I am a chocolate man myself, but the few times I have eaten peach ice cream it tasted exactly the way I figured it was going to taste, which is why I classify this statement as idiosyncratic; that is, peculiar to one individual. The item about foreigners never fishing, or, at any rate, never fishing where you can see them, was given to me last summer by a lady who had just returned from a motor trip through New England. The charming generalization about people

who break into houses popped out of a conversation I overheard between two women, one of whom said it was not safe to leave rye, Scotch or bourbon in your summer house when you closed it for the winter, but it was perfectly all right to leave your wine, since intruders are notoriously men of insensitive palate, who cannot tell the difference between Nuits-St.-Georges and saddle polish. I would not repose too much confidence in this theory if I were you, however. It is one of those Comfortable Conclusions that can cost you a whole case of Château Lafite.

[6] I haven't got space here to go through my entire collection, but there is room to examine a few more items. I'm not sure where I got hold of "Gamblers hate women"—possibly at Bleeck's—but, like "Sopranos drive me crazy," it has an authentic ring. This is not true, I'm afraid, of "You can't trust an electrician" or "Cops off duty always shoot somebody." There may be something in "Dogs know when you're despondent" and "Sick people hear everything," but I sharply question the validity of "Nobody taps his fingers if he's all right" and "People who like birds are queer."

[7] Some twenty years ago, a Pittsburgh city editor came out with the generalization that "Rewrite men go crazy when the moon is full," but this is perhaps a little too special for the layman, who probably doesn't know what a rewrite man is. Besides, it is the abusive type of Sweeping Statement and should not be dignified by analysis or classification.

[8] In conclusion, let us briefly explore "Generals are afraid of their daughters," vouchsafed by a lady after I had told her my General Wavell anecdote. It happens, for the sake of our present record, that the late General Wavell, of His Britannic Majesty's forces, discussed his three daughters during an interview a few years ago. He said that whereas he had millions of men under his command who leaped at his every order, he couldn't get his daughters down to breakfast on time when he was home on leave, in spite of stern directives issued the night before. As I have imagined it, his ordeal went something like this. It would get to be 7 A.M. and then 7:05, and General Wavell would shout up the stairs demanding to know where everybody was, and why the girls were not at table. Presently, one of them would call back sharply, as a girl has to when her father gets out of hand, "For heaven's sake, Daddy, will you be quiet! Do you want to wake the neighbors?" The General, his flanks rashly exposed, so to speak, would fall back in orderly retreat and eat his kippers by himself. Now, I submit that there is nothing in this to prove that the General was afraid of his daughters. The story merely establishes the fact that his daughters were not afraid of him.

[9] If you are going to start collecting Sweeping Statements on your

own, I must warn you that certain drawbacks are involved. You will be inclined to miss the meaning of conversations while lying in wait for generalizations. Your mouth will hang open slightly, your posture will grow rigid, and your eyes will take on the rapt expression of a person listening for the faint sound of distant sleigh bells. People will avoid your company and whisper that you are probably an old rewrite man yourself or, at best, a finger tapper who is a long way from being all right. But your collection will be a source of comfort in your declining years, when you can sit in the chimney corner cackling the evening away over some such gems, let us say, as my own two latest acquisitions: "Jewelers never go anywhere" and "Intellectual women dress funny."

Good hunting. [10]

James Thurber

Which Which

The relative pronoun "which" can cause more trouble than any other word, if recklessly used. Foolhardy persons sometimes get lost in which-clauses and are never heard of again. My distinguished contemporary, Fowler, cites several tragic cases, of which the following is one: "It was rumoured that Beaconsfield intended opening the Conference with a speech in French, his pronunciation of which language leaving everything to be desired . . . ." That's as much as Mr. Fowler quotes because, at his age, he was afraid to go any farther. The young man who originally got into that sentence was never found. His fate, however, was not as terrible as that of another adventurer who became involved in a remarkable which-mire. Fowler has followed his devious course as far as he safely could on foot: "Surely what applies to games should also apply to racing, the leaders of which being the very people from whom an example might well be looked for . . . ." Not even Henry James would have successfully emerged from a sentence with "which," "whom," and "being" in it. The safest way to avoid such things is to follow in the path of the American author, Ernest Hemingway. In his youth he was trapped in a which-clause one time and barely escaped with his mind. He was going along on solid ground until he got into this: "It was the one thing of which, being very much afraid—for whom has not been warned to fear such things—he . . . ." Being a young and powerfully built man, Hemingway was able to fight his way back to where he had started, and begin again. This time he skirted the treacherous morass in this way: "He was afraid of one thing. This was the one thing. He had been warned to fear such things. Everybody has been warned to fear such things." Today Hemingway is alive and well, and many happy writers are following along the trail he blazed. [1]

What most people don't realize is that one "which" leads to another. Trying to cross a paragraph by leaping from "which" to "which" is like Eliza crossing the ice. The danger is in missing a "which" and falling in. A case in point is this: "He went up to a pew which was in the gallery, which brought him under a colored window which he loved and always quieted his spirit." The writer, worn out, missed the last "which"—the one that should come just before "always" in that sentence. But supposing he had got it in! We would have: "He went up to a pew which was in the gallery, [2] which brought him under a colored window which he loved and which always quieted his spirit." Your inveterate whicher in this way gives the effect of tweeting like a bird or walking with a crutch, and is not welcome in the best company.

[3] It is well to remember that one "which" leads to two and that two "whiches" multiply like rabbits. You should never start out with the idea that you can get by with one "which." Suddenly they are all around you. Take a sentence like this: "It imposes a problem which we either solve, or perish." On a hot night, or after a hard day's work, a man often lets himself get by with a monstrosity like that, but suppose he dictates that sentence bright and early in the morning. It comes to him typed out by his stenographer and he instantly senses that something is the matter with it. He tries to reconstruct the sentence, still clinging to the "which," and gets something like this: "It imposes a problem which we either solve, or which, failing to solve, we must perish on account of." He goes to the water-cooler, gets a drink, sharpens his pencil, and grimly tries again. "It imposes a problem which we either solve or which we don't solve and . . . ." He begins once more: "It imposes a problem which we either solve, or which we do not solve, and from which . . . ." The more times he does it the more "whiches" he gets. The way out is simple: "We must either solve this problem, or perish." Never monkey with "which." Nothing except getting tangled up in a typewriter ribbon is worse.

VOCABULARY

derringer	small antique pistol
idiosyncratic	behavior characteristic of an individual
impalpable	difficult to get a grip on
intangible	impossible to perceive through the senses
kippers	smoked herring
monograph	scholarly piece of writing, limited in scope
palate	sense of taste
rapt	deeply absorbed in thought
vouchsafed	granted or guaranteed in a lofty manner
zither	stringed musical instrument
devious	not straightforward; roundabout
foolhardy	foolishly daring; reckless
inveterate	habitual; firmly established
mire	deep mud or slush
morass	a piece of low, soft, watery ground; a bog
treacherous	untrustworthy and unsafe

DESIGN AND MEANING

1. "What a Lovely Generalization!" gives a wealth of specific examples. How does Thurber sort and organize these examples?
2. How does the conclusion of the generalization article bring the reader into the picture?
3. Does Thurber have an underlying serious point about generalizations? What is it?
4. What is the comparison set up in sentence 2 of "Which Which"? Where and how is the comparison carried further? Find two examples of other comparisons used for humorous effect.
5. Thurber gives abundant examples in "Which Which." In each example, can you figure out what the "whiches" refer to?
6. Ernest Hemingway, Henry James, and Eliza crossing the ice all appear in this essay. Research these references to literature sufficiently to explain Thurber's use of them.
7. How seriously does Thurber want readers to take this advice? Is it good advice, in your opinion?

SIMILARITY AND DIFFERENCE

Compare Thurber's writing with Dereck Williamson's in "Wall Covering" (Chapter 5). What similarities do you see in their humor?

SHORT WRITING IDEA

The comparison Thurber develops in "Which Which" between writing and exploring is called an "extended metaphor." Write a paragraph using one of these ideas and developing your comparison further.

1. ______ is like taking a long, dangerous journey.
2. Writing a paper is like ______.
3. ______ is like falling in love.

LONGER WRITING IDEA

Write an essay in which you warn speakers, conversationalists, teachers, or writers against a certain practice or usage that particularly bothers you. Give examples to support your points.

VOCABULARY CHECK

Fill in each blank with a different form of a vocabulary word from the list following "Which Which."

1. Sue's attempts to find a job are ______ in her lack of organization.
2. Marla, when she discovered that Clyde had bugged her office, could barely believe his ______ .
3. Steve's ______ was exemplified when he tried to juggle five raw eggs over his new carpet.
4. Marty ______ succeeded in alienating his roommates and ended up happily living alone.
5. Mark ______ arranged to run out of gas in the country on our last date.

PREREADING EXERCISE

Record in as much detail as possible a dream of yours, a friend's, or a character's in a fictional work.

Sharon Begley

The Stuff That Dreams Are Made Of

As a staff writer for *Newsweek*, Begley has learned to write well under the pressure of a deadline. She has written over 200 articles for the magazine since she signed on. Her topics include everything from astronomy to bacteria, with an emphasis on science and technological developments.

About 90 minutes after you fall asleep tonight, your brain will awaken with a start, crackling with mental electricity. The brainstem, at the base of your skull, will begin firing a random barrage of high-voltage impulses, nonsensical and chaotic, and unleash waves of chemicals that will lap into the forebrain. There the gray matter will desperately seek coherence in these neuroevents, almost as if it were faced with a Rorschach. You are paralyzed, a helpless voyeur of events unfolding just inside your forehead, where images as familiar to Dali as to Jung race by. [1]

You're dreaming. [2]

Before dawn breaks, you will probably experience four more dreams, though in all likelihood their details will never lodge in your conscious memory. Instead the images will disappear, as if into the collective unconscious—for the act of dreaming is part of mankind's evolutionary heritage, so basic that it can be traced back 135 million years. Now, spurred by new research, science is unlocking the mysteries of dreams and using them to probe the secrets of the brain. [3]

For psychotherapists, this nocturnal theater of the mind remains a mother lode of symbols. For scientists, dreams are even more provocative. Some find that dreams may serve as a sort of early-warning system for illness. Others track how dreams start as the simplest of snapshots and grow more complicated as a child ages; by mapping that development psychologists gain insight into the blossoming of cognition. Still other researchers believe that memory may be controlled by the same polysyllabic chemicals that trigger dreams. [4]

For all their promise, dreams seemed, until very recently, like a vaguely disreputable way for a scientist to make a living. Even after the 1953 discovery of the brain state in which dreams occur, [5] "the feeling was dreams were ephemeral things, not something to base solid science on," says Dr. Robert W. McCarley of Harvard Medical School. Once Freudians began to use other paths to the unconscious, dreams became the province of pop culture, the first sign that a new age was dawning. In the 1970s devotees launched newsletters and clubs whose members swapped dreams over herbal tea; they snapped up books that promised to reveal meanings as easily as looking up "tunnel" in the index.

[6] What was a fad is now mainstream. Even executives are asking their dreams to solve business dilemmas. One "creative management" course at the Stanford Business School uses "Living Your Dreams," a book by San Francisco psychologist Gayle Delaney. "We are trying to put to bed the notion of dreams as meaningless epiphenomena of the firing of neurons," says Delaney. Here's how it works. *I was visiting my Uncle Fred and Aunt Jean,* said James Schrager, chief financial officer of a trading firm in San Francisco. He had gone to sleep intent on having a dream about a new wheelchair he'd been working on. *They had all the material goods in the world, but they seemed so very sad.* Although the dream did not tell Schrager how to advance his invention, it told him something else. "He was my favorite uncle," says Schrager. "But he sold out. It showed what's keeping *me* from getting into the state of mind necessary to create"—the same concern with material success that his dream uncle had. Schrager still hasn't invented a better wheelchair, but his dreams did give him an idea for a new business: taking companies public in Japan.

[7] Dreams never seem more powerful than when they solve a problem. Robert Louis Stevenson said he got the idea for Dr. Jekyll and Mr. Hyde in a dream; Elias Howe, trying to invent a machine that sewed, reportedly dreamed he was captured by savages carrying spears with holes in their tips. Upon waking, Howe realized he should put the hole for the thread at the end of the needle, not the middle. Such inspirations truly seem like gifts of the gods, and mere biochemistry can't fully explain the creativity of dreams. It may be that dreams give us greater insight because they weave together, in unique and creative ways, current experiences with ones from the past.

[8] To scientists, dreaming is the collection of mental images that arise during "rapid eye movement" sleep. REM sleep is characterized by darting eye movements, paralyzed limbs and irregular respiration and heartbeat. If sleep-lab volunteers are awakened after every REM episode, 85 to 90 percent of the time they say they were dreaming. Fetuses as young as 23 weeks experience REM sleep, as do all birds and mammals (except the spiny anteater). This suggests that REM developed when these creatures branched off from a

common ancestor, more than 135 million years ago, long before humans were even a glimmer in evolution's eye.

[9] Now dreams fill everyone's nights. Such common dreams as flying, falling or walking naked in public can visit anyone, for these experiences seem to capture universal human aspirations or fears. But dreams also bear the unmistakable stamp of gender. "Dreams of American women have more in common with those of Aboriginal women than they do with those of American men," says Dr. Milton Kramer, director of the Sleep Disorders Center of Greater Cincinnati. In the past, women dreamed more of interior, homey scenes; men of the outdoors. Women's dreams featured more conversation and emotion, and portrayed the dreamer as a victim of aggression. Men's dreams tended toward mechanical images.

[10] *I dreamt I was driving a huge truck into a gas station. I couldn't get close enough to the pumps because another truck was taking up all the available space. I go get a hose to fill my gas tank but it won't reach.* Says Dr. Rosalind Cartwright of the Rush-Presbyterian-St. Luke's Medical Center in Chicago, "No *woman* would dream a sexy dream in those terms."

[11] But men's and women's dreams are becoming more androgynous. Women are dreaming more of the outdoors and of torrid sex. They are as likely as men to dream of themselves as aggressors. Concludes Kramer, "If one accepts the dream as a reflector of inner processes, [these themes] no longer serve to discriminate between the sexes. The sexual revolution may have indeed contributed to meaningful internal change."

[12] Age also influences dreams. In his studies, David Foulkes of Emory University brought 3- and 4-year-olds to his lab. For nine nights he woke them from sound sleep and asked them what they remembered. The children reported snippets, not narratives. "It was like a slide show, with moments frozen in time," says Foulkes. The static images of storybook animals—rabbits, frogs, birds—had little emotional content and the kids themselves made only rare appearances in their own dreams. For the next five years, Foulkes brought the youngsters back for more interrupted dreams. By the age of 5 or 6, some children began dreaming in stories; there was action and movement, but the dreamer still did not star in her own dreams. Only by the age of 7 or 8 did some children, especially brighter ones, put themselves into their dreams. "For the first time the dream proceeds at the psychological as well as the physical level," says Foulkes. By 8 or 9, children dream like adults.

[13] What mental circuits must be wired to create "adult" dreams? One prerequisite seems to be the use of symbols. Dreams aren't replays of specific events, notes Foulkes, but "fusions of pieces of memory and knowledge" that the brain weaves together. This re-

quires an ability to analyze concepts and meld them into novel wholes. Foulkes concludes that "dreaming develops along the same lines, and at roughly the same rate, as waking intelligence." By noting when various abilities blossom, he hopes to use children's dreams to write a timetable of cognitive development.

As every parent racing to the crib of a crying toddler knows, children between 3 and 5 are especially prone to nightmares. So are people who have what psychologists call "thin boundaries": they are acutely sensitive to their own emotions and inner world as well as to others', and are very trusting. "They have a flower-child aspect," says Dr. Ernest Hartmann of Tufts University School of Medicine. They gravitate to the arts and to such creative professions as teaching and therapy. They also suffer many more nightmares than the typical one or two a year. [14]

I was walking in the park but got caught by nightfall. There had been people all around, but they had disappeared. I couldn't find the exit, so called to someone up ahead. He turned, as if to answer, but then started racing toward me. I ran. The distinguishing trait of all nightmares is that the dreamer is endangered. Parents are the exception: they dream their babies are in trouble. [15]

One way to overcome nightmares may be through a technique called lucidity, in which the sleeper recognizes a dream as it's unfolding. The ability to dream "lucidly" comes naturally to just 10 percent or so of the population, and even they report only one lucid dream a month, on average. But lucidity can be learned, claims psychologist Stephen LaBerge of Standford University. He has volunteers wear sleep masks with sensors that detect REM sleep and turn on a red flashing light. When the sleeper sees the light it becomes incorporated into the dream and alerts him that he's dreaming. Alternatively, one can choose some aspect of dreams, ideally a recurring one, and train oneself to recognize that when that situation or image pops up, it's a dream. [16]

Children as young as 5 seem able to learn lucid dreaming, especially to fight off nightmares. *A shark was chasing me in the reservoir,* dreamed the 7-year-old girl. *I was so afraid he was going to eat me.* LaBerge told her that next time she had this recurring nightmare, she should climb onto the shark's back for a ride. She did, and the nightmares stopped. [17]

During REM, most dreamers are immobilized. But Dr. Mark Mahowald and Dr. Carlos Schenck of the Minnesota Regional Sleep Disorders Center have been studying 75 people, primarily elderly men, who are anything but paralyzed: these calm, friendly, happily married men act out violent dreams. [18]

I was deer hunting with my grandfather, says Mel Abel, 75. *The deer wasn't quite dead so I was strangling it.* In reality he was [19] strangling his wife. Donald Dorff, 69, also got into his dream: *I was a halfback. The quarterback lateraled the ball to me. There is this big 280-pound tackle waiting so I was to give him my shoulder and bounce him out of the way.* When he awoke, says Dorff, "I had knocked lamps, mirror and everything else off the dresser, hit my head against the wall and my knee against the dresser." Although the Minnesota researchers aren't sure of the exact cause of the syndrome, they suspect it's neurological or related to aging. They have eliminated it in 90 percent of their patients with clonazepam, a drug prescribed for epilepsy.

One dogma that remains unchallenged is that dreaming of one's own death does *not* portend doom. But there are hints that dreams may whisper something about illness. In a 1987 study, Dr. Robert Smith of Michigan State University analyzed the recent dreams of cardiac patients for references to death, including images of graveyards, and for scenes of separation from family or friends. "Men who dreamed of destruction, mutilation and death, and women who dreamed of separations had worse heart disease than those who didn't," says Smith. Such dreams became more frequent as cardiac problems became more severe. Since the patients didn't know the severity of their condition, it's unlikely that worry shaped their dreams. Perhaps dreams might be used as warning signs of disease. "Dreaming may let us know if something is wrong, warning us of vulnerability," says Hartmann. [20]

Whatever dreams reveal of the body, they seem to provide a peek at the subconscious. But their language is cryptic; interpreting what Delaney calls "their metaphorical, visual language" is akin to literary analysis, a parsing of images, an analysis of symbols. "Dreams are very much like poetry," she says. "You understand them if you get the metaphor." [21]

It was dark, and I was being chased by a man with a knife. When I turned to confront him, I made him come into the light with me so I could see him. When he did, he turned into a puddle. I bent down to taste it. It was cognac. [22]

Delaney asks her client to define and describe every image as if to a Martian, for different images hold different meanings for every dreamer. What is a knife? What is cognac? Then the dreamer summarizes the plot, describes the feelings of the dream and recapitulates the definitions. Last, Delaney asks the client to think which situation in real life the images or feelings resemble. This client realized she had been running from a fear that all men would turn into alcoholics like her father. A similar sequence would mean something else to another person, but would still shine a light on things he might have known only vaguely. "Dreams show us what we don't dare confront directly when we're awake," Delaney says. [23]

Even some scientists who tickle neurons and map brain chemicals have a newfound respect for dreams, largely because of the work of Harvard's McCarley and Dr. J. Allan Hobson. The psychiatrists developed a theory to explain how dreams are generated by neurons during REM sleep and how the mind makes sense of the signals it receives. Dreams, they conclude, are born in the brainstem, which controls such basics as reflexes. In the brainstem are two kinds of neurons known to control sleep, each using a different chemical to communicate. One type uses acetylcholine; they are "on" during REM. The others use norepinephrine and serotonin; they are "off." Only when these latter neurons are turned off can the acetylcholine neurons turn on. Then a dream is born. The acetylcholine neurons send rapid bursts of electrical signals to the cortex, the seat of higher thought and vision. The cortex takes this information and weaves it into a coherent story, say Hobson and McCarley, interpreting the signals by referring to pre-existing memories. [24]

Acetylcholine may be the very stuff that dreams are made of. (The dream cocktail is $C_7H_{17}NO_3$, or 7 parts carbon, 17 hydrogen, 1 nitrogen, 3 oxygen.) The evidence: when researchers led by Hobson and McCarley inject drugs that mimic acetylcholine into the brainstem of cats, they undergo REM sleep. Recently they've shown that the neurons responsible for REM connect with neurons containing acetylcholine emanating from the brainstem. And in people, drugs that increase the availability of acetylcholine hasten the onset of REM and dreams. [25]

Such research draws bitter criticism from researchers who think it dismisses dreams as mere random products of REM sleep. But that may be an unfair reading. In "The Dreaming Brain," published last year, Hobson bends over backward to say dreams are *not* meaningless. To the contrary: he claims that the brain is so "inexorably bent upon the quest for meaning" that it takes essentially random, automatic signals from the brainstem and imbues them with sense. What *kind* of sense reveals the dreamer's "drives, fears and associations," he writes. Far from belittling dreams, Hobson offers a coherent explanation of why dreams are so bizarre, why they are filled with movement and not smells or tastes and why we dream in metaphors. [26]

I dreamed of cleaning out my garage. I took out all the summer furniture and piled it on the street. A man in a pickup came along and started to load up my stuff. I yelled at him and asked what he thought he was doing. He told me, "If you didn't want someone else to take it, you shouldn't have left it out there and available." The patient immediately realized the discarded "stuff" was his wife and [27] children. Call him The Man Who Mistook His Family For Chaises Longues.

[28] Hobson maintains that dreams are full of such vivid images because "the brain works associatively. High-level associations are metaphors, which pack lots of material into an economical unit." The ubiquity of symbols may also reflect how memory works. Since we dream in metaphors, perhaps we store knowledge in that form, too. Studying dream symbols, says Emory's Foulkes, may reveal whether we organize memories by their emotional content, by their appearance or by some other trait.

[29] Physiology may explain other puzzles. Dreams are visually vivid yet nearly devoid of tastes and smells. The reason: it may be that visual neurons, but not taste or olfactory neurons, fire intensely during REM. Also, dreams are bizarre. Hobson argues that's because the cortex receives signals from the brainstem and not the outside world; trying to make a coherent story from chaotic signals produces strange plots and events. They still have a link to real life, however, because the brain draws on actual memories to spin the stories. Finally, dreams seem frenetic, with chases, flights and falls. The reason may be that during REM, neurons in the part of the cortex that control movement fire as rapidly as when the dreamer is awake and active.

[30] During REM sleep, neurons that permit the dream-inducing neurons to buzz with activity are themselves out of action. Normally, they are involved in attention and self-awareness. Hartmann suggests that this dormancy may explain why people remember better in their dreams than they do while awake: with the attention-paying neurons off, remote memories are unusually accessible. But once awake, some 95 percent of dreams vanish. Hobson speculates that's because dreams are stored temporarily in short-term memory, but the chemicals necessary to "print" them in long-term memory are serotonin and norepinephrine, which are shut off during the dream.

[31] Scientists' new respect for dreams has pushed them to ask what these dramas are *for.* Finding an answer is problematic because it is so difficult to tease apart the function of REM from the function of dreams themselves. The sleep of newborns has twice as much REM time as that of 5-year-olds; might REM sleep help the brain develop? In fact, learning a new, challenging skill induces heightened REM activity, and people deprived of REM sleep have trouble recalling things. Some studies show that the more people dream the better they remember a bedtime story. Or perhaps REM is basically restorative: since some neurons are dormant during REM sleep, Tufts's Hartmann says, REM's function may be to rejuvenate

these systems. Indeed, people think better soon after waking, perhaps because dreams prepare us for the challenges of the new day by "rev[ving] our cerebral motor," says Hobson.

Walt Whitman cursed the astronomer for his dispassionate analysis of the stars, for such dry wisdom ruined the joy he felt in the twinkling sky. For those who regard dreams with mystic adoration, explaining them as products of biochemistry is just as insulting. But even hardheaded researchers retain a sense of wonder at these enigmatic missives of the night. Whatever science discovers, dreams will remain among the most beguiling children of the mind. [32]

Sweet dreams. [33]

VOCABULARY

Aboriginal	belonging to a primitive Australian tribe
engimatic	perplexing
epiphenomena	a secondary effect of a physiological event
frenetic	frenzied
lucid	clearly perceived
missives	letters, communications
novel	of a new kind
parsing	describing by identifying parts
portend	foreshadow
Rohrschach	a psychological test consisting of an ink blot which the client imaginatively interprets
ubiquity	presence everywhere

DESIGN AND MEANING

1. How does the first sentence of the essay encourage the reader's involvement?
2. In paragraph 7, the author suggests a reason why dreams give us insight that we may not have in waking life. What is this reason? Does it seem possible to you? Have you ever achieved an insight through a dream?
3. In paragraph 9, how do the characteristics of men's and women's dreams reflect traditional sex roles?
4. How many examples of specific dreams are there in the essay? What general principle does each example illuminate? To see the usefulness of examples, read paragraphs 13–19 aloud, leaving out all examples.

5. List the experts who are cited in the essay. Notice that we accept these people as experts, even though we probably haven't heard their names before. Why? How are their credentials established?
6. Using reference books, find out something about the historical figures mentioned in the essay: Dali, Jung, Robert Louis Stevenson, Dr. Jekyll and Mr. Hyde, Walt Whitman, Elias Howe.

SIMILARITY AND DIFFERENCE

Reread the poems in Chapter 1. Do they support the statements about metaphors in paragraphs 21 and 28 of this essay?

SHORT WRITING IDEA

Summarize Begley's article in 250–300 words. Exchange summaries with two other students and note similarities and differences. Do you all agree on two or three points for inclusion? Can you detect varying emphases among the summaries? Could you write a summary together that all would find satisfactory?

LONGER WRITING IDEA

Many areas of our lives and studies are guided by rules or principles. Your household probably has groundrules; scientific experimentation follows principles; your school has course requirements; even your love relationships have certain mandates. Illustrate the rules or principles guiding one area of your life by giving examples.

Earl Shorris

How 114 Washing Machines Came to the Crow Reservation

Shorris (b. 1936), a free-lance writer concerned with social issues, has published in many national magazines and is presently a contributing editor of *Harper's Magazine.* In the following selection he focuses on defining the problems—both material and psychological—of an individual caught in the toils of government bureaucracy. This account appeared in his book *The Death of the Great Spirit* (1971).

The problems of the Indian are the weights and measures of Roger Stops. He fills saucers with cigarette butts while contemplating them. During the day, he stands behind the counter of his café, drinking coffee, playing with his granddaughter, talking to her in Crow; sometimes he cooks a hamburger or sells bottles of soda pop or shouts to his wife or tells a kid that the jukebox is broken because he is not yet ready to hear it; the whole of his day is pocked with the problems of washing machines: change is needed, the rinse cycle has failed, a machine has spun itself into collapse, and then there are the dryers and children who make too much noise. Through it all, he smokes and schemes and practices the arts of exegesis and nostalgia on everything that touches his life. If only he had a little capital, enough for this machine, which is certain to . . . . [1]

His name is not Stops, but Stops-at-Pretty-Places; and it isn't Roger, not his Indian name; he is really Likes-to-Go-on-the-Warpath. He is a member of the Greasy Mouth clan on both sides, which is unusual for a Crow or any Indian, for it defies the function of the clan system. His wife is Mandan and Hidatsa, both of which are Siouan-speaking people, as are the Crow, but since Roger and his wife cannot easily speak to each other, the language in the home is almost always English. So Roger Stops speaks English to his wife and most of his customers, and Crow to his children and his friends. [2]

He is a man of great bulk, more than six feet tall, wide at the shoulders and deep through the chest; after fifty-one years, his belly has begun to dominate: his shirt separates from his trousers when [3] he stretches; he leaves his dapper brown shoes untied. Among the Crow, Roger Stops is something of a celebrity because his brother died in combat in France during World War II. Roger believes that he survived Korea as well as World War II because the old men who gathered around to name him Likes-to-Go-on-the-Warpath said he would be safe in combat.

He achieved the rank of master sergeant, fighting without being injured, except for his teeth, which were knocked out by a comrade who jumped into his trench feet first. He tells of the incident by way of apologizing for having no teeth now. [4]

After the Korean War, he decided to stay in the Army until he was able to retire, but he became ill. The army doctors diagnosed his illness as cancer of the stomach, operated on him to remove the cancer, then discharged him as incurable. He returned to the reservation to die, his body shriveled and weak at 146 pounds. "I came back here and took sweat baths and prayed," he said, "and I cured myself in the Indian way." He keeps a medicine bundle in his house, but he hesitates when asked about it, saying that he is afraid it will only make white men laugh. "The things in a medicine bundle are things we see in visions," he said: "they have the power of God in them. They don't look like much, a stone or a feather or a piece of fur; whites wouldn't understand." [5]

He calls himself a "dumb savage," saying that he never really went to school, that he preferred to stay outside and play with his "bow and arrows." It is a bitterness befitting a man conceived by Dostoevsky, and in the night, when the café is empty, Roger Stops retreats to his Underground in a Laundromat. He locks himself into a storeroom, sitting on a high stool behind a discarded display counter or reclining on a couch of raw board and rags, filling the room with smoke, sweetly stale, suspended on the steam that pours from the washing machines and dryers, and reading Indian history or law. [6]

The room is further decorated with a single shelf of books, a typewriter on a high stand, and a calendar. Outside, the washing machines and dryers roar and grind, and children shout over them, playing, aware though unconcerned that Stops is in his office reading Felix Cohen's book on Indian law, battling the Bureau of Indian Affairs with bookmarks and underlining. It is a room adjacent to Hell, and in it, contemplative and powerless, Stops turns the pages with enormous and slow hands, seeking the little victories that allow him another day . . . . [7]

The declared purpose of Roger Stops's reading, scheming, and contemplation is "to help my people," but there would seem to be another purpose: the saving of himself. He works hard, two or three hours a day, on a Crow language project, thinking back on the old [8] words, collecting them from his friends and customers, learning the structure and development of his own language, pleased to understand that the Crow words for dog and horse are actually "my horse" and "my real horse," and that they are linguistic proof of the history of domesticated animals among the Crow. He plans to translate the Bible into Crow, though he is not a Christian. There is no payment for the work, and it takes a subtle mind to understand how such an effort can be of help to his people. Though there is little doubt that Roger Stops is capable of such subtle thinking, it is also clear that the intellectual stimulation is a requisite of his own sanity, the lonely joy that sustains him through another day of overdue payments and lost customers . . . .

Brooding and hopelessness are the occupations of Indians: the managed life allows little else: an Indian cannot plan his future, the BIA does that; he cannot decide what to do with his land, his crops, or his herd, the BIA has rules for that; he cannot even enjoy the prerogatives of power within his own tribe, the BIA superintendent has veto power. He is neither a free man nor a captive; weeping and dreaming have the same value in his life. [9]

Roger Stops, soldier, truck driver, and entrepreneur, rejects the psychology of the managed life in his businesses and his attitude toward the BIA. But he cannot escape the reality of it: when he argued with a BIA official, the official was not unpleasant to him, nor did he do anything that could be considered a direct reprisal. Instead, the federal government quite suddenly purchased 114 washing machines and distributed them to the Crows. "I used to make $35 to $37 a day in the laundromat," said Stops, "good money. Now I can't meet my payments. I don't know what to do. The whole tribe is watching me, waiting to see if I make it." [10]

He refuses to pay his water bill, citing an obscure passage in a treaty as his authority. It may cut back on his expenses for a while, but 114 free washing machines is more than he can cope with. He is thinking of turning his laundromat into a recreation center for the young people on the reservation, something beyond the occasional movies shown by the churches and the pinball machines and jukebox that now serve that purpose. The problem is that such a place couldn't support itself . . . . [11]

So he schemes. He has a plan to make money from selling a photographic gimmick to tourists. As a start on the scheme he has built a darkroom in his laundromat. "You wouldn't think a dumb savage could learn that all by himself," he said. He smiles proudly and runs his hands through his hair, like huge combs. It is a gesture of concern encroaching on his pride. Everywhere he turns there are restraining enemies. "I fight the BIA in my own way," he says. "I don't join any of those organizations. But it's hard to fight them, [12] because they can always get you, like the guy with the washing machines. I made trouble for him, so he ruined my business. You can't go to the tribal council and complain because the chairman is in on it. At the tribal fair not one Indian had a concession. I wanted to run a concession, but they asked me for a payoff, and I told them I wouldn't do it."

[13] Even when the federal government seems to be helping, the Indians are, in his view, somehow made to suffer. "I knew a guy in Los Angeles," he says, "who wanted to get into a relocation program. He went to the Bureau, and they told him he had to go back to the reservation to apply for relocation in Los Angeles. He didn't go: he couldn't." And then there is the new Boy Scout camp. The tribe donated one hundred sixty acres of land, and an Office of Economic Opportunity Communication Action Program supplied the money to build a fine camp on the land. Stops describes the camp proudly, giving details of the construction and operation. Then he shakes his head: "The first year it was for Indian kids. Now they say the OEO rules prohibit discrimination because of race. The camp has to be opened up to white kids from Billings. By next summer there won't be room for any Indian kids up there. Another hundred and sixty acres is gone."

[14] When there are visitors to his smoky office, they come with seriocomic deference. Stops once participated in a land-leasing negotiation which raised the rate per acre from ten cents to sixty cents. He once helped to get surplus commodities distributed on the reservation, about which he says, "Our people didn't feel like it was charity. They took it as a victory over the white man. They outsmarted him." Those are his successes; there have also been failures. He is a sorcerer of dubious powers, poring over his ragged books, marking the possibilities, making war on the white man with his own logic.

[15] George Mad Bear, tidy in his windbreaker and cowboy hat in contrast to the thorough dishabille of Stops, takes his wife to the laundromat, visiting in the small office for the duration of one complete washing-machine cycle. He and Stops discuss their victory over the state of Montana. Mad Bear had been notified by the state that he had to pay back taxes and interest for three years during which he was employed by the federal government on the reservation. The Legal Services office on the reservation told him they could not take his case, because his income was too high for him to qualify under the OEO rules. The lawyer, however, did give him some advice: he told Mad Bear to pay the taxes and the penalties, although he admitted that he had no specific information on the subject.

[16] Mad Bear had no knowledge of the law, but he did not under-

stand why he had been singled out to pay state taxes. He took the problem to Roger Stops, who consulted his books and determined that an Indian employed by the federal government and living on a reservation was not obliged to pay taxes to the state of Montana. They wrote a letter to their U.S. representative, who confirmed the opinion. A few weeks later, Mad Bear walked by the Legal Services office. The young lawyer called out to him, "George, about those state taxes, you don't have to pay them. I got the information." Mad Bear said, "Yes, I know. I had them send it to you."

The dissident sorcerer is not the only one who knows, but he is an Indian, he is the one who cares. Where else can those who are governed without their consent turn for help? The enemy of power is surrounded by washing machines and soda pop bottles. His hair is grown long, reaching for his collar. He has no connections among the college students who conduct sit-ins and make rage in the newspapers. His fingernails are thick and rimmed with black. He does not tie his shoes. He is toothless, and fat has begun to round away the character of his face. But he is an ally against the BIA, the OEO, and the officials of the tribe. He can say with them, "They tried to destroy us for five hundred years, and now we're destroying ourselves." Dreams of freedom and self-determination are symbolized in his dissent. [17]

Roger Stops understands his position in the tribe. It is not what he expects of himself, but it is all he can do. "This is the only culture I know," he said. "Everything I do is trying to achieve a higher state in the Indian way. But I was brought up in war, and now I fry hamburgers for a living. I'm degraded in the eyes of my people." [18]

VOCABULARY

dapper	trim and neat
deference	courteous regard or respect
dishabille	state of being untidily or scantily dressed
dissent	to differ in belief or opinion
dissident	a person who disagrees
Dostoevsky	Russian novelist, author of *Notes from the Underground*
exegesis	critical analysis or interpretation
obscure	not well-known
reprisal	an act of retaliation
requisite	something indispensable; a requirement
subtle	capable of making fine distinctions

DESIGN AND MEANING

1. What adjectives would you use to describe the scene set in paragraph 1? List some of the specific details that contribute to your impression.
2. Why does the writer include the material in paragraphs 4 and 5?
3. Notice the examples of the relationship between American whites and Indians in paragraphs 5, 10, and 13. Find examples of what Stops has done or tried to do in other paragraphs. What general statements could you make about whites and Indians after reading the two sets of examples?
4. Identify the pattern of the sentences in paragraph 9.
5. Find examples of visual appeal in descriptions of Stops and the setting. What other senses does the writer appeal to? What are some possible reasons for the extensive use of sensory language in this essay?
6. Is Stops's final statement true or false? What might be his motivation for saying such a thing? Is it an effective closing for the piece?

SIMILARITY AND DIFFERENCE

How does Roger Stops differ from the "Unknown Citizen" in Auden's poem in this chapter? Does the Stops type or the Unknown Citizen type prevail among the people you come in contact with?

SHORT WRITING IDEA

Write a paragraph describing a victory over (or defeat by) authority in your own life.

LONGER WRITING IDEA

Illustrate your relationship with someone significant to you by narrating three examples.

PREREADING EXERCISE

What do the colors prevalent in your wardrobe say about you? Do you think that they reflect your personality accurately?

Marisa Bowe

Black to Basics

Born in 1958 in Minneapolis, Bowe now lives in Brooklyn, New York, and follows the fashion world closely. She is currently working on her first novel. Her main hobby is sewing.

Not all hipsters wear black, but so many do that you'd be forgiven for thinking, upon first passing through Manhattan's Bohemian East Village, that you'd somehow stumbled onto the campus of a large urban undertaker college. [1]

If you ask a hipster why they wear black all the time, they'll say because it doesn't show dirt, or because that way all their clothes match. Maybe one in 100 will admit it's because it's cool. [2]

Black *is* cool; also hip, chic, elegant, sexy, kinky, bad, rebellious, intellectual, mysterious and forbidding. People who wear it think they are, too. My mother wouldn't let me wear black until I was "old enough." No other color's symbolic content is this tangible. [3]

To other people, the hipsters' somber ensembles look unnatural, inappropriate or pretentious—especially during the daytime. It's as if they've broken a rule you didn't know existed until you saw them. The raven-dark silhouette of the hipster, in sharp relief from the hyperactive colors and patterns splashed across the busy backs of most moderns, reads as a confrontation. [4]

To refuse color is to make a statement of difference, even if the hipsters who make that statement cling together in their nonconformity. Although in optical terms black is a void caused by absence of light, its meaning in clothing is more complex than simple negation. Black is a dense signifier, luxuriant with meaning. Tracing its subterranean sartorial pedigree brings to light the historical trajectory of a certain type of social difference, or at least its visible manifestation. [5]

Throughout modern history black has tended to clothe dissidents whose break with the dominant mindset of their time has been on aesthetic and emotional, rather than overtly political, grounds. Often not even politically awake, let alone active, they are nevertheless half-aware of unsatisfactory values being imposed on them. Their dissenting dress advertises a decision to live out their lives according to values that to them seem more honest, more [6] profound and more fulfilling—as if their revolution had already occurred.

Resonant symbol If black is particularly resonant as a symbol, it's because its symbolism derives from a natural phenomenon that even the high-tech humanoid of today can't fully escape: the blackness of night. Night's ancient mythology still punctures the gloss of contemporary mass culture, albeit in the trivialized, déclassé vehicle of the horror novel or film. [7]

The tawdry jumble of stereotypes that stock the genre are fragments from a pre-modern world-view in which night was the kingdom of irrationality—or worse. Night's stranglehold on the Greek imagination stemmed from its sinister link with the eternal darkness of death. In Greek mythology, Death and Sleep were twin brothers, and Death wore a sable robe. Black has stood for the most profound event of every human life since the beginning of Western civilization. [8]

In classical antiquity, black literally meant death: black was worn solely for mourning. Black garments gradually became embedded with spiritual and ascetic connotations. As Christianity took root, monks discovered black's suitability for their habits. Black symbolized their renunciation of the sensual, and their obsession with what happens to the soul after death. Perversely, but significantly, when heretical gnostic and satanist religious cults sprang up advocating knowledge of evil and the irrational, they were denounced as "black magic." [9]

According to Anne Hollander's *Seeing Through Clothes,* it wasn't until the 14th century that the phenomenon known as fashion came of age in Europe. Only then did black evolve from a simple functional symbol, used mainly for rituals, into a color that could be used for creative emotional effect by people who were part of society rather than cloistered from it. [10]

Mild blasphemy As early as the mid-1400s dandyish Burgundian and Italian royalty sported exquisite versions of the latest fashions made entirely of ultra-elegant black—the better to set them off from their gaudy courtiers. For a secular ruler, this petty symbol-theft of both the unworldly nobility of asceticism and the otherworldly aura of satanism had the piquant flavor of mild blasphemy. In other words, it was cool. Due to the great influence of the Burgundian court, black's career as a chic color was launched. [11]

In the late 1500s Shakespeare cast Hamlet in mourning black for the first part of his big starring role. Hamlet's "nighted color," sign of his secret spiritual anguish, was a stunning contrast to the [12] frivolous frippery of his mother's wedding guests. The "inky cloak" tattle-taled on the evil lurking beneath the merriment.

[13] Hamlet's dashingly sepulchral outfit gave him a dark halo of charisma, making him a mesmerizing exemplar of Elizabethan melancholy. Arguably the first major neurotic in European literature, in exile from the happy world of reason, Hamlet was a prototype of the modern alienated hero. *Hamlet* introduced black as the official color of iconoclastic anti-fashion.

[14] The Puritans did their share, too. Their sober black garb highlighted their disgust with their contemporaries' lack of "serious" religious commitment.

[15] Sometime before 1800 the Romantic figure of the wanderer—the remote, poetic soul whose feverish sensibility and nameless unrest made him or her a misfit doomed to solitude—began to haunt Western literature and influence fashionable minds throughout the 19th century. This archetypal modern Outsider wore black, the stigmata of isolation, and plunged headlong into the forbidden, dark underside of life that cheerful bourgeois dullards didn't even know existed.

[16] The Fatal Man and Woman personified the gothic-tinged Romantic Sublime, emanating the unutterable, if not the unspeakable. They struck terror and awe in more timid hearts, and wrecked the lives of fools drawn in by their fascination.

[17] **Sexual outlaws** Lord Byron, legendary, scandalous, Romantic *homme fatal,* made a habit of wearing black. Byron's notorious rep as an insatiable and deviant amorous adventurer—homosexuality and incest got him banished from England—introduced black as the color worn by diabolic sexual outlaws. Black clothes now signified renunciation of ordinary values, of stuffy rules, of the trap of mundane, restrictive, Victorian family life.

[18] Related but not identical to the fatal hero was the dandy. A mere fop to those who misunderstood him, the dandy was made a hero by Baudelaire. Baudelaire, genius psychochronicler of modernity, was an all-black-wearing dandy himself—when he could afford it.

[19] To Baudelaire, dandies were the vanguard of a new aristocracy based on an ineffable superiority more legitimate than mere birthright. He wrote that the subtle and austere appearance of dandies like Beau Brummel—who, according to one account, wore nothing but grey, black and white—conveyed their indifference to the absurd busy industriousness of their contemporaries.

[20] Dandies, said Baudelaire, scorned their era's crass, mediocre materialism, hale and hearty manliness and idolatry of usefulness.

They inhabited an inner world of beauty and emotion that was invisible to cruder minds. Baudelaire, sensing that the human soul was being killed off by Progress, said black was the appropriate hue for an age in mourning, in which "we celebrate all that is being buried."

As the Romantic era gave way to the machine age, black, now weighed down with encrusted historical meanings, slunk into the 20th century, where mass media had been waiting patiently for it. Black sank its greedy teeth into virgin culture. Hollywood vamps wore it as they corrupted innocent youths. Villains wore it as they tied pure maidens to railroad tracks. Criminals wore it as they crept into dowagers' bedrooms. Black has become shorthand for Cinema. [21]

In France, the Left Bank intellectuals of Paris had evolved a bohemian way of life that repudiated both the affluence and the official bourgeois morality of the period. After World War II they began wearing black turtlenecks, mixing a contemporary sense of off-the-rack informality with a Romantic sense of post-bomb doom. Black suited those whose daily occupation was confronting the dark existential void. American bohemians—artists, dancers, students and intellectuals—were quick to ape the look. [22]

Beats get basic The Beats, in love with a misty-mythical image of the black be-bop hipsters whose perceived freedom they sought to emulate, in search of the American Sublime along black asphalt hallucinogenic highways, were also partial to the color. Black was emblematic of all they couldn't find in the aseptic fluorescent offices of the corporate copycat kingdom. [23]

The black leather jacket debuted as a cult fashion item in the late '40s. Violent California motorcycle gangs such as the Hell's Angels, founded in 1950, lifted its powerful machismo from the brutal Nazi SS of Germany. Every rabble-rousing teenage punk in the Western world fell head-over-heels in love with the film version—Marlon Brando in *The Wild One* (1954). Black leather jackets instantly sprouted on the backs of the overtly anti-social. [24]

The spanking-new mass youth culture apparatus was just beginning to market forms of music—black, like the jacket—that uncannily expressed the attitudes of socially and economically disenfranchised young whites. R&B, re-christened "rock'n'roll" for the white market, possessed all the raw sexuality and emotion that had been gelded and lobotomized out of the syrupy songs of the Eisenhower-era soundtrack. Lumpen teens discovered you didn't need to be an egghead to be alienated, and the rocker/Teddy Boy subculture was born. [25]

During the '60s the Warhol demimonde added its hard-edged [26] ironic panache to the tradition of wearing black. Warhol's assistant, the poet Gerard Malanga (or alternately, Jim Morrison of the Doors, depending on whose story you believe) started the rage for black leather pants—a radically erotic departure from the usual drab male repertoire. Edie Sedgwick, Warhol's rich and beautiful female film "Superstar" until she started careening too close to her eventual O.D., did likewise for black tights and T-shirts. Lou Reed, lead singer/songwriter of the Warhol-produced Velvet Underground, lived in black Levis and a black leather jacket.

Counter-counter-culture The other dropouts of the '60s generation, the folk-singing flower children, dreaming of a nostalgic, pastoral utopia, wore all the pretty colors of the rainbow. But the darker-minded deviant urban cockroach-people were into hard-core sexual and chemical kicks—sympathy for the devil and all that—and made black their emblem. [27]

In the '70s, this groovy American *glasnost* was washed away. Corporate values reasserted themselves, choking off alternatives. The most blatant cultural symptom of this was the album-oriented pablum that took over the airwaves. The punks aimed poison black arrows at radio's marsh-mellow heart and let fly. Jeering outcasts, they wore their dole-queue alienation on their sleeves—literally—and made a joke of it. No question of utopia now; the crash-landing of the '60s counterculture it seemed had made a mockery of pure hopes and idealistic politics. [28]

The Ramones, Beach Boys gone bad, resurrected the black leather jacket. The Sex Pistols resuscitated black leather everything, only disconstructed with the help of a little S&M fetishism. Richard Hell and Patti Smith draped their spidery legs in black denim. For a short time, black clothes signalled the emergence of a like-minded underground cadre, intent on exploring the anger, hate, isolation and evil it discovered between the cracks of the official commodity culture's ideology of fun-abundance. [29]

Naturally the fashion industry lapped it up. The economic imperative of growth gives fashion its insatiable craving for novelty without which product obsolescence and turnover wouldn't occur fast enough to keep the industry in the black. When fashion percolates up from the streets, the industry removes clothes with shock value from their social context and presents them as a novel mode of consumption. The constellation of meanings swirling around black exert a pull on almost everybody. And for a few fashion seasons, at least, we all get to be titillated with a little sublimated rebellion. [30]

Inevitably, as chunks of punk's dead body have bit-by-bit been tossed as spice into the mainstream culture processor, black has [31] seeped into the heartland. The carefully manufactured images of the biggest male and female pop stars in the world—Michael Jackson and Madonna—display airbrushed bodies clad in what is now merely conventionally "bad" and "sexy" black leather.

[32] Pink-cheeked suburban teeny-boppers buy peek-a-boo black spandex rocker outfits in every climate-controlled, security-guarded mall in the U.S.A.—on Dad's credit card. In Soho, ambitious yuppie gals peel off their little suits with the perky little bows to try on arty-naughty black avant-garde designer dresses that cost enough to keep a thousand hard-core thrashers in safety pins and swastikas 'til the world ends. Black has gotten corny: the kiss of death.

[33] On the surface of things the probably temporary demise of an insurrectionary fashion may seem an offensively trivial topic. It's hard to care about the color of your jeans when compared to the problems of the homeless, the starving, the violently oppressed. But the stylistics of opposition are a real attempt to negotiate a cultural free space; to visually articulate resistance to the emotional, erotic and intellectual repression that help keep the status quo rigidly in place.

[34] The way the fashion apparatus has denatured black's threat and engulfed its meaning is a telling illustration of a lost battle in what Umberto Eco has called "semiotic guerrilla warfare." To the observant, the struggle that takes place at the level of appearances illuminates the less visible war of ideas that is always being fought between those who shape and enforce official ideology and those who presume to differ.

VOCABULARY

bohemian	unconventional, usually artistic in lifestyle
Burgundian	belonging to a historically powerful area of France
cadre	a key group of persons
declasse	reduced to low status
demimonde	a class of people with no standing in respectable society
gnostic	mystical
hipster	a person who is hip
homme fatal	a dangerous man
iconoclastic	attacking traditional beliefs
lumpen	alienated people with no social status
panache	grand style
sartorial	pertaining to tailoring
semiotic	symbolic

DESIGN AND MEANING

1. List the vivid, emotionally loaded language used in paragraphs 1–4 of "Black to Basics."
2. Make a case for either the last sentence in paragraph 5 or the first sentence in paragraph 6 as the thesis of the essay. How does the thesis predict how the essay will be organized?
3. Give examples of types of people who have worn black in the past. What do they have in common, according to Bowe?
4. What is the author's attitude toward today's fashionable use of black? What words and phrases in paragraphs 30–32 reflect this attitude?
5. How is the style of the essay related to its subject?

SIMILARITY AND DIFFERENCE

Relate the dissident point of view expressed in paragraphs 12–23 to W. H. Auden's poem "The Unknown Citizen."

SHORT WRITING IDEA

Writing of black in the introduction, Bowe asserts, "No other color's symbolic content is this tangible." Even so, write a paragraph discussing the symbolic content of some other color.

LONGER WRITING IDEA

Choose one of the specific names mentioned in the essay (a list follows). Do some research and write about how the figure illustrates an "aesthetic and emotional" dissident nature. Baudelaire, Lord Byron, Hamlet, Marlon Brando, Warhol, Jim Morrison, Edie Sedgwick, Lou Reed, Gerard Malanga, the Ramones, the Sex Pistols, Richard Hell, Patti Smith, Umberto Eco.

poetry

Dorothy Parker

Résumé

Dorothy Parker (1893–1967), celebrated for her sardonic wit, wrote verse, short stories, dramas, and screenplays. "Résumé" (1926) is included in *The Portable Dorothy Parker* (1954).

Razors pain you;
Rivers are damp;
Acids stain you;
And drugs cause cramp.
Guns aren't lawful; [5]
Nooses give;
Gas smells awful;
You might as well live.

Lawrence Ferlinghetti

The World Is a Beautiful Place

Lawrence Ferlinghetti (b. 1919), owner of the famous City Lights Bookstore in San Francisco, gathering place of the "beat poets" of the late nineteen-fifties, satirizes in his poetry the smug hypocrisy of "straight" society. "The World is a Beautiful Place" is included in *A Coney Island of the Mind* (1958).

The world is a beautiful place
to be born into
if you don't mind happiness
not always being
so very much fun [5]
if you don't mind a touch of hell
now and then
just when everything is fine
because even in heaven
they don't sing [10]
all the time
The world is a beautiful place
to be born into
if you don't mind some people dying
all the time [15]
or maybe only starving
some of the time
which isn't half so bad
if it isn't you
Oh the world is a beautiful place [20]
to be born into
if you don't much mind
a few dead minds
in the higher places
or a bomb or two [25]
now and then
in your upturned faces
or such other improprieties
as our Name Brand society
is prey to [30]

with its men of distinction
and its men of extinction
and its priests
and other patrolmen
and its various segregations [35]
and congressional investigations
and other constipations
that our fool flesh
is heir to
Yes the world is the best place of all [40]
for a lot of such things as
making the fun scene
and making the love scene
and making the sad scene
and singing low songs and having inspirations [45]
and walking around
looking at everything
and smelling flowers
and goosing statues
and even thinking [50]
and kissing people and
making babies and wearing pants
and waving hats and
dancing
and going swimming in rivers [55]
on picnics
in the middle of the summer
and just generally
'living it up'
Yes [60]
but then right in the middle of it
comes the smiling
mortician

PREREADING EXERCISE ("The Unknown Citizen")

Think of the general conception of the ideal member of the society you live in. You may not personally agree with this conception, but you see it around you. Make a few lists about this ideal citizen:

10 things he or she would do

10 things he or she would *not* do

10 beliefs he or she would have

10 possessions he or she would have

W. H. Auden

The Unknown Citizen

Wystan Hugh Auden (1907–1973), who was born in England and educated at Oxford, chose American citizenship in 1946. His poetry, which lucidly reflects the troubled era in which he lived, is considered some of the finest of the twentieth century. "The Unknown Citizen" appeared in 1940.

(To JS/07/M/378
This Marble Monument
Is Erected by the State)

He was found by the Bureau of Statistics to be
One against whom there was no official complaint,
And all the reports on his conduct agree
That, in the modern sense of an old-fashioned word, he was a
saint,
For in everything he did he served the Greater Community. [5]
Except for the War till the day he retired
He worked in a factory and never got fired,
But satisfied his employers, Fudge Motors Inc.
Yet he wasn't a scab or odd in his views,
For his Union reports that he paid his dues, [10]
(Our report on his Union shows it was sound)
And our Social Psychology workers found
That he was popular with his mates and liked a drink.
The Press are convinced that he bought a paper every day
And that his reactions to advertisements were normal in every
way [15]
Policies taken out in his name prove that he was fully insured.
And his Health-card shows he was once in hospital but left it cured.
Both Producers Research and High-Grade Living declare
He was fully sensible to the advantages of the Installment Plan
And had everything necessary to the Modern Man, [20]
A phonograph, a radio, a car and a frigidaire.
Our researchers into Public Opinion are content
That he held the proper opinions for the time of year;
When there was peace, he was for peace; when there was war, he
went.
He was married and added five children to the population, [25]

Which our Eugenist says was the right number for a parent of his
generation.
And our teachers report that he never interfered with their
education.
Was he free? Was he happy? The question is absurd:
Had anything been wrong, we should certainly have heard.

DESIGN AND MEANING

1. Look up the word "résumé" and speculate about why Parker chose it as a title.
2. What underlying attitudes toward life, death, and suicide does "Résumé" suggest? How do the examples of suicide methods support those attitudes?
3. Does the narrator of the second poem believe that "the world is a beautiful place"? How does the placement of the examples influence your answer?
4. Explain these phrases: "a few dead minds / in the higher places," "Name Brand society," and "priests / and other patrolmen."
5. What kind of society did the "Unknown Citizen" live in? What specific details and examples tell you about it?
6. After you read the poem, what added meaning can you attach to its title and the opening epitaph?
7. The poem is dated 1940. If it were rewritten today, what different examples of necessities might be in line 21? What else might be changed?
8. Who is the narrator ("we") supposed to be? How is the narrator different from the poet?

SHORT WRITING IDEA

Write a humorous lyric following the form of "Résumé," but ending with the line "You might as well die."

LONGER WRITING IDEA

Reread "The Unknown Citizen" and write a three-paragraph essay. In each paragraph, develop an example of how depersonalization in society has affected you.

Short Story

Walter van Tilburg Clark

The Portable Phonograph

Clark (1909–1971) is known primarily for his fine western novel, *The Ox-Bow Incident,* but he has also written a number of excellent short stories. "The Portable Phonograph," a starkly realistic story of futurist fiction, is taken from his collection *The Watchful Gods and Other Stories* (1941).

The red sunset, with narrow black cloud strips like threats across it, lay on the curved horizon of the prairie. The air was still and cold, and in it settled the mute darkness and greater cold of night. High in the air there was wind, for through the veil of the dusk the clouds could be seen gliding rapidly south and changing shapes. A queer sensation of torment, of two-sided, unpredictable nature, arose from the stillness of the earth air beneath the violence of the upper air. Out of the sunset, through the dead, matted grass and isolated weed stalks of the prairie, crept the narrow and deeply rutted remains of a road. In the road, in places, there were crusts of shallow, brittle ice. There were little islands of an old oiled pavement in the road too, but most of it was mud, now frozen rigid. The frozen mud still bore the toothed impress of great tanks, and a wanderer on the neighboring undulations might have stumbled, in this light, into large, partially filled-in and weed-grown cavities, their banks channeled and beginning to spread into badlands. These pits were such as might have been made by falling meteors, but they were not. They were the scars of gigantic bombs, their rawness already made a little natural by rain, seed, and time. Along the road there were rakish remnants of fence. There was also, just visible, one portion of tangled and multiple barbed wire still erect, behind which was a shelving ditch with small caves, now very quiet and empty, at intervals in its back wall. Otherwise there was no structure or remnant of a structure visible over the dome of the darkling earth, but only, in sheltered hollows, the darker shadows of young trees trying again. [1]

Under the wuthering arch of the high wind a V of wild geese fled south. The rush of their pinions sounded briefly, and the faint, plaintive notes of their expeditionary talk. Then they left a still greater vacancy. There was the smell and expectation of snow, as there is likely to be when the wild geese fly south. From the remote distance, towards the red sky, came faintly the protracted howl and quick yap-yap of a prairie wolf. [2]

North of the road, perhaps a hundred yards, lay the parallel and deeply intrenched course of a small creek, lined with leafless alders and willows. The creek was already silent under ice. Into the bank above it was dug a sort of cell, with a single opening, like the mouth of a mine tunnel. Within the cell there was a little red of fire, which showed dully through the opening, like a reflection or a deception of the imagination. The light came from the chary burning of four blocks of poorly aged peat, which gave off a petty warmth and much acrid smoke. But the precious remnants of wood, old fenceposts and timbers from the long-deserted dugouts, had to be saved for the real cold, for the time when a man's breath blew white, the moisture in his nostrils stiffened at once when he stepped out, and the expansive blizzards paraded for days over the vast open, swirling and settling and thickening, till the dawn of the cleared day when the sky was thin blue-green and the terrible cold, in which a man could not live for three hours unwarmed, lay over the uniformly drifted swell of the plain. [3]

Around the smoldering peat four men were seated cross-legged. Behind them, traversed by their shadows, was the earth bench, with two old and dirty army blankets, where the owner of the cell slept. In a niche in the opposite wall were a few tin utensils which caught the glint of the coals. The host was rewrapping in a piece of daubed burlap four fine, leather-bound books. He worked slowly and very carefully and at last tied the bundle securely with a piece of grass-woven cord. The other three looked intently upon the process, as if a great significance lay in it. As the host tied the cord he spoke. He was an old man, his long, matted beard and hair gray to nearly white. The shadows made his brows and cheekbones appear gnarled, his eyes and cheeks deeply sunken. His big hands, rough with frost and swollen by rheumatism, were awkward but gentle at their task. He was like a prehistoric priest performing a fateful ceremonial rite. Also his voice had in it a suitable quality of deep, reverent despair, yet perhaps at the moment a sharpness of selfish satisfaction. [4]

"When I perceived what was happening," he said, "I told myself, 'It is the end. I cannot take much; I will take these.' " [5]

"Perhaps I was impractical," he continued. "But for myself, I do not regret, and what do we know of those who will come after us? [6]

We are the doddering remnant of a race of mechanical fools. I have saved what I love; the soul of what was good in us is here; perhaps the new ones will make a strong enough beginning not to fall behind when they become clever."

He rose with slow pain and placed the wrapped volumes in the niche with his utensils. The others watched him with the same ritualistic gaze. [7]

"Shakespeare, the Bible, *Moby Dick,* the *Divine Comedy,*" one of them said softly. "You might have done worse, much worse." [8]

"You will have a little soul left until you die," said another harshly. "That is more than is true of us. My brain becomes thick, like my hands." He held the big, battered hands, with their black nails, in the glow to be seen. [9]

"I want paper to write on," he said. "And there is none." [10]

The fourth man said nothing. He sat in the shadow farthest from the fire, and sometimes his body jerked in its rags from the cold. Although he was still young, he was sick and coughed often. Writing implied a greater future than he now felt able to consider. [11]

The old man seated himself laboriously and reached out, groaning at the movement, to put another block of peat on the fire. With bowed heads and averted eyes his three guests acknowledged his magnanimity. [12]

"We thank you, Dr. Jenkins, for the reading," said the man who had named the books. [13]

They seemed then to be waiting for something. Dr. Jenkins understood but was loath to comply. In an ordinary moment he would have said nothing. But the words of *The Tempest,* which he had been reading, and the religious attention of the three made this an unusual occasion. [14]

"You wish to hear the phonograph," he said grudgingly. [15]

The two middle-aged men stared into the fire, unable to formulate and expose the enormity of their desire. [16]

The young man, however, said anxiously, between suppressed coughs, "Oh, please," like an excited child. [17]

The old man rose again in his difficult way and went to the back of the cell. He returned and placed tenderly upon the packed floor, where the firelight might fall upon it, an old portable phonograph in a black case. He smoothed the top with his hand and then opened it. The lovely green-felt-covered disk became visible. [18]

"I have been using thorns as needles," he said. "But tonight, because we have a musician among us"—he bent his head to the young man, almost invisible in the shadow—"I will use a steel needle. There are only three left." [19]

The two middle-aged men stared at him in speechless adoration. [20]

The one with the big hands, who wanted to write, moved his lips, but the whisper was not audible.

"Oh, don't!" cried the young man, as if he were hurt. "The thorns will do beautifully." [21]

"No," the old man said. "I have become accustomed to the thorns, but they are not really good. For you, my young friend, we will have good music tonight." [22]

"After all," he added generously, and beginning to wind the phonograph, which creaked, "they can't last forever." [23]

"No, nor we," the man who needed to write said harshly. "The needle, by all means." [24]

"Oh, thanks," said the young man. "Thanks," he said again in a low, excited voice, and then stifled his coughing with a bowed head. [25]

"The records, though," said the old man when he had finished winding, "are a different matter. Already they are very worn. I do not play them more than once a week. One, once a week, that is what I allow myself. [26]

"More than a week I cannot stand it, not to hear them," he apologized. [27]

"No, how could you?" cried the young man. "And with them here like this." [28]

"A man can stand anything," said the man who wanted to write, in his harsh, antagonistic voice. [29]

"Please, the music," said the young man. [30]

"Only the one," said the old man. "In the long run, we will remember more that way." [31]

He had a dozen records with luxuriant gold and red seals. Even in that light the others could see that the threads of the records were becoming worn. Slowly he read out the titles and the tremendous, dead names of the composers and the artists and the orchestras. The three worked upon the names in their minds, carefully. It was difficult to select from such a wealth what they would at once most like to remember. Finally the man who wanted to write named Gershwin's "New York." [32]

"Oh, no!" cried the sick young man, and then could say nothing more because he had to cough. The others understood him, and the harsh man withdrew his selection and waited for the musician to choose. [33]

The musician begged Dr. Jenkins to read the titles again, very slowly, so that he could remember the sounds. While they were read he lay back against the wall, his eyes closed, his thin, horny hand pulling at his light beard, and listened to the voices and the orchestras and the single instruments in his mind. [34]

When the reading was done he spoke despairingly. "I have forgotten," he complained. "I cannot hear them clearly." [35]

"There are things missing," he explained. [36]

"I know," said Dr. Jenkins. "I thought that I knew all of Shelley by heart. I should have brought Shelley." [37]

"That's more soul than we can use," said the harsh man. "*Moby Dick* is better. [38]

"By God, we can understand that," he emphasized. [39]

The Doctor nodded. [40]

"Still," said the man who had admired the books, "we need the absolute if we are to keep a grasp on anything. [41]

"Anything but these sticks and peat clods and rabbit snares," he said bitterly. [42]

"Shelley desired an ultimate absolute," said the harsh man. "It's too much," he said. "It's no good; no earthly good." [43]

The musician selected a Dubussy nocturne. The others considered and approved. They rose to their knees to watch the Doctor prepare for the playing, so that they appeared to be actually in an attitude of worship. The peat glow showed the thinness of their bearded faces, and the deep lines in them, and revealed the condition of their garments. The other two continued to kneel as the old man carefully lowered the needle onto the spinning disk, but the musician suddenly drew back against the wall again, with his knees up, and buried his face in his hands. [44]

At the first notes of the piano the listeners were startled. They stared at each other. Even the musician lifted his head in amazement but then quickly bowed it again, strainingly, as if he were suffering from a pain he might not be able to endure. They were all listening deeply, without movement. The wet, blue-green notes tinkled forth from the old machine and were individual, delectable presences in the cell. The individual, delectable presences swept into a sudden tide of unbearably beautiful dissonance and then continued fully the swelling and ebbing of that tide, the dissonant inpourings, and the resolutions, and the diminishments, and the little, quiet wavelets of interlude lapping between. Every sound was piercing and singularly sweet. In all the men except the musician there occurred rapid sequences of tragically heightened recollection. He heard nothing but what was there. At the final, whispering disappearance, but moving quietly so that the others would not hear him and look at him, he let his head fall back in agony, as if it were drawn there by the hair, and clenched the fingers of one hand over his teeth. He sat that way while the others were silent and until they began to breathe again normally. His drawn-up legs were trembling violently. [45]

Quickly Dr. Jenkins lifted the needle off, to save it and not to [46] spoil the recollection with scraping. When he had stopped the whirling of the sacred disk he courteously left the phonograph open and by the fire, in sight.

[47] The others, however, understood. The musician rose last, but then abruptly, and went quickly out at the door without saying anything. The others stopped at the door and gave their thanks in low voices. The Doctor nodded magnificently.

[48] "Come again," he invited, "in a week. We'll have the 'New York.' "

[49] When the two had gone together, out towards the rimed road, he stood in the entrance, peering and listening. At first there was only the resonant boom of the wind overhead, and then far over the dome of the dead, dark plain the wolf cry lamenting. In the rifts of clouds the Doctor saw four stars flying. It impressed the Doctor that one of them had just been obscured by the beginning of a flying cloud at the very moment he heard what he had been listening for, a sound of suppressed coughing. It was not near by, however. He believed that down against the pale alders he could see the moving shadow.

[50] With nervous hands he lowered the piece of canvas which served as his door and pegged it at the bottom. Then quickly and quietly, looking at the piece of canvas frequently, he slipped the records into the case, snapped the lid shut, and carried the phonograph to his couch. There, pausing often to stare at the canvas and listen, he dug earth from the wall and disclosed a piece of board. Behind this was a deep hole in the wall, into which he put the phonograph. After a moment's consideration he went over and reached down his bundle of books and inserted it also. Then, guardedly, he once more sealed up the hole with the board and the earth. He also changed his blankets and the grass-stuffed sack which served as a pillow, so that he could lie facing the entrance. After carefully placing two more blocks of peat upon the fire he stood for a long time watching the stretched canvas, but it seemed to billow naturally with the first gusts of a lowering wind. At last he prayed, and got in under his blankets, and closed his smoke-smarting eyes. On the inside of the bed, next the wall, he could feel with his hand the comfortable piece of lead pipe.

VOCABULARY

acrid	sharp, bitter, and stinging
chary	not giving freely; suspicious
doddering	moving unsteadily
loath	reluctant

magnanimity	generosity
pinions	wing feathers
rimed	frosted
shelving	sloping
undulation	a wavy form
wuthering	a dull, roaring sound

DESIGN AND MEANING

1. What details in the first two paragraphs establish a mood? Choose five words that you consider especially important to the mood. What factual background do you get in this opening?
2. Why do the volumes Dr. Jenkins chose to save exemplify "what was good in us is here" (paragraph 6)?
3. The characters of the professor, the writer, and the musician are not drawn in detail, and the fourth character is even more shadowy. Why would Clark leave the characters so vague? What *do* you know about them?
4. What is the significance of the choice between Gershwin and Debussy? What kind of music does each choice exemplify?
5. What does the last paragraph, especially the last sentence, contribute to the meaning of the story?

SIMILARITY AND DIFFERENCE

What difference in purpose can you see between stories like "The Portable Phonograph" or "The Other Side of the Hedge" (Chapter 8) and a story like "Eve in Darkness" (Chapter 1)?

SHORT WRITING IDEA

Find three examples of religious imagery in the story. Explain how each one is appropriate to the meaning of the story.

LONGER WRITING IDEA

Make up a situation in which there is a conflict among three people over money. Describe the conflict, making each of the three people exemplify a distinct attitude toward money.

Analysis

COMPETENT PEOPLE HAVE GOOD powers of analysis. They do not hopelessly see life as a huge wave washing over them; instead, they can identify its force, its volume, its harmless debris, and its stinging jellyfish. They are able to separate a whole into its parts and examine them, a skill that is indispensable for successful living. Even a monumental problem can be solved systematically if you can isolate its parts and think about them one by one.

Analysis is always a part of effective problem solving. Take this topic: Why is it so hard to study English? Rack your brains to think of the component parts of your difficulty in studying. You may come up with three fairly curable contributing factors, like: (1) I have not bought the textbook, (2) the light bulb in my desk lamp has been burned out for three months, and (3) I turn on the television as soon as I get home from class. Then all you have to do is borrow a book, change the bulb, abstain from television, and think up three more rationalizations. Eventually you may get to the heart of the problem, and you will owe this breakthrough to your growing analytical prowess.

Analysis is also indispensable for writing: finding an effective organization depends on the writer's ability to examine a thesis and break it into smaller, related supporting topics. That is why, in a broad sense, the heart of most writing is analytical. Once a thesis is broken down, its parts may include several of the interrelationships we talk about elsewhere in this book—cause, effect, comparison, contrast—and may be developed using any or a combination of the different modes we discuss—narration, illustration, example, definition, process, or classification. Spelling out a process, speculating on cause and effect, arguing a point, interpreting literature, or, for that matter, any writing that tries to explain a problem, a trend, a relationship, or an abstract idea—all of these require analysis. As you begin the writing process, the first movements of the mind are analytical.

Thus, almost any subject is appropriate for analysis. In this section we will see the auto industry analyzed by Paul Blumberg in "Snarling Cars"; the urge to marry analyzed by Mary Kay Blakely in "I Do, I Do, I Do . . ."; Alfred Hitchcock's film *Shadow of a Doubt* analyzed by David Denby in "Walk on the Mild Side"; popular culture analyzed by Peter Andrews in "The Hating Game" and by Roland Barthes in "Toys"; human nature analyzed by Mark Twain in "The Lowest Animal." And Matthew Arnold takes on the meaning of life in general in his poem "Dover Beach."

You will probably not have to assume such burdensome tasks, but the job done by these writers is worthy of study and respect. You will be asked to analyze the analyses and to write a few manageable ones yourself.

essays

Peter Andrews

The Hating Game

A journalist of varied interests, Andrews (b. 1931) has written about sports, married life, country inns, and television in magazines as diverse as his topics. The following selection appeared in the *Saturday Review,* March 29, 1980.

"Did you make whoopee first and then decide to get married or did you decide to get married and then make whoopee?" [1]

This is a typical question asked on *The Newlywed Game,* one of five participation shows producer Chuck Barris is currently inflicting on the television screen. It is also the kind of slop I watched for one week to write this column, so don't expect me to be pleasant. In fact, after putting in 10 or 12 hours watching Chuck Barris shows, I may not even be coherent. [2]

I didn't start out to do a column on Chuck Barris and his works. The original idea was to develop a theory of mine about how it seems to be almost a requirement that nonactors agree to make fools of themselves in order to appear on television. As I saw it, I was going to trace a line from those blank-faced characters at sporting events who point to themselves whenever the camera swings in their direction to contestants on such shows as *The Price Is Right* who come apart at the seams over the excitement of winning a year's supply of birdseed. Then I was going to touch on the serious side and briefly discuss the unseemly rush on the part of half the women in television to take over Shana Alexander's doleful spot on *60 Minutes.* Alexander quit, by the way, not because she and James Kilpatrick were an embarrassment but because she felt she wasn't getting enough money. The apotheosis of these shows, I had supposed, was *Let's Make a Deal,* a program in which the producers take no chances whatsoever. Contestants have to *arrive* dressed like idiots even to be considered. I had not, however, reckoned with the cosmic vulgarity of Chuck Barris. [3]

Besides *The Newlywed Game* Chuck Barris numbers among his creations *The $1.98 Beauty Show, The Gong Show, The Dating Game,* and *Three's a Crowd.* All five attempt to make entertainment out of self-degradation. Without exception they are unremittingly witless, tasteless, illiterate, and stupid—I'm not being obscure here, am I? Additionally, all five Chuck Barris programs display what seems to be his almost psychotic hatred of women. No opportunity is ever missed to show a woman as some sort of Daffy Duck who doubles as the town moron and the community punchboard. Barris shows amount to a systematic assassination of women, and that his victims skip to the executioner's block fairly squealing with delight at the prospect is no defense. [4]

Take the *$1.98 Beauty Show*—in the word of Henny Youngman, "please!" In case you have missed it, the format is simplicity itself, which is probably the only way host Rip Taylor can keep track of it. Taylor, whose entire inventory of comedic devices consists of his single impersonation of a man having a nervous breakdown on his way to a transvestite costume party, reels onstage in a sequined ringmaster's outfit at full screech and then divides his time between delivering satiric introductions and standing to one side shouting incomprehensibly while the women go through their paces. The "contestants," who usually resemble the kinds of ladies the police try to get off the streets before political conventions come to town, dance and sing after a fashion and then parade around in joke-shop bathing suits. And, for something really funny, Taylor brings on a fat lady who waddles around the stage with the vacant expression of a cow who has just been hit on the forehead with a sledgehammer. Finally, for the big boffola finish, *the fat lady wins* while Taylor breaks into hysterics and strews confetti over her capacious bosom. [5]

In comparison, *The Gong Show* is almost austere, combining third-rate professional acts with some truly horrific amateur ones. The principal interest here is that we get to see the master, Chuck Barris himself, who works as his own emcee. At 50, Barris is still the eternal classroom cut-up your parents didn't want you to associate with because he never would amount to anything. And they were right. He never did. Barris is a constant source of amusement to himself as he claps his hands and breaks himself up with gag introductions to the acts, mostly old vaudeville wheezes like "here he is fresh from an engagement on the Astor roof laying tar paper" mixed with a few Barris locker room touches of his own. He introduced one act as "Flash Beaver," which gives you an idea of the humor level Barris is comfortable with. As you might expect, the entertainment is supposed to come not from what the acts do but from their ineptitude, the amusement equivalent of putting turtles on their backs so that you can watch their feet wiggle. [6]

Benumbing as these shows are, I suppose they could be defended as representing at least a perverted attempt at variety entertainment in the slapstick tradition of burlesque. But to get the real, double-dipped Chuck Barris passion for voyeurism combined with self-debasement, you have to include his other shows, which are just crawling with social commentary. [7]

Watching *The Dating Game,* a television update of a forlorn radio show some 30 years past, is like being lashed to a stool in a singles' bar, and if that's your idea of a good time, you're welcome to my seat. In this one, a woman so aroil with passion she is suffused with a precoital glow, gets to talk to but not see three macho types. They in turn try out their lines and the one who weaves the finest seine bags her for the night. On the show I watched, the woman's opening question to all three was, "Imagine I am a beer can and then describe everything you are going to do for me from the time you pick me up until you're finished with me." I'm not making this up. That is what she said. The first guy replied that he was going to treat her like champagne and then he was going to chug-a-lug her . . . . You can figure the rest out for yourself. [8]

My guess is that *The Newlywed Game* is Chuck Barris's personal favorite of his shows. It combines the maximum amount of double entendre with the least amount of intelligence. "Whoopee" questions are, of course, a staple. But every once in a while it goes off into general-interest areas that offer grist for somebody's mill. On one show the women were to guess what their husbands' favorite country in South America was. The first bride passed on the grounds she didn't know what or where South America was, and another guessed his choice would be Africa. Interestingly, one of the husbands, not hers, said his favorite country in South America was Africa. This started me thinking we might have the genesis of a wife-swapping game show on our hands here, but I assume Barris is way ahead of me on that one. [9]

As a matter of fact, Barris is nibbling around the edges of a fun infidelity game show with *Three's a Crowd,* which pits wives against secretaries in knowing who has more sexual information about the lout they are both serving however indifferently. This is the latest of the Barris shows, and the material has become terribly threadbare even by his standards. I am assuming there that most of the "funny" answers contestants come up with have been written for them. Certainly, they have the same tired gag factory smell about them. When the wife and the secretary had to guess where the husband/boss most like to be tickled, the best anyone could come up with was "south of the border." [10]

I have no idea why people should yearn to go on these shows any more than I understand someone who thinks it's funny to get [11] smashed at a party and dance with a lampshade on his head. But the appeal is undoubtedly strong. Barris himself fired the original emcee of *The Gong Show* so he could expose himself on television. Is the desire to be on television so powerful that people will submit to any kind of ridicule just to see themselves? What do these media flashers do when their program is aired? Do they gather their loved ones about them and say, "Now watch Mommy and Daddy make fools of themselves"? I don't know, and, frankly, I don't like to think about it very much.

[12] In an interview, Barris once sounded the traditional schlock-meister's defense for selling garbage. "I produce entertainment shows for the masses, not for the intelligentsia," he said, "I produce entertainment shows the way Robert Hall makes suits."

[13] I take solace in the knowledge that Robert Hall eventually went bankrupt. Perhaps there is some hope for us.

VOCABULARY

apotheosis	a glorified ideal
aroil	violently agitated
austere	lacking ornament or fanciness
capacious	spacious
coherent	capable of logical, understandable speech or thought
doleful	melancholy, or causing sadness
double entendre	double meaning
genesis	beginning or origin
intelligentsia	the educated and enlightened class
lout	a clumsy, stupid fellow
precoital	before sexual intercourse
reckon with	to take into consideration
satiric	using ridicule to attack or expose folly
schlockmeister	a master of trash
seine	a fishing net
self-debasement	lowering oneself in value or dignity
self-degradation	lowering oneself in status or moral condition
solace	comfort or relief
suffused	overspread
unremitting	constant, persistent
unseemly	unbecoming and improper
voyeurism	exaggerated interest in viewing sexual acts

DESIGN AND MEANING

1. How effective are the introductory tactics in this essay?
2. What is Peter Andrews's thesis?
3. How does the writer organize his analysis of the Barris shows?
4. List several examples of strongly connotative words and phrases.
5. Find at least three similes or metaphors in the essay. Are they effective comparisons?
6. Research the references to these people: Shana Alexander, James Kilpatrick, Henny Youngman, and Robert Hall.

SIMILARITY AND DIFFERENCE

What ideas about popular culture would Peter Andrews and Ann Nietzke ("Doin' Somebody Wrong," Chapter 7) probably share?

SHORT WRITING IDEA

Summarize a joke you know and analyze why you think it is funny.

LONGER WRITING IDEA

Analyze the emotional and intellectual appeal of a television series or a set of related television shows.

VOCABULARY CHECK

Use each of the following phrases in a meaningful sentence.

1. an eerie light suffused
2. the unremitting desert sun
3. the genesis of a bad habit
4. is sometimes a solace
5. an austere apartment
6. no longer coherent
7. unseemly behavior at the park
8. reckon with restless children

9. unnecessarily doleful

10. satiric poem about

PREREADING EXERCISE

List as many reasons as you can why people get married. Which ones do you believe are good reasons? Which ones are unrealistic?

Mary Kay Blakely

I Do, I Do, I Do . . .

Born in 1948, Blakely writes mostly about women's issues and the inequalities in our society. She holds a Master's degree from Northern Illinois University and lives in Greenwich, Connecticut. Her freelance works have appeared in *Ms.*, from which this essay was taken, *The New York Times Book Review, Newsday, Woman's Day, Ladies' Home Journal,* and other national publications. She wrote a book called *Wake Me When It's Over* in 1984, about her nine-day coma. She appears frequently on the college circuit as a speaker.

"Do you think we should get married?" the man I love asked the other night. He was not down on bended knee, muscles taut, sweating and anxious about meeting my father. His long, 45-year-old frame was slouched comfortably in our living room couch, a wineglass balanced on the soft plateau of his abdomen, his eyebrows knit in the same thoughtful frown he wore when he clipped his toenails. The question was not designed to make my heart palpitate wildly, and it did not. For three years, the question of marriage has been passing back and forth between us like a deflated volleyball. [1]

It isn't that we aren't in love—we're as madly and passionately in love as two former volleyball players ever expect to be. And we're both periodically seized with the oaty, human urge to make this love official in some way, to enshrine it in gold rings and diamonds, to sign our names to lifetime promises. The problem is that we can't, in good faith, promise to love and honor each other until death do us part. Fifteen years ago we both made that promise to other people—former spouses who are still very much alive. We were in love then, too, but didn't think much about the widely circulated fact that when love is deposited in the institution of marriage, it faces nearly a 45 percent chance of meeting the shredder of divorce. We didn't believe it applied to us. Now, of course, we know. [2]

Even for couples who escape the shredder, however, there are signs that their love hasn't thrived in marriage. Almost half the female respondents to a recent national magazine survey on marital satisfaction concluded they would not again marry their husbands. If nearly half of all marriages now end in divorce, and half of the [3] remainder are really divorces waiting to happen, a bride today has roughly a 25 percent chance of living happily ever after.

[4] How does it happen that 70 percent of us lose track of the love we once felt so passionately? The anonymous wives in that survey described an overwhelming loneliness and reported that sexually . . . well, their lives had gone rather limp. Since women often reach their sexual peak 20 years after men, as one friend bluntly put it, "just as a woman is feeling her friskiest, her husband has found his favorite chair."

[5] According to contemporary analysts, women today are leaving or refusing marriages our grandmothers accepted because we suffer from having "higher expectations." The divorce rate would drop, presumably, if women could be encouraged to want less. This will be a difficult concept to sell, since ours is the first generation of women in history who could afford to have high expectations. Until very recently, women didn't have much choice about marriage if they wanted financial support, children, and lifetime companionship. For better or worse, a husband was the only route to those wishes for our grandmothers. But no more.

[6] Yesterday many women's economic livelihoods used to depend on becoming the wife of a doctor or lawyer or bricklayer. Today we can earn those paychecks ourselves. And that has a remarkable effect on the way a woman with high expectations thinks. An independent income allows women the freedom to think of things in themselves. As Virginia Woolf wrote of the two rights she won in her lifetime, "the vote and the money—the money, I own, seemed infinitely the more important."

[7] The free thinking that begins with an independent income allows women to take advantage of another significant aspect of life that middle-class mores used to assign solely to marriage. During the social revolution of the last decade, women won the right to make their own decisions about whether to reproduce. Women who didn't want children were no longer forced to bear them, and recent discoveries in medical technology have now made it possible for women to conceive without husbands or, excuse me, gentlemen, without penises altogether. With the assistance of modern fertility clinics, a single woman can almost immaculately conceive a child. It isn't easy to raise a child alone—but the unhappy truth is that marriage doesn't guarantee help with child care. The father's rights movement, don't forget, was born during the divorce revolution—the first time many men noticed they had children.

[8] Although some single women over 30 who deliberately conceived out of wedlock have acknowledged that they would have preferred marriage had the "right man" shown up in time, they felt their professions and children provided two thirds of the benefits a

husband had to offer. The only reason they now had to marry, in these revolutionary times, was the promise of lifetime companionship. And here, too, modern life has compromised "till death do us part."

[9] As life expectancies increase, the added years put men and especially women through more seasons of growth and change—not always in the same direction. In *Future Shock,* Alvin Toffler predicted that longer life spans may mean repeated divorces for many of us, and envisioned marriage in the future as serial monogamy. It's a heart-stopping concept for a woman in love, but knowledgeable brides and grooms now have to enter marriage in a state of preparedness for divorce.

[10] What are prenuptial agreements if not a sheepish acknowledgement that love may come to grief someday? For tender-hearted lovers, too romantically involved to think about divorce, many state legislators are considering bills that equitably divide assets acquired during marriage. Like the car insurance required for every driver's license, this type of legislation would provide basic coverage with each marriage license in case of an accident. Settling financial questions in advance, however, doesn't relieve the emotional whiplash couples suffer after the crash.

[11] The greatest tragedy of divorce is that couples finally begin talking again, after it's too late to act upon the truths revealed. After long years of "we don't talk" or "he takes me for granted," divorce brings an onslaught of amazing revelations. The fuzzy assumptions about what each partner meant by the promise to "love and honor" are brought into sharp relief during protracted negotiations about money, children, the value of housework, the insufferability of certain habits, the hours lost to a favorite armchair.

[12] As painful as these revelations were during my own divorce, both my former spouse and I admit they improved our relationship. We had to keep negotiating until we worked out a fair settlement of financial and parental responsibilities. I would have liked to have lived as a wife under the terms we finally established through divorce. Instead of vowing to love and honor until death do us part, I would now promise to talk and argue and state my needs—then maybe love, if I had any energy left.

[13] What other promises should a woman with high expectations make in this perilous age of serial monogamy? Ironically, the qualities of life a bride needs for a happy marriage are exactly what she'll need in the event of divorce. If two independent people who are deeply in love manage to become semimarried and halfway divorced at the same time—if they share housework, child care, and finances from the beginning—it may improve their 25 percent chance of living happily ever after. Since we don't "need" marriage

but nevertheless keep choosing it, perhaps again and again, a woman with the highest expectations might possibly achieve serial monogamy with the same man. That, essentially, was the answer I gave to the man I love, when he posed the critical question the other night. "Yes, I think we should get married. If we live long enough, let's get married several times."

VOCABULARY

equitably	reasonably and fairly
insufferability	unbearableness
mores	unquestioned customs and rules of a group
onslaught	vigorous onset
palpitate	flutter
perilous	dangerous
prenuptial	before marriage
protracted	drawn out

DESIGN AND MEANING

1. How does the marriage proposal described in paragraph 1 differ from the idealized proposal? List as many ways as you can. What do you expect this article to be like after reading the introductory paragraph?
2. List the statistics integrated into the first four paragraphs of the essay.
3. What reason for the divorce rate does the author propose in paragraph 5?
4. In paragraph 5, the author mentions three desires that women might have. Where in the essay are these three desires further developed?
5. The transitions between paragraphs 5 and 6 and between paragraphs 6 and 7 are graceful *echo* transitions. What is echoed from one paragraph to the next?
6. What did the author learn from her divorce (paragraphs 11 and 12)?
7. According to the author, what would be the nature of the ideal marriage? How is it reflected in the last line?

SIMILARITY AND DIFFERENCE

What ideas about humanity does Blakely share with Mark Twain in his essay "The Lowest Animal" (in this chapter)? What would Blakely and Twain disagree about?

SHORT WRITING IDEA

Write a paragraph or two in which you make a comparison between two really unlike things (like the divorce/car accident comparison in paragraph 10). Here are some possibilities: writing an essay and making a sandwich, your dog and your boyfriend, love and hate, government and football.

LONGER WRITING IDEA

For you, what would be the ideal marriage? In preparation for writing this analysis, consider some of these ideas: Where do your ideas about marriage come from (your parents' example, other couples you know, books, films)? What are some things that would *not* be part of the ideal marriage? What actions do you need to take to assure yourself the best possible marriage? If you don't intend to get married, analyze why not.

Paul Blumberg

Snarling Cars

Blumberg (b. 1935), who grew up in Minneapolis, Minnesota, has been for many years a professor of sociology at Queens College of the City University of New York. He is also well established as a writer with a social conscience, whose best-known book, *Inequality in an Age of Decline* (1980), reflects a concern for the social inequities resulting from the lean economic years of the late 1970s. In the following selection Blumberg offers a biting analysis of Detroit's decision-making strategies.

Lincoln-Mercury Cougar Slain

PITTSBURGH (UPI)—*The cougar that served as the Lincoln-Mercury advertising trademark was shot and killed today after it attacked a 9-year-old boy at an automobile show.*—News item. [1]

In this macabre incident, the cougar seized the boy by the neck, pinned him to the ground, resisted all efforts by the trainer to pull him from his prey, and was finally shot to death by an off-duty policeman. The boy, suffering severe neck wounds, was rushed to the hospital in serious condition. He has since recovered. The health of the American automobile industry, however, still hangs in the balance. [2]

For decades, one of Detroit's major advertising ploys was to market its products as instruments of violence. During the entire postwar period, in fact, Detroit's marketing strategy was not to sell automobiles as sensible family transportation, as one might expect in a reasonably civilized society, but as vehicles of mayhem and destruction. [3]

What's in a name? In Detroit's case, plenty. Because over the years, as an auto writer once observed, the very names Detroit managers gave to their cars reveal quite plainly the industry's appeal to motives of violence and aggression. Consider the Oldsmobile *Cutlass,* the Buick *Le Sabre,* the Plymouth *Fury,* the Plymouth *Barracuda*, the Chevrolet Corvette *Stingray*, the Ford Mustang *Cobra,* the American Motors *Matador,* the Mercury *Lynx,* Mercury *Bobcat,* and Mercury *Cougar*—killers all, the last one, this [4] time, almost literally. The theme of violence in these names has a cunning economic logic behind it. As we now know, Detroit management's guiding theology during the postwar era was: big car, big profit; small car, small profit. And what better way to sell big, powerful cars than to link them in the public's mind with the libidinal release of destructive impulses?

[5] In the postwar auto industry, as the horsepower race heated up, the managers of each company dropped ever-larger and hungrier engines into ever-bigger, heavier, and more option-laden automobiles. As late as 1970, 85 percent of U.S. cars were sold with V-8 engines. Consequently, as one sage assessed the peculiar logic of the American automobile industry, Detroit sold a 5,000-pound car to a 100-pound woman so she could drive one block to buy a one-pound loaf of bread. When Marx wrote of the anarchy of production under capitalism, he knew whereof he spoke, though he lived before Detroit management had honed the principle to perfection.

[6] Of all the gadgets on the Road Locomotives (as Consumers Union called these American behemoths thirty years ago), none so clearly opens a window into the mind of the Detroit executive as the design of the speedometer. In keeping with management's appeal to raw power rather than sensible transportation, the speedometer had to show speeds of 120, 140, or 150 miles per hour—far faster, of course, than was safe, legal, or even possible for most cars. But when you scale up a small gauge with speeds to 150 m.p.h., the numbers must all be crammed so close together that it's difficult to read any of them. Here in a nutshell (or a dial) were management's values: style and libido over engineering logic. And while Detroit managers were busy refining these priorities with tail fins and sleek but dangerous hardtop convertibles (whose roofs, lacking a center pillar, might collapse if the car rolled over), foreign manufacturers were making disc brakes and radial tires.

[7] When Detroit's managers are accused of foisting the Road Locomotives on the American public and thus being unprepared for the small-car revolution, they neatly shift the blame to the public. The postwar dinosaurs weren't their idea, they protest; they were simply giving their customers what they wanted. This, the consumer sovereignty argument, overlooks the fact that consumer taste does not develop in a vacuum but is shaped by manufacturers through massive advertising. In one recent year, the auto industry spent $700 million on TV ads, $340 million more on newspaper ads, and $225 million for magazine advertising—well over $1 billion in just one year (not counting the money spent on radio, billboards, and other forms of advertising). Throughout the postwar years Detroit spent comparable billions fashioning public taste for the gas guzzlers, and then proceeded to satisfy that taste.

[8] Of course, public taste cannot be totally programmed by advertising. Ford failed to generate much interest in the Edsel, and some new and highly promoted products do occasionally fail. Nonetheless, though massive advertising cannot guarantee demand for individual products, there is no question that the billions Detroit spent after World War II pushing the big, heavy, powerful V-8s did in fact create the taste and habit for these cars. Because of postwar affluence, which allowed an ethic of conspicuous waste, and because of the underlying macho element in American culture, there was a basic public receptivity to the marketing strategy of selling murder on wheels. But if the ground was fertile, Detroit management sowed the seeds and carefully tended the fields.

[9] In 1949 the U.A.W.'s research and engineering people published an article, "A Motor Car Named Desire," that called on Detroit to build a small, light, affordable car, suitable for postwar urban America. They cited a contemporary opinion survey taken by the Society of Automotive Engineers, which showed that 60 percent of Americans wanted the U.S. auto industry to produce a small car. Specifically, the U.A.W. proposed a car about 170 inches in length, weighing about 2,000 pounds, with a small six- or four-cylinder engine that would get more than 25 miles to the gallon. In other words, the U.A.W. proposed a car almost identical in conception to the Datsuns, Toyotas, and Hondas now inundating America. Had Detroit heeded the U.A.W.'s advice then, it would now have the experience to meet and beat the small-car competition from abroad, rather than belatedly struggling to catch up. But it ignored the suggestion; in fact, it responded to Walter Reuther's presumption with a bold assertion of executive power meant to keep the union in its place and to protect the principle of managerial prerogative. In its contract with the U.A.W. in 1950, and in every contract thereafter, G.M. inserted a clause stipulating the "Rights of Management." It provided that "the products to be manufactured, the location of plants, the schedules of production, the methods, processes and means of manufacturing are solely and exclusively the responsibility of the Corporation."

[10] When sensible, small-car transportation became necessary after the 1973 OPEC embargo, Detroit was unprepared. By hooking the American consumer on far bigger and more powerful cars than were rational or necessary, Detroit became the victim of its own shortsightedness and masterminded its own collapse. Until 1955 Detroit had the U.S. auto market all to itself; foreign imports comprised less than 1 percent of sales. But in the late 1950s the U.S. was invaded by a horde of insects—the Volkswagen beetles. And between 1955 and 1960, foreign auto imports rose to nearly 7 percent of sales. Though opposed in principle to building small, inexpensive

cars, Detroit management realized that it had to offer the American public something to offset the growing popularity of the Volkswagen, the other small European cars, and the initial flow of Japanese cars. So at the end of the 1950s Detroit introduced its own compact cars—the Plymouth Valiant, Ford Falcon, Chevrolet Corvair, and the like.

[11] These practical American compacts sold well, and the foreign car tide began to recede. By 1965 imports accounted for a smaller share of the U.S. market than they had in 1960. But Detroit executives were so hooked on the big-is-beautiful formula that they said, in effect, "Well, we'll build these compacts if we have to, but they're going to be the biggest, widest, heaviest, most powerful, most expensive compacts the world has ever seen." Each year U.S. compacts got bigger, more powerful, more loaded with options, and more costly. The U.S. auto industry was so successful in building the world's biggest compacts that it eventually abandoned the small-car field altogether. Into this vacuum came the European cars again, and with them the Japanese—this time for keeps. Foreign imports rose from just 5.5 percent of sales in 1965 to 23 percent in 1970. With that kind of a foothold the imports now could not be dislodged. But if Detroit management had stayed with the compacts in the 1960s and redirected its advertising to wean Americans from the gospel of speed, power, and mayhem, the U.S. industry could have overcome or at least minimized the foreign car challenge, perhaps forestalled the protectionist tide, and might even have started exporting significant numbers of cars itself.

[12] Friends of the U.S. auto industry like to argue that protectionism would never have become an issue if the working men and women who build the cars weren't so greedy. Detroit cannot compete with the Japanese, it is alleged, because American workers earn $8 an hour more than Japanese workers. Most objective observers agree, however, that the presumed $8-an-hour wage difference has been exaggerated and omits such things as the substantial housing subsidies Japanese companies provide for their workers. Although U.S. workers are more highly paid, wage differences between the U.S. and Japan probably amount to less than $500 per car, which is virtually offset by duty and the cost of shipping from Japan to the U.S.

[13] Moreover, low price is not the reason foreign cars are selling here. In fact, foreign cars sold in the U.S., which years ago were cheaper than American cars, are now on the average more expensive than American cars. Commerce Department figures show that in the last quarter of 1981 the average selling price of an American car was $9,012, and the average selling price of a foreign car sold here was $9,318. Japanese companies are selling cars in this coun-

try primarily because they have the product, and they have the product because they've had long experience making it. American companies don't.

[14] The lesson of Detroit's decline is clear: just as war is too important to leave to the generals, business is too important to leave to the managers. Detroit management has failed; their marketing strategy has been cynical and antisocial for at least a generation; their world view is obsolete. Until recently the idea of economic democracy—the participation of workers, consumers, and the public in corporate decisionmaking—was a radical, utopian dream. Today it may be an economic necessity.

[15] The paradox of all this is that Detroit management's prime concern with the bottom line by selling big cars for big profits proved in the long run to be extremely unprofitable. Had saner voices among workers, consumers, and the public prevailed, a sensible automobile for urban America would probably have been produced decades ago, which might have saved the U.S. auto industry from its present debacle. Ironically, production for use would have been more profitable than production for profit.

[16] A final note: recently Dodge management introduced a new small truck. They call it the Dodge *Rampage*. These guys will never change.

VOCABULARY

anarchy	disorder
behemoth	huge monster
foist	force
hone	sharpen
libidinal	having to do with the libido, sex drive
macabre	gruesome
mayhem	intentional crippling
OPEC	Organization of Petroleum Exporting Countries
prerogative	choice
sage	wise person
U.A.W.	United Auto Workers
utopian	involving imaginary perfection

DESIGN AND MEANING

1. Analyze the evidence Blumberg uses to support his analysis of Detroit's failure. Evidence usually falls into one or more of these

groups: examples, cases, instances, statistics, facts, logical reasoning, testimony of experts. Find examples of at least four of these types of evidence in the essay. Is the evidence sufficient?

2. According to Blumberg, what were Detroit's main errors?
3. What audience of readers does Blumberg have in mind? How much do they know about cars? About economics? What would he have to alter to write the essay for a less knowledgeable audience?
4. Where is the thesis directly stated? Do you think its placement is effective, or would you have preferred it in a traditional, earlier place?
5. What is an "ethic of conspicuous waste"? Name some examples of conspicuous waste in the world today.

SIMILARITY AND DIFFERENCE

How does Blumberg establish a more rational tone than Andrews does in "The Hating Game"? Where does the strength of Blumberg's feeling show in his essay?

SHORT WRITING IDEA

"Snarling Cars" opens with a quoted newspaper clipping. In your local newspaper, find a clipping that might be an intriguing opening for an essay. Tell what the essay's subject might be. Here's an evocative classified ad from a local weekly:

> MAIZE COLORED PROM DRESS for sale, with jacket, worn 1 hour, size 9. $50. 417-286-3986 after 5 p.m. Stoutland. B9*

LONGER WRITING IDEA

The U.A.W. submitted a proposal to Detroit management in 1949 which might have saved the industry from trouble. Is your workplace, school, or family headed for trouble unless some changes are made? Write a proposal identifying a problem and outlining a possible solution.

essays

PREREADING EXERCISE ("Walk on the Mild Side")

In class, focus on a recent or classic movie that is quite popular. Make a list of reasons for its appeal. Does it have any detractors? What are their complaints?

David Denby

Walk on the Mild Side

Engrossed in film criticism, Denby (b. 1938) reviews movies and writes books about the industry and the people in it. A staff movie reviewer for *The New York Times,* he has reviewed over 1000 films and endured countless more he chose not to write about. He has written a number of film review anthologies and edited *The 400 Blows* (1969), a book on Francois Truffaut, the noted French director.

Alfred Hitchcock often mentioned *Shadow of a Doubt* as one of his favorites among his American films. And yet this extraordinary 1943 movie is far from his most popular or famous work. Everyone knows the irresistibly florid kitsch triumph *Rebecca* and the glamorous, debonair *To Catch a Thief* and *North by Northwest.* The momma-done-tol'-me, house-on-a-hill shocker *Psycho* has passed into universal pop iconography, like *Gone With the Wind* or *Casablanca;* the theatrical revivals of *Rear Window* and *Vertigo* in 1983 confirmed their standing as disturbing, devious, psychologically complex investigations of voyeurism and obsession. *Notorious* and *Strangers on a Train,* both great films, represent high points, respectively, of Hitchcock's erotic sophistication and his perverse wit; both are far better known than *Shadow of a Doubt,* which has now receded into the semi-limbo of Hitchcock's early-'40s movies, along with *Suspicion, Saboteur,* and *Spellbound,* all inferior works (though by Hitchcock's standards only). [1]

Why the obscurity of so wonderful a movie? Possibly because *Shadow of a Doubt,* with its small-town setting and family theme, its nagging dinner-table conversations and prosaic atmosphere, feels thoroughly embedded in the values of the American '40s. Like so many movies of the period, it celebrates innocence and community and identifies threats to American goodness. It's not racy and fast like so much of Hitchcock, not easy fun, and sometimes we may be skeptical of the innocence of this place, with its library and friendly neighborhood policeman and orderly streets. But in *Shadow of a Doubt,* the town of Santa Rosa, California, has no dark side. (It has a dull side, however, and dullness is suggestively presented as the father of darkness.) [2]

Something else about the movie may make it seem a little bland to modern tastes. Though utterly self-assured, even masterly, in [3] technique, *Shadow of a Doubt* is not one of Hitchcock's classics of labyrinthine and insinuating design, not one of the films in which cinematic strategies themselves or illusion or the perils of voyeurism become the subject of the movie. The preoccupation of art with its own means is characteristic of the most challenging works of modernism, in movies as well as in literature and painting; in Hitchcock's case, an obsession with technique goes along with the manipulative coldness that became the insignia of his peculiar chic. We're often titillated and fascinated by the antihuman in his movies, the deadpan outrageousness of *Vertigo* or *The Birds* or many others. But *Shadow of a Doubt* is a Hitchcock rarity, a humanist movie—possibly his only humanist movie. It is an ironic fable of innocence; perhaps Hitchcock's high regard for the film reflects his recognition of its unique plainness and moral fervor.

Plainness, in the sense of ordinariness, is in fact one of its subjects. In the first scene, Charles Oakley (Joseph Cotten) lies on a bed in a cheap boardinghouse in Philadelphia, wearing a double-breasted suit, smoking a cigar, money strewn around him. He's laid out like a corpse—almost finished. Pursued by the police for unspecified crimes, he pulls himself together and decides to go to Santa Rosa to hide out with his sister and her family. At the very same time, his niece, Charlie Newton (Teresa Wright), who is named after him, wires him asking him to visit. The vibrant Charlie, who is perhaps nineteen, has been lying (like Uncle Charlie) on a bed, fully dressed, complaining of the boredom of family life. Her connection with her distant, peripatetic uncle goes deep—she thinks of herself as his spiritual twin, linked telepathically and by temperament, too. [4]

Charlie is a romantic convinced that ordinary life is a prison. An imperious yet deeply generous person, she vibrates with indignation on behalf of her mother (Patricia Colinge), whom she sees as trapped in the soul-killing routine of child-rearing and housework and the general banality of small-town life. Mrs. Newton would never put it that way herself, but for her, as for her daughter, Uncle Charlie represents the adventure and brilliance of the great, wide world, and she's thrilled—renewed, really—by his sudden reappearance in her life. Mrs. Newton's belief in Uncle Charlie is a key structural element in the fable, because once young Charlie begins to understand who her uncle really is—a murderer of wealthy widows—she refrains from exposing him in part because she's sure the truth would kill her mother. Even at her age, Charlie senses that innocence must be protected. [5]

The movie was written by Thornton Wilder, whose classic play about a typical American community, *Our Town,* Hitchcock greatly admired. The two men worked together closely on the screenplay, [6] but Wilder—a very different writer from Hitchcock's usual type of hard-nosed professional—is probably responsible for the film's tone of affectionate satire. Wilder's sensitivity is something rare in American movies. He jokes about people who are set in their ways, limited, even childish, yet he does it without the rasp of ridicule. Mrs. Newton is furiously pedantic about her cooking, and her husband, a drooping, whimsical bank teller (Henry Travers, the essence of bourgeois inanition), plays a strange game with a mousy neighbor who keeps dropping in (Hume Cronyn)—the two men make up outlandish ways of killing each other. An actual murderer sleeps under the Newton roof, yet the two crime addicts have no inkling of it; for all their talk, they don't know that murder actually exists.

[7] Hitchcock brings off the smalltown atmosphere with surprising delicacy and grace—a lilt of affection—but the drama of the film lies in the relationship between the two Charlies. There's a novelistic richness to Charles Oakley. Joseph Cotten uses his elegance—the svelte, narrow, long line of his body, the cherubic lips and eyes, the surprisingly dark voice—in one of the more convincing interpretations of nastiness ever put on the screen. Uncle Charlie is silkily charming but cynical, patronizing, deeply insulting. Cruelty in movies is usually too broad and conventionally motivated. Uncle Charlie, however, has not only a cruel temperament but a cruel point of view. Genial and sociable, he is nevertheless tormented by the awfulness of existence. "Do you know the world is a foul sty? Do you know if you ripped the fronts off houses you'd find swine? The world's a hell," he rants in the extraordinary, Iago-like aria that he delivers to his niece in a cheap bar. In a way, his view is appealing. There's a war on and a depression recently over—the movie's opening shots, moving from downtown Philadelphia to some shabby back streets, remind us of a world of obscure failure outside Santa Rosa. Uncle Charlie, unlike the people of Santa Rosa, at least knows that violence and failure exist. But his view is debased by self-justification. Preying on the susceptibilities of women, he uses his distaste for the contemporary world to create an illusion of gracious manners and romance. His charm colludes insinuatingly with deception and weakness.

[8] He is viewed icily, while young Charlie is portrayed with a tenderness and an alertness to tremulous, uncertain states of feeling that is unique in Hitchcock's work. She flirts with Charlie, and he actually slips a ring onto her finger, teasing her, trying to enlist her in his cause. He almost succeeds. After she finds out who he is, she can't bring herself to simply turn him in. For her, a complex issue of honor is at stake, and here Hitchcock is at his most brilliantly psychological. In a magnificent scene, Charlie accompanies her uncle back to the house after his horrifying outburst in the bar;

she's shocked yet also thrilled by his nightmarish view of life. But then, as he goes inside, Hitchcock's camera stays with her; she hears him bantering with her mother and sees him carrying her kid sister piggyback up the stairs, and she turns slowly, facing us in anguish, appalled that she has helped this viper slide into her family fortress. It is one of the truly heart-wrenching moments in a Hitchcock film, one of the rare times when this consummately perverse artist produces a surge of emotion in solidarity with home, family, and order, against the dark forces of life.

Uncle Charlie tries to kill his niece and then tries again, and *Shadow of a Doubt* turns into a very good thriller. But right to the end the moral interest of the story lies in young Charlie's divided feelings. Able at last to despise her uncle, she remains unwilling to shatter her mother's illusions, so she forces him to leave town. Hitchcock has never shown greater warmth and delicacy than in the great moment when Uncle Charlie announces that he's leaving and Charlie, torn between relief and anger, witnesses with misery her mother's disappointment. Uncle Charlie, it turns out, has been a great success in Santa Rosa; the con man has triumphed again. He has donated money to charity and given an inspiring speech to the local businessmen. [9]

When Uncle Charlie dies after a final struggle with his niece, the local minister eulogizes him as a great man, and Charlie says nothing to dispel the illusion. She won't disturb the town's childish ignorance of life; she's still, in her way, loyal to Uncle Charlie's view. "He said people like us had no idea what the world was really life," she says wonderingly, thinking that perhaps he had a point. Innocence, in *Shadow of a Doubt,* is an incomparable blessing, like strength or good health, but it's also morally inadequate, precisely because it can't take into account the existence of a man like Uncle Charlie. *Shadow of a Doubt* is a *film noir* without a single predigested generic touch. Everything in it is freshly conceived and fully felt, everything has weight—the movie is genuinely serious in its ironies and paradoxes. It is one of Hitchcock's greatest films, even though no one will ever call it "quintessentially Hitchcockian." [10]

VOCABULARY

aria	an elaborate melody
banality	lack of freshness or originality
bourgeois	lacking in refinement
chic	stylishness
debonair	gracious and charming

dispel	to drive off
eulogizes	praises highly someone dead
film noir	a movie, usually a mystery, with pessimistic undercurrents reflected in its style
florid	ornate
humanist	concerned with human welfare and dignity
Iago	villain of Shakespeare's *Othello,* famous for his vicious speeches behind his victims' backs
iconography	system of symbols
inanition	lack of vigor
kitsch	popular art of little or no value
labyrinthine	intricate
obscurity	lack of prominence
pedantic	overemphasizing rules and minor details
peripatetic	traveling about
prosaic	unimaginative
quintessentially	perfectly showing the essence of something
semi-limbo	a place for half-forgotten things
susceptibilities	emotional vulnerabilities
voyeurism	gratification, especially sexual, through secretly watching others

DESIGN AND MEANING

1. What two reasons are advanced in paragraphs 2 and 3 for the relative unpopularity of *Shadow of a Doubt?*
2. What kind of innocence does each member of the Newton family possess?
3. Notice how Denby weaves together plot summary and his own comments on the film. Label each sentence in paragraphs 5, 6, and 8 either *plot detail* or *commentary.* Which sentences are difficult to label? Why? How would the article be different if Denby knew that his readers had seen the film?
4. How is *Shadow of a Doubt* different from other Hitchcock films? How is it similar? Use quotations from the article to answer these questions.
5. Make a list of words Denby uses as opposites of innocence. Relate the contents of each paragraph in the essay to the idea of innocence and its opposites.

SIMILARITY AND DIFFERENCE

"Walk on the Mild Side" is similar to a narrative in that it follows a chronological order, from the beginning of the film to the end. What is the difference between this essay and Howard's, King's, and Guillain's in Chapter 2?

SHORT WRITING IDEA

The title of Denby's article is a take-off on another title. Find out what that title is and explain why the reference to it is appropriate for this article.

LONGER WRITING IDEA

Write an essay explaining a theme or conflict often encountered in the work of a certain director, playwright, actor, author, or other artist. Refer abundantly to the artist's works.

Mark Twain

The Lowest Animal

America's favorite humorist, Mark Twain (1835–1910) was often outraged by the less-than-admirable behavior of what he called "the mangy human race." When he was in these moods, the tone of his writing changed markedly. The following selection, although written in 1896, was not published until long after his death, in a collection called *Letters from the Earth* (1962).

In August, 1572, similar things were occurring in Paris and elsewhere in France. In this case it was Christian against Christian. The Roman Catholics, by previous concert, sprang a surprise upon the unprepared and unsuspecting Protestants, and butchered them by thousands—both sexes and all ages. This was the memorable St. Bartholomew's Day. At Rome the Pope and the Church gave public thanks to God when the happy news came. [1]

During several centuries hundreds of heretics were burned at the stake every year because their religious opinions were not satisfactory to the Roman Church. [2]

In all ages the savages of all lands have made the slaughtering of their neighboring brothers and the enslaving of their women and children the common business of their lives. [3]

Hypocrisy, envy, malice, cruelty, vengefulness, seduction, rape, robbery, swindling, arson, bigamy, adultery, and the oppression and humiliation of the poor and the helpless in all ways have been and still are more or less common among both the civilized and uncivilized peoples of the earth. [4]

For many centuries "the common brotherhood of man" has been urged—on Sundays—and "patriotism" on Sundays and weekdays both. Yet patriotism *contemplates the opposite of a common brotherhood.* [5]

Woman's equality with man has never been conceded by any people, ancient or modern, civilized or savage. [6]

I have been studying the traits and dispositions of the "lower animals" (so-called), and contrasting them with the traits and dispositions of man. I find the result humiliating to me. For it obliges me to renounce my allegiance to the Darwinian theory of the Ascent of Man from the Lower Animals; since it now seems plain to me that the theory ought to be vacated in favor of a new and truer one, [7] this new and truer one to be named the *De*scent of Man from the Higher Animals.

In proceeding toward this unpleasant conclusion I have not guessed or speculated or conjectured, but have used what is commonly called the scientific method. That is to say, I have subjected every postulate that presented itself to the crucial test of actual experiment, and have adopted it or rejected it according to the result. Thus I verified and established each step of my course in its turn before advancing to the next. These experiments were made in the London Zoological Gardens, and covered many months of painstaking and fatiguing work. [8]

Before particularizing any of the experiments, I wish to state one or two things which seem to more properly belong in this place than further along. This is in the interest of clearness. The massed experiments established to my satisfaction certain generalizations, to wit: [9]

1. That the human race is of one distinct species. It exhibits slight variations—in color, stature, mental caliber, and so on—due to climate, environment, and so forth; but it is a species by itself, and not to be confounded with any other. [10]
2. That the quadrupeds are a distinct family, also. This family exhibits variations—in color, size, food preferences and so on; but it is a family by itself. [11]
3. That the other families—the birds, the fishes, the insects, the reptiles, etc.—are more or less distinct, also. They are in the procession. They are links in the chain which stretches down from the higher animals to man at the bottom. [12]

Some of my experiments were quite curious. In the course of my reading I had come across a case where, many years ago, some hunters on our Great Plains organized a buffalo hunt for the entertainment of an English earl—that, and to provide some fresh meat for his larder. They had charming sport. They killed seventy-two of those great animals; and ate part of one of them and left the seventy-one to rot. In order to determine the difference between an anaconda and an earl—if any—I caused seven young calves to be turned into the anaconda's cage. The grateful reptile immediately crushed one of them and swallowed it, then lay back satisfied. It showed no interest in the calves, and no disposition to harm them. I tried this experiment with other anacondas; always with the same result. The fact stood proven that the difference between an earl and an anaconda is that the earl is cruel and the anaconda isn't; and that the earl wantonly destroys what he has no use for, but the anaconda doesn't. This seems to suggest that the anaconda was [13] not descended from the earl. It also seemed to suggest that the earl was descended from the anaconda, and had lost a good deal in the transition.

[14] I was aware that many men who have accumulated more millions of money than they can ever use have shown a rabid hunger for more, and have not scrupled to cheat the ignorant and the helpless out of their poor servings in order to partially appease that appetite. I furnished a hundred different kinds of wild and tame animals the opportunity to accumulate vast stores of food, but none of them would do it. The squirrels and bees and certain birds made accumulations, but stopped when they had gathered a winter's supply, and could not be persuaded to add to it either honestly or by chicane. In order to bolster up a tottering reputation the ant pretended to store up supplies but I was not deceived. I know the ant. These experiments convinced me that there is this difference between man and the higher animals: he is avaricious and miserly, they are not.

[15] In the course of my experiments I convinced myself that among the animals man is the only one that harbors insults and injuries, broods over them, waits till a chance offers, then takes revenge. The passion of revenge is unknown to the higher animals.

[16] Roosters keep harems, but it is by consent of their concubines; therefore no wrong is done. Men keep harems, but it is by brute force, privileged by atrocious laws which the other sex were allowed no hand in making. In this matter man occupies a far lower place than the rooster.

[17] Cats are loose in their morals, but not consciously so. Man, in his descent from the cat, has brought the cat's looseness with him but has left the unconsciousness behind—the saving grace which excuses the cat. The cat is innocent, man is not.

[18] Indecency, vulgarity, obscenity—these are strictly confined to man; he invented them. Among the higher animals there is no trace of them. They hide nothing; they are not ashamed. Man, with his soiled mind, covers himself. He will not even enter a drawing room with his breast and back naked, so alive are he and his mates to indecent suggestion. Man is "The Animal that Laughs." But so does the monkey, as Mr. Darwin pointed out; and so does the Australian bird that is called the laughing jackass. No—Man is the Animal that Blushes. He is the only one that does it—or has occasion to.

[19] At the head of this article* we see how "three monks were burnt to death" a few days ago, and a prior "put to death with atrocious cruelty." Do we inquire into the details? No; or we should find out

* The newspaper clippings reporting atrocities in Crete, which Twain intended to use as epigraphs for this essay, have been lost.

that the prior was subjected to unprintable mutilations. Man—when he is a North American Indian—gouges out his prisoner's eyes; when he is King John, with a nephew to render untroublesome, he uses a red-hot iron; when he is a religious zealot dealing with heretics in the Middle Ages, he skins his captive alive and scatters salt on his back; in the first Richard's time he shuts up a multitude of Jew families in a tower and sets fire to it; in Columbus's time he captures a family of Spanish Jews and—but *that* is not printable; in our day in England a man is fined ten shillings for beating his mother nearly to death with a chair, and another man is fined forty shillings for having four pheasant eggs in his possession without being able to satisfactorily explain how he got them. Of all the animals, man is the only one who is cruel. He is the only one that inflicts pain for the pleasure of doing it. It is a trait that is not known to the higher animals. The cat plays with the frightened mouse; but she has this excuse, that she does not know that the mouse is suffering. The cat is moderate—unhumanly moderate; she only scares the mouse, she does not hurt it; she doesn't dig its eyes, or tear off its skin, or drive splinters under its nails—man-fashion; when she is done playing with it she makes a sudden meal of it and puts it out of its trouble. Man is the Cruel Animal. He is alone in that distinction.

The higher animals engage in individual fights, but never in organized masses. Man is the only animal that deals in that atrocity of atrocities, War. He is the only one that gathers his brethren about him and goes forth in cold blood and with calm pulse to exterminate his kind. He is the only animal that for sordid wages will march out, as the Hessians did in our Revolution, and as the boyish Prince Napolean did in the Zulu war, and help to slaughter strangers of his own species who have done him no harm and with whom he has no quarrel. [20]

Man is the only animal that robs his helpless fellow of his country—takes possession of it and drives him out of it or destroys him. Man has done this in all the ages. There is not an acre of ground on the globe that is in possession of its rightful owner, or that has not been taken away from owner after owner, cycle after cycle, by force and bloodshed. [21]

Man is the only Slave. And he is the only animal who enslaves. He has always been a slave in one form or another, and has always held other slaves in bondage under him in one way or another. In our day he is always some man's slave for wages, and does the man's work; and this slave has other slaves under him for minor wages, and they do *his* work. The higher animals are the only ones who exclusively do their own work and provide their own living. [22]

Man is the only Patriot. He sets himself apart in his own coun- [23]

try, under his own flag, and sneers at the other nations, and keeps multitudinous uniformed assassins on hand at heavy expense to grab slices of other people's countries, and keep *them* from grabbing slices of *his*. And in the intervals between campaigns he washes the blood off his hands and works for "the universal brotherhood of man"—with his mouth.

Man is the Religious Animal. He is the only Religious Animal. He is the only animal that has the True Religion—several of them. He is the only animal that loves his neighbor as himself, and cuts his throat if his theology isn't straight. He has made a graveyard of the globe in trying his honest best to smooth his brother's path to happiness and heaven. He was at it in the time of Caesars, he was at it in Mahomet's time, he was at it in the time of the Inquisition, he was at it in France a couple of centuries, he was at it in England in Mary's day, he has been at it ever since he first saw the light, he is at it today in Crete—as per the telegrams quoted above*—he will be at it somewhere else tomorrow. The higher animals have no religion. And we are told that they are going to be left out, in the Hereafter. I wonder why? It seems questionable taste. [24]

Man is the Reasoning Animal. Such is the claim. I think it is open to dispute. Indeed, my experiments have proven to me that he is the Unreasoning Animal. Note his history, as sketched above. It seems plain to me that whatever he is he is *not* a reasoning animal. His record is the fantastic record of a maniac. I consider that the strongest count against his intelligence is the fact that with that record back of him he blandly sets himself up as the head animal of the lot: whereas by his own standards he is the bottom one. [25]

In truth, man is incurably foolish. Simple things which the other animals easily learn, he is incapable of learning. Among my experiments was this. In an hour I taught a cat and a dog to be friends. I put them in a cage. In another hour I taught them to be friends with a rabbit. In the course of two days I was able to add a fox, a goose, a squirrel and some doves. Finally a monkey. They lived together in peace; even affectionately. [26]

Next, in another cage I confined an Irish Catholic from Tipperary, and as soon as he seemed tame I added a Scotch Presbyterian from Aberdeen. Next a Turk from Constantinople; a Greek Christian from Crete; an Armenian; a Methodist from the wilds of Arkansas; a Buddhist from China; a Brahman from Benares. Finally, a Salvation Army Colonel from Wapping. Then I stayed away two whole days. When I came back to note results, the cage of Higher Animals was all right, but in the other there was but a chaos of [27]

* See note, page 161.

gory odds and ends of turbans and fezzes and plaids and bones and flesh—not a specimen left alive. These Reasoning Animals had disagreed on a theological detail and carried the matter to a Higher Court.

VOCABULARY

anaconda	a long, heavy snake of the boa family
atrocious	cruel, brutal
avaricious	greedy for riches
bolster	to prop up
caliber	degree of worth
chicane	trickery
concert	mutual understanding; arrangement
concubine	a woman who is forced to live with a man without marriage
confounded	lumped together
contemplate	to think about or look at intently
Darwinian theory	the idea of evolution: that humans developed from earlier and lower forms of life
gory	bloody
heretic	a person who holds beliefs opposed to church dogma
larder	supply of food
occasion	a need arising from circumstances
particularize	to give details
postulate	an axiom or basic principle
rabid	raging, violent
render	to cause to become
renounce	to give up
scrupled	was unwilling because of conscience
sordid	mercenary, grasping, meanly selfish
theology	system of religion
totter	to be unsteady
to wit	namely
wanton	senseless, unprovoked, unrestrained
zealot	a person who is excessively enthusiastic.

VOCABULARY CHECK

Write the other forms of each word, using a dictionary.

1. heretic (n., person) ______ (n., quality) ______ (adj.)

2. scruple (v. or n.) ______ (adj.) ______ (n., quality)
3. avaricious (adj.) ______ (n.) ______ (adv.)
4. atrocious (adj.) ______ (n.) ______ (adv.)
5. theology (n.) ______ (n., person) ______ (adj.)

DESIGN AND MEANING

1. What are the components in Twain's analysis of humanity's inferiority?
2. What are two of Twain's methods of supporting his contentions?
3. How does the writer make his analysis sound scientific? Why do you think he does this?

SIMILARITY AND DIFFERENCE

Twain's "Boyhood Remembered" in Chapter 1 is very different from this essay. Can you find any similarities that would suggest the two selections were written by the same person?

SHORT WRITING IDEA

In a focused free writing, list the qualities of the ideal roommate, dinner date, novel, Saturday afternoon, parent, or child.

LONGER WRITING IDEA

Write an essay establishing the preferability of one animal to others. Consider the options of being humorous or pseudoscientific.

PREREADING EXERCISE ("Toys")

What was your favorite toy as a child? Write a short essay describing the toy, explaining what you did with it, and speculating on why it was your favorite.

Roland Barthes

Toys

A prominent French literary critic, sociologist, and journalist, Barthes (1915–1980) analyzed signs and symbols to determine their influence in popular culture. The following essay is taken from his collection entitled *Mythologies*, first published in Paris in 1957 and translated into English in 1972.

French toys: one could not find a better illustration of the fact that the adult Frenchman sees the child as another self. All the toys one commonly sees are essentially a microcosm of the adult world; they are all reduced copies of human objects, as if in the eyes of the public the child was, all told, nothing but a smaller man, a homunculus to whom must be supplied objects of his own size. [1]

Invented forms are very rare: a few sets of blocks, which appeal to the spirit of do-it-yourself, are the only ones which offer dynamic forms. As for the others, French toys *always mean something*, and this something is always entirely socialized, constituted by the myths or the techniques of modern adult life: the Army, Broadcasting, the Post Office, Medicine (miniature instrument-cases, operating theatres for dolls), School, Hair-Styling (driers for permanent-waving), the Air Force (Parachutists), Transport (trains, Citroëns, Vedettes, Vespas, petrol-stations), Science (Martian toys). [2]

The fact that French toys *literally* prefigure the world of adult functions obviously cannot but prepare the child to accept them all, by constituting for him, even before he can think about it, the alibi of a Nature which has at all times created soldiers, postmen and Vespas. Toys here reveal the list of all the things the adult does not find unusual: war, bureaucracy, ugliness, Martians, etc. It is not so much, in fact, the imitation which is the sign of an abdication as its literalness: French toys are like a Jivaro head, in which one recognizes, shrunken to the size of an apple, the wrinkles and hair of an adult. There exist, for instance, dolls which urinate; they have an oesophagus, one gives them a bottle, they wet their nappies; soon, no doubt, milk will turn to water in their stomachs. This is meant to prepare the little girl for the causality of house-keeping, to "condition" her to her future role as mother. However, faced with [3] this world of faithful and complicated objects, the child can only identify himself as owner, as user, never as creator; he does not invent the world, he uses it: there are, prepared for him, actions without adventure, without wonder, without joy. He is turned into a little stay-at-home house-holder who does not even have to invent the mainsprings of adult causality; they are supplied to him ready-made: he has only to help himself, he is never allowed to discover anything from start to finish. The merest set of blocks, provided it is not too refined, implies a very different learning of the world: then, the child does not in any way create meaningful objects, it matters little to him whether they have an adult name; the actions he performs are not those of a user but those of a demiurge. He creates forms which walk, which roll, he creates life, not property: objects now act by themselves, they are no longer an inert and complicated material in the palm of his hand. But such toys are rather rare: French toys are usually based on imitation, they are meant to produce children who are users, not creators.

The bourgeois status of toys can be recognized not only in their forms, which are all functional, but also in their substances. Current toys are made of a graceless material, the product of chemistry, not of nature. Many are now moulded from complicated mixtures; the plastic material of which they are made has an appearance at once gross and hygienic, it destroys all the pleasure, the sweetness, the humanity of touch. A sign which fills one with consternation is the gradual disappearance of wood, in spite of its being an ideal material because of its firmness and its softness, and the natural warmth of its touch. Wood removes, from all the forms which it supports, the wounding quality of angles which are too sharp, the chemical coldness of metal. When the child handles it and knocks it, it neither vibrates nor grates, it has a sound at once muffled and sharp. It is a familiar and poetic substance, which does not sever the child from close contact with the tree, the table, the floor. Wood does not wound or break down; it does not shatter, it wears out; it can last a long time, live with the child, alter little by little the relations between the object and the hand. If it dies, it is in dwindling, not in swelling out like those mechanical toys which disappear behind the hernia of a broken spring. Wood makes essential objects, objects for all time. Yet there hardly remain any of these wooden toys from the Vosges, these fretwork farms with their animals, which were only possible, it is true, in the days of the craftsman. Henceforth, toys are chemical in substance and colour; their very material introduces one to a coenaesthesis of use, not pleasure. These toys die in fact very quickly, and once dead, they have no posthumous life for the child.

VOCABULARY

abdication	surrender
bourgeois	conventionally middle-class
causality	the interrelation between cause and effect
coenaesthesis	general awareness
consternation	dismay, shock
demiurge	a minor god
fretwork	decorative carving
homunculus	a little man; a dwarf
inert	without power to move or act
Jivaro	tribe of South American Indians who shrink the heads of captured enemies
microcosm	a miniature world
posthumous	after death
prefigure	to suggest beforehand
sever	to part or separate
Vosges	a mountain range in northeastern France

DESIGN AND MEANING

1. What are the psychological effects of French toys on children, in Barthes's opinion? What kind of people are the children influenced to grow up to be?
2. What kind of toys would Barthes prefer to see? Why?
3. Summarize the topic of each paragraph of the essay. Identify development by specific details, comparison-contrast, and cause-effect.

SIMILARITY AND DIFFERENCE

What concepts about childhood do Barthes and Larry King ("Getting 'Em Ready for Darrell," in Chapter 2) share?

SHORT WRITING IDEA

List the qualities you would look for in the perfect toy.

LONGER WRITING IDEA

Take a field trip to the toy section of a department store, or watch the toy ads on children's television. Analyze the kinds of conditioning current American toys give children.

poetry

Matthew Arnold

Dover Beach

Matthew Arnold (1822–1888), the renowned and influential critic and poet, was educated at Oxford where he later became professor of poetry. "Dover Beach," which reflects the spiritual upheaval caused by Darwin's discoveries, was published in 1867.

The sea is calm tonight.
The tide is full, the moon lies fair
Upon the straits;—on the French coast the light
Gleams and is gone; the cliffs of England stand,
Glimmering and vast, out in the tranquil bay. [5]
Come to the window, sweet is the night-air!
Only, from the long line of spray
Where the sea meets the moon-blanched land,
Listen! you hear the grating roar
Of pebbles which the waves draw back, and fling, [10]
At their return, up the high strand,
Begin, and cease, and then again begin,
With tremulous cadence slow, and bring
The eternal note of sadness in.

Sophocles long ago [15]
Heard it on the Aegean, and it brought
Into his mind the turbid ebb and flow
Of human misery; we
Find also in the sound a thought,
Hearing it by this distant northern sea. [20]

The Sea of Faith
Was once, too, at the full, and round earth's shore
Lay like the folds of a bright girdle furled.
But now I only hear
Its melancholy, long, withdrawing roar, [25]

Retreating, to the breath
Of the night-wind, down the vast edges drear
And naked shingles of the world.

Ah, love, let us be true
To one another! for the world, which seems [30]
To lie before us like a land of dreams,
So various, so beautiful, so new,
Hath really neither joy, nor love, nor light,
Nor certitude, nor peace, nor help for pain;
And we are here as on a darkling plain [35]
Swept with confused alarms of struggle and flight,
Where ignorant armies clash by night.

DESIGN AND MEANING

1. What is the atmosphere or mood of "Dover Beach"? What establishes it?
2. What is the logic of the stanza division in "Dover Beach"?
3. What comparison is developed in stanza 3 in "Dover Beach"? How does this concept lead to the persona's thoughts in stanza 4?

SIMILARITY AND DIFFERENCE

Contrast the diction in "Dover Beach" and "The World Is a Beautiful Place" (Chapter 3). What are some factors that may account for the differences you see?

Short Story

PREREADING EXERCISE ("The Untold Lie")

Think of a few times in your life that you've asked other people for advice. Choose one of them to describe in writing. Whom did you choose to ask? Why? What does your choice of adviser reveal, if anything?

Short Story

Sherwood Anderson

The Untold Lie

Anderson (1876–1941), a midwesterner who first established himself in a small Ohio town as a successful businessman, walked out of his office one day and never came back. He moved to Chicago, a center of literary activity in the early twentieth century, and began a new career as a writer. "The Untold Lie" is a chapter from his masterpiece, *Winesburg, Ohio* (1919), a loosely structured novel, which resembles a group of short stories interrelated by characters and theme.

Ray Pearson and Hal Winters were farm hands employed on a farm three miles north of Winesburg. On Saturday afternoons they came into town and wandered about through the streets with other fellows from the country. [1]

Ray was a quiet, rather nervous man of perhaps fifty with a brown beard and shoulders rounded by too much and too hard labor. In his nature he was as unlike Hal Winters as two men can be unlike. [2]

Ray was an altogether serious man and had a little sharp-featured wife who had also a sharp voice. The two, with half a dozen thin-legged children, lived in a tumbledown frame house beside a creek at the back end of the Wills farm where Ray was employed. [3]

Hal Winters, his fellow employee, was a young fellow. He was not of the Ned Winters family, who were very respectable people in Winesburg, but was one of the three sons of the old man called Windpeter Winters who had a sawmill near Unionville, six miles away, and who was looked upon by everyone in Winesburg as a confirmed old reprobate. [4]

People from the part of Northern Ohio in which Winesburg lies will remember old Windpeter by his unusual and tragic death. He got drunk one evening in town and started to drive home to Unionville along the railroad tracks. Henry Brattenburg, the butcher, who lived out that way, stopped him at the edge of town and told [5] him he was sure to meet the down train but Windpeter slashed at him with his whip and drove on. When the train struck and killed him and his two horses a farmer and his wife who were driving home along a nearby road saw the accident. They said that old Windpeter stood up on the seat of the wagon, raving and swearing at the onrushing locomotive, and that he fairly screamed with delight when the team, maddened by his incessant slashing at them, rushed straight ahead to certain death. Boys like George Willard and Seth Richmond will remember the incident quite vividly because, although everyone in our town said that the old man would go straight to hell and that the community was better off without him, they had a secret conviction that he knew what he was doing and admired his foolish courage. Most boys have seasons of wishing they could die gloriously instead of just being grocery clerks and going on with their humdrum lives.

But this is not the story of Windpeter Winters nor yet of his son Hal who worked on the Wills farm with Ray Pearson. It is Ray's story. It will, however, be necessary to talk a little of young Hal so that you will get into the spirit of it. [6]

Hal was a bad one. Everyone said that. There were three of the Winters boys in the family, John, Hal, and Edward, all broad-shouldered big fellows like old Windpeter himself and all fighters and woman-chasers and generally all-around bad ones. [7]

Hal was the worst of the lot and always up to some devilment. He once stole a load of boards from his father's mill and sold them in Winesburg. With the money he bought himself a suit of cheap, flashy clothes. Then he got drunk and when his father came raving into town to find him, they met and fought with their fists on Main Street and were arrested and put into jail together. [8]

Hal went to work on the Wills farm because there was a country school teacher out that way who had taken his fancy. He was only twenty-one then but had already been in two or three of what were spoken of in Winesburg as "women scrapes." Everyone who heard of his infatuation for the school teacher was sure it would turn out badly. "He'll only get her into trouble, you'll see," was the word that went around. [9]

And so these two men, Ray and Hal, were at work in a field on a day in the late October. They were husking corn and occasionally something was said and they laughed. Then came silence. Ray, who was the more sensitive and always minded things more, had chapped hands and they hurt. He put them into his coat pockets and looked away across the fields. He was in a sad, distracted mood and was affected by the beauty of the country. If you knew the Winesburg country in the fall and how the low hills are all splashed with yellows and reds you would understand his feeling. He began [10] to think of the time, long ago when he was a young fellow living with his father, then a baker in Winesburg, and how on such days he had wandered away to the woods to gather nuts, hunt rabbits, or just to loaf about and smoke his pipe. His marriage had come about through one of his days of wandering. He had induced a girl who waited on trade in his father's shop to go with him and something had happened. He was thinking of that afternoon and how it had affected his whole life when a spirit of protest awoke in him. He had forgotten about Hal and muttered words. "Tricked by Gad, that's what I was, tricked by life and made a fool of," he said in a low voice.

As though understanding his thoughts, Hal Winters spoke up. "Well, has it been worth while? What about it, eh? What about marriage and all that?" he asked and then laughed. Hal tried to keep on laughing but he too was in an earnest mood. He began to talk earnestly. "Has a fellow got to do it?" he asked. "Has he got to be harnessed up and driven through life like a horse?" [11]

Hal didn't wait for an answer but sprang to his feet and began to walk back and forth between the corn shocks. He was getting more and more excited. Bending down suddenly he picked up an ear of yellow corn and threw it at the fence. "I've got Nell Gunther in trouble," he said. "I'm telling you, but you keep your mouth shut." [12]

Ray Pearson arose and stood staring. He was almost a foot shorter than Hal, and when the younger man came and put his two hands on the older man's shoulders they made a picture. There they stood in the big empty field with the quiet corn shocks standing in rows behind them and the red and yellow hills in the distance, and from being just two indifferent workmen they had become all alive to each other. Hal sensed it and because that was his way he laughed. "Well, old daddy," he said awkwardly, "come on, advise me. I've got Nell in trouble. Perhaps you've been in the same fix yourself. I know what everyone would say is the right thing to do, but what do you say? Shall I marry and settle down? Shall I put myself into the harness to be worn out like an old horse? You know me, Ray. There can't anyone break me but I can break myself. Shall I do it or shall I tell Nell to go to the devil? Come on, you tell me. Whatever you say, Ray, I'll do." [13]

Ray couldn't answer. He shook Hal's hands loose and turning walked straight away toward the barn. He was a sensitive man and there were tears in his eyes. He knew there was only one thing to say to Hal Winters, son of old Windpeter Winters, only one thing that all his own training and all the beliefs of the people he knew would approve, but for his life he couldn't say what he knew he should say. [14]

At half-past four that afternoon Ray was puttering about the barnyard when his wife came up the land along the creek and called him. After the talk with Hal he hadn't returned to the cornfield but worked about the barn. He had already done the evening chores and had seen Hal, dressed and ready for a roistering night in town, come out of the farmhouse and go into the road. Along the path to his own house he trudged behind his wife, looking at the ground and thinking. He couldn't make out what was wrong. Every time he raised his eyes and saw the beauty of the country in the failing light he wanted to do something he had never done before, shout or scream or hit his wife with his fists or something equally unexpected and terrifying. Along the path he went scratching his head and trying to make it out. He looked hard at his wife's back but she seemed all right. [15]

She only wanted him to go into town for groceries and as soon as she had told him what she wanted began to scold. "You're always puttering," she said. "Now I want you to hustle. There isn't anything in the house for supper and you've got to get to town and back in a hurry." [16]

Ray went into his own house and took an overcoat from a hook back of the door. It was torn about the pockets and the collar was shiny. His wife went into the bedroom and presently came out with a soiled cloth in one hand and three silver dollars in the other. Somewhere in the house a child wept bitterly and a dog that had been sleeping by the stove arose and yawned. Again the wife scolded. "The children will cry and cry. Why are you always puttering?" she asked. [17]

Ray went out of the house and climbed the fence into a field. It was just growing dark and the scene that lay before him was lovely. All the low hills were washed with color and even the little clusters of bushes in the corners by the fences were alive with beauty. The whole world seemed to Ray Pearson to have become alive with something just as he and Hal had suddenly become alive when they stood in the corn field staring into each other's eyes. [18]

The beauty of the country about Winesburg was too much for Ray on that fall evening. That is all there was to it. He could not stand it. Of a sudden he forgot all about being a quiet old farm hand and throwing off the torn overcoat began to run across the field. As he ran he shouted a protest against his life, against all life, against everything that makes life ugly. "There was no promise made," he cried into the empty spaces that lay about him. "I didn't promise my Minnie anything and Hal hasn't made any promise to Nell. I know he hasn't. She went into the woods with him because she wanted to go. What he wanted she wanted. Why should I pay? Why should Hal pay? Why should anyone pay? I don't want Hal to [19] become old and worn out. I'll tell him. I won't let it go on. I'll catch Hal before he gets to town and I'll tell him."

Ray ran clumsily and once he stumbled and fell down. "I must catch Hal and tell him," he kept thinking, and although his breath came in gasps he kept running harder and harder. As he ran he thought of things that hadn't come into his mind for years—how at the time he married he had planned to go west to his uncle in Portland, Oregon—how he hadn't wanted to be a farm hand, but had thought when he got out West he would go to sea and be a sailor or get a job on a ranch and ride a horse into Western towns, shooting and laughing and waking the people in the houses with his wild cries. Then as he ran he remembered his children and in fancy felt their hands clutching at him. All of his thoughts of himself were involved with the thoughts of Hal and he thought the children were clutching at the younger man also. "They are the accidents of life, Hal," he cried "They are not mine or yours. I had nothing to do with them." [20]

Darkness began to spread over the fields as Ray Pearson ran on and on. His breath came in little sobs. When he came to the fence at the edge of the road and confronted Hal Winters, all dressed up and smoking a pipe as he walked jauntily along, he could not have told what he thought or what he wanted. [21]

Ray Pearson lost his nerve and this is really the end of the story of what happened to him. It was almost dark when he got to the fence and he put his hands on the top bar and stood staring. Hal Winters jumped a ditch and coming up close to Ray put his hands into his pockets and laughed. He seemed to have lost his own sense of what had happened in the corn field and when he put up a strong hand and took hold of the lapel of Ray's coat he shook the old man as he might have shaken a dog that had misbehaved. [22]

"You came to tell me, eh?" he said. "Well, never mind telling me anything. I'm not a coward and I've already made up my mind." He laughed again and jumped back across the ditch. "Nell ain't no fool," he said. "She didn't ask me to marry her. I want to marry her. I want to settle down and have kids." [23]

Ray Pearson also laughed. He felt like laughing at himself and all the world. [24]

As the form of Hal Winters disappeared in the dusk that lay over the road that led to Winesburg, he turned and walked slowly back across the fields to where he had left his torn overcoat. As he went some memory of pleasant evenings spent with the thin-legged children in the tumble-down house by the creek must have come into his mind, for he muttered words. "It's just as well. Whatever I told him would have been a lie," he said softly, and then his form also disappeared into the darkness of the fields. [25]

VOCABULARY

incessant constant
reprobate a scoundrel

DESIGN AND MEANING

1. What elements of this narrative make it sound like a story told out loud by a native of a small town?
2. What is the basic conflict the story deals with? Is the conflict resolved?
3. What relationship does the anecdote about Windpeter have to the rest of the story?
4. Why is the beauty of the fall scenery such a strong presence in the story?
5. Explain Ray's words to himself at the closing. Is he right?

SIMILARITY AND DIFFERENCE

Describe the similarities of form, style, and meaning between this story and "I Stand Here Ironing" (Chapter 2).

SHORT WRITING IDEA

Write a paragraph relating a piece of gossip just as you would out loud. Analyze what you would change to make the paragraph regular informal prose.

LONGER WRITING IDEA

Describe an experience in which you had to give advice to someone. Analyze why you gave the advice you did, whether it was good or bad advice, and how the advisee responded.

Process

FIXING A BROKEN SEWER TILE, learning to type, breathing smog, and falling in love—all have at least two things in common. First, all are enlightening experiences. Second, all involve a process of some sort. A process is a continuing development, usually one that can be written about in steps or stages. Whether you know it or not, you are very familiar with process writing.

For example, if you needed to fix a broken sewer tile and had no willing friends or relatives with experience in such matters, you would go to the public library and find a book telling you how to do it. (Actually, first you would call several contractors; then after you found out how much they planned to charge, you would head for the library.) This handy "how-to" book would describe the process you should follow to fix your tile. You can see the necessity of completeness and accuracy in process writing: you do not want to end up standing in a smelly 8-foot-deep hole in the back yard with no idea what to do next. Back at the library, you might also check out books on how to type, how to make tempura, how to lose 10 pounds in ten days, or how to improve your love life.

Besides the "how-to" kind of process writing, there is another kind that describes processes. An essay titled "How I Finally Learned to Type" could be a descriptive narrative, instead of a list of instructions. Narrative and process writing are closely related because both follow chronological order. A description of what happens in your body after you inhale smog involves process writing; so does an account of stages in the course of falling in or out of love, even though you have little if any control over either process.

Since process writing, like narrative writing, involves a sequence of time and action, you need to think about your explanation carefully before beginning your first draft. A scratch outline is absolutely necessary. Just a numbered list of steps will do, but you need to write the steps in the order that they occur, which may not be the same order in which they happen to flit through your mind. Once you have an outline, you can go back and add steps in the right places when you remember something that you left out. You can see the obvious advantage in starting a process paper at least a day ahead of time to give your unconscious mind a chance to nudge any forgotten details into your memory so that you can add them to your list.

Perhaps the chief challenge in process writing involves explaining each step fully and clearly. Here are some tips that may help you with development.

1. **Define terms.** In parentheses or in a concise sentence, define any word that would be unfamiliar to most of your readers or any common word that you're using in an unfamiliar way, like "cursor" and "mouse," if you're explaining to a novice how to use a word processor.
2. **Be specific.** Remember that in writing, you must make yourself clear without those gestures and grimaces you use to convey meaning in conversation. Instead of "Strip the insulation off a *short* piece of wire," you need to write "Strip the insulation off a *1-inch* piece of wire."
3. **Include reasons.** Instead of simply noting, "The carburetor mixes gas and air," you can help your readers understand the process by writing, "The carburetor mixes gas and air to make the most highly combustible combination possible, so it can be easily ignited by the spark plugs."
4. **Include don'ts.** If there happens to be a common (or uncommon but disastrous) mistake that people can make in pursuing the process you are describing, you had better warn your readers. For instance, "Do not stick your fingers in the fusebox unless you have pulled out the main fuse" is handy advice.
5. **Mention possible pitfalls.** Whenever things are likely to go wrong despite your careful directions, let your readers know about it. When describing the process of making bread, you should note that if the water is too hot, it will kill the yeast and the dough won't rise.

One more tip. After you have finished your process paper, try to find someone to read it carefully and tell you whether every step is perfectly clear and whether you've left anything important out.

Good process writing gives you a sense of order and completeness. Poor process writing leaves you, literally or metaphorically, standing in a hole wondering what to do next. The selections that follow allow you to study the features and variety of first-rate process composition; the writing suggestions then invite you to practice doing it yourself.

essays

Kurt Vonnegut, Jr.

How to Write with Style

Kurt Vonnegut, Jr., (b. 1922) conveys in his novels a sense of the absurdity of human existence. His sometimes zany fiction is admired by serious literary critics and the reading public alike. "How to Write with Style" appeared as an advertisement for the International Paper Company.

Newspaper reporters and technical writers are trained to reveal almost nothing about themselves in their writings. This makes them freaks in the world of writers, since almost all of the other ink-stained wretches in that world reveal a lot about themselves to readers. We call these revelations, accidental and intentional, elements of style. [1]

These revelations tell us as readers what sort of person it is with whom we are spending time. Does the writer sound ignorant or informed, stupid or bright, crooked or honest, humorless or playful—? And on and on. [2]

Why should you examine your writing style with the idea of improving it? Do so as a mark of respect for your readers, whatever you're writing. If you scribble your thoughts any which way, your readers will surely feel that you care nothing about them. They will mark you down as an egomaniac or a chowderhead—or, worse, they will stop reading you. [3]

The most damning revelation you can make about yourself is that you do not know what is interesting and what is not. Don't you yourself like or dislike writers mainly for what they choose to show you or make you think about? Did you ever admire an empty-headed writer for his or her mastery of the language? No. [4]

So your own winning style must begin with ideas in your head. [5]

1. Find a Subject You Care About

Find a subject you care about and which you in your heart feel [6] others should care about. It is this genuine caring, and not your games with language, which will be the most compelling and seductive element in your style.

[7] I am not urging you to write a novel, by the way—although I would not be sorry if you wrote one, provided you genuinely cared about something. A petition to the mayor about a pothole in front of your house or a love letter to the girl next door will do.

2. Do Not Ramble, Though

[8] I won't ramble on about that.

3. Keep It Simple

[9] As for your use of language: Remember that two great masters of language, William Shakespeare and James Joyce, wrote sentences which were almost childlike when their subjects were most profound. "To be or not to be?" asks Shakespeare's Hamlet. The longest word is three letters long. Joyce, when he was frisky, could put together a sentence as intricate and as glittering as a necklace for Cleopatra, but my favorite sentence in his short story "Eveline" is this one: "She was tired." At that point in the story, no other words could break the heart of a reader as those three words do.

[10] Simplicity of language is not only reputable, but perhaps even sacred. The *Bible* opens with a sentence well within the writing skills of a lively fourteen-year-old: "In the beginning God created the heaven and the earth."

4. Have the Guts to Cut

[11] It may be that you, too, are capable of making necklaces for Cleopatra, so to speak. But your eloquence should be the servant of the ideas in your head. Your rule might be this: If a sentence, no matter how excellent, does not illuminate your subject in some new and useful way, scratch it out.

5. Sound Like Yourself

[12] The writing style which is most natural for you is bound to echo the speech you heard when a child. English was the novelist Joseph Conrad's third language, and much that seems piquant in his use of English was no doubt colored by his first language, which was Polish. And lucky indeed is the writer who has grown up in Ireland, for the English spoken there is so amusing and musical. I myself grew up in Indianapolis, where common speech sounds like a band

saw cutting galvanized tin and employs a vocabulary as unornamental as a monkey wrench.

In some of the more remote hollows of Appalachia, children still grow up hearing songs and locutions of Elizabethan times. Yes, and many Americans grow up hearing a language other than English, or an English dialect a majority of Americans cannot understand. [13]

All these varieties of speech are beautiful, just as the varieties of butterflies are beautiful. No matter what your first language, you should treasure it all your life. If it happens not to be standard English, and if it shows itself when you write standard English, the result is usually delightful, like a very pretty girl with one eye that is green and one that is blue. [14]

I myself find that I trust my own writing most, and others seem to trust it most, too, when I sound most like a person from Indianapolis, which is what I am. What alternatives do I have? The one most vehemently recommended by teachers has no doubt been pressed on you, as well: to write like cultivated Englishmen of a century or more ago. [15]

6. Say What You Mean to Say

I used to be exasperated by such teachers, but am no more. I understand now that all those antique essays and stories with which I was to compare my own work were not magnificent for their datedness or foreignness, but for saying precisely what their authors meant them to say. My teachers wished me to write accurately, always selecting the most effective words, and relating the words to one another unambiguously, rigidly, like parts of a machine. The teachers did not want to turn me into an Englishman after all. They hoped that I would become understandable—and therefore understood. And there went my dream of doing with words what Pablo Picasso did with paint or what any number of jazz idols did with music. If I broke all the rules of punctuation, had words mean whatever I wanted them to mean, and strung them together higgledy-piggledy, I would simply not be understood. So you, too, had better avoid Picasso-style or jazz-style writing, if you have something worth saying and wish to be understood. [16]

Readers want our pages to look very much like pages they have seen before. Why? This is because they themselves have a tough job to do, and they need all the help they can get from us. [17]

7. Pity the Readers

They have to identify thousands of little marks on paper, and make sense of them immediately. They have to *read,* an art so difficult [18] that most people don't really master it even after having studied it all through grade school and high school—twelve long years.

[19] So this discussion must finally acknowledge that our stylistic options as writers are neither numerous nor glamorous, since our readers are bound to be such imperfect artists. Our audience requires us to be sympathetic and patient teachers, ever willing to simplify and clarify—whereas we would rather soar high above the crowd, singing like nightingales.

[20] That is the bad news. The good news is that we Americans are governed under a unique Constitution, which allows us to write whatever we please without fear of punishment. So the most meaningful aspect of our styles, which is what we choose to write about, is utterly unlimited.

8. For Really Detailed Advice

[21] For a discussion of literary style in a narrower sense, in a more technical sense, I commend to your attention *The Elements of Style,* by William Strunk, Jr., and E. B. White (Macmillan, 1979). E. B. White is, of course, one of the most admirable literary stylists this country has so far produced.

[22] You should realize, too, that no one would care how well or badly Mr. White expressed himself, if he did not have perfectly enchanting things to say.

Edward T. Thompson

How to Write Clearly

Thompson (b. 1928), who has served as an editor of two engineering journals and of the *Reader's Digest,* is himself a writer for national magazines. "How to Write Clearly" appeared as an advertisement for the International Paper Company.

If you are afraid to write, don't be. [1]

If you think you've got to string together big fancy words and high-flying phrases, forget it. [2]

To write well, unless you aspire to be a professional poet or novelist, you only need to get your ideas across simply and clearly. [3]

It's not easy. But it *is* easier than you might imagine. [4]

There are only three basic requirements: [5]

First, you must *want* to write clearly. And I believe you really do, if you've stayed this far with me. [6]

Second, you must be willing to *work hard.* Thinking means working and that's what it takes to do anything well. [7]

Third, you must know and follow some *basic guidelines.* [8]

If, while you're writing for clarity, some lovely, dramatic or inspired phrases or sentences come to you, fine. Put them in. [9]

But then with cold, objective eyes and mind ask yourself: "Do they detract from clarity?" If they do, grit your teeth and cut the frills. [10]

Follow Some Basic Guidelines

I can't give you a complete list of *dos* and *don'ts* for every writing problem you'll ever face. [11]

But I can give you some fundamental guidelines that cover the most common problems. [12]

1. Outline what you want to say I know that sounds grade-schoolish. But you can't write clearly until, *before you start,* you know where you will stop. [13]

Ironically, that's even a problem in writing an outline (i.e., knowing the ending before you begin). [14]

So try this method. [15]

- On 3″ × 5″ cards, write—one point to the card—all the points you need to make. [16]
- Divide the cards into piles—one pile for each group of points *closely related* to each other. (If you were describing an automobile, you'd put all the points about mileage in one pile, all the points about safety in another, and so on.) [17]
- Arrange your piles of points in a sequence. Which are most important and should be given first or saved for last? Which must you present before others in order to make the others understandable? [18]
- Now, *within* each pile, do the same thing—arrange the *points* in logical, understandable order. [19]

There you have your outline, needing only an introduction and conclusion. [20]

This is a practical way to outline. It's also flexible. You can add, delete or change the location of points easily. [21]

2. Start where your readers are How much do they know about the subject? Don't write to a level higher than your readers' knowledge of it. [22]

CAUTION: Forget that old—and wrong—advice about writing to a 12-year-old mentality. That's insulting. But do remember that your prime purpose is to *explain* something, not prove that you're smarter than your readers. [23]

3. Avoid jargon Don't use words or expressions, phrases known only to people with specific knowledge or interests. [24]

Example: A scientist, using scientific jargon, wrote, "The biota exhibited a one hundred percent mortality response." He could have written: "All the fish died." [25]

4. Use familiar combinations of words A speech writer for President Franklin D. Roosevelt wrote, "We are endeavoring to construct a more inclusive society." F. D. R. changed it to, "We're going to make a country in which no one is left out." [26]

CAUTION: By familiar combinations of words, I do *not* mean incorrect grammar. *That* can be *un*clear. Example: John's father says he can't go out Friday. (Who can't go out? John or his father?) [27]

5. Use "first-degree" words These words immediately bring an image to your mind. Other words must be "translated" through the first-degree word before you see the image. Those are second/third-degree words. [28]

[29]

First-degree words	Second/third-degree words
face	visage, countenance
stay	abide, remain, reside
book	volume, tome, publication

First-degree words are usually the most precise words, too. [30]

6. Stick to the point Your outline—which was more work in the beginning—now saves you work. Because now you can ask about any sentence you write: "Does it relate to a point in the outline? If it doesn't, should I add it to the outline? If not, I'm getting off the track." Then, full steam ahead—on the main line. [31]

7. Be as brief as possible Whatever you write, shortening—*condensing*—almost always makes it tighter, straighter, easier to read and understand. [32]

Condensing, as *Reader's Digest* does it, is in large part artistry. But it involves techniques that anyone can learn and use. [33]

- *Present your points in logical ABC order:* Here again, your outline should save you work because, if you did it right, your points already stand in logical ABC order—A makes B understandable, B makes C understandable and so on. To write in a straight line is to say something clearly in the fewest possible words. [34]
- *Don't waste words telling people what they already know:* Notice how we edited this: "Have you ever wondered how banks rate you as a credit risk? ~~You know, of course, that it's some combination of facts about your income, your job, and so on. But actually~~, many banks have a scoring system . . . ." [35]
- *Cut out excess evidence and unnecessary anecdotes:* Usually, one fact or example (at most, two) will support a point. More just belabor it. And while writing about something may remind you of a good story, ask yourself: "Does it *really help* to tell the story, or does it slow me down?" [36]

(Many people think *Reader's Digest* articles are filled with anecdotes. Actually, we use them sparingly and usually for one of two reasons: either the subject is so dry it needs some "humanity" to give it life; or the subject is so hard to grasp, it needs anecdotes to help readers understand. If the subject is both lively and easy to grasp, we move right along.) [37]

- *Look for the most common word wasters:* windy phrases. [38]

[39]

Windy phrases	Cut to . . .
at the present time	now
in the event of	if
in the majority of instances	usually

- *Look for passive verbs you can make active:* Invariably, this produces a shorter sentence. "The cherry tree *was* chopped down by George Washington." (Passive verb and nine words.) "George Washington *chopped* down the cherry tree." (Active verb and seven words.) [40]
- *Look for positive/negative sections from which you can cut the negative:* See how we did it here: "The answer ~~does not rest with carelessness or incompetence. It lies largely in~~ is having enough people to do the job." [41]
- Finally, to write more clearly by saying it in fewer words: when you've finished, stop. [42]

VOCABULARY

appalling	causing horror, shock, or dismay
anecdotal	full of little stories
bromide	a trite saying
callous	insensitive
cantankerous	bad-tempered and quarrelsome
chowderhead	a person with a mind like thick soup
cogent	forceful and convincing
compelling	forceful enough to inspire action
delete	to take out
dissent	to disagree
eloquence	vividness, grace, and persuasiveness of expression

higgledy-piggledy	disorderly and jumbled
illuminate	to make clear
inexorable	not capable of being changed, influenced, or stopped
profound	intellectually or emotionally deep
reputable	respectable
revelation	a striking insight
unambiguous	perfectly clear; having only one meaning
vacuity	emptiness
vehement	having intense feeling or strong passion

DESIGN AND MEANING

1. In each of the essays, point out three places in which the writer takes his own advice.
2. Writing a paper is a process with many stages. What parts of the process does each selection here emphasize?
3. What pieces of advice on writing do the selections share?
4. Thompson's and Vonnegut's essays were written to appear in International Paper Company advertisements in popular magazines. These advertisements were each laid out in six columns across two pages and included four pictures. How did knowledge of how their pieces would be used affect Thompson's and Vonnegut's writing?

SIMILARITY AND DIFFERENCE

How does the kind of writing Vonnegut and Thompson discuss differ from diary writing and personal letter writing?

SHORT WRITING IDEA

Choose a paragraph in need of improvement from some of your earlier writing. Using the advice of these writers, revise the paragraph.

LONGER WRITING DATA

Make an outline for a paper on any subject, using Thompson's method.

VOCABULARY CHECK

Is the italicized vocabulary word used correctly? *Yes* or *no*?

1. Fred must present *compelling* resons to get Lupita to move to Arkansas with him.
2. His *unambiguous* arguments confuse and perplex her.
3. A *vehement* statement is likely to be boring.
4. It is difficult to ignore a *cogent* statement.
5. Vonnegut believes that nineteenth-century Englishmen had *eloquence*.
6. *Vacuity* is an important quality for a good writer.
7. Fred's cabin in Arkansas has neither hot water nor electricity, an environment Lupita finds *appalling*.
8. Verses on humorous greeting cards are usually *profound*.

PREREADING EXERCISE

Which of your five senses is most important to you? Why?

Andrew Potok

Dash and Me

Potok has more Dash in his life now that he shares his waking hours with a seeing-eye dog. His book, *My Life with Goya*, came out in 1986 and was widely reviewed. He recounts the experience of having to depend on a seeing-eye dog and the bonding that resulted.

I am right-handed, right everything. That side of my body—hand, arm, leg, even ear—is better developed than the other. But it's all changing. My left hand, clutching a leash and harness, now is sensitive to every movement, every distraction, every thought that passes through the amazing mind of a dog. My body has been extended by some 36 sleek inches, terminating, at our very tip, with Dash's long, handsome black nose. [1]

Once I relied on steel-toed boots to protect me from obstacles, and I was never surprised by a new test of my threshold of pain. Now my dog leads the way. My head is held high, my chest is thrust forward, and my old bruises are healing. But there are new aches and pains: shinsplints, a pulled groin muscle, something that feels like a shoulder separation, all because of our breakneck speed, as Dash and I fly through the world together. Aerodynamically, we are the Concorde of the blind travelers' world. [2]

Just as I have been extended in the formulation of a new, longer body, so has my dog's spatial awareness been extended to include the space that I fill, an extra two and a half feet of width to his right and some four feet above his head. For Dash is trained not only to take me around parking meters and fire hydrants, but also to arc around overhanging tree branches. I nearly wept the first time we moved together through a line at an airline ticket counter. A dog has no reason not to proceed straight under the velvet cordons, but Dash knew that now he carried extra baggage and that I, with all my human height, would have to follow the prescribed path. [3]

When I first considered training with a guide dog, my wife, Charlotte, said that she was jealous. [4]

"Jealous? Jealous of what?" I asked, amazed. [5]

"That damn dog is going to take my place," she said. Well, one year later, I can't deny that there are grounds for jealousy. If you entered the privacy of my bedroom, you would see that Charlotte [6] sleeps on my left, Dash on my right, though he is some two feet below us on his rug. There he is, present and listening to every whispered sweetness, perhaps watching everything too. At times during the night, when I haven't felt the nudge of his wet nose for a while, I will fish around for the feel of him, just to keep in touch.

[7] But, alas, jealousy can run both ways. Dash is absolutely mad about Charlotte. Recently, when I caught him lying on the bed next to her, I yanked him off, then got down on all fours to lecture him, to point things out, to help him distinguish between our two worlds. "Hey," I said, "this rug is yours, the bed is mine. I won't sleep on your rug, you keep off the bed." I do tend to anthropomorphize, but I swear he accepted my words with a sigh. Repentant, he went to sleep on his imitation Navaho rug. The next day, after his early feeding, I was making two cups of coffee to take upstairs. Dash, as usual, bolted ahead of me to plant his morning kiss on Charlotte's sleeping face. By the time I arrived, I encountered an unbelievable scene: Dash, understanding very well that the rug was his domain, had dragged the thing up on the bed and was happily asleep next to Charlotte. Cause for jealousy? You bet. But what comfort to entrust one's life to a beast with a scheming mind like that.

[8] My visual problem is retinitis pigmentosa, an inherited blight of the retina, the flimsy screen at the back of the eye that receives visual images from the world outside. The disease is relentlessly progressive, taking away vision in unpredictable increments. Just when I think I've finally adjusted to certain losses, back it comes again, bringing with it an even more diminished world and the nearly forgotten depressions and rages.

[9] Last summer, when I began to crash into doorjambs inside my house in Vermont and when the dirt road down to my office blurred into fragments of gray field on either side, I knew that the time to ask for help had come again. Like a fungus, I was becoming too accustomed to a lethargic dependence. I needed to shake things up, to start taking risks again. A bit frightened, I called The Seeing Eye, Inc., in Morristown, N.J.

[10] Until then, I'd been an expert at denial. White canes were easy. They could be folded into briefcases, hidden inside long raincoats. If discovered, I could swear that they belonged to someone else. But a dog? "My blind friend is sick. I am walking his dog." In harness? Now there could be no turning back. I was finally going public with my blindness.

[11] On the plane to Newark I realize that the purpose of this journey is to meet, to bond with, a dog. I recall our sweet, departed mutt Charlie, and terror fills my heart. Am I really going to entrust my life to a beast from the same genus as Charlie? For 20,000 years of

domestication, these pets, these *mere* pets, have slobbered and growled, snored and scratched by the heat of fireplaces, hardly fit to lead, to make decisions, to make no mistakes. In despair, I order a noontime martini from the flight attendant.

I unpack to the sound of howling, barking dogs outside my window. This mansion is spacious, even elegant, and scrubbed so clean that I can't imagine the presence of dogs here. The Seeing Eye was founded in 1929 and is supported today by an endowment of more than $60 million. On a manicured 55 acres in northwestern New Jersey, the institute operates a breeding station for Labrador retrievers and shepherds, kennels that house some 160 dogs in training or awaiting training, a converted mansion serving as a residence for 20 students and trainers, and offices for a staff of 90. About 230 blind people pass through here annually, each making a token payment of $150 for the first dog and $50 for each subsequent one. The Seeing Eye pays the students' round-trip fare from anywhere in the U.S. or Canada and covers the cost of the training, the dog, and the students' room and board for a month. [12]

By late afternoon all 16 of us are here—six for our first dog; the rest, calling themselves retreads, are replacing retired or deceased dogs with new ones. Davis Duty, a judge from Arkansas, is here for his seventh! We novices listen breathlessly to the veterans' stories of total devotion in the face of flood, blizzard or locusts, stories of unbearable cuteness, uncanny intelligence. [13]

Kris Verdi, small and wiry, is my instructor. "This morning, I will be your dog," she announces, handing me a leash, the other end of which, I suppose at first, she puts around her neck. "You're going to walk Juno, Mr. Potok," she tells me. We are all Miss, Mrs. and Mr. here, the formality a tradition since the early days of The Seeing Eye when, we are told, blind people often felt like worthless outcasts. [14]

"Juno, heel," I tell Verdi tentatively, then, "Good dog," hoping that no one is watching. We climb into a van and drive into the streets of Morristown. Verdi teaches me to correct her errant behavior with a sharp yank of the leash. I do it, hoping that I have not decapitated her. (Later I learn she is holding the leash and harness in her hand.) "Harder, Mr. Potok," she says, "I hardly felt that." As she stops at curbs I offer the prescribed "attagirls" and "good dogs." On a long straightaway on Maple Street, we are both running. [15]

"Can you take this pace?" [16]

"Easy," I tell her. This walk and a long questionnaire, answered some months before, will determine the match of individual dog to individual student. [17]

The day's wait for a dog seems interminable. My new friend Jo [18]

Taliaferro, a Presbyterian minister nicknamed The Rev and here for her third dog, whispers that she will die if she doesn't get a shepherd. "You can take a shepherd out to a good restaurant," she says. "I love those stand-up ears, that sleek nose. A Lab is a leisure dog."

The room where we are all gathered feels electric. Kris Verdi jokes about a cane-burning ceremony, then begins to read from a list. "Miss Taliaferro, your dog's name is Cocoa, a female chocolate Labrador retriever." Jo holds back her tears. "Mr. Duty, your dog is Eddie, a male shepherd, black and tan. Mr. Potok," she continues, "your dog's name is Dash, a black male shepherd with a little bit of tan." [19]

Each of us is called in separately to meet his dog. I shake as I take the leash of my new partner. "Dash," I say, patting his broad head. He turns toward Kris as if to ask: "What do you want me to do with this idiot?" [20]

As I tell my new dog what an interesting person I am, I am paralyzed by the realization that he and I will be together, inseparable, for some 10 years. I am overcome by the desire to call it all off, to run. [21]

Later at dinner, the 16 of us, our knives and forks clattering politely on porcelain plates, carry on a genteel, yet cheerful conversation, while under the tables lie 16 very quiet, confused dogs. [22]

Seeing Eye dogs do not urinate or defecate. They "park." After the dogs eat, and also at 10:30 a.m. and 8 p.m., our instructors shout down the hallways, "Park time." We rush to give our dogs bowls of water and go down the stairs to the broad asphalt terrace known as The Park. Here each of us stands in an appointed spot with our dogs circling on long leashes around us, sniffing the ground, getting into the mood to park. [23]

"Mr. Potok, Dash is doing a two," Verdi shouts from the sidelines. Our three instructors have shovels at the ready. [24]

"Cocoa did a one," cries Jo proudly, already beginning to love her Lab. [25]

With the possible exception of when my children were babies, I have never been so intimately in touch with every morsel that enters and exits a body. Whatever Dash's extraordinary exploits of body or mind, they are fueled by four cups daily of Purina Field 'n Farm, plus several bowls of water. I feel guilty about his meager daily fare. No more deserving than he, I require herring fillets and chilled Stolichnaya, just for starters. When my partner licks my fingers for the pungent trace of Camembert—which, unless he has even more resources than I can imagine, he will never snack on—I am a little embarrassed. [26]

At the age of two months, the Labrador and German shepherd [27] puppies bred here are given to 4-H families in the area. Over the course of a year the dogs are housebroken and loved, and learn basic obedience. They are returned to The Seeing Eye for four months of intensive training, including three to four weeks with their new masters. The crucial activity of stopping at every up curb and down curb is repeated over and over again—the basis of the dog's function, the fundamental safety procedure. The animals learn the "left," "right" and "forward" commands and are praised for everything done correctly. The dog must also have the intelligence to disobey the master's mistaken command. "Even sighted people can be distracted and cross a street into traffic," we are told.

On the busy sidewalks of Morristown, I gape through my mud-splattered bits of vision, unable to see enough to check on Dash as he races toward the curb. I want desperately to trust him, but my inclination is to put my free hand in front of my face in case we walk into a tree. Kris Verdi, always a few steps behind me, says, "Relax, Mr. Potok. You're tight as a drum." Exercising all my will, I give myself up to my dog. It's like jumping from an airplane, praying the parachute will open. [28]

Dash and I fly down the sidewalk. My hand still darts to my face as I feel trees breeze by us. And then, like cartoon characters, we come to a screeching halt at the curb. "Lots of praise, Mr. Potok," Kris advises. "Dash is doing a terrific job." I want to get on my hands and knees, to kiss him all over, but instead I give him a dignified, "Attaboy, Dash." I listen hard for the direction of the traffic. "Dash, forward," I tell my partner tentatively, and we speed across the street without incident. [29]

"It's a Zen experience," says Don Steelman, a Texas attorney who is here for his fourth dog. Zen it may sometimes be, but there are also moments of panic and pain. When Dash smacks me head-on into a parking meter, I am furious, indignant, as well as bloodied. As hard as it has been for most of us to exercise leash corrections properly, not wanting to hurt our precious dogs, I now wish that my left arm were made of steel. I want to hurt him. "How could you do this to me?" I scream. "Do you call this *bonding*, you miserable cur?" [30]

"Good correction, Mr. Potok," Kris says quietly. [31]

Five blocks later, as Dash stops neatly at a curb, my praise sounds thin and phony. I am still furious. "Dash has no idea why you're still angry, Mr. Potok," Verdi tells me. "You must learn to forget your anger right after you correct." I think of the misery she might have prevented in my life among humans if she had always been around to instruct me. [32]

Hurtling along South Street, Dash comes to a stop at a car blocking the sidewalk. "Hup, up," I tell him, in this case meaning, [33]

"Find your way carefully past this obstacle." Slowly, he begins to take me around the rear of the car. Suddenly he jerks me backward, his body taut and watchful. Behind me, Verdi, like a proud mother, tells me what had just happened. Apparently a plume of exhaust in his face warned my wonderful dog that the car was about to back up.

Kris Verdi parks the van, and we're off into the streets of New York City, her idea of hell. "Go anywhere you like, Mr. Potok," she says with apparent distaste. "It's your city." [34]

Having grown up in New York, I know my way around. Especially since I've become blind, I take a certain pride in my awareness of place. Perversely, Dash and I lead Kris east on 42nd Street, trash blowing in our faces. We turn up Sixth Avenue, and on the corner of 49th, as we wait for the light to change, a voice from across the street shouts at me: "Hey, fella, you can cross now." Unsuspecting, I say, "Forward." But Dash doesn't respond. "Hup, up," I say uncertainly. With his large pointed ears moving like radar, my dog stands motionless. Finally I realize that the unsolicited advice comes from a maniac whose satisfaction would have been complete had we been flattened by a truck. Trembling, I turn to Verdi. She too is shaken. "No big surprise to me," she stammers. [35]

Dash threads our way through crowds, through the dark labyrinths of scaffolding, through two floors of Bloomingdale's, alongside the horses and pigeons of Central Park South. Twice on Seventh Avenue we are yelled at, called every name in the book. I'm not sure why some people react so angrily. Perhaps Dash looks too much like a police dog, or perhaps blind people are a safe repository of uncontrolled hatred. Still, it takes my breath away. [36]

Our month, as tough and disciplined as basic training, is over. It's time to get on with it, to see if all this works in the real world, the world without instructors trailing us, the world of crowded subways, territorial dogs and drunk drivers. [37]

The trainers take their charges back to Newark Airport. Kris calls me Andy for the first time. We hug in saying goodbye, and I feel a tear on her cheek. As much as we have liked each other, the tears are for Dash, once her dog, now mine. [38]

The Seeing Eye has sent a letter to my family advising on proper homecoming behavior: Keep emotions down on arrival, greet the dog quietly, do not follow the team down the street to see how man and dog work. This is enough to arouse the curiosity of three of my children and several friends. The first night home, we are 14 at dinner. I try to manage Dash's confusion, taking him upstairs from time to time where the two of us can be alone. Charlotte says it's as if I were the mom bringing the baby home from the hospital and she the father, more observer than participant, allowed to smile [39] from a distance. If so, I'm like a first-time mom, anxious about making a wrong move.

[40] We begin to establish our daily routine, down the hill to my office in the morning, back home at night. I have not walked alone in the dark since I was a child. But then this doesn't feel like walking—it's flying, flying through space, the winter stars breezing by.

[41] Problems arise. I find I tend to let Dash get away with minor infractions, such as a semiprotective growl or two, or a turning of his head to check whether Charlotte is still walking with us. At a small local restaurant, I'm having too nice a time to notice that my guide dog has wandered over to the next table, just to be friendly. After three months my permissiveness has created an intractable situation. Dash is now easily distracted, restless, on edge. In two weeks I am supposed to fly to the West Coast to lecture on writing. I'm not sure I want to go.

[42] We make a trial run to Cambridge, Mass., where the sidewalks are piled high with snow or slick with ice. On the stretches of clear pavement, Dash is frenetic and runs curbs, putting us both at great risk. In a coffee shop, he barks from under the table, and as I try to correct him, shaking his head by the scruff, clamping my hands around his muzzle, Charlotte says that everyone in the place is glaring at me. To complete the unpleasantness of these few days, someone smashes our car windows during the night.

[43] "He's still a puppy," Charlotte says as we are driving back to Vermont early the next morning. "Be patient."

[44] My anger won't go away. "He's useless," I snarl, though Kris Verdi's words—"Dash doesn't know why you're still angry"—resound in my ears. But I don't know where to put all this feeling. I can't bear the fact that Dash and I are not a perfect team, amazing to watch, the envy of all.

[45] I call The Seeing Eye and they, in their wisdom and goodness, propose sending a trainer to fix things before my Oregon trip. I am relieved but then gripped with fear that they will take Dash away.

[46] The deus ex machina from Morristown is named Peggy Gibbon. We go out to eat, restaurants being the scene of some of Dash's more egregious offenses: barking, growling, pulling me into tables. But in the streets of Montpelier and Burlington, with Peggy shadowing our every move, he performs faultlessly. Dash and I do best when we are watched and graded, soothed by instruction. Perceiving my dog through Gibbon's eyes, I realize that Dash is taking on *my* nervousness, *my* anxieties. Though I do the worrying, we both pace about, too impatient and overwrought to take things one step at a time. "He's a terrific dog," she informs me, "but he's still a puppy. Keep working hard with him. Be consistent and patient."

Her reinforcement is like an elixir, though I am close to losing my determination to struggle, to keep it all together. "I'm so tired," I tell Charlotte after Gibbon's departure. "Just managing my blindness, keeping oriented, aware, upright, saps all my energy." [47]

We have a perfect flight to the West Coast. Dash is neatly tucked away in front of me. Not only is no one near us allergic to dogs, but his cuteness gets me free drinks. [48]

In Portland we are asked to appear on a morning TV show. To my horror, the studio is full of cats—cats and the trainers who cleverly teach them to eat their Friskies on camera. It's a soap opera version of the Peaceable Kingdom. Yet in the midst of this idiocy, Dash somehow keeps his cool. I am told that he looks beautiful on the screen, but I know that he's thinking what I'm thinking: "If this is the real world, I want out." [49]

At the city library, my first lecture goes well, though Dash is not thrilled to share the stage with me. He is unable to resist his impulse to pace or grumble his displeasure. To him, the applause that follows my talk must be like a rising cloud of pigeons, for he stiffens, glares, seems ready to pounce. [50]

The next day at Reed College, our partnership becomes unglued. The campus is a bouillabaisse of dogs into which Dash pulls me, barking as he goes. Inside the chapel, our audience includes not only students and faculty but also a contingent of blind people with dogs. Dash is inconsolable. During my entire lecture, this member of the dog elite paces behind me, moaning and groaning steadily. I try to cover up for my unruly beast, though I feel like a mother at the end of her rope, clothes splattered with food, the glint of madness in her eyes, excusing her screaming brat on grounds of exhaustion. [51]

Recuperating in Vermont, I get a phone call from Debbie Purtee, a fellow student from The Seeing Eye. She too is feeling desperate. Brownie, her Lab, cannot stop sniffing. "It's not only garbage cans, Andy," Debbie says, "it's *everything*. We're walking down the street, and she goes after strangers. She pulls me to lampposts, you name it." I begin to tell her of my woes with Dash. "I haven't told you half of it," Debbie continues. "Brownie can't control her bowels either. I'm so embarrassed." She sounds close to tears. [52]

What a relief to my aching soul to know that I am not alone. Every one of us must be having problems, I conclude. After all, they did tell us that it would take months, maybe more, to form a good working unit. I call the Arkansas law offices of Davis Duty, the dog veteran who was the envy of us all. "Listen to this, Andy," Davis says. "The other day Eddie and I did our 'shoot the dog' trick before a class of sixth graders, and let me tell you, he died with real verve." [53]

In the spring our friend Noma gives Charlotte and me her elegant New York apartment for a month. "You and Dash can practice working in the city," Noma suggests. We drive to the city, my computer equipment, with its huge screen, its enlarging components, speech synthesizer, all taking up most of the car space. Dash barely fits between the printer and a box of books. [54]

"Aren't you worried about Dash wrecking the place?" I had asked Noma. [55]

"It's all right," she had assured me, "there's nothing to wreck." [56]

One evening I decide to leave Dash at home while we visit friends, but the moment Charlotte and I are on the sidewalk, I begin to worry. [57]

"What can happen?" Charlotte says. "Relax." [58]

"Relax? Are you crazy? We should go back," I snap as a taxi stops in front of us. I'm angry for a thousand reasons, one of them being that, without my dog, I am totally dependent on my wife. [59]

At our friends' house, I am preoccupied, fretting about my dog's undeserved abandonment, his undoubted vengeful fury. My mind's eye begins to focus on the precious objects in the apartment: the archaic Greek warrior's mask on the mantel, the Magritte bottle, the Egyptian funerary barge on the dining table, the Giacometti lamp. As soon after dinner as we can extricate ourselves, I whisk Charlotte away. In the cab, I begin to assess the possible damage, adding up my debt by increments of tens of thousands of dollars. But inside the apartment, as Dash pirouettes around us with the sheer joy of seeing us again, everything seems to be intact, everything except the guest room, which is piled high with heaps of a fibrous material. It turns out to be the underpad of the beautiful silk rug on its floor. Interpreter of my dog's language, I understand his message clearly: "This time it's this worthless old rag, but leave me alone again and the Spanish Renaissance bedstead is toothpicks." [60]

It is time to try the subway. I walk out of the building, head a few blocks east. Dash stops at every curb. "How does he know when to cross? Can he see the lights?" I am asked by strangers. "I have to listen to traffic," I tell them. "I determine when it's safe to go." [61]

Dash stops at the top of the stairs leading down into the station. I instruct him to proceed. We make our way in the direction of the token booth, needing help to locate the window, though I can make out the pattern of the shiny tops of the turnstiles. I feel around for the slot, drop my token in and cajole my dog through the barrier. Once on the platform, I have Dash sit while we await our train. I feel good to have made it this far, but I am also in a sweat, knowing I can't make any wrong moves, nothing in the direction of the tracks. [62]

When the train rumbles into the station, Dash takes me to the opening door, pulls me inside, brushing me against a sea of exiting passengers. As we begin to move, a young woman helps me to a seat. Dash takes the opportunity to sprawl on the gritty floor, occupying, it seems to me, all the available space end to end. I try to pull him up but, totally relaxed, he won't budge. I stand, pulling him upright, but with a weary sigh he falls to the floor like a bag of potatoes. At Astor Place, I'm thrilled to get off and be led toward daylight. [63]

I ask directions to Tower Records. A man with a heavy New York accent points this way and that. "I'm blind," I tell him. "Hey, fella, I'm sorry," he says and continues giving me directions with his hands. Inside the store, we are escorted to the chamber music section; the items on my list are plucked from the shelves. We leave with tapes in a shopping bag, the simplest of occurrences in the normal world but to me a glorious victory. [64]

Dash and I meander uptown. In Union Square Park, a toddler stands in his path, and Dash, a sucker for kids, goes straight for him and licks his face. "Leash correct him now," I hear Kris Verdi warn inside my head, but I can't do it. I delight in the knowledge that my beast, terrifying to some on the street, is recognized by the children of the world as a pushover. We walk to 34th Street, get back on the subway uptown. Near home I find a wine shop, where I buy a bottle of Taittinger to commemorate this triumph with Charlotte. [65]

All three of us are happy to return to Vermont. Dash goes around the house smelling everything. He tears through the upstairs rooms, bouncing off the walls like a maniac. Out of breath, he settles down on his rug, where I offer him the rawhide bone I have saved for his homecoming. Late that night I sit in the living room, listening to a Mozart trio, Dash sprawled across my feet. [66]

Because of him I have tasted real freedom. I bend to touch him, loving the feel of his elegant long nose. He takes my hand in his mouth, chewing on it playfully, making singing puppy noises. I strain to see his eyes. I want to communicate my love in words, not just through inflection and play. Why can't he understand words if he's so damn smart? I want to talk of my gratitude for what he's already given me, all he has yet to give. I want to tell him how sorry I am that he won't ever be allowed to play with the dogs in the park, chase cats or sniff lampposts. Neutered, he won't woo bitches, nor will I let him exercise his territorial aggressiveness, all a distraction from his work, our safety. Because he is so precious and essential to my life, I can never let him run free. [67]

Dash changes his position at my feet. "Enough of this," he seems [68] to say, and I realize that I even love his aloofness. Every day we seem to know more and more about each other, more ways to make each other happy. We will keep learning, for we have a whole life ahead of us and a lot of work to get done.

VOCABULARY

aerodynamically	in relation to objects and air motion
anthropomorphize	to give human qualities to an animal
bouillabaisse	fish stew
cajole	persuade by promises or flattery
egregious	extraordinarily bad
elixir	cure-all
frenetic	frantic or frenzied
increments	mathematical increases
intractable	stubborn; hard to work with
labyrinth	a puzzling maze of paths or passages
lethargic	drowsy; sluggish
pirouettes	dancing twirls
repentant	remorseful
repository	a place where things are stored
spatial	pertaining to space

DESIGN AND MEANING

1. How does the introductory paragraph use unusual tactics to gain your attention and good will?
2. What process is described in this essay—or are more than one process interwoven?
3. What do the details in paragraph 3 do for a sighted person?
4. Why do you think there is a leap in time between paragraphs 10 and 11? Notice, too, that from paragraph 11 on, the author uses present tense, even though the events are clearly in the past. Why do you think he does this?
5. This essay is occasionally broken by white-space breaks between paragraphs. Look those over and see whether you can come up with an explanation for them.
6. The whole process Potok covers in this essay must have been filled with incident: thus, he had to choose which incidents to relate in detail and which to leave out. Choose one of the anec-

dotes he relates and explain why it was significant enough to put in the essay.

SIMILARITY AND DIFFERENCE

How does "Dash and Me" differ from the other selections in this chapter?

SHORT WRITING IDEA

If you have ever trained a pet or a child, some of Potok's experiences probably seem familiar. Relate an incident you remember clearly from your experience. See the anecdotes in paragraphs 30–33, 42–44, and 50–51 as examples.

LONGER WRITING IDEA

Write an essay about the process of getting used to some new condition of life: a move, illness, office reorganization, marriage, prison, career change, additions to the family.

Roy Hoffman

How to Say Thank You

Roy Hoffman (b. 1953), a native of Alabama who began his career as features editor for the Tulane University newspaper, now lives in New York City where he works as a free-lance writer. The author of two novels, *Almost Family* and *Jona's Way*, Hoffman has also contributed articles to many popular magazines. The essay reprinted here appeared in *Esquire* magazine in September 1982.

Most of us will acknowledge that saying thank you is a gesture of decency—and survival—for anyone wandering a foreign realm. What educated American, no matter how parochial, doesn't know *gracias, danke*, and *merci*? Curiously, though, when the time comes to say thank you to someone in our own land, many of us fall mute. When the kid at the gas station washes our windshield, our office colleague covers a blunder, or our sweetheart serves us a dinner of rump roast and claret, we tend to suffer selective amnesia. [1]

Of course, there are a thousand ways to say thank you. And there are times when the spoken word is not enough. [2]

When someone sends you a gift, a thank-you note acts both as a thank-you and as a kind of receipt. It is also called for when someone has you in his home who usually doesn't; when someone entertains you for a weekend; when someone does you a special favor; or when you know deep in your bones that if you don't send a note you'll be prickled by guilt whenever you see the person you didn't thank. Of course, you can always thank someone by phone, but unless you know the person well or see him frequently, a note is more intimate. As with birthday greetings and congratulations, the phone has a way of taking some of the fizz out of thank-yous. [3]

As a literary form, thank-you notes are rather like haiku. How can you cram into only three lines a description of a vegetable dicer, your sentiment about it, and a touch of gratitude that you'll never have to chop onions again? Actually, the note need not be terse, but it should be *brief*. It should also be personal, mentioning some specific virtue of the gift, like the ideal spacing of teeth in the moustache comb. Above all, the note should be prompt and should never begin, "I'm sorry for not writing sooner," since it's obvious you should have written sooner. My mother always contended that it was never too late to send a thank-you note, but, like all gracious [4] gals of her generation, she never tarried more than a few days anyway. It's my feeling that a thank-you note sent within a week or two of a gift or event is okay; a month is pushing it. If I've let two months slip by and still haven't buckled down, I usually let it slide and resign myself to being thought of forever as an ungrateful slob.

Caveat emptor: Card companies still presume that only teenage girls send thank-you notes; they adorn them with baskets of flowers, bounding squirrels, or tinselly rivers. Another style of commercial card—plain and white, with THANK YOU stamped on the front—is fine to send only if you're thanking somebody for bar mitzvah cuff-links. My own preference is for blank notepaper or, for chummier thank-yous, cards or postcards with catchy pictures on the front. [5]

A thank-you gift is classier by far than a thank-you note, but it's also trickier, since gifts cost money and money, of course, can be counted. The thank-you gift is appropriate when someone's done you a huge favor or has shown you extended hospitality. Like any gift, it is best when it has a personal signature—if you're from New Orleans, pralines; from Vermont, maple syrup. You can combine the thank-you gift with the house present, showing up with a bottle of Scotch at your friend's beach house, then sending a note after your visit. But sending a gift after your stay still means more than showing up with it—it means you're still with your friends in spirit. [6]

Thank-you gifts should never be too lavish, though. Since a thank-you is, when you get down to it, a way of paying off a debt, the object is *not* to put the other person in *your* debt. If a friend takes you skiing a few times and you reciprocate by sending him a new down jacket, he'll love the jacket but probably be uncomfortable at now being in debt to you. He'll feel *forced* to take you skiing again and will resent you for it. [7]

When it comes to a business thank-you, think long and hard before sending a gift. I've heard embarrassing tales of movie directors and magazine editors receiving expensive wallets, bunches of roses, and baskets of gourmet food after throwing the smallest amount of work the way of some poor actor or writer. This is gratitude's dirty side—a thank-you as buttering up or bribery. Unless an employer helps you a great deal with your work, avoid sending a thank-you gift and go with the note—one that tells your boss why you've enjoyed working with him. If you do send a gift, don't make it too personal. In my opinion, tickets to a ball game or a play are better than a shirt or a hat. You're not romancing, simply thanking. [8]

If you're a boss, giving thank-you gifts to your employees, except on special occasions, might seem like an effort to hush them with trinkets. Thank an employee verbally, with a memo that other employees will see, or, best of all, by giving him an afternoon off. [9]

A lunch or dinner is often just the right way to say thank you—and not only in business relationships.

Saying thank you is such a simple act that it's surprising it's not as common as saying good morning or nodding hello. Certainly, it's an act that we need more of—one that will help us all get through the day a little more easily, even a little less selfishly. [10]

VOCABULARY

caveat emptor — Latin for "Let the buyer beware," usually a warning to consumers
parochial — limited or narrow in outlook
terse — succinct, curt

DESIGN AND MEANING

1. Make a concise list of thank-you *dos* and *don'ts* from Hoffman's article.
2. Construct a sentence outline of the essay.
3. How does the ending gracefully bring the subject to a close? How does it relate to the opening?
4. What other things might be included in this essay that would help you more with your thank-yous?

SIMILARITY AND DIFFERENCE

Compare the style of this article with the style of Twain's, Bradbury's, or Selzer's article. *Style* usually includes considerations of sentence length and type, word choice (formal or informal? common or unusual? long or short?), and rhythm and sound.

SHORT WRITING IDEA

Write a thank-you note to an appropriate person. This could be a surprise!

LONGER WRITING IDEA

Explain a custom of American etiquette to someone from another culture, country, or planet. Include an explanation of proper occasions and *dos* and *don'ts*, as Hoffman does.

Dereck Williamson

Wall Covering

A free-lance journalist who writes with humor about life and its ironies, Williamson publishes articles in many popular magazines. He also writes amusing "do-it-yourself" books full of useful, tongue-in-cheek advice. The following selection is taken from *The Complete Book of Pitfalls: A Victim's Guide to Repairs, Maintenance, and Repairing the Maintenance* (1971).

Over the years, starting even before Adolf Hitler, paperhanging has gotten a million laughs. In the movies, great rolls of paper curl up over people who fall off ladders covered with paste as dogs chase cats around the room. It's what advertising copy writers call "a laff riot." [1]

People who have done their own wallpapering rarely even chuckle at the antics on the silver screen. They remember great rolls of curling paper causing them to fall off ladders on dogs and cats covered with paste. (Never mind what modifies what, you picky grammarians; *everything* was covered with paste.) [2]

In recent years the job of wall decorating has become a little easier, but paperhanging is still nothing to be sneezed at. Especially when you're trying to line up the edges. [3]

The most difficult job is preparing the surface. The very thought makes the brain cringe. So many more jobs would get done around the home if you didn't have to "prepare the surface" first. By the time you get a surface prepared, all enthusiasm for the project at hand has disappeared. Remember Uncle Percy who invited you and all the other kids for a Sunday drive? As you gathered around he said, "First we must wash the car . . . ." [4]

Many people have such severe hangups about preliminary work that they flee from place to place all their lives, leaving a trail of unprepared surfaces behind them. Or else they tackle the job without preparing the surface. That's possible in a paperhanging project, but it's not a good idea. Chances are you'll run into trouble. Putting new paper on old paper is risky unless the old paper is still adhering firmly. And you know it isn't. Deep in your heart you know the old paper is loose and cracked and awful. [5]

Too many layers of wallpaper can give a closed-in feeling. Many city apartments have been papered over so many times that there's no room in the rooms. A good rule of thumb is that if both elbows [6] touch walls—and you're standing in the room the long way—you should remove all the old wallpaper and start all over again. However, if you have unusually long elbows, you might possibly get away with one more layer of paper.

To remove old layers of wallpaper you need old clothes, a wide putty knife, and a compulsive urge to destroy. You loosen up the paper either by soaking it with hot water or using a wallpaper steamer. You rent the latter at a paint store, not a shipping office. [7]

Do-it-yourself books say the job is messy, but that it goes fast once you start. Only the first part is true. Have you ever heard of a messy job going fast? You'll be steaming and soaking and scraping and slopping and slushing and slogging around that room for days. Only two things will relieve the boredom. The first is the layer by layer discovery of what hideous taste the previous tenants had. The other is the prospect of finding a million dollar bill or an original Van Gogh between the wall and first layer of paper, a logical hiding place for money and paintings. [8]

As you wield the scraper, be careful not to gouge the walls. Not only will the Van Gogh be ruined, but you'll have to fill up the holes before you put on the new paper. [9]

Cracks and holes should be filled with spackling compound and sanded smooth after dry. The next step is to apply a coat of wall size, a gluelike substance which seals the surface and also fills in small depressions. Like your ears and eyes. [10]

Materials you'll need for papering are a paste brush and bucket, a sponge, a plumb line, chalk, a stepladder, a yardstick, scissors, razor blades, a smoothing brush, a seam roller, and the same putty knife you used for wallgouging. [11]

Instructions that come with the wallpaper tell you that a long, clean, flat work surface is essential for preparing the paper. The illustration shows a smiling man standing at a banquet table, brushing paste on an endless strip of paper. He is wearing a necktie. Do you know anybody who wears a necktie when he applies wallpaper paste? [12]

Face the fact that paperhanging is a grubby job, and that you won't have enough space to work in. If you're lucky, you'll find room someplace to set up a lone card table, and you'll make do with that. Afterward, the table won't be any good for card-playing. Each time you shuffle, the bottom card will stick to the table. You'll have to play with an incomplete deck, stopping every few hands to steam and scrape cards. [13]

There are formulas for estimating the amount of paper you'll need, but they don't take into account dog and cat damage. Your best bet is to supply the dealer with your room dimensions, plus window and door measurements, and a list of household pets. The [14] dealer will give you enough rolls of paper to do the room. Make sure he has more of the same pattern on hand.

Start papering next to a door. (Don't paper over the door.) From the door frame, measure out a distance of one inch less than the width of the paper, and make a mark. Then, using the chalked plumb line, snap a perfectly vertical line against the wall. Then go to bed. That's quite enough for one day. [15]

When you return to the room several months later, maybe someone will have already papered it. Or taken away the rolls of paper and applied a decent coat of whitewash. If not, you've got to start hanging the wallpaper. [16]

Cut off a piece from the roll the distance from floor to ceiling plus about eight inches to allow trimming on the top and bottom. Then lay the paper face down on the work table and start brushing paste on the back, as the remainder of the roll falls off the table into the fresh bucket of paste. [17]

After plucking out the roll and flinging it against the wall in a blind rage, finish applying paste to the first strip and then start on exposed parts of your body. Remove your clothes and cover yourself completely with paste. Now you are ready to (1) go out in the street and dance, or (2) apply the first strip of paper to the wall. If you choose to be dull and hang paper, here's the technique: [18]

Carefully line up the first strip so the edge touches the chalk line, and smooth it out against the wall. It helps if you apply the paste on one half of the paper's length first, fold it over loosely paste side to paste side, and then do the same thing with the other half. It also helps if you don't lose your head as you're trying to hold the paper up against the wall and unfold it at the same time. [19]

Once the paper is lined up, use a smoothing brush or damp sponge to flatten out the strip and remove bubbles and wrinkles. Then carefully trim off the top and bottom with a razor blade, and wipe off the excess paste. [20]

Some paper comes with untrimmed edges, and you use a long straightedge to trim off the selvage. That's done while the paper is on the table. Next time, get smart and buy paper already trimmed. [21]

Each succeeding layer of paper is applied to the wall just a tiny bit away from the preceding one, and then sort of nudged over in place so it matches up. Press the edges down with the seam roller. Before you put paste on the next strip, the books say to hold it up against the wall to make sure it will match up with the other piece. To do this, just pull the roll apart until one hand is up against the ceiling molding and the other hand is against the baseboard. Then go out in the kitchen and eat a bunch of bananas. [22]

Save leftover strips and use them around windows and doors. Remove wall fixtures and switch plates, paper over them, and then [23] cut out the openings later if you can find them. Some people carefully paper each individual switch plate, making sure it exactly fits in with the wall pattern. This type of person Simonizes the inside of his glove compartment, and fills unused pegboard holes with Plastic Wood.

One kind of paper comes with the paste already applied. You put a water trough on the floor, soak each precut strip in the water for a minute, then slowly pull one end out of the trough, unrolling the paper and climbing the ladder and scratching your nose and lighting a cigarette. The trough gets moved along the floor as you apply successive strips. Try to keep your feet out of it. [24]

When you come to the corner, take the paper around to the next wall about an inch. Before starting on the new wall, make another chalk mark if you can find the plumb bob under all that rubble. [25]

In order to paper ceilings it takes two people, both insane. If you're thinking of papering your ceiling you don't need instructions, you need a doctor. [26]

Today, the home decorator has a huge assortment of wall coverings to choose from, in every imaginable pattern, color, and material. The secret of modern decorating is to apply something that looks like something else. There are plastic coverings that look like cloth, cloth coverings that look like tile, tile coverings that look like metal, metal coverings that look like wood, and wood coverings that look like plastic. And vice versa. You can also get fiberglass panels that look like real rocks cemented together. So far, they haven't tried to make real rocks look like anything else, but they're working on it. [27]

You don't need water, paste, or tools to apply many of the modern materials. You just stick them on, after peeling off a protective backing. In a jiffy you can cover your walls with imitation bricks, your refrigerator with imitation wood, your windows with imitation chair caning, and your chairs with imitation stained glass windows. [28]

But even with stick-on materials, ceilings are almost impossible to get right. You might try nailing up the fake fiberglass rock panels, though. In this nuclear age, a stone ceiling gives you a sense of security. [29]

VOCABULARY

adhere	to stick fast
plumb bob	a lead weight hung at the end of a string, used to determine a vertical line by gravity
selvage	a specially defined edge of fabric or paper

DESIGN AND MEANING

1. What qualities of "do-it-yourself" home decorating manuals does Williamson make fun of? Has Williamson ever put up wallpaper himself?
2. Why is "laff" spelled that way in paragraph 1?
3. Point out some examples of exaggeration used for humorous effect. What other sources of humor did you find in the essay?
4. Could you really put up wallpaper using these directions? What elements resemble the format of serious instructions? What elements do not?

SIMILARITY AND DIFFERENCE

Analyze Williamson's writing in the light of Thompson's and Vonnegut's advice.

SHORT WRITING IDEA

Write a paragraph telling a fellow student how to prepare to do homework.

LONGER WRITING IDEA

Give the *real* instructions for some task you have found to be more difficult than the directions or instructions admitted.

John E. Eichenlaub

How to Fight Cold-Proneness

Dr. Eichenlaub practiced medicine for many years as an old-fashioned family doctor before deciding in 1953 to extend his services by writing advice about home remedies. Besides his helpful book, *A Minnesota Doctor's Home Remedies for Common and Uncommon Ailments* (1960), from which this selection is taken, he has published a number of articles in popular magazines.

Almost anyone can substantially reduce his exposure to cold germs and substantially increase his resistance to them. If you are particularly subject to colds, home measures to counteract this tendency usually prove especially worthwhile. These measures are more effective than any cold shot yet devised and involve absolutely no medical expense or risk. [1]

You cannot dodge cold germs simply by avoiding people who sneeze and cough. Colds spread mainly before complaints begin and reach you mainly from members of your own family or close circle of friends. A few germs, even of the worst possible kind, do you no harm. It takes thousands or millions of germs, all from the same germ family, to set up disease. Even one less than the crucial number leads to no trouble at all. You can cut down the spread of germs through mouth moisture, improperly sanitized dishes, and close quarters in the firm knowledge that even a few less germs spread may mean a great deal less sickness in your household. [2]

Protect your nose lining against cold germs. Some home measures for preventing colds are just common sense: enough rest, well-chosen foods, and sufficient warm clothing. Science can add two tremendous aids: extra help for your body's main shield against cold germs, which is your nose lining, and heightened resistance through cold-fighting morale. [3]

How your nose lining protects you against germs. Your nose lining spreads an invisibly thin sheet of sticky mucus over the entire inside of your nose. When you breathe in germs, most of them stick in the sheet of mucus. Tiny sweeper cells continually brush the mucus back into your throat. A brand new sheet forms every six minutes or so. Meanwhile sweepings pile up at the back [4] of your throat until they make a glob big enough for you to swallow. Your stomach acids kill the germs.

In the wintertime, the dry, heated air turns your nose lining's mucus blanket to crusts. It may even dry the nose lining until it cracks, providing completely free access to germs. Moisturization prevents this effect, and thus increases your nose lining's resistance. [5]

How can you moisturize your nose lining? Three main methods are worthwhile: [6]

[7]

1. *Add moisture to heated air.* Humidifiers or moisturizing pans on the radiators are worthwhile. They at least take the edge off the dryness of indoor air. They cannot do the whole job, since thorough home air moisturization requires evaporation of several gallons of water each day.
2. *Turn down the heat.* When you warm air from 68 degrees to 80 degrees, you increase its drying power more than fourfold. It's best to heat your nose only to 68 degrees and put on extra sweaters or heavier clothes for bodily warmth. At night you can cool your bedroom five or ten degrees by turning heat down or by ventilation. That gives your nose lining a rest from too-dry, overheated air. Extra blankets keep your body comfortably warm. [8]
3. *Use home-made moisturizing nose spray.* You can banish dry crusts and help your nose's defense by using this moisturizing spray: [9]

   1 tablespoon glycerin, obtained from any drugstore without prescription.

   1½ tablespoons 70% alcohol (rubbing alcohol strength).

   1 teaspoon table salt.

   1 pint tap or distilled water.

If your tap water has a heavy odor of chlorine, let it stand overnight in an open vessel. Mix the ingredients and stir until salt is thoroughly dissolved. Pour into clean bottle and stopper firmly. [10]

Get a plastic pocket atomizer for about 35¢ at the drugstore, fill it with this solution, and use it several times a day as needed. [11]

Last-minute action to ward off a cold. Can you tell when a cold is just coming on? If you can, you may be able to stop some colds from getting a real start. [12]

The first thing to try is moisturizing spray (see above). Spray the inside of your nose thoroughly every hour or two. Keep warm and get a good night's sleep. This program alone will stop some colds in their tracks. [13]

If you have enough colds to make it worthwhile, one other [14] medicine might help you. It's a combination of codeine and papaverine, which are available on prescription only. When used at the first sign of a cold, it sometimes stops the nose lining responses which allow germs to get a foothold. When you next see your doctor, ask if you should have this material on hand and how you should use it when you feel a cold coming on.

[15] **Fight colds by mental measures.** Parts of your brain actually govern your circulation and many other bodily functions through which you fight off germs. Your emotional state greatly influences these functions. It can thus help or hurt your resistance to all kinds of infection. This effect is very strong. Just thinking you are liable to get a cold may tip the balance and make you fall victim to one.

[16] A research expert proved the importance of emotions to the origin of colds without even trying. He wanted to grow cold germs in the laboratory. In order to tell whether the germs were present in his culture solution, he decided to spray some into a few people's noses. The subjects were left in hospital rooms and protected from new infections until any strong germs they already had acquired would have shown up. (Some cold germs are probably present in most people's throats at all times, but not enough to cause a cold so long as their resistance is normal.) Then he sprayed a few people with ordinary water telling them the stuff was loaded with germs. One out of five promptly came down with a cold.

[17] The rest of the experiment proved that strong cold germs were present in the doctor's other mixture. But this very first step proved a point which is very important to you. It means that even weak cold germs can be helped along by mental forces until they overcome your resistance. When you get chilled or feel a draught, the chances are that you say to yourself: "Now I'm in for it! I'll have a cold tomorrow for sure!" That conviction itself causes concern and emotional response which actually help to give you the cold.

[18] **Build your cold-fighting morale.** You can protect yourself against two thirds of all colds by building cold-fighting morale. That's what a team of researchers at Michigan found out when they were experimenting with a new cold vaccine. They thought they had an effective product and designed tests to prove the fact. One group of people got the vaccine. Another group got nothing, and still another got distilled water, being told that they were getting cold shots.

[19] When the results were in, the people who took the cold shots reported only one third as many colds as the ones who had nothing at all. But the ones who got the distilled water had even less! The conviction that they would get less colds actually cut tremendously the number of colds these people suffered!

[20] What does this mean to you? Certainly not that your colds aren't

real: they're real, germ-caused infections. But your resistance may be affected so much by concern about old superstitions that you have many colds which you could otherwise fight off.

This need not be. You can use mental forces to *increase* your resistance instead of impair it. You can build your cold-fighting morale to the point where you have many less colds per year. [21]

How to build cold-fighting morale. Cold-fighting morale is best built on one firm conviction: *nothing that happens to you can give you a cold*. You need never say to yourself: "Drat it! I did thus-and-so, so now I'll probably get a cold!" Absolutely none of the common experiences you might note can give you a cold. [22]

Let's look at some of the ideas science has explored in reaching this conclusion: [23]

Draughts, night air, and going without a hat do not cause colds. The lining of your nose is definitely affected by nerve and emotional balance. Your nose can get stopped up or runny on the basis of pure nerve reflex when you are exposed to wind or cold. It can get stopped up and runny after any uncomfortable nerve-tickling exposure, even through slight draughts. But unless worry or concern add further burdens, your nose lining will usually get back to normal before the ever-present cold germs actually get a start. [24]

Chilling doesn't cause colds. When I was only a child, I remember my aunt stomping her feet one day as she came in the front door. [25]

"Brrrr—" she said. "I'm chilled clean through. Have a cold tomorrow, like as not." [26]

The next day, sure enough! She had a cold. But today's science says that my aunt probably already had the cold germs in her body, and those germs were already starting disease when she first walked in my door saying "Brrrr—." My aunt almost certainly felt chilly because of a beginning cold; she didn't get the cold because of the chill. But millions of people are positive that whenever they get chilled a cold will certainly follow. If they actually do get chilled, not simply get chilly sensations because of a beginning cold, how many of them actually suffer a cold, not because of the chill, but because of fearful certainty that they are headed for the sickbed? [27]

Have confidence in your body's powers. Of course, it pays to dress yourself warmly to avoid extreme exposure. But it pays to have confidence in your body, too. Take reasonable measures to avoid chilling, then shrug your shoulders and forget it if you find that you've been uncomfortably cool. [28]

Other people's colds aren't easy to catch. Suppose a stranger sneezes at you in a store. What are your chances of getting a cold? [29]

Actually, almost none at all. Children, who take little care to dodge other people's germs, get colds four times out of five when [30] they are right in the household with a cold victim. But as an adult, you will *escape* four times out of five even if you are in close family contact with a cold. Moreover, most people who sneeze or cough at you in public have already passed the early days when their cold can still be spread and could not give you germs no matter how hard they tried. Many people sneeze or cough because of conditions which are impossible to spread, like allergy. Your chance of catching a stranger's cold is almost zero, but your chance of worrying yourself into a cold after he's sneezed in your face is considerable indeed, unless you have become convinced that colds are rarely spread through such contact.

Cold-fighting morale can really protect you. If you are convinced that nothing is likely to cause colds, you won't suffer psychologically induced ones. You will probably also increase your resistance against whatever cold-causing germs you meet. So whenever you find yourself thinking that what has just happened might cause a cold, repeat to yourself several times: "Nothing that happens to me can give me a cold. Not draughts, not chilling, not even a victim's sneeze! Nothing that happens to me can give me a cold!" As you go about your daily activities, have confidence in your body's powers of resistance. You will still occasionally meet an overwhelming number of cold germs and suffer an infection. But you can throw off the bulk of cold germs without even a sniffle. [31]

DESIGN AND MEANING

1. What methods does Eichenlaub use to help you follow his organization?
2. This selection contains fairly technical information. What does the writer do to make it interesting and understandable to nonexperts?
3. Process writing often involves other kinds of development, too. In this piece, find at least one point supported in each of these ways: cause-and-effect reasoning, example, statistical fact, and logical reasoning.

SIMILARITY AND DIFFERENCE

What similarities can you see among Eichenlaub's, Vonnegut's, and Thompson's selections in this chapter? Why do you think these similarities exist?

SHORT WRITING IDEA

Write a one-page outline of Eichenlaub's essay.

LONGER WRITING IDEA

Reread paragraphs 4 and 5. Research any other natural process, and explain it in a way almost anyone could understand. Some possibilities: how clouds form, how bees swarm, how hair turns gray.

Jonathan Miller

Your Reflex Systems

An Englishman of many talents, Miller took his medical degree in 1959 but soon diversified. He has been a coauthor and costar of an internationally popular musical review, a director of opera and Shakespearean plays, a writer for the *New Yorker* and *Partisan Review*, and a research fellow in the history of medicine at University College, London. The following selection is taken from his book about the human body, *The Body in Question* (1978), which was brilliantly dramatized in a thirteen-hour BBC television series starring Dr. Miller.

The inside of the body—blood vessels, heart, intestine, lungs and bladder—is liberally studded with instruments capable of registering changes in pressure, temperature and chemical composition. But none of these meters has any dials: they are not meant to be read by human consciousness, but are linked up with the reflex systems which obey automatically. Although you can sometimes, when the variations are extreme, become aware of the adjustments going on inside, most of the time you are quite unconscious of the hectic activity. When you start to exercise, your heart automatically speeds up in order to supply the working muscles with the blood they need. But you don't make the decision to speed up your heart. You simply choose to run, and the reflex arrangements automatically take care of the rest. And when you stop running, you don't have to remember to switch off your heart: as the sensory messages stop arriving from the muscles, the heart begins to slow down automatically; one of the first signs that something is wrong with the circulation is that it takes the heart longer than normal to slow down after exercise. [1]

This principle applies most of all to systems which have a closed cycle: the circulation of the blood, for instance, which follows an unbroken sequence without coming into immediate contact with the outside world; the blood vessels are constantly adjusting themselves, redistributing blood from the skin, the muscles and so forth. When you need to lose heat, the radiators of the skin flush with warm blood, whereas when you need to conserve heat, the blood vessels contract and the skin whitens and cools. You can sometimes feel the results of all this, but you are not actually conscious of the fact of contraction or expansion. You can't blush at will. [2]

Certain cycles, however, open directly into the outside world, and in these cases we are made aware of the sensations in order to introduce voluntary control of what happens. Take the urinary system. The kidneys manufacture urine from the blood, following biochemical instructions which never enter our consciousness. If the body is short of water for some reason, the urine is automatically reduced in volume and becomes more concentrated. If it is short of salt, the kidneys reabsorb as much as they can. The blood is continually being monitored or tasted by sense organs linked up to systems which do everything they can to maintain the *status quo*. All this is quite automatic: the urine sweeps into the bladder through the ureter, and, although there are muscles to help it on its way, we are quite unaware of their action. In animals which live in the sea, the urine can flow straight out into the environment without the animal having to pay any attention. Such carelessness isn't possible on dry land: an unsupervised flow of urine would soon ulcerate the skin, and before long, infections would backtrack into the ureter. Land animals have therefore developed a muscular reservoir for holding the urine until it can be thrown clear in one go. In lower animals, this act is more or less automatic, but in animals like cats and dogs the sensations of a full bladder arouse enough of their attention to cause them quite complicated behavior, and in species which live in communities, like ours, the part played by consciousness is even more important. What happens is this: the urine accumulates unnoticed until the pressure begins to stretch small sense organs embedded in the wall of the bladder; in an untrained infant, these impulses bring about an automatic reflex; in an adult, the sensations rise into consciousness, and etiquette takes care of the rest. In patients suffering from a broken back, the messages between bladder and brain are interrupted, and their urine accumulates until it reaches a critical pressure, at which point the bladder opens automatically, regardless of where the patient happens to be. [3]

The same principle of dual control applies to the intestine, except that this system is open to negotiation at two ends. Although it is automatic throughout its huge length, it still has to be filled and emptied at the right moment, and at both points this involves a conscious transaction with the world. The feelings of hunger and taste allow us to negotiate for the right meal, whereas the sensation of a full rectum reminds us when to visit the lavatory. Between these two archways of conscious sensation lies the vast unconscious Amazon of the intestine. All its movements are quite automatic. (Which is just as well—imagine what it would be like if you had to supervise the passage of food through its whole length.) Fortunately, [4] the muslces of the intestine move of their own accord, and the peristaltic waves follow one another in an orderly fashion.

[5] But we have to pay a price for this labour-saving efficiency. When anything goes wrong, neither the quality nor the location of the sensation tells what is happening. A kidney stone, for instance, produces an agonising pain, but unless you have had it before and know that this is the sort of pain you get with a stone, you are almost bound to be mystified by it. In one way or another, this applies to all our innards—heart, lungs, intestines. In emergencies, the sensations and feelings may be extremely vivid and can in fact monopolize our attention altogether, but the feelings we get are almost entirely uninformative. Designed to work without conscious instruction, these interior systems are at a loss for words when they try to speak up for themselves. And, to make it worse, the vocabulary of internal sensation is so small that several illnesses have to share the same feelings. Breathlessness may be the result of anaemia, pneumonia or heart failure. A bad internal haemorrhage with concealed loss of blood produces symptoms almost indistinguishable from a sudden fall in blood sugar. Nausea may arise from food poisoning, kidney failure, appendicitis, brain tumour or migraine.

[6] Although our experience in our body is so vague and muddy, our mind does everything it can to intensify the images with which it is supplied—like the computers which sharpen the pictures sent from distant planets. In the absence of any immediate knowledge of our own insides, most of us have improvised an imaginary picture in the hope of explaining the occasional feelings which escape into consciousness. Our mind, it seems, prefers a picture of some sort to having to live through the chaos of sensations that would otherwise seem absurd.

DESIGN AND MEANING

1. Although Miller's writing is not full of unfamiliar words, probably you found that you needed to read this selection more slowly and thoughtfully than the preceding ones in this chapter. Looking back, speculate about why it required this extra effort.
2. Point out three examples of cause-and-effect development within the essay.
3. Miller gives excellent transitions between paragraphs. Tell how each one ties into an idea in the preceding paragraph and establishes its relationship to the new topic.

4. Explain the extended comparison in paragraph 5.

SIMILARITY AND DIFFERENCE

Speculate on the reasons for difference in paragraph length among the selections so far in this chapter.

SHORT WRITING IDEA

Pretend you are rewriting this selection for junior high school students. Revise the first three sentences. Your revision will probably be longer than the original.

LONGER WRITING IDEA

Eichenlaub's and Miller's pieces describe natural processes. The same techniques are used to describe mechanical processes. Write an essay explaining how a mechanical process works: a fountain pen, an automatic choke, a three-way light bulb, a piano key.

poetry

Robert Frost

Departmental

A respected poet who also enjoys popular acclaim, Frost (1874–1963) typically wrote on simple, homely subjects. In this selection he adopts a satirical stance.

An ant on the table cloth
Ran into a dormant moth
Of many times his size
He showed not the least surprise.
His business wasn't with such. [5]
He gave it scarcely a touch,
And was off on his duty run.
Yet if he encountered one
Of the hive's enquiry squad
Whose work is to find out God [10]
And the nature of time and space,
He would put them onto the case.
Ants are a curious race;
One crossing with hurried tread
The body of one of their dead [15]
Isn't given a moment's arrest—
Seems not even impressed.
But he no doubt reports to any
With whom he crosses antennae,
And they no doubt report [20]
To the higher up at court.
Then word goes forth in Formic:
"Death's come to Jerry McCormic,
Our selfless forager Jerry.
Will the special Janizary [25]
Whose office it is to bury
The dead of the commissary
Go bring him home to his people.

Lay him in state on a sepal.
Wrap him for shroud in a petal. [30]
Embalm him with ichor of nettle.
This is the word of your Queen."
And presently on the scene
Appears a solemn mortician;
And taking formal position [35]
With feelers calmly atwiddle,
Seizes the dead by the middle,
And heaving him high in air,
Carries him out of there.
No one stands round to stare. [40]
It is nobody else's affair.

It couldn't be called ungentle.
But how thoroughly
departmental.

VOCABULARY

commissary	branch of the army that provides food and supplies to the troops
curious	arousing interest due to strangeness
dormant	lying still
enquiry	an investigation
forager	one who searches for food and provisions
formic	relating to ants
ichor	a thin fluid
janizary	a loyal or submissive follower
nettle	a weed with stinging hairs
sepal	a green, leaflike part of a flower

DESIGN AND MEANING

1. How is the strict rhyme scheme of this poem appropriate for its subject matter?
2. Do you think the poem has a moral or message? What could it be?
3. What is the function of the first example of ant behavior, the encounter with the moth?
4. This poem has an unusual mixture of formal and informal lan-

guage. Point out examples of each. What effect does the mixture have on you?

SIMILARITY AND DIFFERENCE

The denotative (dictionary) meaning of the word "departmental" is simply "arranged into departments." How does that contrast with the connotative (emotional) meaning of the word in the context of this poem?

SHORT WRITING IDEA

Using "Departmental" as a pattern, write a four- or six-line poem describing the habits or personality of a creature of your choice.

LONGER WRITING IDEA

You have written descriptions of natural and mechanical processes. Now try a description of a social process, like courtship, giving a party, breaking up, making friends, or learning table manners.

PREREADING EXERCISE

Read the first nine paragraphs of Chopin's "The Story of an Hour," which follows, and then stop. Write a brief plot line explaining what you think will happen in the remainder of the story.

Short Story

Kate Chopin

The Story of an Hour

Chopin (1851–1904) did not begin to write until she was left widowed with five children at the age of thirty-two. During the next sixteen years, she produced several volumes of short stories and an exquisite feminist novella, *The Awakening* (1899), which was received with outrage by the critics. "The Story of an Hour" first appeared in *Vogue* magazine in 1894.

Knowing that Mrs. Mallard was afflicted with a heart trouble, great care was taken to break to her as gently as possible the news of her husband's death. [1]

It was her sister Josephine who told her, in broken sentences; veiled hints that revealed in half concealing. Her husband's friend Richards was there, too, near her. It was he who had been in the newspaper office when intelligence of the railroad disaster was received, with Brently Mallard's name leading the list of "killed." He had only taken the time to assure himself of its truth by a second telegram, and had hastened to forestall any less careful, less tender friend in bearing the sad message. [2]

She did not hear the story as many women have heard the same, with a paralyzed inability to accept its significance. She wept at once, with sudden, wild abandonment, in her sister's arms. When the storm of grief had spent itself she went away to her room alone. She would have no one follow her. [3]

There stood, facing the open window, a comfortable, roomy arm-chair. Into this she sank, pressed down by a physical exhaustion that haunted her body and seemed to reach into her soul. [4]

She could see in the open square before her house the tops of trees that were all aquiver with the new spring life. The delicious breath of rain was in the air. In the street below a peddler was crying his wares. The notes of a distant song which some one was singing reached her faintly, and countless sparrows were twittering in the eaves. [5]

There were patches of blue sky showing here and there through the clouds that had met and piled one above the other in the west facing her window. [6]

She sat with her head thrown back upon the cushion of the chair, quite motionless, except when a sob came up into her throat and shook her, as a child who has cried itself to sleep continues to sob in its dreams. [7]

She was young, with a fair, calm face, whose lines bespoke repression and even a certain strength. But now there was a dull stare in her eyes, whose gaze was fixed away off yonder on one of those patches of blue sky. It was not a glance of reflection, but rather indicated a suspension of intelligent thought. [8]

There was something coming to her and she was waiting for it, fearfully. What was it? She did not know; it was too subtle and elusive to name. But she felt it, creeping out of the sky, reaching toward her through the sounds, the scents, the color that filled the air. [9]

Now her bosom rose and fell tumultuously. She was beginning to recognize this thing that was approaching to possess her, and she was striving to beat it back with her will—as powerless as her two white slender hands would have been. [10]

When she abandoned herself a little whispered word escaped her slightly parted lips. She said it over and over under her breath: "free, free, free!" The vacant stare and the look of terror that had followed it went from her eyes. They stayed keen and bright. Her pulses beat fast, and the coursing blood warmed and relaxed every inch of her body. [11]

She did not stop to ask if it were or were not a monstrous joy that held her. A clear and exalted perception enabled her to dismiss the suggestion as trivial. [12]

She knew that she would weep again when she saw the kind, tender hands folded in death; the face that had never looked save with love upon her, fixed and gray and dead. But she saw beyond that bitter moment a long procession of years to come that would belong to her absolutely. And she opened and spread her arms out to them in welcome. [13]

There would be no one to live for her during those coming years; she would live for herself. There would be no powerful will bending hers in that blind persistence with which men and women believe they have a right to impose a private will upon a fellow-creature. A kind intention or a cruel intention made the act seem no less a crime as she looked upon it in that brief moment of illumination. [14]

And yet she had loved him—sometimes. Often she had not. What did it matter! What could love, the unsolved mystery, count [15] for in face of this possession of self-assertion which she suddenly recognized as the strongest impulse of her being!

"Free! Body and soul free!" she kept whispering. [16]

Josephine was kneeling before the closed door with her lips to the keyhole, imploring for admission. "Louise, open the door! I beg; open the door—you will make yourself ill. What are you doing, Louise? For heaven's sake open the door." [17]

"Go away. I am not making myself ill." No; she was drinking in a very elixir of life through the open window. [18]

Her fancy was running riot along those days ahead of her. Spring days and summer days, and all sorts of days that would be her own. She breathed a quick prayer that life might be long. It was only yesterday she had thought with a shudder that life might be long. [19]

She arose at length and opened the door to her sister's importunities. There was a feverish triumph in her eyes, and she carried herself unwittingly like a goddess of Victory. She clasped her sister's waist, and together they descended the stairs. Richards stood waiting for them at the bottom. [20]

Some one was opening the front door with a latchkey. It was Brently Mallard who entered, a little travel-stained, composedly carrying his grip-sack and umbrella. He had been far from the scene of the accident, and did not even know there had been one. He stood amazed at Josephine's piercing cry; at Richards' quick motion to screen him from the view of his wife. [21]

But Richards was too late. [22]

When the doctors came they said she had died of heart disease—of joy that kills. [23]

VOCABULARY

composed	calm, tranquil
elixir	an imaginary substance which prolongs life and health indefinitely
elusive	hard to grasp
fancy	imagination
implore	to ask or beg earnestly
importunity	a persistent request
reflection	serious thought
save	except
spent	worn out
suspension	a temporary cancellation
tumultuous	turbulent, wild and disturbed
unwittingly	unknowingly

DESIGN AND MEANING

1. What words would you use to describe the process that goes on in this story?
2. What are some contrasts between Louise's old life and the new life she imagines? What details are unstated but suggested about her old life?
3. What does the open window signify?
4. What does the last sentence add to the message of the story?

SIMILARITY AND DIFFERENCE

This story was first published in *Vogue* magazine in 1894. What differences might there be between the way readers reacted then and now? What similarities? Would a women's magazine be likely to publish this story today?

SHORT WRITING IDEA

After reading the story, you can derive a second meaning from the opening words, "Mrs. Mallard was afflicted with a heart trouble." Explain both meanings in a paragraph.

LONGER WRITING IDEA

Record the sequence of your emotions after a particularly striking event or discovery: a death, news of your pregnancy, an unexpectedly failed exam, a revealed secret.

VOCABULARY CHECK

For each numbered item, write a complete sentence using the phrase in a reasonable way.

1. a composed face
2. the elusive concept
3. implored pitifully
4. unwittingly revealed
5. after long reflection

Hernando Telléz

Just Lather, That's All

Hernando Telléz (1908–1965), a native of Bogota, Colombia, worked primarily as a journalist editing several of the leading magazines and newspapers in that strife-torn country. He is now acknowledged as one of the finest short story writers in the Spanish language. His best-known story, "Just Lather, That's All," which is reprinted here, also appears in many anthologies of great Spanish stories.

He said nothing when he entered. I was passing the best of my razors back and forth on a strop. When I recognized him I started to tremble. But he didn't notice. Hoping to conceal my emotion, I continued sharpening the razor. I tested it on the meat of my thumb, and then held it up to the light. At that moment he took off the bullet-studded belt that his gun holster dangled from. He hung it up on a wall hook and placed his military cap over it. Then he turned to me, loosening the knot of his tie, and said, "It's hot as hell. Give me a shave." He sat in the chair. [1]

I estimated he had a four-day beard. The four days taken up by the latest expedition in search of our troops. His face seemed reddened, burned by the sun. Carefully, I began to prepare the soap. I cut off a few slices, dropped them into the cup, mixed in a bit of warm water, and began to stir with the brush. Immediately the foam began to rise. "The other boys in the group should have this much beard, too." I continued stirring the lather. [2]

"But we did all right, you know. We got the main ones. We brought back some dead, and we've got some others still alive. But pretty soon, they'll all be dead." [3]

"How many did you catch?" I asked. [4]

"Fourteen. We had to go pretty deep into the woods to find them. But we'll get even. Not one of them comes out of this alive, not one." [5]

He leaned back on the chair when he saw me with the lather-covered brush in my hand. I still had to put the sheet over him. No doubt about it, I was upset. I took a sheet out of a drawer and knotted it around my customer's neck. He wouldn't stop talking. He probably thought I was in sympathy with his party. [6]

"The town must have learned a lesson from what we did the other day," he said. [7]

"Yes," I replied, securing the knot at the base of his dark, sweaty neck. [8]

"That was a fine show, eh?" [9]

"Very good," I answered, turning back for the brush. The man closed his eyes with a gesture of fatigue and sat waiting for the cool caress of the soap. I had never had him so close to me. The day he ordered the whole town to file into the patio of the school to see the four rebels hanging there, I came face to face with him for an instant. But the sight of the mutilated bodies kept me from noticing the face of the man who had directed it all, the face I was now about to take into my hands. It was not an unpleasant face, certainly. And the beard, which made him seem a bit older than he was, didn't suit him badly at all. His name was Torres. Captain Torres. A man of imagination, because who else would have thought of hanging the naked rebels and then holding target practice on certain parts of their bodies? I began to apply the first layer of soap. With his eyes closed, he continued. "Without any effort I could go straight to sleep," he said, "but there's plenty to do this afternoon." I stopped the lathering and asked with a feigned lack of interest: "A firing squad?" "Something like that, but a little slower." I got on with the job of lathering his beard. My hands started trembling again. The man could not possibly realize it, and this was in my favor. But I would have preferred that he hadn't come. It was likely that many of our faction had seen him enter. And any enemy under one's roof imposes certain conditions. I would be obliged to shave that beard like any other one, carefully, gently, like that of any customer, taking pains to see that no single pore emitted a drop of blood. Being careful to see that the little tufts of hair did not lead the blade astray. Seeing that his skin ended up clean, soft, and healthy, so that passing the back of my hand over it I couldn't feel a hair. Yes, I was secretly a rebel, but I was also a conscientious barber, and proud of the preciseness of my profession. And this four-day's growth of beard was a fitting challenge. [10]

I took the razor, opened up the two protective arms, exposed the blade and began the job, from one of the sideburns downward. The razor responded beautifully. His beard was inflexible and hard, not too long, but thick. Bit by bit the skin emerged. The razor rasped along, making its customary sound as fluffs of lather mixed with bits of hair gathered along the blade. I paused a moment to clean it, then took up the strop again to sharpen the razor, because I'm a barber who does things properly. The man, who had kept his eyes closed, opened them now, removed one of his hands from under the sheet, felt the spot on his face where the soap had been cleared off, and said, "Come to the school today at six o'clock." "The same thing as the other day?" I asked horrified. "It could be better," he replied. [11]

"What do you plan to do?" "I don't know yet. But we'll amuse ourselves." Once more he leaned back and closed his eyes. I approached him with the razor poised. "Do you plan to punish them all?" I ventured timidly. "All." The soap was drying on his face. I had to hurry. In the mirror I looked toward the street. It was the same as ever: the grocery store with two or three customers in it. Then I glanced at the clock: two-twenty in the afternoon. The razor continued on its downward stroke. Now from the other sideburn down. A thick, blue beard. He should have let it grow like some poets or priests do. It would suit him well. A lot of people wouldn't recognize him. Much to his benefit, I thought, as I attempted to cover the neck area smoothly. There, for sure, the razor had to be handled masterfully, since the hair, although softer, grew into little swirls. A curly beard. One of the tiny pores could be opened up and issue forth its pearl of blood. A good barber such as I prides himself on never allowing this to happen to a client. And this was a first-class client. How many of us had he ordered shot? How many of us had he ordered mutilated? It was better not to think about it. Torres did not know that I was his enemy. He did not know it nor did the rest. It was a secret shared by very few, precisely so that I could inform the revolutionaries of what Torres was doing in the town and of what he was planning each time he undertook a rebel-hunting excursion. So it was going to be very difficult to explain that I had him right in my hands and let him go peacefully—alive and shaved.

[12] The beard was now almost completely gone. He seemed younger, less burdened by years than when he had arrived. I suppose this always happens with men who visit barber shops. Under the stroke of my razor Torres was being rejuvenated—rejuvenated because I am a good barber, the best in town, if I may say so. A little more lather here, under his chin, on his Adam's apple, on this big vein. How hot is it getting! Torres must be sweating as much as I. But he is not afraid. He is a calm man, who is not even thinking about what he is going to do with the prisoners this afternoon. On the other hand, I, with this razor in my hands, stroking and re-stroking this skin, trying to keep blood from oozing from these pores, can't even think clearly. Damn him for coming, because I'm a revolutionary and not a murderer. And how easy it would be to kill him. And he deserves it. Does he? No! What the devil! No one deserves to have someone else make the sacrifice of becoming a murderer. What do you gain by it? Nothing. Others come along and still others, and the first ones kill the second ones and they the next ones and it goes on like this until everything is a sea of blood. I could cut his throat just so, zip! zip! I wouldn't give him time to complain and since he has his eyes closed he wouldn't see the glistening knife

blade or my glistening eyes. But I'm trembling like a real murderer. Out of his neck a gush of blood would spout onto the sheet, on the chair, on my hands, on the floor. I would have to close the door. And the blood would keep inching along the floor, warm, ineradicable, uncontainable, until it reached the street, like a little scarlet stream. I'm sure that one solid stroke, one deep incision, would prevent any pain. He wouldn't suffer. But what would I do with the body? Where would I hide it? I would have to flee, leaving all I have behind, and take refuge far away, far, far away. But they would follow until they found me. "Captain Torres' murderer. He slit his throat while he was shaving him—a coward." And then on the other side. "The avenger of us all. A name to remember. (And here they would mention my name.) He was the town barber. No one knew he was defending our cause."

And what of all this? Murderer or hero? My destiny depended on the edge of this blade. I can turn my hands a bit more, press a little harder on the razor, and sink it in. The skin would give way like silk, like rubber, like the strop. There is nothing more tender than human skin and the blood is always there, ready to pour forth. A blade like this doesn't fail. It is my best. But I don't want to be a murderer, no sir. You came to me for a shave. And I perform my work honorably. . . . I don't want blood on my hands. Just lather, that's all. You are an executioner and I am only a barber. Each person has his own place in the scheme of things. That's right. His own place. [13]

Now his chin had been stroked clean and smooth. The man sat up and looked into the mirror. He rubbed his hands over his skin and felt it fresh, like new. [14]

"Thanks," he said. He went to the hanger for his belt, pistol, and cap. I must have been very pale; my shirt felt soaked. Torres finished adjusting the buckle, straightened his pistol in the holster, and after automatically smoothing down his hair, he put on the cap. From his pants pocket he took out several coins to pay me for my services. And he began to head toward the door. In the doorway he paused for a moment, and turning to me said: [15]

"They told me that you'd kill me. I came to find out. But killing isn't easy. You can take my word for it." And he headed on down the street.

VOCABULARY

ineradicable	not able to be erased
strop	a strip of leather used for sharpening razors

DESIGN AND MEANING

1. Reread the first three sentences of the story. How do they ensnare your interest? What background material do you infer from them?
2. What are your first impressions of the barber and the customer? How do you get those impressions?
3. What is the central conflict? How is it resolved? How does the ending add a new dimension to the conflict?
4. In the barber's thought process, what are the arguments for and against killing his customer?
5. Why is there such sensual description of the customer's skin and hair? Why does the narrator repeat that he is a very good barber?
6. Is the twist at the end a gimmick or a meaningful addition? Explain your answer.

SIMILARITY AND DIFFERENCE

Compare the point of view (whose mind the story is told through) of "Just Lather, That's All" and "The Story of an Hour." Try to rewrite or retell passages from each with the points of view reversed.

SHORT WRITING IDEA

Add one more paragraph to "Just Lather, That's All."

LONGER WRITING IDEA

Write about a time when you had an opportunity to do something you might want to do but that might also conflict with your principles. Trace your thought process as you made your decision.

Classification

"I HAVE TO SORT THIS OUT," you hear people say when they run into one of life's stickier problems. "Julia has no sense of priorities," Julia's friends remark as she buys fresh shrimp with the rent money. And when asked what her next-door neighbor is like, our friend Pam says, "Oh, he's a granola."

A what? Well, it seems as though whenever we encounter an assortment of things—whether ideas or expenses or neighbors—we tend to classify them into tidy groups. It gives us a comforting sense of order and often helps us think straight. We can decide which ideas are most valuable to us in solving a problem; we can choose which expenses are essential and which are not. As for a granola, that's Pam's verbal shorthand for the type of person who takes the baby along in a back carrier on hikes and is building a solar greenhouse—and eats granola, of course.

A classification essay usually devotes one section to each category. The section can stretch from one paragraph to many, but ordinarily the sections on the major categories are about equal in length. Strays here and there that fail to fit into the writer's classification system may be dealt with in the introduction or conclusion. Skillful writers will often develop each section parallel to the others. For example, let's say that Pam jokingly classifies her neighbors into "granolas," "junior execs," and "one-big-happy-families." If she writes that the granolas eat yogurt and zucchini, then she would mention in the junior-exec section that they eat steak and Caesar salad, and she would report in the one-big-happy-family section that they eat casseroles made with cream of mushroom soup and molded Jell-O desserts. This parallel development helps the reader follow the distinctions among the groups and cuts down on the writer's need for transitional devices. (Of course, people defy classification into such handy groupings, and we should avoid forcing stereotypes on them in serious writing.)

One thing you have to be careful about when you classify any topic is choosing your basis for division into categories. Here are some clues that may save you from disaster.

1. **Know the difference between useful and useless bases of division.** Classifying history teachers into those who wear black socks and those who wear dark blue socks is useless. The grouping is not significant because it has nothing to do with teaching or history. But classifying history teachers into those who lecture and those who use a question-discussion format could be significant because it may reveal the teachers' philosophies and their attitudes toward the subject and the students.
2. **The division should cover everything you claim it covers.** If, for instance, you know of several history teachers who are not strictly lecturers and not really question-discussion types either, you can't pretend these people don't exist just to make your classification tidy. At least *mention* exceptions, even if you don't give them as much space as you give the major divisions.
3. **The basis of division should not shift.** If you can see a problem with the classification below, you already understand this warning.

   Types of Aardvarks
   a. The fuzzy aardvark
   b. The hairless aardvark
   c. The friendly aardvark

   Notice that the first two types of aardvarks are divided according to physical characteristics, whereas the last type is defined by its personality. You can see the worry this causes: Can a hairless aardvark be friendly? Are fuzzy aardvarks ill-tempered? How much hair does a friendly aardvark have? It simply won't do.

4. **The divisions should have parallel or equal rank.** The classification below illustrates a problem in rank:

   Types of Recorded Music
   a. Classical
   b. Easy listening
   c. The Rolling Stones

   Although the Rolling Stones do represent a type distinct from classical and easy listening, the category is not parallel to the others—it is far too small. It should be "rock 'n' roll" or "hard rock" with the Rolling Stones used as an example.

5. **The subject and its divisions should be suitable to the length of the essay.** Whole books have been written on the types and qualities of heroes. If you are shooting for a 750-word paper, you should narrow your categories to "Types of Heroes on TV Crime Shows" or "Eliot Rosewater's Heroic Qualities." On the other hand, if you find that you'll be able to devote fewer than fifty words to each classification you've chosen, that is nature's way of telling you to change topics or to consolidate groups.

Also, be sure that you can think of someone who would like to read your essay. Often, classifications are humorous or informative. Try to think of someone or some group who would be amused by your paper or learn from the information.

The classification writing you will read in this chapter demonstrates the wide range possible in style, subject, and purpose. The writing ideas will give you some practice. Before you set pen to paper, though, be sure you know how to spell *category.*

essays

Laurence Sheehan

Fighting Bugs Organically

Lawrence Sheehan, a regular contributor to *Harper's Magazine* and to the *Atlantic Monthly's* "Life and Letters" section, usually writes about sports and gardening. The following selection appeared in *Harper's Magazine* in April of 1979.

A vegetable garden is a lovesome thing, said the poet, but what about bugs and pests? How can we protect our bounty from invaders without resorting to using the pesticides and insecticides that ravage soil and spring leaks in our ozone layer? . . . [1]

There are many effective non-chemical-company methods for debugging the garden. Some are new, some old, but all are safe and sane and may be used without fear of upsetting Nature's balance. Repeat, none are chemical! They have been endorsed by one or more members [of our garden club]. [2]

Hand-to-Hand Combat

We lightly refer to these methods as "hand-to-hand combat" because members are expected to get out into the garden proper and actually fight the pests attacking their crops. [3]

If you have slugs, set out trays of warm beer. Attracted by the yeasty smell, slugs will fall into the trays and drown. Many thanks to our dear friend and neighbor over in Redding, Ruth Stout, for this clever idea, which she dreamed up in '06. [4]

If you have aphids, lay out Reynolds Wrap on the ground around the plants. Caught between skies—one real, one reflected—the aphids become disoriented and shortly drop dead, utterly mad. [5]

The single best hand-to-hand combat method of organic pest control is to pick the bugs off the plants with your fingers. But don't drop them on the ground and trample them or many will survive. Either deposit them in a pail containing laundry detergent (no [6] phosphates, please) and put the lid on it so they will suffocate. Or drop them in kerosene and set a match to it when you have a sufficient quantity.

Hired-Guns Approach

Continuing our "warfare" analogy, this method refers to using natural enemies of the unwanted intruders. Two of our personal favorites are ladybugs and green lacewings. [7]

Ladybugs may be purchased by mail order for less than $1 per thousand. They devour forty to fifty aphids per day. The down side is you may have to buy in *aphids* come August, to keep your ladybugs fat and happy. [8]

Green lacewings are excellent against scale insects and mealybugs. They lay eggs at night and their babies look like tiny alligators when they hatch. They also may be obtained in quantity from a reputable entomologist. It is impressive to see them tearing through a mealybug infestation. [9]

Praying mantises make another good gardener's ally, as they will destroy any and all caterpillars or mites that you "mite" have in the garden. We don't count them among our favorites simply because they terrify us and they have ever since we were children. [10]

Other creatures that will keep your slug and snail population to a minimum, and therefore should be welcomed in the garden, are geese, ducks, snakes, shrews, and bats. [11]

Biological Warfare

Now we come to some more recent trends in nonchemical pest control. [12]

Special sicknesses have been developed that attack two of the organic gardener's most persistent enemies—the cabbage worm and the Japanese beetle. [13]

Bacillus thuringiensis is the one to order for your cabbage worms. It comes in spray form and should be applied directly to the soil at the base of plants. Soon your worms catch a kind of terminal whooping cough. *Bacillus thuringiensis* is said to be as devastating in its limited range (unfortunately, only cabbage worms are vulnerable) as was the Plague of Middle Ages lore and legend. [14]

Milky spore disease (trade name Doom) is your choice for Japanese beetles. It should be introduced into the garden soil and surrounding lawn areas in the fall. It turns the young larvae of the beetles completely white while they are trying to hibernate, and they do not live to see another spring. [15]

One drawback to milky spore is it does nothing about *this* year's [16] beetles. To deal with them, we recommend trying a method based on the recent discovery that when a beetle is suffering a violent death, it emits a noxious element that can be collected and used as a toxic dose against other beetles.

[17] Here's how to go about it. Take a dozen mature beetles and put them in your blender with a tablespoon of lukewarm water. Set on "coarse chop" for ninety seconds. If you have a Cuisinart, use the No. 3 setting. Take the resulting batch, add a quart of water, mix thoroughly, and transfer to your home sprayer. Now spray garden areas where the beetles are feeding. Watch them drop!

Conclusion

[18] Science marches on. We have recently read that it may not be long before the only thing we'll have to do to control insects in the garden is to plant the correct hybrids of the vegetables we want. For example, researchers have now developed a type of bush bean that has long hairs on it that actually catch leafhoppers and strangle them before they can eat the beans. Is it unrealistic, then, to hope for a new pepper plant variety that will come with its own natural anti-aircraft system to stave off wasps, or a breed of corn with tiny land mines here and there among the kernels, to get the crows?

[19] In the meantime, we must depend on the various pest-management methods previously discussed to keep garden and conscience clear during the growing season.

VOCABULARY

analogy	an explanation based on comparison
disoriented	mentally confused
entomologist	a person who studies insects
lore	traditional knowledge on a certain subject
shrew	a small, mouselike mammal

DESIGN AND MEANING

1. Sheehan uses the word *we* and its forms to refer to himself. This is a convention called the *editorial "we"* which was common in the days when use of the word *I* was considered too informal for essayists and use of *one* to refer to the writer was too formal to suit the purpose. The *editorial "we"* still crops up once in a while today, as it does in this selection. What do you think of it? Would you prefer that he had used *I* or *one*? Why or why not?

2. What are the three parts of Sheehan's classification?
3. How is the warfare analogy carried through the essay?
4. Point out several elements of Sheehan's writing that reflect his personality and humor.

SIMILARITY AND DIFFERENCE

Does this section fulfill the requirements of a good process essay? Which selection in Chapter 5 is it most like?

SHORT WRITING IDEA

In outline form, classify the cartoon strips in your Sunday funny papers.

LONGER WRITING IDEA

Write an essay describing three methods of doing something—studying, getting breakfast, cleaning your room, writing an essay, or driving parents crazy during a car trip, for example.

Judith Viorst

Friends, Good Friends—and Such Good Friends

Judith Viorst, a successful journalist who also publishes light verse, is a contributing editor of *Redbook* magazine. Her articles usually concern the problems of married couples in dealing with each other and with their children. The following essay first appeared in *Redbook* in 1977.

Women are friends, I once would have said, when they totally love and support and trust each other, and bare to each other the secrets of their souls, and run—no questions asked—to help each other, and tell harsh truths to each other (no, you can't wear that dress unless you lose ten pounds first) when harsh truths must be told. [1]

Women are friends, I once would have said, when they share the same affection for Ingmar Bergman, plus train rides, cats, warm rain, charades, Camus, and hate with equal ardor Newark and Brussels sprouts and Lawrence Welk and camping. [2]

In other words, I once would have said that a friend is a friend all the way, but now I believe that's a narrow point of view. For the friendships I have and the friendships I see are conducted at many levels of intensity, serve many different functions, meet different needs and range from those as all-the-way as the friendship of the soul sisters mentioned above to that of the most nonchalant and casual playmates. [3]

Consider these varieties of friendship: [4]

1. Convenience friends. These are the women with whom, if our paths weren't crossing all the time, we'd have no particular reason to be friends: a next-door neighbor, a woman in our car pool, the mother of one of our children's closest friends or maybe some mommy with whom we serve juice and cookies each week at the Glenwood Co-op Nursery. [5]

Convenience friends are convenient indeed. They'll lend us their cups and silverware for a party. They'll drive our kids to soccer when we're sick. They'll take us to pick up our car when we need a lift to the garage. They'll even take our cats when we go on vacation. As we will for them. [6]

But we don't, with convenience friends, ever come too close or tell too much; we maintain our public face and emotional distance. "Which means," says Elaine, "that I'll talk about being overweight but not about being depressed. Which means I'll admit being mad but not blind with rage. Which means that I might say that we're pinched this month but never that I'm worried sick over money." [7]

But which doesn't mean that there isn't sufficient value to be found in these friendships of mutual aid, in convenience friends. [8]

2. Special-interest friends. These friendships aren't intimate, and they needn't involve kids or silverware or cats. Their value lies in some interest jointly shared. And so we may have an office friend or a yoga friend or a tennis friend or a friend from the Women's Democratic Club. [9]

"I've got one woman friend," says Joyce, "who likes, as I do, to take psychology courses. Which makes it nice for me—and nice for her. It's fun to go with someone you know and it's fun to discuss what you've learned, driving back from the classes." And for the most part, she says, that's all they discuss. [10]

"I'd say that what we're doing is *doing* together, not being together," Suzanne says of her Tuesday-doubles friends. "It's mainly a tennis relationship, but we play together well. And I guess we all need to have a couple of playmates." [11]

I agree. [12]

My playmate is a shopping friend, a woman of marvelous taste, a woman who knows exactly *where* to buy *what,* and furthermore is a woman who always knows beyond a doubt what one ought to be buying. I don't have the time to keep up with what's new in eyeshadow, hemlines and shoes and whether the smock look is in or finished already. But since (oh, shame!) I care a lot about eyeshadow, hemlines and shoes, and since I don't *want* to wear smocks if the smock look is finished, I'm very glad to have a shopping friend. [13]

3. Historical friends. We all have a friend who knew us when . . . maybe way back in Miss Meltzer's second grade, when our family lived in that three-room flat in Brooklyn, when our dad was out of work for seven months, when our brother Allie got in that fight where they had to call the police, when our sister married the endodontist from Yonkers and when, the morning after we lost our virginity, she was the first, the only, friend we told. [14]

The years have gone by and we've gone separate ways and we've little in common now, but we're still an intimate part of each other's past. And so whenever we go to Detroit we always go to visit this friend of our girlhood. Who knows how we looked before our teeth were straightened. Who knows how we talked before our voice got [15] un-Brooklyned. Who knows what we ate before we learned about artichokes. And who, by her presence, puts us in touch with an earlier part of ourself, a part of ourself it's important never to lose.

[16] "What this friend means to me and what I mean to her," says Grace, "is having a sister without sibling rivalry. We know the texture of each other's lives. She remembers my grandmother's cabbage soup. I remember the way her uncle played the piano. There's simply no other friend who remembers those things."

[17] 4. Crossroads friends. Like historical friends, our crossroads friends are important for *what was*—for the friendship we shared at a crucial, now past, time of life. A time, perhaps, when we roomed in college together; or worked as eager young singles in the Big City together; or went together, as my friend Elizabeth and I did, through pregnancy, birth and that scary first year of new motherhood.

[18] Crossroads friends forge powerful links, links strong enough to endure with not much more contact than once-a-year letters at Christmas. And out of respect for those crossroads years, for those dramas and dreams we once shared, we will always be friends.

[19] 5. Cross-generational friends. Historical friends and crossroads friends seem to maintain a special kind of intimacy—dormant but always ready to be revived—and though we may rarely meet, whenever we do connect, it's personal and intense. Another kind of intimacy exists in the friendships that form across generations in what one woman calls her daughter-mother and her mother-daughter relationships.

[20] Evelyn's friend is her mother's age—"but I share so much more than I ever could with my mother"—a woman she talks to of music, of books, and of life. "What I get from her is the benefit of her experience. What she gets—and enjoys—from me is a youthful perspective. It's a pleasure for both of us."

[21] I have in my own life a precious friend, a woman of 65 who has lived very hard, who is wise, who listens well; who has been where I am and can help me understand it; and who represents not only an ultimate ideal mother to me but also the person I'd like to be when I grow up.

[22] In our daughter role we tend to do more than our share of self-revelation; in our mother role we tend to receive what's revealed. It's another kind of pleasure—playing a wise mother to a questing younger person. It's another very lovely kind of friendship.

[23] 6. Part-of-a-couple friends. Some of the women we call our friends we never see alone—we see them as part of a couple at couples' parties. And though we share interests in many things and respect each other's views, we aren't moved to deepen the relationship. Whatever the reason, a lack of time or—and this is more

likely—a lack of chemistry, our friendship remains in the context of a group. But the fact that our feeling on seeing each other is always, "I'm *so* glad she's here" and the fact that we spend half the evening talking together says that this too, in its own way, counts as a friendship.

[24] (Other part-of-a-couple friends are the friends that came with the marriage, and some of these are friends we could live without. But sometimes, alas, she married our husband's best friend; and sometimes, alas, she *is* our husband's best friend. And so we find ourself dealing with her, somewhat against our will, in a spirit of what I'll call *reluctant* friendship.)

[25] 7. Men who are friends. I wanted to write just of women friends, but the women I've talked to won't let me—they say I must mention man-woman friendships too. For these friendships can be just as close and as dear as those that we form with women. Listen to Lucy's description of one such friendship:

[26] "We've found we have things to talk about that are different from what he talks about with my husband and different from what I talk about with his wife. So sometimes we call on the phone or meet for lunch. There are similar intellectual interests—we always pass on to each other the books that we love—but there's also something tender and caring too."

[27] In a couple of crises, Lucy says, "he offered himself, for talking and for helping. And when someone died in his family he wanted me there. The sexual, flirty part of our friendship is very small, but *some*—just enough to make it fun and different." She thinks—and I agree—that the sexual part, though small, is always *some,* is always there when a man and a woman are friends.

[28] It's only in the past few years that I've made friends with men, in the sense of a friendship that's *mine,* not just part of two couples. And achieving with them the ease and the trust I've found with women friends has value indeed. Under the dryer at home last week, putting on mascara and rouge, I comfortably sat and talked with a fellow named Peter. Peter, I finally decided, could handle the shock of me minus mascara under the dryer. Because we care for each other. Because we're friends.

[29] 8. There are medium friends, and pretty good friends, and very good friends indeed, and these friendships are defined by their level of intimacy. And what we'll reveal at each of these levels of intimacy is calibrated with care. We might tell a medium friend, for example, that yesterday we had a fight with our husband. And we might tell a pretty good friend that this fight with our husband made us so mad that we slept on the couch. And we might tell a very good friend that the reason we got so mad in that fight that we slept on the couch had something to do with that girl who works in his office.

But it's only to our very best friends that we're willing to tell all, to tell what's going on with that girl in his office.

The best of friends, I still believe, totally love and support and trust each other, and bare to each other the secrets of their souls, and run—no questions asked—to help each other, and tell harsh truths to each other when they must be told. [30]

But we needn't agree about everything (only 12-year-old girl friends agree about *everything*) to tolerate each other's point of view. To accept without judgment. To give and to take without ever keeping score. And to *be* there, as I am for them and as they are for me, to comfort our sorrows, to celebrate our joys. [31]

DESIGN AND MEANING

1. How does Viorst signal the division points in this classification? What are some alternative methods? Why do you think she chose this method?
2. In the opening of the essay, what ideas does Viorst say she is giving up? How does this rejection lead into her thesis? How does the opening relate to the closing paragraphs?
3. Within the classification, Viorst develops her points through narration, definition, example and illustration, comparison and contrast, and cause-and-effect reasoning. Find one example of each kind of development.
4. Identify three passages in which the writer uses repetition of phrases or sentence structure. Why is the repetition acceptable instead of awkward?

SIMILARITY AND DIFFERENCE

What similarities in form can you find among all the essay selections in this chapter?

SHORT WRITING IDEA

Using Viorst's classification system, sort your own friends into categories. Do the categories also apply to your friends? If not, invent and describe a new category to suit yourself.

LONGER WRITING IDEA

Viorst writes of different intensities of friendship. There are also different intensities of aversion (dislike). Write an essay classifying aversions—to foods, teachers, doctors, social situations, violence, or anything that brings out various levels of distaste in people.

PREREADING EXERCISE

As part of an interplanetary exchange program, an extraterrestrial being comes to live with you. What types of things in your everyday life will you need to explain?

Betty Lee Sung

Bicultural Conflict

Born in Baltimore, Sung teaches Asian studies at City College of New York. She has written extensively on the problems of Chinese immigrants in the United States and the adjustments that their descendants are still making. She sees research on the expanding Chinese-American population as fascinating and important.

[1] The moment a child is born, he begins to absorb the culture of his primary group; these ways are so ingrained they become a second nature to him. Imagine for a moment how wrenching it must be for an immigrant child who finds his cumulative life experiences completely invalidated, and who must learn a whole new set of speech patterns and behaviors when he settles in a new country. The severity of this culture shock is underlined by Teper's definition of culture:

> [2] Culture is called a habit system in which "truths" that have been perpetuated by a group over centuries have permeated the unconscious. This basic belief system, from which "rational" conclusions spring, may be so deeply ingrained that it becomes indistinguishable from human perception—the way one sees, feels, believes, knows. It is the continuity of cultural assumptions and patterns that gives order to one's world, reduces an infinite variety of options to a manageable stream of beliefs, gives a person a firm footing in time and space, and binds the lone individual to the communality of a group.

[3] The language barrier was the problem most commonly mentioned by the immigrant Chinese among whom I have conducted field research. Language looms largest because it is the conduit through which people interact with other people. It is the means by which we think, learn, and express ourselves. Less obvious is the basis upon which we speak or act or think. If there are bicultural conflicts, these may engender problems and psychological difficulties, which may not be immediately apparent but may nevertheless impact on the development of immigrant children.

[4] This article will address some of the cultural conflicts that commonly confront the Chinese child in the home and, particularly, in the schools. Oftentimes, teachers and parents are not aware of these conflicts and ascribe other meanings or other motives to the

child's behavior, frequently in a disapproving fashion. Such censure confuses the child and quite often forces him to choose between what he is taught at home and what is commonly accepted by American society. In his desire to be accepted and to be liked, he may want to throw off that which is second nature to him; this may cause anguish and pain not only to himself but also to his parents and family. Teachers and parents should be aware of these differences and try to help the children resolve their conflicts, instead of exacerbating them.

Aggressiveness and Sexuality

[5] In Chinese culture, the soldier, or the man who resorts to violence, is at the bottom of the social ladder. The sage or gentleman uses his wits, not his fists. So the Chinese child is taught not to fight. The American father will take his son out to the backyard and give him a few lessons in self-defense at the age of puberty. He teaches his son that the ability to fight is a sign of manhood. The Chinese parent teaches his son the exact opposite: Stay out of fights. Yet, when the Chinese child goes to the school playground, he becomes the victim of bullies who pick on him and call him a sissy. New York's teenagers can be pretty tough and cruel. If the child goes home with bruises and a black eye, his parents will yell at him and chastise him. What is he to do? The unresolved conflict about aggressive behavior is a major problem for Chinese-American males. They feel that their masculinity has been affected by their childhood upbringing.

[6] What do the teachers or monitors do? In most instances, they are derisive of the Chinese boys. "Why don't the Chinese fight back?" they exclaim. "Why do they stand there and just take it?" This derision only shames the Chinese boys, who feel that their courage is questioned. This bicultural conflict may be reflected in the self-hatred of some Asian-American male activists who condemn the passivity of our forefathers in response to the discrimination and oppression they endured. Ignorant about their cultural heritage, the activists want to disassociate themselves from such "weakness," and they search for historical instances in which Asians put up a brave but costly and oftentimes futile fight to prove their manhood. The outbreak of gang violence may be another manifestation of the Chinese male's efforts to prove that he is "macho" also. He may be overcompensating for the derision that he has suffered.

[7] In American schools, sexuality is a very strong and pervasive force. Boys and girls start noticing each other in the junior highs; at the high school level, sexual awareness is very pronounced. School is as much a place for male/female socialization as it is an

institution for learning. Not so for the Chinese. Education is highly valued, and it is a serious business. To give their children an opportunity for a better education may be the primary reason why the parents push their children to study, study, study. Interest in the opposite sex is highly distracting and, according to some old-fashioned parents, improper. Dating is an unfamiliar concept and sexual attractiveness is underplayed, not flaunted as it is according to American ways.

This difference in attitudes and customs poses another dilemma for both the Chinese boys and girls. In school, the white, black, or Hispanic girls like to talk about clothes, makeup, and the dates they had over the weekend. They talk about brassiere sizes and tampons. The popular girl is the sexy one who dates the most. She is the envy of the other girls. [8]

For the Chinese girl, the openness with which other girls discuss boys and sex is extremely embarrassing. Chinese girls used to bind their breasts, not show them off in tight sweaters. Their attitude toward the opposite sex is quite ambivalent. They feel that they are missing something very exciting when other girls talk about phone calls from their boyfriends or about their dates over the weekends, yet they will shy away and feel very uncomfortable if a boy shows an interest in them. [9]

Most Chinese parents have had no dating experience. Their marriages were usually arranged by their own parents or through matchmakers. Good girls simply did not go out with boys alone, so the parents are very suspicious and apprehensive about their daughters dating, and they watch them very carefully. Most Chinese girls are not permitted to date, and for the daring girl who tries to go out against her parents' wishes, there will be a price to pay. [10]

It is no easier for Chinese boys. The pressure to succeed in school is even greater than for girls, and parental opposition to dating is even more intense. Naturally, the parents want their children to adhere to the old ways. Some children do not agree with their parents and have to carry on their high school romances on the sly. These children are bombarded by television, advertisements, stories, magazines, and real-life examples of boy-girl attraction. The teenager is undergoing puberty and experiencing the instinctive urges surging within him or her. In this society they are titillated, whereas in China they are kept under wraps until they are married. [11]

The problem is exacerbated when teachers make fun of Chinese customs and the parents. I saw an instance of this at one of the Chinatown schools. A young Chinese girl had been forbidden by her parents to walk to school with a young Puerto Rican boy who [12] was in the habit of accompanying her every day. To make sure that the parents were being obeyed, the grandmother would walk behind the girl to see that she did not walk with the boy. Grandma even hung around until her granddaughter went into class, and then she would peer through the window to make sure all was proper before she went home.

[13] Naturally, this was embarrassing for the girl, and it must have been noticed by the homeroom teacher. He exploded in anger at the little old lady and made some rather uncomplimentary remarks about this being the United States and that Chinese customs should have been left in China. To my mind, this teacher's attitude and remarks could only push the daughter farther away from her parents. What he could have done was explain to the girl, or even to the entire class, the cultural values and traditions of her parents, so that she could understand how they thought and why they behaved in such a fashion. Putting down the parents and their customs is the worst thing he could have done.

Sports

[14] The Chinese attitude toward sports is illustrated by an oft-told joke about two Englishmen who were considered somewhat mad. The two lived in Shanghai where they had gone to do business. In the afternoons, they would each take a racquet, go out in the hot sun, and bat a fuzzy ball across the net. As they ran back and forth across the court, sweat would pour from their faces, and they would be exhausted at the end of the game. To the Chinese onlookers standing on the side, this was sheer lunacy. They would shake their heads in disbelief and ask: "Why do these crazy Englishmen work so hard? They can afford to hire coolies to run around and hit the ball for them." The Chinese attitude toward sports has changed considerably, but it still does not assume the importance that it enjoys in American life.

[15] Turn on any news program on radio or television, and you will find one-third of the air time devoted to sports. Who are the school heroes? The football quarterback, the track star, the baseball pitcher. What are the big events in school? The games. What is used to rally school spirit? The games.

[16] Yet in the traditional Chinese way of thinking, development of the mental faculties was more important than development of the physique. The image of a scholar was one with a sallow face and long fingernails, indicating that he spent long hours with his books and had not had to do physical labor. Games that required brute strength, such as football and boxing, were not even played in China. Kung fu or other disciplines of the martial arts did not call

for physical strength as much as concentration, skill, and agility. In the minds of many Chinese, sports are viewed as frivolous play and a waste of time and energy. Add to this the generally smaller physique of the Chinese immigrant student in comparison to his classmates, and we do not find many of them on any of the school teams.

What does this mean to the Chinese immigrant students, especially the boys? On the one hand, they may think that the heavy emphasis upon sports is a displaced value. They may want to participate, but they are either too small in stature or unable to devote the time necessary for practice to make the school teams. If the "letter men" are the big wheels, the Chinese student will feel that his kind are just the little guys. But most important of all, an entire dimension of American school is lost to the Chinese immigrant children. [17]

Tattling

Should one report a wrongdoing? Should one tell the teacher that a schoolmate is cheating on his exam? Should one report to the school authorities that a fellow student is trying to extort money from him? The American values on this score are ambiguous and confusing. For example, in the West Point scandal a few years ago, most of the cadets involved were not cheaters themselves, but they knew about the cheating and did not report it to the authorities. Their honor code required that they tell, but the unwritten code among their fellow cadets said that they should not tattle or "fink." If they had reported the cheating of their fellow cadets they would have been socially ostracized. There is a dilemma for the American here as well. [18]

This bicultural conflict was noted by Denise Kandel and Gerald S. Lesser in the book, *Youth in Two Worlds,* in which their reference groups were Danish and American children. The Danish children, like the Chinese, feel duty bound to report wrongdoing. There is no dichotomy of consequences here. Authorities and peers are consistent in their attitude in this respect, and this consistency helps to maintain social control. The teacher cannot be expected to have four pairs of eyes and see everything. The parents cannot be everywhere at once to know what their child is doing during the day. If the siblings or schoolmates will help by reporting wrongdoing, the task of teaching the child is shared and made easier for the adults. But when social ostracism stands in the way of enforcing ethical values, an intense conflict ensues and contributes to the breakdown of social control. [19]

Demonstration of Affection

[20] A commonly voiced concern among Chinese children is, "My parents do not love me. They never kiss or hug me. They are so cold, distant, and remote." The children long for human warmth and affection because they see it on the movie and television screens, and they read about it in books and magazines. Because their experiences with mother and father and the other members of the family as well are so formal and distant, they come to the conclusion that love is lacking. In China, where such behavior is the norm, children do not question it. But in this country, where expressions of affection are outwardly effusive and commonly exhibited, they feel deprived.

[21] This lack of demonstrative affection extends also to the spouse and friends. To the Chinese, physical intimacy and love are private matters never exhibited in public. Even in handshaking, the traditional Chinese way was to clasp one's own hands in greeting. Kissing and hugging a friend would be most inappropriate, and to kiss one's spouse in public would be considered shameless and ill-mannered.

[22] Nevertheless, Chinese children in this country are attracted to the physical expressions of love and affection. While they crave it for themselves, they are often unable to reciprocate or be demonstrative in their relations with their own spouses, children, or friends because of their detached emotional upbringing.

[23] In the schools, this contrast in culture is made all the sharper because of the large numbers of Hispanics. In general, the Hispanics are very outgoing and are not the least bit inhibited about embracing, holding hands, or kissing even a casual acquaintance. The Chinese children may interpret these gestures of friendliness as overstepping the bounds of propriety, but more often than not they wish they could shed their reserve and reach out to others in a more informal manner.

[24] On the other hand, the aloofness of the Chinese students is often wrongly interpreted as unfriendliness, standoffishness, as a desire to keep apart. If all the students in the schools were made aware of these cultural differences, they would not misread the intentions and behavior of one another.

Education

[25] That education is a highly prized cultural value among the Chinese is commonly known, and the fact that Chinese children generally do well scholastically may be due to the hard push parents exert in this direction. None of this means, however, that these children do not experience a bicultural conflict regarding education when they

see that the bright student is not the one who is respected and looked up to in American schools. Labels such as "bookworm," "egghead," and "teacher's pet" are applied to the intelligent students, and these terms are not laudatory, but derisive. When parents urge their children to study hard and get good grades, the children know that the payoff will not be social acceptance by their schoolmates. The rewards are not consistent with values taught at home.

Nevertheless, the Chinese immigrant high school students indicated in their survey questionnaire that they prized the opportunity to get an education. In fact, they identified the opportunity to get a free education as one of the most important reasons why they are satisfied with their schoolwork. Of 143 students who said that they were satisfied with their schoolwork, 135 mentioned this one factor. Education is not easily available to everyone in China, Hong Kong, or Taiwan. It is attained at great personal sacrifice on the part of the parents. It is costly and it is earned by diligence and industry on the part of the student. In this country, school is free through high school. Everyone has to go to school until sixteen years of age in New York, for example. It is not a matter of students trying to gain admittance by passing rigorous entrance exams, but a matter of the authorities trying to keep the dropout rates low that characterizes the educational system here. [26]

This is ground also for conflict, however, since what is free and easy to get is often taken lightly. New York State's academic standards are lower than those in Hong Kong or Taiwan, and the schoolwork is easier to keep up with. As a result, there is less distinction attached to being able to stay in school or graduate. What the Chinese immigrant students prize highly has less value in the larger society, and again the newcomers to this country start to have doubts about the goals that they are striving for. [27]

Thrift

Twelve, perhaps thirteen, banks can be found within the small core area of New York's Chinatown. When the Manhattan Savings Bank opened a new branch in October 1977 it attracted to its coffers $3 million within a few months' time. Most of the large banks are aware that Chinatown is fertile ground for the accumulation of capital because the Chinese tend to save more of what they earn than other ethnic groups in America, in spite of the fact that their earnings are small. [28]

Two major factors encourage the growth of savings among Chinese immigrants. One is the sense of insecurity common to all immigrants, who need a cushion for the uncertainties that they feel acutely. The other is the esteem with which thrift is regarded by [29] the Chinese. A person who is frugal is thought of more highly than is one who can sport material symbols of success.

[30] I was once sent on an assignment to cover the story of a very wealthy Chinese man from Bangkok who was reputed to own shipping lines, rice mills, and many other industries. He was a special guest of the United States Department of State, and that evening he was to be honored at the Waldorf-Astoria. I found this gentleman in a very modestly-priced midtown hotel. When he extended his hand to shake mine, I saw that his suit sleeves were frayed.

[31] The value placed upon thrift poses acute bicultural conflict for Chinese immigrant children who see all about them evidence of an economic system that encourages the accumulation and conspicuous consumption of material possessions. A very important segment of the consumer market is now the teenage population. The urge to have stylish clothes, a stereo, a camera, a hi-fi-radio, sports equipment, and even a car creates a painful conflict in the child who is enticed by television and other advertising media, but whose parents reserve a large percentage of their meager earnings for stashing away in the banks.

[32] In school, the girl who gets money to spend on fashionable dresses and the latest rock record feels more poised and confident about herself than do her less materially fortunate classmates. She is also admired, complimented, and envied. In the Chinese community, on the other hand, a Chinese girl who spent a lot of money on clothes and frivolities would soon be the object of grapevine gossip, stigmatized as a less-than-desirable prospective wife or daughter-in-law, whereas praises would be sung for the more modestly dressed girl who saved her money.

[33] From my students I hear a commonly voiced complaint about their parents as "money-hungry." They give their children very little spending money. They do not buy fashionable clothing; rather, they buy only serviceable garments in which the children are ashamed to be seen. The Chinese home is generally not furnished for comfort or aesthetics, so when Chinese children visit the homes of their non-Chinese friends and compare them with their own living quarters, they feel deprived and ashamed of their parents and their family. They certainly do not want to bring their friends home to play, and the teenagers may themselves stay away from home as much as possible, feeling more comfortable with their peers in clubhouses or on the streets.

[34] The contrast in spending attitudes between the underdeveloped economy from which many Chinese immigrants have come and the American economy, which emphasizes mass and even wasteful consumption, is very sharp, and it creates many an unresolved conflict in the children, who do not realize that cultural differences lie

behind it. They think that their parents value money more than they care for their children, and exhibit this by denying material possessions that give them pleasure and status in the eyes of their peers.

[35] Credit is another concept foreign to immigrants from the Far East. If one does not have the money, one should not be tempted to buy. Credit is borrowing money, and borrowing should be resorted to only in extreme emergencies. The buy now, pay later idea goes against the Chinese grain. So the Chinese families postpone buying until they have saved up enough to cover the entire purchase price. This attitude is fairly common even when it comes to the purchase of a home. The family will scrimp and economize, putting aside a large portion of its income for this goal, denying itself small pleasures along the way for many, many years until the large sum is accumulated. To the Chinese way of thinking, this singleness of purpose shows character, but to the more hedonistic American mind, this habit of thrift may appear asinine and unnecessary.

Dependency

[36] In her study, "Socialization Patterns among the Chinese in Hawaii," Nancy F. Young noted the prolonged period of dependency of the children commonly found in the child-rearing practices of the Chinese in Hawaii. She wrote:

> Observations of Chinese families in Hawaii indicate that both immigrant and local parents utilize child-rearing techniques that result in parent-oriented, as opposed to peer-oriented, behavior . . . . Chinese parents maximize their control over their children by limiting their experiences with models exhibiting nonsanctioned behavior.

Analyzing and comparing the results of the Chance Independence Training Questionnaire that she administered to six ethnic groups and local (American-born) Chinese as well as immigrant Chinese, she found the mean age of independent training for American-born Chinese to be the lowest (6.78 years), while that for immigrant Chinese to be the highest (8.85 years). Among other ethnic groups in Young's study, the mean age of independence training ranged as follows: Jewish, 6.83; Protestant, 6.87 years; Negro, 7.23 years; Greek, 7.67 years; French-Canadian 7.99 years; and Italian, 8.03 years.

[38] Immigrant mothers exercise constant and strict supervision over their children. They take the children wherever they go, and babysitters are unheard of. They prefer their children to stay home rather than go out to play with their friends. Friends are carefully screened by the mother, and the child is not expected to do things

for himself until about two years beyond the mean age that a Jewish mother would expect her child to do for himself.

[39] On the other hand, American-born Chinese parents expect their children to cut the apron strings sooner than any of the other ethnic groups surveyed. Young did not elaborate and explain why, but it seems that Chinese parents who are American-born have assimilated the American values of independence at an early age and may even have gone overboard in rearing their own children. There are areas of dependence and independence in which Young found divergence. The immigrant Chinese child is expected to be able to take care of himself at an earlier age, but he is discouraged from socializing with people outside the family until a much later age.

[40] The extremes exhibited between the American-born and immigrant Chinese may be indicative of the bicultural conflict that the Chinese in this country feel. As children, they may have felt that their parents were overprotective; this was frequently mentioned by the teachers to whom we talked. We saw evidence of this in the elementary schools—the previously mentioned practice of mothers coming to the school from the garment factories during their own lunch hours to feed their children lunch. Many walked their children to and from school, even as late as the junior high level, but it was not clear to us whether the parents were justifiably afraid for their children's safety from the gangs or whether they were being overprotective. The teachers thought the mothers were smothering the children and restricting their freedom of action. By adolescence, the children must have felt the same. They were chafing against parental control over what they presumed to be their own business, while the parents thought they were merely doing their parental duty.

[41] Teachers and parents do not agree on this score, with the result that parental authority is often undermined by a teacher's scoffing attitude. A personal experience of my own reveals how damaging this can be to a parent's ability to maintain some kind of control over the growing teenager.

[42] My seventeen-year-old son was coming home late at night, and I found it hard to fall asleep until he was home. I did not feel that he should be up so late, nor did I wish my sleep to be disturbed. My son objected strenuously to a curfew of midnight during the week and 1 A.M. on the weekends. His objection was based on the fact that no other teenagers he knew had such restrictions, that most get-togethers did not get going until 11 P.M., and that he would be the "wet blanket" if he left early. I understood his concerns and tried to get the parents of his friends to agree to a uniform time when the group should break up and go home to bed. I felt that if everybody had to go, my son would not mind leaving.

To my utter surprise, not one of the parents felt that boys or girls of seventeen years of age should have a curfew. They felt that I was being too strict and overprotective and that it was time for me to cut the apron strings. The worst part of it was that my conversation with the parents got back to my son, who immediately and gleefully confronted me with, "See, none of the other parents agree with you. You are the only old-fashioned, strict one." This lack of understanding on the part of the other parents in telling my son about our conversation undermined my authority. From that day, I was unable to set hours for him anymore. [43]

The Chinese value of respect for one's elders and for authority is common knowledge and needs no further elaboration here. We have already mentioned that the Chinese immigrant children encountering the disrespect accorded teachers and school authorities for the first time in American classrooms find themselves extremely upset and dismayed. In our interviews with the students, this concern was voiced frequently. [44]

Challenging established authority has been a notable feature of youth culture over the past two decades. The parents, the teachers, the police, the government, the church—all authority figures in the past—have been knocked down and even reviled. Violence against teachers is the leading problem in schools across the nation. If students do not have respect for the teacher, neither will they have respect for the knowledge that the teacher tries to impart. The issue is a disturbing one, not only for the immigrant children but for the entire American society as well. [45]

Heroes, Heroines, and Individualism

Who are the people who are praised, admired, looked up to, and revered? The idols of different cultures are themselves different types of people, and the values of a society may be deduced from the type of people who are respected and emulated in that culture. In the United States, the most popular figures are movie, television, and stage stars, sports figures, politicians, successful authors, inventors, and scientists; probably in that order. Who are the heroes and heroines of China? If we use literature as a guide, they are the filial sons or daughters, the sacrificing mother, the loyal minister, the patriot or war hero who saves his country, and revolutionaries who overthrow despotic rulers and set up their own dynasties. Even in modern China, the persons honored and emulated are the self-sacrificing workers who put nation above self. [46]

Priests, ministers, and rabbis once commanded prestige in this country, but the status of these men of God has declined. In China, monks or priests have always occupied lowly positions. In contrast [47] to the United States, in China actors are riffraff. Women did not act in the theater, so men had to play the female roles. Western influence has brought about changes in the pseudo-Chinese cultures of Hong Kong and Singapore and stage performers and movie stars are now popular and emulated, but this was not always so.

[48] As a rule, Chinese heroes and heroines were people of high moral virtues, and they set the standards of conduct for others. In this country, the more sensational the exposé of the private lives of our national leaders or entertainment figures, the more our curiosity is aroused. How movie stars retain their popularity in spite of the relentless campaigns to strip them naked is very difficult for someone not brought up in the United States to comprehend. An old adage says, "No man is a hero to his valet." Yet, the very fact that American heroes and heroines survive and thrive on notoriety and self-confession can only mean that the American people admire such behavior. One might say, Chinese heroes are saints; American heroes are sinners.

[49] Noted anthropologist Francis L.K. Hsu has written extensively about individualism as a prominent characteristic of American life. According to Hsu, the basic ingredient of rugged individualism is self-reliance. The individual constantly tells himself and others that he controls his own destiny and that he does not need help from others. The individual-centered person enjoins himself to find means of fulfilling his own desires and ambitions.

[50] Individualism is the driving force behind the competitiveness and creativity that has pushed this nation forward. Loose family ties, superficial human relationships, little community control, and weak traditions have given the individual leeway to strike out on his own without being hindered by sentimentality, convention, and tradition. Self-interest has been a powerful incentive.

[51] In contrast, Dr. Hsu contends, the Chinese are situation-centered. Their way of life encourages the individual to find a satisfactory adjustment with the external environment of men and things. The Chinese individual sees the world in relativistic terms. He is dependent upon others and others are dependent upon him. Like bricks in a wall, one lends support to the other and they all hold up the society as a whole. If even one brick becomes loose, the wall is considerably weakened; interlocked, the wall is strong. The wall is the network of human relations. The individual subordinates his own wishes and ambitions for the common good.

[52] Dr. Kenneth Abbott, in his book *Harmony and Individualism,* also points out that the Western ideas of creativity and individualism are not accented in Chinese and must be held within accepted norms. One of the reasons for this is the importance ascribed to maintenance of harmony. Harmony is the key concept in all rela-

tionships between god(s) and man and between man and man. It is the highest good.

To the Chinese, the sense of duty and obligation takes precedence over self-gratification. It is not uncommon to find Chinese teenagers handing over their entire paychecks to their parents for family use or for young Chinese males to pursue a course of study chosen for them by their parents rather than one of their own choosing. Responsibility toward distant kin is more keenly felt by the Chinese than by other Americans. Honor and glory accrue not only to the individual but to all those who helped him climb the ladder. This sense of being part of something greater than oneself gives the Chinese a feeling of belonging and security in the knowledge that they do not stand alone. On the other hand, individual freedom of action is very much restricted. [53]

Some of the better known problems that confront a Chinese immigrant to these shores, such as respect for elders, modesty and humility, and male superiority, were omitted here because they have been dealt with at length elsewhere. The foregoing examples—aggressiveness, sexuality, sports, tattling, demonstration of affection, education, thrift, independence training, respect for authority, heros and heroines, and individualism—represent other important areas of bicultural conflict that confront Chinese newcomers to these shores. [54]

VOCABULARY

asinine — lacking in common sense
conduit — channel
hedonistic — devoted to pleasure

DESIGN AND MEANING

1. How does Sung establish who her main audience is?
2. What categories of bicultural conflict are discussed in the essay? What categories are *not* discussed? How is the structure of the essay clarified for the reader?
3. Do you think that the author prefers either American or Chinese culture in any category, or does she present both cultures evenhandedly?
4. Mark places where personal experience is used as support and places where other sources are used. What authorities are cited? How do you know that they are authorities?

5. What are some solutions to the problems of bicultural conflict?
6. Which category of conflict did you find particularly interesting, surprising, or revealing? If you wanted to know more, what would you do?

SIMILARITY AND DIFFERENCE

Find instances of narration, description, illustration, example, and analysis within this essay of classification.

SHORT WRITING IDEA

Expand on the definition of *culture* in paragraph 2 with at least one example.

LONGER WRITING IDEA

Perhaps you yourself have been thrust into contact with a culture that is "foreign" to you. It may not be as extremely different as the Chinese culture from the American; it may be a culture different due to class background, ethnic customs, sex or sexual preference, religious belief, hierarchy of values, or intellectual persuasion. Write about the categories of difference you see between your culture and the foreign one. If you have not had this experience, interview someone who has—perhaps an exchange student—with the goal of writing about cultural differences.

John Hope Franklin

Slavery and Brutality

The grandson of a runaway slave, Franklin (b. 1915) is a distinguished educator and historian who writes compellingly of the black history he has studied and lived. The following is an excerpt from his book *From Slavery to Freedom* (1947).

It cannot be denied that as old as the institution of slavery was, human beings had not, by the nineteenth century, brought themselves to the point where they could be subjected to it without protest and resistance. Resistance has been found wherever the institution of slavery existed, and Negro slavery in the United States was no exception. Too frequently, there were misunderstanding, suspicion, and hatred which were mutually shared by master and slave. Indeed, they were natural enemies, and on many occasions they conducted themselves as such. There are numerous examples of kindness and understanding on the part of the owner as well as docility—which may be more accurately described as accommodation—and tractability on the part of the slave. But this was an unnatural relationship and was not, by the nature of things, inherent in the system. [1]

The brutality which apparently was inherent in a system of human exploitation existed in every community where slavery was established. The wastefulness and extravagance of the plantation system made no exception of human resources. Slaves were for economic gain, and if beating them would increase their efficiency—and this was generally believed—then, the rod and lash should not be spared. Far from being a civilizing force, moreover, the plantation bred indecency in human relations; and the slave was the immediate victim of the barbarity of the system which exploited the sex of the women and the work of everyone. Finally, the psychological situation which was created by the master-slave relationship stimulated terrorism and brutality because the master felt secure in his position and because he frequently interpreted his role as calling for that type of conduct. Many masters as well as slaves got the reputation of being "bad," and their prevalence did nothing to relieve the tension which everywhere seemed to be mounting as the institution developed. [2]

The laws that were for the purpose of protecting the slaves were few and seldom enforced. It was almost impossible to secure a conviction of a master who mistreated his slave. Knowing that, the master was inclined to take the law into his own hands. Overseers were generally known for their brutality, and the accounts of abuse and mistreatment on their part as well as on the part of hirers are numerous. Masters and mistresses were, perhaps, almost as guilty. In 1827 a Georgia grand jury brought in a true bill of manslaughter against a slaveowner for beating his slave to death, but he was acquitted. Several years later Thomas Sorrell of the same state was found guilty of killing one of his slaves with an ax, but the jury recommended him to the mercy of the court. In Kentucky a Mrs. Maxwell had wide reputation for beating her slaves on the face as well as the body, women as well as men. There is, also, the shocking account of Mrs. Alpheus Lewis who burned her slave girl around the neck with hot tongs. Drunken masters had little regard for their slaves, the most sensational example of which is the Kentucky owner who dismembered his slave and threw him piece by piece into the fire. One Mississippi master dragged from the bed a slave whom he suspected of theft and inflicted over one thousand lashes on him. Repeated descriptions of runaways contain phrases such as "large scar on hip," "no marks except those on his back," "much scarred with the whip," and "will no doubt show the marks of a recent whipping"; they suggest a type of brutality that doubtless contributed toward the slave's decision to abscond. [3]

To the demonstrations of brutality as well as to the very institution of slavery itself the Negro reacted in various ways. Thanks to the religion of his master he could be philosophical about the whole thing and escape through ritual and song. His emphasis on otherworldliness in his songs certainly suggested grim dissatisfaction with his worldly status. "Dere's a Great Camp Meetin' in de Promised Land," "Look Away in de Heaven, Lord," "Fo' My Soul's Goin to Heaven Jes' Sho's You Born," and "Heaven, Heaven, Everybody Talkin' 'Bout Heaven Ain't Goin' There" are only a few of the songs which slaves sang in the hope that their burdens would be relieved in the next world. As long as he was in this world he had to make the most of the unfavorable situation by loafing on the job, feigning illness in the fields and on the auction block, and engaging in an elaborate program of sabotage. The slave was so hard on the farming tools that special ones were developed for him. He drove the animals with a cruelty that suggested revenge, and he was so ruthless in his destruction of the crops that the most careful supervision was necessary to insure their survival until harvest time. He burned forests, barns, and homes to the extent that members of the [4] patrol [for protecting property] were frequently fearful of leaving home lest they be visited with revenge in the form of destruction of their property by fire.

[5] Self-mutilation and suicide were popular forms of resistance to slavery. Slaves cut off their toes, hands, and mutilated themselves in other ways so as to render themselves ineffective as workers. One Kentucky slave carpenter, for example, cut off one of his hands and the fingers of the other when he learned that he was to be sold down the river. There are several instances of slaves having shot themselves in the hand or foot, especially upon being recovered after running away. The number of suicides seems relatively large, and certainly they were widespread. Slaves fresh from Africa committed suicide in great numbers. In 1807 two boatloads of newly arrived Negroes in Charleston starved themselves to death. When his slave woman was found dead by her own hanging in 1829, a Georgia planter was amazed since he saw no reason why she should want to take her own life. When two Louisiana slaves were returned to their master after having been stolen in 1858 they unbound themselves and drowned themselves in the bayou. One of the South's wealthiest planters, Charles Manigault, lost a slave by a similar act when the overseer threatened him with punishment. Sometimes slave mothers killed their own children to prevent them from growing up in slavery.

[6] Much more disturbing to the South were the numerous instances of slaves doing violence to the master class. Poisoning was always feared, and perhaps some planters felt a real need for an official taster. As early as 1761 the Charleston *Gazette* remarked that the "Negroes have begun the hellish act of poisoning." Arsenic and other similar compounds were used. Where they were not available, slaves are known to have resorted to mixing ground glass in the gravy for their masters' table. Numerous slaves were convicted for murdering their masters and overseers, but some escaped. In 1797 a Screven County, Georgia, planter was killed by his newly imported African slaves. Another Georgia master was killed by his slave who stabbed him sixteen times. The slave was later burned alive. The slave of William Pearce of Florida killed his master with an axe when Pearce sought to punish him. One Mrs. Carolina Turner of Kentucky was choked to death by a slave whom she was flogging. Though the citizenry had long complained of Mrs. Turner's merciless brutality in dealing with her slaves, her killer was summarily hanged for his deed. The times that overseers and masters were killed by slaves in the woods or fields were exceedingly numerous, as the careful reading of almost any Southern newspaper will reveal.

VOCABULARY

abscond	to leave quickly and secretly
accommodation	adaptation to a situation
barbarity	cruel and brutal behavior
docility	obedience and manageability
feign	to pretend
indigenous	occurring naturally in an area
inherent	basic, inborn
lest	for fear that
sabotage	intentional destruction or waste
tractability	submissiveness and compliance

DESIGN AND MEANING

1. What are the four kinds of brutality resulting from slavery that Franklin describes?
2. What is the writer's most frequent method of supporting paragraph topics?
3. In paragraphs 1 and 2, point out transitional terms that show these relationships between ideas: contrast, expansion, emphasis, conclusion.
4. Explain the statement (in paragraph 2), "The wastefulness and extravagance of the plantation system made no exception of human resources."

SIMILARITY AND DIFFERENCE

Although this selection appeals to your emotions, it seems more objective than "Fighting Bugs Organically" and "Friends." Why?

SHORT WRITING IDEA

List the information that a reader must already be familiar with in order to understand "Slavery and Brutality."

LONGER WRITING IDEA

Classify the kinds of responses to roles set up in an institution you are familiar with: cliques or gangs, family, school, prison, courtship, marriage.

VOCABULARY CHECK

The suffix "-ity" and its variations usually indicate that a word is a *noun.* Thus, root words that are *adjectives* transform to nouns with the addition of "-ity," and the nouns often denote the quality the adjective describes.

docile (adj.) docility (n.)
tractable (adj.) tractability (n.)
barbaric (adj.) barbarity (n.)

Using a dictionary, fill in the missing noun or adjective.

1. possible (adj.) ______ (n.)
2. solemn (adj.) ______ (n.)
3. ______ (adj.) rationality (n.)
4. ______ (adj.) validity (n.)
5. authentic (adj.) ______ (n.)

poetry

PREREADING EXERCISE ("Do Not Go Gentle into That Good Night")

When good men die their goodness does not perish,
But lives though they are gone. As for the bad,
All that was theirs dies and is buried with them.
—Euripides, *Temenidae*. Frag. 734.

We are all kept and fed for death, like a herd of swine to be slain without reason.
—Palladas, *Greek Anthology*. Bk. x. epig. 85.

Death is an angel with two faces:
To us he turns
A face of terror, blighting all things fair;
The other burns
With glory of the stars, and love is there.
—T. C. Williams, *A Thanatopsis*.

What differences do you see among the three quotations above? Which of the quotations above reflects your own thoughts about death most closely? Copy the quotation you choose and write a paragraph elaborating on its meaning.

poetry

Dylan Thomas

Do Not Go Gentle into That Good Night

The great Welsh poet Dylan Thomas (1919–1953) enjoyed enormous acclaim in America for his vibrant, lyrical verse. The singer Bob Dylan chose his stage name in honor of Thomas. The following poem, addressed to Thomas's father, was written in 1951.

Do not go gentle into that good night,
Old age should burn and rave at close of day;
Rage, rage against the dying of the light.

Though wise men at their end know dark is right,
Because their words had forked no lightning they [5]
Do not go gentle into that good night.

Good men, the last wave by, crying how bright
Their frail deeds might have danced in a green bay,
Rage, rage against the dying of the light.

Wild men who caught and sang the sun in flight, [10]
And learn, too late, they grieved it on its way,
Do not go gentle into that good night.

Grave men, near death, who see with blinding sight
Blind eyes could blaze like meteors and be gay,
Rage, rage against the dying of the light. [15]

And you, my father, there on the sad height,
Curse, bless, me now with your fierce tears, I pray.
Do not go gentle into that good night.
Rage, rage against the dying of the light.

DESIGN AND MEANING

1. What four kinds of men are described in stanzas 2, 3, 4, and 5?
2. What do the phrases "that good night" and "dying of the light" stand for?
3. What image is repeated in different forms in stanzas 2, 3, 4, and 5?
4. Why do you think each line of the poem rhymes with "day" or "night"?

SIMILARITY AND DIFFERENCE

Compare the ideas of "Do Not Go Gentle" and Richard Selzer's "An Absence of Windows" in Chapter 2.

SHORT WRITING IDEA

Write a paragraph explaining the paradox (seeming contradiction) in line 17: how can his father's tears both curse and bless him?

LONGER WRITING IDEA

Describe three or four different attitudes toward a part of life: birth, childhood, adolescence, parenthood, middle age, old age, death.

Short Story

Anton Chekhov

The Darling

A Russian physician who gave up medicine when he became a renowned literary artist, Chekhov (1860–1904) is most famous as a dramatist but has also been influential as a writer of short fiction. "The Darling," written in 1899, appeared in *The Darling and Other Stories* (1916).

Olenka Plemyannikova, the daughter of a retired collegiate assessor, was sitting on her porch, which gave on the courtyard; deep in thought. It was hot, the flies were persistent and annoying, and it was pleasant to think that it would soon be evening. Dark rainclouds were gathering in the east and there was a breath of moisture in the wind that occasionally blew from that direction. [1]

Kukin, a theater manager who ran a summer garden known as The Tivoli and lodged in the wing of the house, was standing in the middle of the courtyard, staring at the sky. [2]

"Again!" he was saying in despair. "It's going to rain again! Rain every day, every day, as if to spite me! It will be the death of me! It's ruin! Such a frightful loss every day!" [3]

He struck his hands together and continued, turning to Olenka: [4]

"There, Olga Semyonovna, that's our life. It's enough to make you weep! You work, you try your utmost, you wear yourself out, you lie awake nights, you rack your brains trying to make a better thing of it, and what's the upshot? In the first place, the public is ignorant, barbarous. I give them the very best operetta, an elaborate spectacle, first-rate vaudeville artists. But do you think they want that? It's all above their heads. All they want is slapstick! Give them trash! And then look at the weather! Rain almost every evening. It starts raining on the tenth of May, and it has kept up all May and June. It's simply terrible! The public doesn't come, but don't I have to pay the rent? Don't I have to pay the artists?" [5]

The next day toward evening the sky would again be overcast and Kukin would say, laughing hysterically: [6]

"Well, go on, rain! Flood the garden, drown me! Bad luck to me in this world and the next! Let the artists sue me! Let them send me to prison—to Siberia—to the scaffold! Ha, ha, ha!" [7]

The next day it was the same thing all over again. [8]

Olenka listened to Kukin silently, gravely, and sometimes tears would come to her eyes. In the end his misfortunes moved her and she fell in love with him. He was a short, thin man with a sallow face and wore his hair combed down over his temples. He had a thin tenor voice and when he spoke, his mouth twisted, and his face perpetually wore an expression of despair. Nevertheless he aroused a genuine, deep feeling in her. She was always enamored of someone and could not live otherwise. At first it had been her papa, who was now ill and sat in an armchair in a darkened room breathing with difficulty. Then she had devoted her affections to her aunt, who used to come from Bryansk every other year. Still earlier, when she went to school she had been in love with her French teacher. She was a quiet, kind, soft-hearted girl, with meek, gentle eyes, and she enjoyed very good health. At the sight of her full pink cheeks, her soft white neck with a dark birthmark on it, and the kind artless smile that came into her face when she listened to anything pleasant, men said to themselves, "Yes, not half bad," and smiled too, while the ladies present could not refrain from suddenly seizing her hand in the middle of the conversation and exclaiming delightedly, "You darling!" [9]

The house in which she lived all her life and which was to be hers by her father's will was situated on the outskirts of the city on what was known as Gypsy Road, not far from The Tivoli. In the evening and at night she could hear the band play and skyrockets go off, and it seemed to her that it was Kukin fighting his fate and assaulting his chief enemy, the apathetic public. Her heart contracted sweetly, she had no desire to sleep, and when he returned home at dawn, she would tap softly at her bedroom window and, showing him only her face and one shoulder through the curtain, give him a friendly smile. [10]

He proposed to her, and they were married. And when he had a look at her neck and plump firm shoulders, he struck his hands together, and exclaimed, "Darling!" [11]

He was happy, but as it rained on their wedding day and the night that followed, the expression of despair did not leave his face. [12]

As a married couple, they got on well together. She presided over the box office, looked after things in the summer garden, kept accounts and paid salaries; and her rosy cheeks, the radiance of her sweet artless smile showed now in the box office window, now in the wings of the theater, now at the buffet. And she was already telling her friends that the theater was the most remarkable, the [13] most important, and the most essential thing in the world, and that it was only the theater that could give true pleasure and make you a cultivated and humane person.

[14] "But do you suppose the public understands that?" she would ask. "What it wants is slapstick! Yesterday we gave 'Faust Inside Out,' and almost all the boxes were empty, and if Vanichka and I had put on something vulgar, I assure you the theater would have been packed. Tomorrow Vanichka and I are giving 'Orpheus in Hell.' Do come."

[15] And what Kukin said about artists and the theater she would repeat. Like him she despised the public for its ignorance and indifference to art; she took a hand in the rehearsals, correcting the actors, kept an eye on the musicians, and when there was an unfavorable notice in the local paper, she wept and went to see the editor about it.

[16] The actors were fond of her and called her "the darling" and "Vanichka-and-I." She was sorry for them and would lend them small sums, and if they cheated her, she cried in private but did not complain to her husband.

[17] The pair got on just as well together when winter came. They leased the municipal theater for the season and sublet it for short periods to a Ukrainian troupe, a magician, or a local dramatic club. Olenka was gaining weight and beamed with happiness, but Kukin was getting thinner and more sallow and complained of terrible losses, although business was fairly good during the winter. He coughed at night, and she would make him drink an infusion of raspberries and linden blossoms, rub him with eau de Cologne and wrap him in her soft shawls.

[18] "What a sweet thing you are!" she would say quite sincerely, smoothing his hair. "My handsome sweet!"

[19] At Lent he left for Moscow to engage a company of actors for the summer season, and she could not sleep with him away. She sat at the window and watched the stars. It occurred to her that she had something in common with the hens: they too stayed awake all night and were disturbed when the cock was absent from the henhouse. Kukin was detained in Moscow, and wrote that he would return by Easter, and in his letters he sent instructions about The Tivoli. But on the Monday of Passion Week, late in the evening, there was a sudden ominous knock at the gate; someone was banging at the wicket as though it were a barrel—boom, boom, boom! The sleepy cook, her bare feet splashing through the puddles, ran to open the gate.

[20] "Open, please!" someone on the other side of the gate was saying in a deep voice. "There's a telegram for you."

[21] Olenka had received telegrams from her husband before, but

this time for some reason she was numb with fright. With trembling hands she opened the telegram and read the following:

"Ivan Petrovich died suddenly today awaiting prot instructions tuneral Tuesday." [22]

That is exactly how the telegram had it: "tuneral," and there was also the incomprehensible word "prot"; the signature was that of the director of the comic opera company. [23]

"My precious!" Olenka sobbed. "Vanichka, my precious, my sweet! Why did we ever meet! Why did I get to know you and love you! To whom can your poor unhappy Olenka turn?" [24]

Kukin was buried on Tuesday in the Vagankovo Cemetery in Moscow. Olenka returned home on Wednesday, and no sooner did she enter her room than she sank onto the bed and sobbed so loudly that she could be heard in the street and in the neighboring courtyards. [25]

"The darling!" said the neighbors, crossing themselves. "Darling Olga Semyonova! How the poor soul takes on!" [26]

Three months later Olenka was returning from Mass one day in mourning and very sad. It happened that one of her neighbors, Vasily Andreich Pustovalov, the manager of Babakeyev's lumberyard, who was also returning from church, was walking beside her. He was wearing a straw hat and a white waistcoat, with a gold watch-chain, and he looked more like a landowner than a businessman. [27]

"There is order in all things, Olga Semyonovna," he was saying sedately, with a note of sympathy in his voice; "and if one of our dear ones passes on, then it means that this was the will of God, and in that case we must keep ourselves in hand and bear it submissively." [28]

Having seen Olenka to her gate, he took leave of her and went further. All the rest of the day she heard his sedate voice, and as soon as she closed her eyes she had a vision of his dark beard. She liked him very much. And apparently she too had made an impression on him, because a little later a certain elderly lady, whom she scarcely knew, called to have coffee with her, and no sooner was she seated at table than the visitor began to talk about Pustovalov, saying that he was a fine, substantial man, and that any marriageable woman would be glad to go to the altar with him. Three days later Pustovalov himself paid her a visit. He did not stay more than ten minutes and he said little, but Olenka fell in love with him, so deeply that she stayed awake all night burning as with fever, and in the morning she sent for the elderly lady. The match was soon arranged and then came the wedding. [29]

As a married couple Pustovalov and Olenka got on very well together. As a rule he was in the lumberyard till dinnertime, then [30] he went out on business and was replaced by Olenka, who stayed in the office till evening, making out bills and seeing that orders were shipped.

"We pay twenty per cent more for lumber every year," she would say to customers and acquaintances. "Why, we used to deal in local lumber, and now Vasichka has to travel to the province of Mogiley for timber regularly. And the freight rates!" she would exclaim, putting her hands to her cheeks in horror. "The freight rates!" [31]

It seemed to her that she had been in the lumber business for ages, that lumber was the most important, the most essential thing in the world, and she found something intimate and touching in the very sound of such words as beam, log, batten, plank, box board, lath, scantling, slab . . . [32]

At night she would dream of whole mountains of boards and planks, of endless caravans of carts hauling lumber out of town to distant points. She would dream that a regiment of beams, 28 feet by 8 inches, standing on end, was marching in the lumberyard, that beams, logs, and slabs were crashing against each other with the hollow sound of dry wood, that they kept tumbling down and rising again, piling themselves on each other. Olenka would scream in her sleep and Pustovalov would say to her tenderly: "Olenka, what's the matter, darling? Cross yourself!" [33]

Whatever ideas her husband had, she adopted as her own. If he thought that the room was hot or that business was slow, she thought so too. Her husband did not care for entertainments and on holidays stayed home—so did she. [34]

"You are always at home or in the office," her friends would say. "You ought to go to the theater, darling, or to the circus." [35]

"Vasichka and I have no time for the theater," she would answer sedately. "We are working people, we're not interested in such foolishness. What good are these theaters?" [36]

On Saturdays the two of them would go to evening service, on holidays they attended early Mass, and returning from the church they walked side by side, their faces wearing a softened expression. There was an agreeable aroma about them, and her silk dress rustled pleasantly. At home they had tea with shortbread, and various kinds of jam, and afterwards they ate pie. Every day at noon, in the yard and on the street just outside the gate, there was a delicious smell of *borshch* and roast lamb or duck, and on fast days there was the odor of fish, and one could not pass the Pustovalov gate without one's mouth watering. [37]

In the office the samovar was always boiling and the customers were treated to tea with doughnuts. Once a week the pair went to the baths and returned side by side, both with red faces. [38]

"Yes, everything goes well with us, thank God," Olenka would [39] say to her friends. "I wish everyone were as happy as Vasichka and I."

[40] When Pustovalov went off to the provinces of Mogilev for timber, she missed him badly and lay awake nights, crying. Sometimes, in the evening, a young army veterinary, by the name of Smirnin, who rented the wing of their house, would call on her. He chatted or played cards with her and that diverted her. What interested her most was what he told her about his domestic life. He had been married and had a son, but was separated from his wife because she had been unfaithful to him, and now he hated her; he sent her forty rubles a month for the maintenance of the child. And listening to him, Olenka would sigh and shake her head: she was sorry for him.

[41] "Well, God keep you," she would say to him as she took leave of him, going to the stairs with him, candle in hand. "Thank you for relieving my boredom, and may the Queen of Heaven give you health!"

[42] She always expressed herself in this sedate and reasonable manner, in imitation of her husband. Just as the veterinary would be closing the door behind him, she would recall him and say:

[43] "You know, Vladimir Platonych, you had better make up with your wife. You ought to forgive her, at least for your son's sake! I am sure the little boy understands everything."

[44] And when Pustovalov came back, she would tell him in low tones about the veterinary and his unhappy domestic life, and both of them would sigh and shake their heads and speak of the boy, who was probably missing his father. Then by a strange association of ideas they would both turn to the icons, bow down to the ground before them and pray that the Lord would grant them children.

[45] Thus the Pustovalovs lived in peace and quiet, in love and harmony for six years. But one winter day, right after having hot tea at the office, Vasily Andreich went out without his cap to see about shipping some lumber, caught a chill and was taken sick. He was treated by the best doctors, but the illness had its own way with him, and he died after four months. Olenka was a widow again.

[46] "To whom can I turn now, my darling?" she sobbed when she had buried her husband. "How can I live without you, wretched and unhappy as I am? Pity me, good people, left all alone in the world—"

[47] She wore a black dress with white cuffs and gave up wearing hat and gloves for good. She hardly left the house except to go to church or to visit her husband's grave, and at home she lived like a nun. Only at the end of six months did she take off her widow's weeds and open the shutters. Sometimes in the morning she was seen with her cook going to market for provisions, but how she lived

now and what went on in her house could only be guessed. People based their guesses on such facts as that they saw her having tea with the veterinary in her little garden, he reading the newspaper aloud to her, and that, meeting an acquaintance at the post office, she would say:

"There is no proper veterinary inspection in our town, and that's why there is so much illness around. So often you hear of people getting ill from the milk or catching infections from horses and cows. When you come down to it, the health of domestic animals must be as well cared for as the health of human beings." [48]

She now repeated the veterinary's words and held the same opinions about everything that he did. It was plain that she could not live even for one year without an attachment and that she had found new happiness in the wing of her house. Another woman would have been condemned for this, but of Olenka no one could think ill: everything about her was so unequivocal. Neither she nor the veterinary mentioned to anyone the change that had occurred in their relations; indeed, they tried to conceal it, but they didn't succeed, because Olenka could not keep a secret. When he had visitors, his regimental colleagues, she, pouring the tea or serving the supper, would begin to talk of the cattle plague, or the pearl disease, of the municipal slaughterhouses. He would be terribly embarrassed and when the guests had gone, he would grasp her by the arms and hiss angrily: [49]

"I've asked you before not to talk about things that you don't understand! When veterinaries speak among themselves, please don't butt in! It's really annoying!" [40]

She would look at him amazed and alarmed and ask, "But Volodichka, what shall I talk about?" [51]

And with tears in her eyes she would hug him and beg him not to be angry, and both of them were happy. [52]

Yet this happiness did not last long. The veterinary left, left forever, with his regiment, which was moved to some remote place, it may have been Siberia. And Olenka remained alone. [53]

Now she was quite alone. Her father had died long ago, and his armchair stood in the attic, covered with dust and minus one leg. She got thinner and lost her looks, and passers-by in the street did not glance at her and smile as they used to. Obviously, her best years were over, were behind her, and now a new kind of life was beginning for her, an unfamiliar kind that did not bear thinking of. In the evening Olenka sat on her porch, and heard the band play at The Tivoli and the rockets go off, but this no longer suggested anything to her mind. She looked apathetically at the empty courtyard, thought of nothing, and later, when night came, she [54] would go to bed and dream of the empty courtyard. She ate and drank as though involuntarily.

[55] Above all, and worst of all, she no longer had any opinions whatever. She saw objects about her and understood what was going on, but she could not form an opinion about anything and did not know what to talk about. And how terrible it is not to have any opinions! You see, for instance, a bottle, or the rain, or a peasant driving in a cart, but what is the bottle for, or the rain, or the peasant, what is the meaning of them, you can't tell, and you couldn't, even if they paid you a thousand rubles. When Kukin was about, or Pustovalov or, later, the veterinary, Olenka could explain it all and give her opinions about everything you like, but now there was the same emptiness in her head and in her heart as in her courtyard. It was weird, and she felt as bitter as if she had been eating wormwood.

[56] Little by little the town was extending in all directions. Gypsy Road was now a regular street, and where The Tivoli had been and the lumberyards, houses had sprung up and lanes had multiplied. How swiftly time passes! Olenka's house had taken on a shabby look, the roof was rusty, the shed sloped, and the whole yard was invaded by burdock and stinging nettles. Olenka herself had aged and grown homely. In the summer she sat on the porch, feeling empty and dreary and bitter, as before; in the winter she sat by the window and stared at the snow. Sometimes at the first breath of spring or when the wind brought her the chime of church bells, memories of the past would overwhelm her, her heart would contract sweetly and her eyes would brim over with tears. But this only lasted a moment, and then there was again emptiness and once more she was possessed by a sense of the futility of life; Trot, the black kitten, rubbed against her and purred softly, but Olenka was not affected by these feline caresses. Is that what she needed? She needed an affection that would take possession of her whole being, her soul, her mind, that would give her ideas, a purpose in life, that would warm her aging blood. And she would shake the kitten off her lap, and say irritably: "Scat! Scat! Don't stick to me!"

[57] And so it went, day after day, year after year, and no joy, no opinion! Whatever Mavra the cook would say, was well enough.

[58] One hot July day, toward evening, when the cattle were being driven home and the yard was filled with clouds of dust, suddenly someone knocked at the gate. Olenka herself went to open it and was dumbfounded at what she saw: at the gate stood Smirnin, the veterinary, already gray, and wearing civilian clothes. She suddenly recalled everything and, unable to control herself, burst into tears, silently letting her head drop on his breast. She was so agitated

that she scarcely noticed how the two of them entered the house and sat down to tea.

"My dear," she murmured, trembling with joy, "Vladimir Platonych, however did you get here?" [59]

"I have come here for good," he explained. "I have retired from the army and want to see what it's like to be on my own and live a settled life. And besides, my son is ready for high school. I have made up with my wife, you know." [60]

"Where is she?" [61]

"She's at the hotel with the boy, and I'm out looking for lodgings." [62]

"Goodness, Vladimir Platonych, take my house! You don't need to look further! Good Lord, and you can have it free," exclaimed Olenka, all in a flutter and beginning to cry again. "You live here in the house, and the wing will do for me. Heavens, I'm so glad!" [63]

The next day they began painting the roof and whitewashing the walls, and Olenka, her arms akimbo, walked about the yard, giving orders. The old smile had come back to her face, and she was lively and spry, as though she had waked from a long sleep. Presently, the veterinary's wife arrived, a thin, homely lady with bobbed hair who looked as if she were given to caprices. With her was the little boy, Sasha, small for his age (he was going on ten), chubby, with clear blue eyes and dimples in his cheeks. [64]

No sooner did he walk into the yard than he began chasing the cat, and immediately his eager, joyous laughter rang out. [65]

"Auntie, is that your cat?" he asked Olenka. "When she has little ones, please give us a kitten. Mama is terribly afraid of mice." [66]

Olenka chatted with him, then gave him tea, and her heart suddenly grew warm and contracted sweetly, as if this little boy were her own son. And in the evening as he sat in the dining-room doing his homework, she looked at him with pity and tenderness and whispered: [67]

"My darling, my pretty one, my little one! How blond you are, and so clever!" [68]

"An island," he was reciting from the book, "is a body of land entirely surrounded by water." [69]

"An island is a body of land . . ." she repeated and this was the first opinion she expressed with conviction after so many years of silence and mental vacuity. [70]

She now had opinions of her own, and at supper she had a conversation with Sasha's parents, saying that studying in high school was hard on the children, but that nevertheless the classical course was better than the scientific one because a classical edu- [71]

cation opened all careers to you: you could be either a doctor or an engineer.

Sasha started going to high school. His mother went off to Kharkov to visit her sister and did not come back; every day his father left town to inspect herds and sometimes he stayed away for three days together, and it seemed to Olenka that Sasha was wholly abandoned, that he was unwanted, that he was being starved, and she moved him into the wing with her and settled him in a little room there. [72]

For six months now Sasha has been living in her wing. Every morning Olenka comes into his room; he is fast asleep, his hand under his cheek, breathing quietly. She is sorry to wake him. [73]

"Sashenka," she says sadly, "get up, my sweet! It's time to go to school." [74]

He gets up, dresses, says his prayers, and sits down to his breakfast: he drinks three glasses of tea and eats two large doughnuts, and half a buttered French roll. He is hardly awake and consequently cross. [75]

"You haven't learned the fable, Sashenka," says Olenka, looking at him as though she were seeing him off on a long journey. "You worry me. You must do your best, darling, study. And pay attention to your teachers." [76]

"Please leave me alone!" says Sasha. [77]

Then he walks down the street to school, a small boy in a big cap, with his books in a rucksack. Olenka follows him noiselessly. [78]

"Sashenka!" she calls after him. He turns around and she thrusts a date or a caramel into his hand. When they turn into the school lane, he feels ashamed at being followed by a tall stout woman; he looks round and says: "You'd better go home, auntie; I can go alone now." [79]

She stands still and stares after him until he disappears at the school entrance. How she loves him! Not one of her former attachments was so deep; never had her soul surrendered itself so unreservedly, so disinterestedly and with such joy as now when her maternal instinct was increasingly asserting itself. For this little boy who was not her own, for the dimples in his cheeks, for his very cap, she would have laid down her life, would have laid it down with joy, with tears of tenderness. Why? But who knows why? [80]

Having seen Sasha off to school, she goes quietly home, contented, tranquil, brimming over with love; her face, grown younger in the last six months, beams with happiness; people meeting her look at her with pleasure and say: [81]

"Good morning, Olga Semyonovna, darling! How are you, darling?" [82]

"They make children work so hard at high school nowadays," she says, as she does her marketing. "Think of it: yesterday in the first form they had a fable to learn by heart, a Latin translation and a problem for homework. That's entirely too much for a little fellow." [83]

And she talks about the teachers, the lessons, the textbooks—saying just what Sasha says about them. [84]

At three o'clock they have dinner together, in the evening they do the homework together, and cry. When she puts him to bed, she takes a long time making the sign of the cross over him and whispering prayers. Then she goes to bed and thinks of the future, distant and misty, when Sasha, having finished his studies, will become a doctor or an engineer, will have a large house of his own, horses, a carriage, will marry and become a father. She falls asleep and her dreams are of the same thing, and tears flow down her cheeks from her closed eyes. The black kitten lies beside her purring: Purr-purrr-purrr. [85]

Suddenly there is a loud knock at the gate. Olenka wakes up, breathless with fear, her heart palpitating. Half a minute passes, and there is another knock. [86]

"That's a telegram from Kharkov," she thinks, beginning to tremble from head to foot. "Sasha's mother is sending for him from Kharkov—O Lord!" [87]

She is in despair. Her head, her hands, her feet grow chill and it seems to her that she is the most unhappy woman in the world. But another minute passes, voices are heard: it's the veterinary returning from the club. [88]

"Well, thank God!" she thinks. [89]

Little by little the load rolls off her heart and she is again at ease; she goes back to bed and thinks of Sasha who is fast asleep in the next room and sometimes shouts in his sleep: [90]

"I'll give it to you! Scram! No fighting!" [91]

VOCABULARY

cracknels	pieces of crisply fried pork fat
dearth	scarcity
entrenchments	surrounding trenches built for protection
gravity	seriousness
icon	a sacred image or figure
lodge	a small house, especially one for a servant
ominous	threatening and sinister
sedate	calm and unemotional

DESIGN AND MEANING

1. What are the four types of men Olenka loves? What does her attachment to all of them reveal about her character?
2. What elements of each episode are treated in parallel fashion? What details differ?
3. How do Sasha's words at the end of the story and Olenka's treatment of the cat contribute to understanding the nature of Olenka's love?
4. Why do you think Chekhov used the title "The Darling"?

SIMILARITY AND DIFFERENCE

Compare and contrast Mrs. Mallard in "The Story of an Hour" (Chapter 5) and Olenka in "The Darling."

SHORT WRITING IDEA

Write a paragraph on your idea of Olenka's definition of love.

LONGER WRITING IDEA

Even the best-integrated person has different selves that come out in different situations. Write an essay telling about your different selves and what environments bring them out.

Definition

A GOOD DEFINITION CAN BE EITHER COMFORTING OR DISTURBING: it can clarify your thinking and ease your mind, or it can shake up your long-held and little-considered ideas. Either way, definition concerns meaning and therefore has a place in every kind of writing. Making your terms clear is a duty you take on whenever you use language.

You should define any word if your intended readers probably don't know its meaning. The special vocabulary of certain vocations, hobbies, and social groups usually needs definition. Labeling someone an "oralist" can be quite misleading if your reading audience knows nothing of education for the deaf. A quick definition can be handled by adding a word or two in parentheses after the term, as you will see us do in the following paragraph.

You should also define what you mean when any abstract, ambiguous, or controversial terms figure importantly in your writing. Serious miscommunications can occur when audience and writer do not share the same idea about what a word or phrase means, either *connotatively* (by its associations) or *denotatively* (by its direct meaning). Consider, for instance, the connotations of these words: *daddy, father,* and *old man.* All denote "male parent" but their understood meanings are quite different. The phrase "good writing" seems clear, doesn't it? Yet three English teachers can argue endlessly about what constitutes good writing if teacher A thinks that good writing is whatever clearly communicates the writer's ideas; if teacher B thinks that good writing not only communicates clearly but does so using correct grammar, punctuation, and mechanics; and if teacher C thinks that good writing is not only correct and communicates clearly, but does so with sparkle, wit, and zing.

Sometimes you may want to define a term not just to achieve clarity but as a challenge in itself. You can devote several hundred words to investigating the nature or essential qualities of just one word or phrase. Consider, for example, that you are trying to define what the word "friend" means to you. You would probably use one or more of the following techniques:

1. You would give descriptive details. You might list specific qualities that you think a friend must possess and provide descriptive illustrations.
2. You would use narrative examples. You might tell the story of how your friend Stan showed up at your house unexpectedly on a Saturday night and volunteered to stay with your children so that you could go to a party.
3. You would compare. "A friend is like a mirror" or "A friend is a safe port in a storm," you might say, and then elaborate.
4. You would contrast. By telling what a friend is *not,* you could show the distinction between friends, acquaintances, and buddies.

Using an apt combination of those four techniques, you could write anything from a paragraph to an entire essay of definition.

In the following selections, you will see how professional writers put these same strategies to use in defining subjects as various as migraines, madness, and mistresses.

essays

Ambrose Bierce

Wisdom from The Devil's Dictionary

An irreverent California journalist and short-story writer, Bierce (1842–1914) compiled these caustic definitions in his *Devil's Dictionary* (1906) while serving as a correspondent in Washington, D.C. His fame rests almost solely on his popular story set during the Civil War, "An Occurrence at Owl Creek Bridge."

admiration, n. Our polite recognition of another's resemblance to ourselves. [1]

bore, n. A person who talks when you wish him to listen. [2]

consult, v. t. To seek another's approval of a course already decided on. [3]

diplomacy, n. The patriotic art of lying for one's country. [4]

distance, n. The only thing that the rich are willing for the poor to call theirs and keep. [5]

heaven, n. A place where the wicked cease from troubling you with talk of their personal affairs, and the good listen with attention while you expound your own. [6]

miracle, n. An act or event out of the order of nature and unaccountable, as beating a normal hand of four kings and one ace with four aces and a king. [7]

DESIGN AND MEANING

1. In your desk dictionary, look up each of the words Bierce defines. What is the basic difference between Bierce's definitions and those in the dictionary? In what situations would Bierce's definitions be more useful?
2. Analyze why each Bierce definition is humorous.

WRITING IDEA

Write three *Devil's Dictionary*-style definitions. Some possible choices are "freedom," "intelligence," "perverted," "nice," "foolish," "potential," "overemotional," "fanatic," "honest"—words that have strong subjective meanings. Compare your definitions with the ones in the dictionary.

Judy Syfers

Why I Want a Wife

Judy Syfers, a free-lance writer, says that her own experience, plus discouraging advice received from male teachers, inspired her to compose the following essay, which first appeared as the "Backpage" feature in *Ms.* magazine in December of 1971 and has since been widely reprinted.

I belong to that classification of people known as wives. I am A Wife. And, not altogether incidentally, I am a mother. [1]

Not too long ago a male friend of mine appeared on the scene fresh from a recent divorce. He had one child, who is, of course, with his ex-wife. He is looking for another wife. As I thought about him while I was ironing one evening, it suddenly occurred to me that I, too, would like to have a wife. Why do I want a wife? [2]

I would like to go back to school so that I can become economically independent, support myself, and, if need be, support those dependent upon me. I want a wife who will work and send me to school. And while I am going to school I want a wife to take care of my children. I want a wife to keep track of the children's doctor and dentist appointments. And to keep track of mine, too. I want a wife to make sure my children eat properly and are kept clean. I want a wife who will wash the children's clothes and keep them mended. I want a wife who is a good nurturant attendant to my children, who arranges for their schooling, makes sure that they have an adequate social life with their peers, takes them to the park, the zoo, etc. I want a wife who takes care of the children when they are sick, a wife who arranges to be around when the children need special care, because, of course, I cannot miss classes at school. My wife must arrange to lose time at work and not lose the job. It may mean a small cut in my wife's income from time to time, but I guess I can tolerate that. Needless to say, my wife will arrange and pay for the care of the children while my wife is working. [3]

I want a wife who will take care of *my* physical needs. I want a wife who will keep my house clean. A wife who will pick up after my children, a wife who will pick up after me. I want a wife who will keep my clothes clean, ironed, mended, replaced when need be, and who will see to it that my personal things are kept in their proper place so that I can find what I need the minute I need it. I [4] want a wife who cooks the meals, a wife who is a *good* cook. I want a wife who will plan the menus, do the necessary grocery shopping, prepare the meals, serve them pleasantly, and then do the cleaning up while I do my studying. I want a wife who will care for me when I am sick and sympathize with my pain and loss of time from school. I want a wife to go along when our family takes a vacation so that someone can continue to care for me and my children when I need a rest and change of scene.

[5] I want a wife who will not bother me with rambling complaints about a wife's duties. But I want a wife who will listen to me when I feel the need to explain a rather difficult point I have come across in my course of studies. And I want a wife who will type my papers for me when I have written them.

[6] I want a wife who will take care of the details of my social life. When my wife and I are invited out by my friends, I want a wife who will take care of the babysitting arrangements. When I meet people at school that I like and want to entertain, I want a wife who will have the house clean, will prepare a special meal, serve it to me and my friends, and not interrupt when I talk about things that interest me and my friends. I want a wife who will have arranged that the children are fed and ready for bed before my guests arrive so that the children do not bother us. I want a wife who takes care of the needs of my guests so that they feel comfortable, who makes sure that they have an ashtray, that they are passed the hors d'oeuvres, that they are offered a second helping of the food, that their wine glasses are replenished when necessary, that their coffee is served to them as they like it. And I want a wife who knows that sometimes I need a night out by myself.

[7] I want a wife who is sensitive to my sexual needs, a wife who makes love passionately and eagerly when I feel like it, a wife who makes sure that I am satisfied. And, of course, I want a wife who will not demand sexual attention when I am not in the mood for it. I want a wife who assumes the complete responsibility for birth control, because I do not want more children. I want a wife who will remain sexually faithful to me so that I do not have to clutter up my intellectual life with jealousies. And I want a wife who understands that *my* sexual needs may entail more than strict adherence to monogamy. I must, after all, be able to relate to people as fully as possible.

[8] If, by chance, I find another person more suitable as a wife than the wife I already have, I want the liberty to replace my present wife with another one. Naturally, I will expect a fresh, new life; my wife will take the children and be solely responsible for them so that I am left free.

When I am through with school and have a job, I want my wife to quit working and remain at home so that my wife can more fully and completely take care of a wife's duties. [9]

My God, who *wouldn't* want a wife? [10]

VOCABULARY

adherence	undeviating attachment; sticking to
entail	to make necessary
nurturant	nourishing; encouraging growth; taking care of
peer	an equal
replenish	to fill again

DESIGN AND MEANING

1. According to what principles does Syfers organize the details of her definition into paragraphs?

2. Think of at least two reasons for the frequent repetition of the words "I want a wife."

3. What kind of person is the "I" in this essay? What kind of person is the wife?

4. What is the purpose of Syfers's definition?

5. Many people would agree that this definition is exaggerated. Assuming that the writer was aware of this exaggeration, why do you think she did it?

SIMILARITY AND DIFFERENCE

Compare the main points of "I Want a Wife" and "The Story of an Hour" in Chapter 5.

SHORT WRITING IDEA

Write a paragraph defining a human role: friend, confidant, mistress, critic, teacher, mentor, enemy.

LONGER WRITING IDEA

Go to your local bookstore and review the text of greeting cards designed for wives, husbands, or mothers. Putting together the ideas you find, write an essay defining a wife, a husband, or a mother as viewed by the greeting card industry.

F. L. Lucas

Brevity

The noted British scholar F. L. Lucas (1894–1967) was a Fellow of the Royal Society of Literature and a lecturer at King's College, Cambridge, who wrote many distinguished works of literary criticism and a book on writing entitled *Style* (1955). The following advice on brevity is taken from an essay, "On the Fascination of Style," published in *Holiday* magazine in March 1960.

People who would not dream of stealing a penny of one's money turn not a hair at stealing hours of one's life. But that does not make them less exasperating. Therefore there is no excuse for the sort of writer who takes as long as a marching army corps to pass a given point. Besides, brevity is often more effective; the half can say more than the whole, and to imply things may strike far deeper than to state them at length. And because one is particularly apt to waste words on preambles before coming to the substance, there was sense in the Scots professor who always asked his pupils—"Did ye remember to tear up that fir-r-st page?" [1]

Here are some instances that would only lose by lengthening: [2]

> *It is useless to go to bed to save the light, if the result is twins.* (Chinese proverb.)
>
> *My barn is burnt down—*
> *Nothing hides the moon.* (Complete Japanese poem.)
>
> *Je me regrette.* (Dying words of the high-living Vicomtesse d'Houdetot.)
>
> *I have seen their backs before.* (Wellington, when French marshals turned their backs on him at a reception.)
>
> *Continue until the tanks stop, then get out and walk.* (Patton to the Twelfth Corps, halted for fuel supplies at St. Dizier, 8/30/44.)

Or there is the most laconic diplomatic note on record: when Philip of Macedon wrote to the Spartans that, if he came within their borders, he would leave not one stone of their city, they wrote back the one word—"If."

VOCABULARY

brevity	shortness
exasperate	to irritate or annoy extremely
laconic	using few words
preamble	an introductory statement

DESIGN AND MEANING

1. What is Lucas's basic method of clarifying his definition of brevity?
2. How could you apply the Scots professor's question to your essay writing?

SIMILARITY AND DIFFERENCE

Lucas's advice is similar to Thompson's and Vonnegut's in Chapter 5. How is it different?

SHORT WRITING IDEA

Write lengthier explanations of two of Lucas's examples.

LONGER WRITING IDEA

Define a slang term or saying (like "nothing to write home about," "put the moves on," "between a rock and a hard place," "not playing with a full deck") by giving examples of its proper use or application.

Wayne W. Dyer

Immobilization

Besides being employed as a therapist and counselor, Dyer, a clinical psychologist, has written a popular book to help people identify their emotional problems and then change their behavior to alleviate the difficulties. The following selection is taken from Dr. Dyer's best-seller, *Your Erroneous Zones*, published in 1976.

As you consider your potential for choosing happiness, keep in mind the word *immobilization* as the indicator of negative emotions in your life. You might believe that anger, hostility, shyness and other similar feelings are worth having at times, and so you want to hang on to them. Your guide should be the extent to which you are in any way immobilized by the feeling. [1]

Immobilization can range from total inaction to mild indecision and hesitancy. Does your anger keep you from saying, feeling, or doing something? If so, then you are immobilized. Does your shyness prevent you from meeting people you want to know? If so, you are immobilized and missing out on experiences that are rightfully yours. Is your hate and jealousy helping you to grow an ulcer or to raise your blood pressure? Does it keep you from working effectively on the job? Are you unable to sleep or make love because of a negative present-moment feeling? These are all signs of immobilization. *Immobilization:* A state, however mild or serious, in which you are not functioning at the level that you would like to. If feelings lead to such a state, you need to look no further for a reason to get rid of them. [2]

Here is a brief checklist of some instances in which you may be immobilized. They range from minor to major states of immobility. [3]

You are immobilized when . . . [4]

You can't talk lovingly to your spouse and children though you want to.

You can't work on a project that interests you.

You don't make love and would like to.

You sit in the house all day and brood.

You don't play golf, tennis, or other enjoyable activities because of a leftover gnawing feeling.

You can't introduce yourself to someone who appeals to you.

You avoid talking to someone when you realize that a simple gesture would improve your relationship.

You can't sleep because something is bothering you.

Your anger keeps you from thinking clearly.

You say something abusive to someone that you love.

Your face is twitching, or you are so nervous that you don't function the way your would prefer.

[5] Immobilization cuts a wide swath. Virtually all negative emotions result in some degree of self-immobility, and this alone is a solid reason for eliminating them entirely from your life. Perhaps you are thinking of occasions when a negative emotion has a payoff, such as yelling at a young child in an angry voice to emphasize that you do not want him to play in the street. If the angry voice is simply a device for emphasis and it works, then you've adopted a healthy strategy. However, if you yell at others not to make a point, but because you are internally upset, then you've immobilized yourself, and it's time to begin working at new choices that will help you to reach your goal of keeping your child out of the street without experiencing feelings that are hurtful to you.

VOCABULARY

abusive damaging
indicator a sign, symptom, or index of something
swath a long broad strip, like the path left behind a lawn mower
virtually essentially, practically

DESIGN AND MEANING

1. What words in the first sentence catch your interest?
2. Identify the rhetorical technique used in paragraph 2. What effect does it have?
3. Consider the organization and spacing of the list in paragraph 4. What are some other possibilities for presenting this list? Would any be more effective?
4. Define the phrase "cut a wide swath," using clues from its context in paragraph 5.
5. How does the contrast in the closing paragraph clarify the definition of "immobilization"?

6. Look up the dictionary definition of "immobilization." What similarities and differences are there with Dyer's definition? Do you think Dyer's extension of the definition is appropriate to the word's dictionary meaning?

SIMILARITY AND DIFFERENCE

What is the similarity between the way Syfers extends the definition of "wife" in this chapter and the way Dyer extends the definition of "immobilization"?

SHORT WRITING IDEA

Write a paragraph defining a term mainly by means of contrast with another similar term or terms (for example, "shyness" and "reticence," "ignorance" and "stupidity," "anxious" and "eager," "religious" and "devout," "beautiful" and "attractive," "patriotism" and "chauvinism").

LONGER WRITING IDEA

Think of a subject that you know more about than many others might. Choose terms from that subject area and define them.

Examples:

Journalism: *lead, kicker, justified*

Cooking: *boil, simmer, scald*

Football: *end-around, shotgun, wingback*

Television: *dissolve, voiceover, share*

PREREADING EXERCISE

"My husband doesn't hit me, but he curses me all the time and won't let me see my relatives or friends. He refuses to give me spending money or let me buy diapers for the baby unless I beg him for it." Is the woman who reports this a victim of wife abuse?

Michael Greene and Beverly Rainbolt

He Doesn't Hit Me, But . . .

A married couple living in New Orleans, Greene and Rainbolt specialize in writing about child care, parenting, and other social-psychological subjects. In several years as freelance writers, they have drawn on a professional background of abuse counseling for their insights. Their book, *Behind the Veil of Silence: Family Violence and Alcohol Abuse,* was published in 1990. They are also writing a book on emotional abuse.

Every day millions of women suffer physical abuse. But millions more suffer nonphysical abuse, and they are not even sure that what they are subjected to by the man in their life *is* abuse. [1]

Counselors in battered-women's shelters report countless phone calls from women who say, "I'm not sure I fit into your program. My husband doesn't hit me, but he curses me all the time and won't let me see my relatives or friends. He refuses to give me spending money or let me buy diapers for the baby unless I beg him for it." [2]

Women who are cursed, isolated, and raped by their husbands truly are battered women. What makes the situation worse is that the nonphysical forms of abuse are not specifically illegal. For example, only recently have married women been legally entitled to bring charges against husbands who force them to have sex against their will. [3]

The situation becomes even more complicated when a woman is being verbally, psychologically, or economically abused, since these sorts of things are open to interpretation. What may be a form of verbal abuse to one person will be simply loud noise to another. [4]

However, there are ways nonphysically battered women can determine if they are being abused. The important thing to remember is that the primary purpose or aim of abuse, in whatever form it might take, is to gain and maintain power and control over someone else. [5]

Abuse Takes Many Forms

Many people believe that physical abuse is the most damaging form of violence one person can commit against another. It is as if people will not believe abusive behavior occurs unless there are bruises, broken arms and black eyes. Yet battered women report that nonphysical abuse can be more horrible, demoralizing, and difficult to recover from than abuse that leaves visible scars.

Economic abuse: Many abusers keep their partners at an economic disadvantage. This serves a dual purpose. It allows the abuser enormous control over the material aspects of the home, including items that his partner truly needs, and it prevents the abused person from escaping the situation. [6]

An economically abused woman is often forced to hand over any money she might earn or inherit. Property, such as an automobile or a house, is kept in her husband's name, as are checking and savings accounts. Often, she will have no idea how much money is available, because the abuser insists on controlling the checkbook and paying all the bills. [7]

Since the abused woman has no ready cash, she is literally forced to beg for needed personal items on a daily basis. Of course, if she can't control enough money to purchase shoes, dresses, or even underwear, there is little or no chance that she will be able to access the large amount of money required to leave and start a new life. [8]

Emotional abuse: This form of abuse occurs when a man damages the self-worth of his partner. The abuser makes his partner feel guilty or worthless, thus making her feel that she deserves abuse. [9]

Very often, an abuser makes a woman feel guilty for behavior she has no control over. For example, he will say, "If you loved me, you wouldn't mind if I drank (or gambled or had affairs)." [10]

Sexual abuse: A woman is being sexually abused if her partner treats her like a sex object or coerces or forces her to perform sexual acts that she finds distasteful or uncomfortable. Marital rape—when a husband forces his wife to have sex against her will—is a common form of sexual abuse, and one that until recently was not brought out into the open. [11]

Isolation: This form of abuse occurs when the woman is limited as to whom she may see or what she may do. Perhaps she is forbidden to talk to her relatives or close female friends. She may not be allowed to watch certain television programs and movies or read certain books and magazines. [12]

Anger and intimidation: Since control and power are the real reasons for abuse, anger and intimidation are almost always present in an abusive situation. For example, an abuser will destroy [13] valued personal property—heirlooms, clothes, pictures—to show what will happen if his partner tries to assert herself. Often, the abuser will kill or maim a pet to make his point.

Most abused women report feeling like they're walking on eggshells when their spouse is upset. This results from never knowing what will trigger anger. [14]

Psychological abuse: A woman is psychologically abused when her partner constantly tells her that she is less than human. This is a brainwashing technique that terrorists use on hostages. The abuser tells the woman that she is ugly, sexually unattractive, stupid, or generally incapable of having a life of her own. Eventually, the woman begins to believe that she cannot function without the abuser—that he is right and she is nothing without him. Because she is often isolated from the outside world, the abused woman has little or no chance to hear supportive, positive messages. [15]

Are You Being Abused?

Due to the enforced isolation, shame, and guilt of an abusive relationship, many women don't know if they are truly being abused. Here are some questions that women who suspect they are being abused should ask themselves: [16]

1. Do you often doubt your judgment or wonder if you are "crazy"? [17]
2. Are you often afraid of your partner? [18]
3. Do you express your opinion less and less frequently? [19]
4. Are you afraid of other people? [20]
5. Do you spend less and less time with other people? [21]
6. Do you ask his permission to spend money, become involved in activities outside the home, or socialize with friends? [22]
7. Do you fear doing the wrong thing or getting into trouble? [23]
8. Have you lost confidence in your ability to cope with problems? [24]
9. Are you increasingly depressed? [25]
10. Do you feel trapped and powerless? [26]

If you find yourself answering yes to many of these questions, there is a good chance you are being abused and are beginning to change as a result of the abuse. [27]

Seeking Help and Support

One of the first—and hardest—things for an abused woman to learn is that she cannot change anyone's behavior except her own. [28]

Since she cannot change his behavior, it is the situation that she must change. In order to do that, she will have to change how she feels about herself. She will need to feel that she is worth taking care of and that she can muster the power to regain control of her life. It will also be important for the woman to know that as she grows in self-confidence and independence, her husband or lover will feel threatened by the loss of control and, no doubt, increase his abusive efforts to regain and maintain his control over her.

Most battered-women's programs offer counselor-facilitated support groups and individual counseling for nonphysically abused women and usually their services are offered free of charge. Some hospitals, especially those specializing in women's health care and those with chemical-dependency programs, offer support groups for women. Another source of information and support that an abused woman needs is the self-help and women's sections of bookstores and libraries. The market has been almost overwhelmed in the last few years with books targeted for the emotionally abused woman. [29]

No matter what program, or programs, a woman chooses to seek help through, or even if she decides on individual professional therapy, it is universally agreed that the most important aspect in changing her life is for her to believe that she is a worthwhile human being. [30]

Every Woman's Bill of Rights

- Every woman has the right to be treated with respect by everyone. [31]
- Every woman has the right to take charge of her life. [32]
- Every woman has the right to make decisions that will ensure her safety and protection and that of her children. [33]
- Every woman has the right to respect herself at all times. [34]
- Every woman has the right to be heard. [35]
- Every woman has the right to compliment, praise, and pat herself on the back every day. [36]
- Every woman has the right to be her own best friend. [37]

New Ways to Think about Yourself

Because the abused woman has received such overwhelming messages about what a "bad" person she is, it will take concentrated and determined effort for her to combat those messages with opposing ones. One way to do this is to stand in front of a mirror, at [38] least once a day, and repeat out loud affirmative statements, such as

- I am not to blame for being abused. [39]
- I am not the cause of someone else's violent behavior. [40]
- I do not like or want to be abused. [41]
- I am a worthwhile person. [42]
- I deserve to be treated with respect. [43]
- I do have power over my own life. [44]
- I can use my own power to take good care of myself. [45]
- I can decide what is best for me. [46]
- I can make changes in my life. [47]
- I can ask others to help me because I am not alone. [48]
- I am worth the work it takes to change. [49]
- I deserve to make sure my life is safe and happy. [50]

DESIGN AND MEANING

1. How do the authors establish the importance of their definition?
2. What are the problems of defining something like nonphysical abuse? What other terms are difficult to define?
3. Note that the authors use many headings and subheadings. What purpose do they serve? If you were paging through a magazine and saw this article with no headings or subheadings, would it make a difference?
4. This article not only defines a problem but offers possible solutions. What are some of them?
5. What could an abusive man do to identify his problem and deal with it?

SIMILARITY AND DIFFERENCE

Look at Dyer's definition, "Immobilization," in this chapter. List as many similarities and differences as you can between his definition and Greene and Rainbolt's.

SHORT WRITING IDEA

Find a letter in Ann Landers, Dear Abby, or some other advice column from a woman whom you would consider abused according to Greene and Rainbolt's definition. Using their advice, write a reply letter.

LONGER WRITING IDEA

Use the overall structure of Greene and Rainbolt's article to define and make recommendations about a different common problem such as procrastination, poor reading skills, an eating disorder, self-centeredness, shopping addiction, or the doormat syndrome.

Joan Didion

In Bed

A native Californian, Didion (b. 1934) has been an editor at *Vogue* magazine but is now famous as a novelist and essayist. Her astute criticisms of the American social scene have appeared in many national magazines. The following selection is from her collection of essays entitled *The White Album* (1979).

Three, four, sometimes five times a month, I spend the day in bed with a migraine headache, insensible to the world around me. Almost every day of every month, between these attacks, I feel the sudden irrational irritation and the flush of blood into the cerebral arteries which tell me that migraine is on its way, and I take certain drugs to avert its arrival. If I did not take the drugs, I would be able to function perhaps one day in four. The physiological error called migraine is, in brief, central to the given of my life. When I was 15, 16, even 25, I used to think that I could rid myself of this error by simply denying it, character over chemistry. "Do you have headaches *sometimes? frequently? never?*" the application forms would demand. "Check one." Wary of the trap, wanting whatever it was that the successful circumnavigation of that particular form could bring (a job, a scholarship, the respect of mankind and the grace of God), I would check one. "*Sometimes,*" I would lie. That in fact I spent one or two days a week almost unconscious with pain seemed a shameful secret, evidence not merely of some chemical inferiority but of all my bad attitudes, unpleasant tempers, wrong-think. [1]

For I had no brain tumor, no eyestrain, no high blood pressure, nothing wrong with me at all: I simply had migraine headaches, and migraine headaches were, as everyone who did not have them knew, imaginary. I fought migraine then, ignored the warnings it sent, went to school and later to work in spite of it, sat through lectures in Middle English and presentations to advertisers with involuntary tears running down the right side of my face, threw up in washrooms, stumbled home by instinct, emptied ice trays onto my bed and tried to freeze the pain in my right temple, wished only for a neurosurgeon who would do a lobotomy on house call, and cursed my imagination. [2]

It was a long time before I began thinking mechanistically [3] enough to accept migraine for what it was: something with which I would be living, the way some people live with diabetes. Migraine is something more than the fancy of neurotic imagination. It is an essentially hereditary complex of symptoms, the most frequently noted but by no means the most unpleasant of which is a vascular headache of blinding severity, suffered by a surprising number of women, a fair number of men (Thomas Jefferson had migraine, and so did Ulysses S. Grant, the day he accepted Lee's surrender), and by some unfortunate children as young as two years old. (I had my first when I was eight. It came on during a fire drill at the Columbia School in Colorado Springs, Colorado. I was taken first home and then to the infirmary at Peterson Field, where my father was stationed. The Air Corps doctors prescribed an enema.) Almost anything can trigger a specific attack of migraine: stress, allergy, fatigue, an abrupt change in barometric pressure, a contretemps over a parking ticket. A flashing light. A fire drill. One inherits, of course, only the predisposition. In other words I spent yesterday in bed with a headache not merely because of my bad attitudes, unpleasant tempers and wrongthink, but because both my grandmothers had migraine, my father has migraine and my mother has migraine.

[4] No one knows precisely what it is that is inherited. The chemistry of migraine, however, seems to have some connection with the nerve hormone named serotonin, which is naturally present in the brain. The amount of serotonin in the blood falls sharply at the onset of migraine, and one migraine drug, methysergide, or Sansert, seems to have some effect on serotonin. Methysergide is a derivative of lysergic acid (in fact Sandoz Pharmaceuticals first synthesized LSD-25 while looking for a migraine cure), and its use is hemmed about with so many contraindications and side effects that most doctors prescribe it only in the most incapacitating cases. Methysergide, when it is prescribed, is taken daily, as a preventive; another preventive which works for some people is old-fashioned ergotamine tartrate, which helps to constrict the swelling blood vessels during the "aura," the period which in most cases precedes the actual headache.

[5] Once an attack is under way, however, no drug touches it. Migraine gives some people mild hallucinations, temporarily blinds others, shows up not only as a headache but as a gastrointestinal disturbance, a painful sensitivity to all sensory stimuli, an abrupt overpowering fatigue, a strokelike aphasia, and a crippling inability to make even the most routine connections. When I am in a migraine aura (for some people the aura lasts fifteen minutes, for others several hours), I will drive through red lights, lose the house keys, spill whatever I am holding, lose the ability to focus my eyes

or frame coherent sentences, and generally give the appearance of being on drugs, or drunk. The actual headache, when it comes, brings with it chills, sweating, nausea, a debility that seems to stretch the very limits of endurance. That no one dies of migraine seems, to someone deep into an attack, an ambiguous blessing.

My husband also has migraine, which is unfortunate for him but fortunate for me: perhaps nothing so tends to prolong an attack as the accusing eye of someone who has never had a headache. "Why not take a couple of aspirin," the unafflicted will say from the doorway, or "I'd have a headache, too, spending a beautiful day like this inside with all the shades drawn." All of us who have migraine suffer not only from the attacks themselves but from this common conviction that we are perversely refusing to cure ourselves by taking a couple of aspirin, that we are making ourselves sick, that we "bring it on ourselves." And in the most immediate sense, the sense of why we have a headache this Tuesday and not last Thursday, of course, we often do. There certainly is what doctors call a "migraine personality," and that personality tends to be ambitious, inward, intolerant of error, rather rigidly organized, perfectionist. "You don't look like a migraine personality," a doctor once said to me. "Your hair's messy. But I suppose you're a compulsive housekeeper." Actually my house is kept even more negligently than my hair, but the doctor was right nonetheless: perfectionism can also take the form of spending most of a week writing and rewriting and not writing a single paragraph. [6]

But not all perfectionists have migraine, and not all migrainous people have migraine personalities. We do not escape heredity. I have tried in most of the available ways to escape my own migrainous heredity (at one point I learned to give myself two daily injections of histamine with a hypodermic needle, even though the needle so frightened me that I had to close my eyes when I did it), but I still have migraine. And I have learned now to live with it, learned when to expect it, how to outwit it, even how to regard it, when it does come, as more friend than lodger. We have reached a certain understanding, my migraine and I. It never comes when I am in real trouble. Tell me that my house is burned down, my husband has left me, that there is gunfighting in the streets and panic in the banks, and I will not respond by getting a headache. It comes instead when I am fighting not an open but a guerrilla war with my own life, during weeks of small household confusions, lost laundry, unhappy help, canceled appointments, on days when the telephone rings too much and I get no work done and the wind is coming up. On days like that my friend comes uninvited. [7]

And once it comes, now that I am wise in its ways, I no longer fight it. I lie down and let it happen. At first every small apprehen- [8]

sion is magnified, every anxiety a pounding terror. Then the pain comes, and I concentrate only on that. Right there is the usefulness of migraine, there in that imposed yoga, the concentration on the pain. For when the pain recedes, ten or twelve hours later, everything goes with it, all the hidden resentments, all the vain anxieties. The migraine has acted as a circuit breaker, and the fuses have emerged intact. There is a pleasant convalescent euphoria. I open the windows and feel the air, eat gratefully, sleep well. I notice the particular nature of a flower in a glass on the stair landing. I count my blessings.

VOCABULARY

aphasia	partial or total loss of ability to use language
avert	to prevent
cerebral	relating to the brain
circumnavigation	the act of making one's way around; bypassing
contraindication	a danger; something not advisable
contretemps	an awkward incident
debility	bodily weakness
derivative	a compound formed from another
euphoria	a sense of great well-being and joy
a given	a dependable premise; something absolutely certain
hemmed in	restricted
imposed	forced
incapacitate	to disable
insensible	not capable of perception or feeling
lobotomy	removal of the frontal lobe of the brain
mechanistic	assuming that physical and chemical things alone can explain everything in life
predisposition	tendency
vascular	relating to blood vessels
wary	carefully watchful
wrongthink	unconventional, possibly evil, thoughts

DESIGN AND MEANING

1. What elements of the common definition of migraine does Didion consider wrong? What elements does she consider right or partly right?

2. As well as defining migraine, Didion describes the process she underwent in dealing with it. What are the stages of that process?
3. What audience do you think Didion was writing for in this essay? What evidence led you to your answer?
4. Find at least four places in which Didion lists specific details to support or clarify a general statement.
5. Explain the closing of the essay, focusing on the image of the circuit breaker and fuses.

SIMILARITY AND DIFFERENCE

What similarity of purpose do Didion and Syfers ("I Want a Wife" in this chapter) share? What differences are there in their writing styles?

SHORT WRITING IDEA

Using information from this essay, write a paragraph in reply to someone who says that migraine victims "bring it on themselves."

LONGER WRITING IDEA

Write an essay in which you clear up the definition of some commonly misunderstood concept—such as femininity or masculinity, freedom, love, intelligence, happiness, or progress.

VOCABULARY CHECK

Complete each sentence in a reasonable way.

1. Claude's mechanistic theory of love is
2. Luis was involved in a contretemps about
3. Susie's mother constantly warns her about the family predisposition toward
4. Marla's activities at parties are hemmed in by
5. Clyde experienced debility after
6. I think strictly imposed mealtimes are
7. Euphoria often comes from

8. To avert disaster, we

9. At taverns, Marla is wary of

10. Parental resistance is a given when children

PREREADING EXERCISE ("Defining Mental Illness")

We often casually call things "crazy": "My sister wore a crazy new sweater to court," "The party at Bruno's was really crazy," "Bruno is crazy about my sister." The word is used to describe nonconformist behavior, humorous or hectic situations, oddity of all kinds, even really good times. Why is this? Write a short essay in which you attempt to explain why *crazy* is so widely used in informal speech.

Thomas Szasz

Defining Mental Illness

Born in Hungary, Szasz (b. 1920) is now a professor of psychiatry at the SUNY Medical Center in Syracuse, New York. He has published four books and numerous articles in popular as well as professional journals. The following definition of mental illness is taken from an essay entitled "Our Despotic Laws Destroy the Right to Self-Control," which was printed in *Psychology Today* in December of 1974.

Our political system is based, or so it seems to me, on the proposition that each person has, or ought to have, an absolute right to make his own decisions so long as he does not harm anyone else. "Unalienable" is the way the Founding Fathers put it. [1]

Americans seem to have forgotten this lofty idea. Dispirited by the unceasing efforts that self-reliance demands, and at the same time dazzled by the victories of science, especially over disease, we have come to believe that, at long last, the experts have discovered Plato's Absolute Good—and that it is called mental health. As a result, we have accepted despotic laws prescribing involuntary confinement in both prisons and mental hospitals for acts that harm no one except, sometimes, the person who chooses to commit them . . . . [2]

Blinding Ourselves

In addition to its influence on the law, the medical-psychiatric complex has made a profound impact on the ways we think and talk about our own lives. When we disagree with what a man says or how he lives, we're likely to say he has a neurosis or psychosis, disguising our disagreement by attributing it to disease . . . . [3]

What we call mental illness is often an illegitimate figure of speech. For example, if a person talks to God, he is said to be praying; but if he says that God is talking to him, he is said to be schizophrenic. This formula applies to countless claims, called psychiatric symptoms, and to countless counterclaims called psychiatric diagnoses. How then do I account for the popularity of the notion of mental illness? By viewing it as a key symbol in the ideology and imagery of psychiatry, one of our most important modern religions. [4]

Bread, Sex, Meaning

In short, mental illness is nothing more than a myth that hides and makes more palatable the moral conflicts in human relations. I have repeatedly asserted that there is no such thing as mental illness, but have never denied that people—and I mean all of us some of the time, and some of us all of the time—have serious problems coping with life and with each other. We should recognize these problems and conflicts for what they are: questions of existence and meaning, freedom and dignity, power and prestige—not health and disease. Freud knew this and said so when he acknowledged that his case histories read more like the work of a novelist than of a medical doctor. Jung knew this and said so when he reasserted that men and women cannot live by bread and sex alone, but need also meaning and significance. But psychiatrists have proceeded to ignore them, and today, particularly in this country, people tend to think of all their problems of living as psychiatric diseases, suspect that everyone is at least a little "sick in the head," and believe that some sort of treatment is the answer. We've come to the point where we view life as an illness that begins with conception and ends with death, requiring skillful assistance from medical and mental-health professionals at every step of the way. [5]

The medical-psychiatric complex has grown in the last decades into a Government monopoly that probably exceeds the defense industry in its power to control our lives. With a strong voice in public policy and legislative decisions, and with vast Federal funds to educate us and give us therapy when we get out of line, mental-health professionals have truly become a class of philosopher-kings. We can fight their influence in two ways. We can continue our dialogue with the professionals themselves, trying to make them recognize how they corrupt their traditional roles as healers and deprive us of our sacred rights as free Americans. But more important, we can demand that the principles written into the Constitution be made the real operating principles of our system of justice by eliminating those laws that prevent citizens from exercising self-determination over their own minds, bodies and lives. For so long as those laws stand, we will not be able to live—indeed, many of us will not want to live—as free citizens in a free society. [6]

VOCABULARY

despotic	tyrannical
dispirited	depressed
figure of speech	an imaginative, nonliteral expression

ideology	the ideas characteristic of a certain system or way of thinking
palatable	agreeable or pleasant

DESIGN AND MEANING

1. Szasz says that the common label for "serious problems coping with life and with each other" is "mental illness." He disagrees with the label; this essay is an antidefinition. What error does Szasz see in the label "mental illness"?
2. In Szasz's opinion, what is the danger of believing that we require "skillful assistance from medical and mental-health professionals at every step of the way" (paragraph 5)?
3. What meanings are suggested in the phrasing of "psychiatry, one of our most important modern religions," and "vast Federal funds to educate us and give us therapy when we get out of line"?
4. In many of his writings, Szasz defends a person's right to commit suicide. Why do you think he does?

SIMILARITY AND DIFFERENCE

Compared with the four selections before it in this chapter, Szasz's essay is more of an antidefinition. Explain its difference from the other definitions.

SHORT WRITING IDEA

Write a paragraph defining what Szasz means by "moral conflicts in human relations" in paragraph 5.

LONGER WRITING IDEA

For a few days, record all of the actions and statements you hear referred to as "crazy" "nutty," "insane," or other such terms. Then write an essay defining these terms in their everyday use.

poetry

Emily Dickinson

Much Madness Is Divinest Sense

Emily Dickinson (1830–1886), whose striking, inventive poetry was in her day too modern to be appreciated, wrote hundreds of unpublished poems. Today she is recognized as one of the two great American poets of the nineteenth century. "Much Madness is divinest Sense—" was probably written in 1862.

Much Madness is divinest Sense—
To a discerning Eye—
Much Sense—the starkest Madness—
'Tis the Majority
In this, as All, prevail— [5]
Assent—and you are sane—
Demur—you're straightway dangerous—
And handled with a Chain—

Anne Sexton

You All Know the Story of the Other Woman

Anne Sexton (1928–1974), like her friend Sylvia Plath, was tormented by mental breakdowns, obsessed with death, and finally driven to suicide. Her sometimes surrealistic images, which she said stemmed from her unconscious, make her poetry difficult but compelling.

It's a little Walden.
She is private in her breathbed
as his body takes off and flies,
flies straight as an arrow.
But it's a bad translation. [5]
Daylight is nobody's friend.
God comes in like a landlord
and flashes on his brassy lamp.
Now she is just so-so.
He puts his bones back on, [10]
turning the clock back an hour.
She knows flesh, that skin balloon,
the unbound limbs, the boards,
the roof, the removable roof.
She is his selection, part time. [15]
You know the story too! Look,
when it is over he places her,
like a phone, back on the hook.

VOCABULARY

assent — to express acceptance of and agreement with an idea
demur — to raise an objection; to hesitate to agree
discerning — having good judgment and understanding

DESIGN AND MEANING

1. How is madness defined in Emily Dickinson's poem? How is this definition similar to that presented by Thomas Szasz?

2. Write out Dickinson's poem using conventional punctuation and capitalization. How does this version differ from the original?
3. Explain the reference contained in the lines "It's a little Walden./ . . . But it's a bad translation" in Anne Sexton's poem. What is the antecedent of the word "it"?
4. How does "You All Know the Story of the Other Woman" define the "other woman"?
5. What attitude is suggested by the closing image of the poem?

SHORT WRITING IDEA

Write a paragraph explaining the significance of the comparisons in lines 6–8 of "You All Know the Story of the Other Woman."

LONGER WRITING IDEA

Define an emotion, atmosphere, or condition by using a series of comparisons. Some possibilities: depression, euphoria, gloom, boredom, infatuation, restlessness, anticipation.

Comparison and Contrast

As a manner of thinking, comparison and contrast involve the kind of analysis you use when making decisions or choices. You organize your thoughts into lists of the positive and negative points for each alternative and make your decision by mentally comparing your lists. Thus you gain control over minor areas of your life—what science course to take, what brand of English muffins to buy, whether to put up a rack for the paper towels or leave them out on the counter. Logical comparison is the intelligent alternative to strategies like flipping coins.

As a rhetorical choice, a comparison and contrast approach allows you to order your material effectively to make your point. In comparison and contrast writing, you will be revealing and explaining the similarities and differences between two comparable items. (*Comparable* means having some basic likeness: you wouldn't choose to compare a computer with a Kleenex, for instance.) Of course, you should do all of this revealing and explaining with a purpose. Here are some possible purposes for comparing things:

To explain something your readers do not know about, when you have thought of something comparable that they do know about.

For example, Seymour Krim's "Men in Bondage on an Easter Morning" depends on our acquaintance with a typical middle-class family's Easter celebration in order to show us what Easter is like behind bars. Assuming that many of us know the myths about black families, Lerone Bennett, Jr., presents us with the contrasting realities.

To convince your readers that one thing is superior to another, or that you prefer it for good reasons.

In Adrienne Rich's "Living in Sin," the narrator finds that her fantasy of life with her lover is a good deal preferable to the reality. And Deairich Hunter, by aligning himself with the wimpy ducks, shows us in "Ducks vs. Hard Rocks" that being a macho hard rock leads to a dead end—often quite literally.

To comment on the underlying differences between two superficially similar things or people.

In Katherine Anne Porter's story, "Rope," you see a seemingly happy young couple become locked in combat: is it really over a piece of rope?

To comment on the similarities between things that seem different.

For instance, the roles prescribed for men and women in the lyrics of country music distinctly contrast, but in "Doin' Somebody Wrong" Ann Nietzke points out how the lyrics serve the same purpose for both sexes: they romanticize the ugly realities of life.

To explain the reasons for the similarities or differences between two things.

The superiority of newer cars over older ones, for example, provides the basis for J. Baldwin's comparison in "They Don't Make Them Like They Used To."

Organization assumes a greater importance than usual in comparison and contrast writing because readers bring with them certain expectations. Whether focusing on differences or similarities, most writers tend to employ a couple of basic ways of organizing their material. If, for instance, you decide to humorously contrast the relative merits of toads and snakes as household pets, you could simply list and illustrate all the companionable characteristics of toads first. Then, using a single transition (something like "Snakes, on the other hand, seldom inspire affection"), you repeat the characteristics for snakes, emphasizing their lack of congeniality. Your conclusion needs only to prod your reader to observe that, indeed, as you have shown, toads do make more lovable pets than snakes and don't bite in the bargain. In the following pages you will see this pattern used by Edna St. Vincent Millay in her poem, "The Spring and the Fall."

That is the easy way—a method well-suited, by the way, for writing essay exams. A sharper contrast can be established by setting up your comparison point by point. Let's go back to our argument that toads make more desirable pets than snakes. You could establish a two-point contrast of their personality traits and their physical appearance this way. Under the first point, you might mention that snakes have unappealing personalities. They are messy, forever sloughing off their skin; introverted and noncommunicative; and they speak only in a menacing hiss. Toads, on the other hand, are known to be clean and tidy; placid and undeceptive; and they speak in a warm, friendly croak. Under the second point—their physical appearance—you could assert that snakes are loathsome to look at: they have beady eyes with a fixed, glassy stare; a hideous forked tongue; and they are uncommonly difficult to cuddle. Now, toads, as everyone knows, come with large, languid eyes; quaintly bowed legs; and they are plump, soft, and snuggly. If you fail to convince your readers with such an astute contrast, they must surely harbor an unreasonable prejudice against toads. You will find this alternating pattern of organization loosely employed by J. Baldwin in "They Don't Make Them Like They Used To (Thank Goodness)."

But before you begin planning what to say, think about your prospective audience. Try to decide who would benefit or get pleasure from reading your comparison and contrast writing. If you can't think of anyone, you had better switch subjects. Remember also that when you are finished, your readers should respond with an "Aha!" and not a "So what?" Otherwise, your topic was probably not well chosen or your comparison not skillfully worked out.

The following essays, poems, and stories will provide you with a further chance to study comparison and contrast patterns, while the suggested activities following each selection will give you a chance to practice the mode yourself.

essays

Deairich Hunter

Ducks vs. Hard Rocks

Hunter has moved back to Wilmington, Delaware, since writing about what life is like for black teenagers in Brooklyn. This essay appeared as *Newsweek*'s "My Turn" feature in August of 1980.

Although the chaos and viciousness of the Miami riot happened months ago, the chaos and viciousness of daily life for many inner-city black people goes on and on. It doesn't seem to matter where you are, though some places are worse than others. A few months ago I left my school in Wilmington, Del., moved to Brooklyn, N.Y., and really began to understand. [1]

After you stay in certain parts of New York for awhile, that chaos and viciousness gets inside you. You get used to seeing the younger guys flashing pistols and the older ones shooting them. It's not unusual to be walking down the street or through the park and see somebody being beaten or held up. It's no big deal if someone you know is arrested and beat up by the cops. [2]

In my four months in Brooklyn I was mugged three times. [3]

Although such events may seem extraordinary to you, they are just a part of life in almost any minority neighborhood. It seems like everybody knows how to use some kind of weapon, whether it's a pair of nun-chucks (two round sticks attached by a chain) or an ice pick. As long as it will do the job, you can use it. [4]

School and street: In Brooklyn you fall into one of two categories when you start growing up. The names for the categories may be different in other cities, but the categories are the same. First, there's the minority of the minority, the "ducks," or suckers. These are the kids who go to school every day. They even want to go to college. Imagine that! School after high school! They don't smoke cheeb (marijuana) and they get zooted (intoxicated) after only one can of beer. They're wasting their lives waiting for a dream that won't come true. [5]

The ducks are usually the ones getting beat up by the majority group—the "hard rocks." If you're a real hard rock, you have no worries, no cares. Getting high is as easy as breathing. You just rip off some duck. You don't bother going to school; it's not necessary. You just live with your mom until you get a job—that should be any time a job comes looking for you. Why should you bother to go look for it? Even your parents can't find work. [6]

I guess the barrier between the ducks and the hard rocks is the barrier of despair. The ducks still have hope, while the hard rocks are frustrated. They're caught in the deadly, dead-end environment and can't see a way out. Life becomes the fast life—or incredibly boring—and death becomes the death that you see and get used to every day. They don't want to hear any more promises. They believe that's just the white man's way of keeping them under control. [7]

Bravado: Hard rocks do what they want to do when they want to do it. When a hard rock goes to prison it builds up his reputation. He develops a bravado that's like a long, sad joke. But it's all lies and excuses. It's a hustle to keep ahead of the fact that he's going nowhere. [8]

Actually, there is one more category, but this group is not really looked upon as human. They're the junkies. They all hang together, but they don't actually have any friends. Everybody in the neighborhood knows that a drug addict would cut his own throat if he could get a fix for it. So everybody knows junkies will stab you in the back for a dollar. [9]

A guy often becomes a junkie when he tries to get through the despair barrier and reach the other side alone. Let's say a hard rock want to change, to better himself, so he goes back to school. His friends feel he's deserting them, so they desert him first. The ducks are scared of him and won't accept him. Now this hard rock is alone. If he keeps going to school, somebody who is after him out of spite or revenge will probably catch him and work him over. The hard rock has no way to get back. His way of life is over; he loses his friends' respect, becoming more and more of an outcast. Then he may turn to drugs. [10]

I guess the best way to help the hard rocks is to help the ducks. If the hard rocks see the good guys making it, maybe they will change. If they see the ducks, the ones who try, succeed, it might bring them around. The ducks are really the only ones who might be able to change the situation. [11]

The problem with most ducks is that after years of effort they develop a negative attitude, too. If they succeed, they know they've got it made. Each one can say he did it by himself and for himself. No one helped him and he owes nobody anything, so he says, "Let [12] the hard rocks and the junkies stay where they are"—the old every-man-for-himself routine.

What the ducks must be made to realize is that it was this same attitude that made the hard rocks so hard. They developed a sense of kill or be killed, abuse or be abused, take it or get taken. [13]

The hard rocks want revenge. They want revenge because they don't have any hope of changing their situation. Their teachers don't offer it, their parents have lost theirs, and their grandparents died with a heartful of hope but nothing to show for it. [14]

Maybe the only people left with hope are the only people who can make a difference—teens like me. We, the ducks, must learn to care. As a 15-year-old, I'm not sure I can handle all that. Just growing up seems hard enough. [15]

DESIGN AND MEANING

1. What is Hunter's thesis—that is, what is the main point in making the contrast between ducks and hard rocks? Where does Hunter come closest to stating his thesis? Is the placement effective?
2. Why does Hunter bring up the junkies, even though they are not either of his two main groups? Do you think the junkie section is necessary to make the main point?
3. Hunter was fifteen when he wrote this essay. How do you think his age is related to the ideas in his essay? How does his youth affect you?
4. Paragraph 3 consists of only one sentence. Why is it not part of either the paragraph preceding it or the one after it?
5. The writing style of this essay is informal and conversational. Point out what words and phrases make it that way.

SIMILARITY AND DIFFERENCE

Why might "Ducks vs. Hard Rocks" fit into Chapter 6 as well as here?

SHORT WRITING IDEA

Choose one paragraph from Hunter's essay and rewrite it in a very formal style.

LONGER WRITING IDEA

Most high school students perceive at least two contrasting groups among the student population. Describe two such groups from your own high school (or college) days. Then analyze whether you now think the categorization was true or oversimplified, just or unfair.

Ann Nietzke

Doin' Somebody Wrong

A midwesterner presently living in California who has been a contributing editor for *Human Behavior* magazine, Nietzke usually writes analyses of various aspects of popular culture. The following selection is an excerpt from "Doin' Somebody Wrong," which appeared in *Human Behavior* in November of 1975.

Nowhere in country, I think, does the relationship between diminished personhood and sadness become more apparent than in the work of Tammy Wynette, for her voice conveys a little teardrop in every syllable, and most of the syllables add up to portrayals of women who feel "I am nothing, my man is everything." So Tammy is full of advice on how to hold your man. "There's no secret, just some little things to do," she says and recommends that you start his day out right with a little loving smile, support him, understand him and let him know that you think he's "better than the rest." A woman is supposed to maintain this attitude no matter how badly the man treats her. "Sometimes," Tammy sings, "I lay in bed and cry, cry, cry," but she insists, "for better or worse, I took him 'til the day I die." [1]

Women who treat men similarly, however, women who do any "slippin' around," may very well get shot as punishment (Johnny Cash's "Kate" and Claude King's "Laura"), because men view women as their sexual property. Surely this is partly because the men work so hard to pay for everything else that they must feel they are paying as well for their women, who wait passively at home. Tex Ritter sings, for example, "I've had enough of your two-timing / You've had enough of my bankroll," and Bobby Bare complains of "Alimony, same old blues in it / I'm payin' for it while someone else is usin' it." For whatever reasons, a woman who cheats, even if she isn't killed for it, is very rarely forgiven in country. Over and over and over again men are driven to the bottle by their unfaithful women ("My heart is breaking like the tiny bubbles / She's actin' single, I'm drinkin' doubles"). [2]

The Good Woman-Bad Woman split is, in fact, a major theme in the music, because the married men are constantly tempted by "honky-tonk angels" of various types who, I gather, are generally better lays than their wives ("She's the one I love," Mel Street tells [3] one, "but you make me feel more like a man"). While many do give in to temptation, they often suffer from the conflict within themselves: "Lord, I'm only human, and I can feel the glow," Jim Mundy sings. "My body's saying yes but my heart is saying no."

[4] The happiest songs narrated by married men, therefore, are those in which the conflict is resolved for them by a wife who can be sexy at the appropriate times. The best known example of these is probably Charlie Rich's "Behind Closed Doors," in which his woman is always a "lady" until he gets her behind closed doors where no one sees what goes on, where she lets her hair hang down and makes him glad he's a man. Jerry Wallace brags of a similar ideal setup in "I've Got So Many Wives at Home," for his wife, too, is both lady and satisfying lover, and "If I need a devil, as all men sometimes do / You got just enough to make me love the devil out of you."

[5] It is taken for granted by both men and women in country music that men have to be "the way they are," while women have to be what their men want them to be. In "I Can't Be Myself," Merle Haggard implies he'll be leaving a woman who wants him to change. George Jones demands, "Take Me As I Am," and Billy Edd Wheeler says straight out, "If you're expectin' me to change my old ways for the new / Baby, don't hold your breath until I do." Dottie West, however, is pictured on one of her album covers as a paper doll about to be cut out by a huge pair of scissors held by a big male hand ("Take your scissors and take your time / And cut along the dotted line"). She begs her man to keep his scissors handy and trim her edges now and then, and "Fit me in with all your plans / For I want to be what I'm cut out to be."

[6] It would appear from such examples that the men have a good deal of ego strength and personal pride, but a close look at many lyrics by both male and female singers reveals to what a great extent men rely on their women for emotional support and for a sense of "manhood" ("Whenever I'm down you come around / And you make me feel like a man"). The male counterpart of Tammy Wynette's "Stand By Your Man" is not "Stand By Your Woman" but rather, "Only a Woman Like You [Can Make a Man of Me]," a woman capable of turning even small dreams into "the greatest thing."

[7] Whatever power women do have in the world of country music stems, I think, from this twisted emotional setup, and I find a subtle but definite thread of contempt for men running through a number of female songs. Tammy Wynette advises, "If you love him, be proud of him / 'Cause after all he's *just a man*" and elsewhere admits that she's "quit lookin' for a perfect man / 'Cause there ain't any more of them." Obviously, if men need women to make men of them, then

without women they are nothing but little boys ("I'd love to just deceive em', playing' with 'em like a toy / Then leave 'em like a little boy"). So, although "It's a Man's World," as Diana Trask sings, "He's got an awful lot of little boy in him / He wants to have his way." And little boys, of course, have to be mothered ("Baby me, baby, as only you can do").

[8] One reason men need so much emotional support is that they are not supposed to do anything so "unmanly" as to feel or express deep emotion themselves. Although men in country do a whole lot of crying, mostly boozy crying, they are nearly always ashamed of it and a little surprised at their own capacity for hurt. Johnny Cash sings of a man "six-foot-six" who weighed 235 pounds but who cried "like a whipped pup" and was "brought down to his knees" by "A Thing Called Love." It is implied that this is a very strange occurrence. The idea is stated as bluntly as possible by Waylon Jennings, when he warns his woman, "Don't mistake my tenderness for any sign of weakness in your man." All of this places the burden of emotion squarely on the woman. "I will feel your loneliness and I will feel your pain," Jeannie C. Riley promises, and Jerry Wallace loves his woman, he tells her, because "If I hurt, it makes you cry."

[9] The price men pay, however, for the questionable benefit of keeping women at home to be mothers and emotional buffers for themselves is a great one, for in order to maintain some kind of balance, this arrangement also requires men to be daddies to their little girl-women, who can't take care of themselves financially or any other way. Dottie West sings an incredible song called "Everything's a Wreck [Since You're Gone]," in which a home turns into a disaster area when the man of the house leaves. The wife can't start the mower or unstop the sink or change a fuse or paint a room or even call a TV repairman so she can watch "Edge of Night." (My gut reaction was, "Christ, no wonder he left her—she's an idiot.")

[10] In song after song by such singers as Charlie Rich and Charley Pride, men express anxieties about whether they are materially successful enough to keep their women happy ("I don't know how to tell her I didn't get that raise in pay today / I know how very much she wanted that dress in Baker's window"). The men age fast and wear themselves down trying to pay for the fancy clothes and new cars and houses they are convinced their wives want. George Jones thinks of giving up since he can't get ahead: "I work hard and I work overtime / And I'm still deep in debt."

[11] Even if a man gets rich, however, there is no guarantee he can keep his woman, for he also has the pressure of responsibility to satisfy her sexuality. Tammy Wynette sings of having "satin sheets to lie on" and a "big long Cadillac" and "tailor-mades upon her

back," yet she is going to leave her rich man for another because he doesn't "keep her satisfied." For their part, the women have to learn all the tricks of catching and holding a man, because the Other Woman, portrayed in country music as Enemy Number One, is always out there waiting to steal him away ("She's a whole lot better lookin' than me and you / And she can do things to a man you never dreamed a woman can do").

In short, both men and women in country music have a hard life, made worse by the limited ways in which they see themselves and each other. For comfort, they retreat into their respective fantasy worlds. The women "watch their stories on TV every day / And eat at McDonald's once a week to get away," and read movie magazines ("They say to have her hair done Liz flies all the way to France / And Jackie's seen in a discotheque doin' a brand new dance"). The men romanticize themselves as "lovable losers, no-account boozers and honky-tonk heroes," studs who value their "Low Down Freedom," who can love women and leave 'em and be happy on the road as wandering gypsies. The prison records and down-and-out images of such singers as Merle Haggard and Johnny Paycheck and Johnny Cash (before he got on the religion bandwagon) appeal to these fantasies. [12]

The central male image in country, alas, is probably still the cowboy. "It ain't easy bein' a cowboy in this day and time," say the album notes of Waylon Jennings's *Honky-Tonk Heroes*. But Jennings ("tough and mean and wild") manages to be one, and "the cowboy will live on just as long as there is the sound of music." The authentic cowboys of the country-music world, though, are the truck drivers, who represent a perfect fusion of the cowboy myth and working-class reality. [13]

There are scores and scores of trucking songs and, in many of them, it becomes obvious that the truckers are cowboys, trucks are their horses, highways are the plains, truck stops are saloons and waitresses are saloon girls. In song after song, the monotony and sheer hard work of being a trucker are romanticized into something noble and exciting through stories of how trucks serve the nation, of how drivers help and rescue fellow travelers, of how they speed and manage to outsmart Smokey the Bear (state police) with their CB radios and especially of how every waitress in every truck stop finds every driver absolutely irresistible. Although often the men remain loyal to their wives at home and don't take advantage of this, they do seem to think about it quite a bit ("I could have a lot of women, but I'm not that kind of guy"). Narrating as a trucker's wife, Tammy Wynette sings, "Last night he called from Dallas / He was havin' a beer at the Crystal Palace / And he said, honey, you [14] won't be alone for long." He's calling to tell her he's going to bring his "big ol' engine" home to her, even though there are "a million chicks" out there who want to make love with him. And Tammy, as always, is patiently waiting, waiting, waiting at home for her man in order to give him "everything he needs."

VOCABULARY

boozer	one who drinks quantities of alcohol
fusion	joining or merging of two or more things
respective	distinct, separate
romanticize	to give an event a more pleasant or more emotional coloring than it really had; to idealize

DESIGN AND MEANING

1. Notice that Nietzke consistently writes conventional paragraphs—topic sentence first, followed by explanations and examples. After surveying the opening sentences of all the paragraphs, can you see Nietzke's method of organization?
2. How do both men and women romanticize their drab lives in country music?
3. What are the various advantages and disadvantages of being a man or a woman according to country lyrics? Are the lyrics a true picture of life in any sense?
4. What is the effect on you of Nietzke's plentiful direct quotations from country songs?
5. Study the examples of lyrics. What is there about the way country lyricists use language that makes their songs so appealing?
6. What is Nietzke's tone, her attitude toward her material? How can you tell?

SIMILARITY AND DIFFERENCE

Compare the ideas about male and female relationships in country music with the couple's behavior in the story "Rope" at the end of this chapter.

SHORT WRITING IDEA

Listen for an hour or so to a "top 40" or other popular radio station. Write down statements or suggestions about the nature of men and women that popular music today makes.

LONGER WRITING IDEA

Choose a small area of popular culture to study: campus fashions, daytime television shows, short stories in women's or men's magazines, or the music of a certain rap group, for example. Following Nietzke's pattern, write an essay about images of men and women in the area of popular culture you choose. If you prefer, you can compare and contrast the images of adults and children or adults and teenagers.

VOCABULARY CHECK

The suffix "-ize" means that the word it appears in is a *verb;* usually the root of the word is another part of speech. The suffix "-ion," according to the same principles, makes a root word a *noun*. So we have:

romantic (adj.)—emotionally pleasant
romanticize (verb)—to make emotionally pleasant
fuse (verb)—to bring together two or more things
fusion (noun)—a blend of two or more things

After looking at the definition of the following root words, see if you can fill in the definitions of the words with suffixes. Use a dictionary if you have difficulty.

contrite (adj.)—sorry, remorseful
contrition (noun)— ________

ideal (adj.)—perfect
idealize (verb)— ________

delete (verb)—to leave out
deletion (noun)— ________

traditional (adj.)—conventional
traditionalize (verb)— ________

PREREADING EXERCISE

List all the labels you can think of that people might place on you (correctly or not): college student, egghead, jock, frat rat, headbanger, feminist, socialist, deadhead, computer nerd, snob, altruist, and so on.

Lerone Bennett, Jr.

The 10 Biggest Myths about the Black Family

Born in 1928 in Mississippi, Bennett lives in Chicago where he works as the senior editor of *Ebony* magazine. He has written over ten books concerning the history and progress of blacks in America, chronicling the dark deeds that white Americans would best like to forget. He holds a doctorate in literature from Marquette University.

In propaganda against the Negro since emancipation in this land," W.E.B. Du Bois said, "we face one of the most stupendous efforts the world ever saw to discredit human beings, an effort involving universities, history, science, social life and religion." [1]

Nowhere is this more clearly visible than in the pervasive and continuing effort to discredit Black fathers, mothers, and children. And it is scarcely possible to understand the problems and enduring strengths of the Black family if we do not at the least make an effort to understand and dispel the misconceptions, myths and outright lies men and women have invented to hide themselves from Black reality and American racism. There are, of course, scores of misconceptions about Black sexuality and Black kinship networks, but the vast propaganda campaign against the Black family is generally organized around ten major myths. [2]

1. **Raw and uncontrolled sex,** according to the biggest and most pervasive myth, **is at the root of the Black family problem.** [3]

This is the most enduring of all lies about Blacks, and sociologists and historians froth at the mouth and strain at the leash of synonymity ("riotous debauchery," "unbridled passions," "wild and primitive emotions") in passionate attempts to express this academic and political voyeurism. For most, if not almost all, critics of the Black family, there is always at the back of the mind this myth, this image of Black America as Babylon, where the Studs and Sapphires are *always* making babies, where—in the words of the myth—"They do it, honey, right out in the middle of the streets." And one of the most challenging problems we face is confronting scholars, journalists and politicians, who have repeatedly used the [4]

Black family to exorcise the demons of their own sexuality and the guilt of their complicity in oppression. What makes this so difficult is that we are dealing here with a magical idea that is impervious to "facts." There are, in fact, no facts in this area, for there has never been a systematic analysis of the sexual differences between American Blacks and American Whites. And the few facts we have (see Robert Staples, "Black Male Sexuality," EBONY, August 1983) contradict the super-sex theory of Black history and suggest that the differences between racial groups are relatively small, especially when you correct for economic and historical differences. More to the point, Blacks, according to the statistics, are not even in the running in the areas of wife-swapping and other experiments of the Sexual Revolutions.

2. **The root cause of the problem,** according to the second most widely disseminated myth, **is loose morals.** [5]

This myth has a thousand lives and has surfaced repeatedly in the last 300 years. It has even seduced some Black writers, male and female, who have created a new and curiously popular literature based on the idea that Black America is a vast emotional wasteland populated by hustlin' men and maimed women. [6]

In this instance, as in the preceding one, we are dealing with explosive emotions that exist in areas of the psyche that cannot be reached by the light of evidence. Some Blacks, for example, have children out of wedlock, but so do millions of Whites, including stars who are celebrated by the same media which browbeat and humiliate poor Blacks. The mythmakers know this, but they cannot be convinced by "facts," for their knowledge precedes the facts and makes the facts. And when they say that Blacks are immoral, they mean that there is a Black way and a White way of making babies and a Black way and a White way of being immoral. [7]

A case in point is the controversy over illegitimacy. For a common impression to the contrary notwithstanding, Black America has always condemned unrestrained sexual expression and has insisted—with a singular lack of support from the American government and White institutions—on stable and responsible mating patterns between knowledgeable and economically qualified parents. But Black America has refused to follow White America in the barbarous practice of condemning infants. It has said, to its credit, that there are no illegitimate children, only illegitimate parents and, it must be added, illegitimate societies which make it impossible for parents to find the work and wherewithal (the day-care centers and the network of supporting images and institutions) to become responsible parents. [8]

Another important point is that there have been marked changes in the last 15 years in the marriage and childbearing patterns of *both* Black and White young women in the United States. In a letter to *The New York Times*, Constance A. Nathanson, a professor of population dynamics in the Johns Hopkins University School of Hygiene and Public Health, said: "These changes, however, have been more profound among Whites than among Blacks; in 1983 there were, for the first time, more births to single white than to single black teen-agers." She added: "The tradition of finding the causes of social ills in the victims of those ills, and particularly in their supposed inadequacies as spouses and parents, has a long history in America. The true causes, however, lie deeply imbedded in our social and economic structure." [9]

Assuredly, and this is the point we want to make: the real moral problem is our failure to deal with those causes and not some mysterious self-perpetuating "pathology" in the Black family or the Black community. [10]

3. **Blacks lack a family tradition and came to America without a sense of morality and a background of stable sexual relationships.** [11]

Far from harming Blacks, this myth maintains, Whites did them a favor by transporting them from an oversexed land to a hospitable climate of cottonfields, chastity, and nuclear families. Cottonfields apart, there is not a word of truth in this. In fact, Blacks came from an ancient culture where there were stable and non-European marriage patterns and where men and women were not cursed by the sexual demons that pursued the Puritans and the sexual demons that pursue the sons and daughters of the Puritans. Two other points are relevant. The first is that polygamy was sanctioned in some of these cultures, although in practice the poor, like the poor everywhere, contented themselves with monogamy. The second is that this non-Puritan, non-uptight ethos was the basis of the great synthesis Africans made of African and European forms. This synthesis began with a revealing family pact that seems to have bound together all slaves who came over on the same ship. For, according to scholar Orlando Patterson, "it was customary for children to call their parents' shipmates 'uncle' and 'aunt,' " and for men and women to "*look upon each other's children mutually as their own* [my emphasis]." [12]

Thus contrary to the myth, the African-American adventure began not in chaos, but in love and in a *higher* morality. And it began in a way with the story of Antoney and Isabell, two of the first Black immigrants to English America, who married in Vir- [13]

ginia in 1623 or 1624. Isabell was soon brought to bed with what was probably the first Black child born in English America. In 1624, the child, a boy named William, was baptized in Jamestown. And since his parents were for all practical purposes free, the Black family in America was born not in slavery but in freedom.

From all this it is clear that the Black American family is the product of a particular history and that *we must explain the family by the history and not the history by the family.* [14]

4. **The bonds of the Black family were destroyed in slavery.** [15]

Certain scholars, Daniel Patrick Moynihan in particular, have argued that the problems of the Black family are rooted in the slave experience and a 300-year "cycle of self-perpetuating pathology." But Moynihan and his followers misread the plantation records and the tracks of the Black spirit, and pathfinding studies by Herbert G. Gutman (*The Black Family in Slavery and Freedom*) and other scholars, Black and White, have destroyed that myth and established three major points: [16]

1. Most slaves lived in families headed by a father and a mother and "large numbers of slave couples lived in long marriages," some for 30 years or more. [17]
2. In slavery (and afterward), Blacks were more open and honest about sex, but they did not condone indiscriminate mating and begetting. And although premarital sex was fairly common, the slave community expected a pregnancy to be followed by marriage. [18]
3. In slavery (and afterwards), slave marriages were buttressed by extended family groupings that seemed to include most members of Slave Row. Slave children, according to numerous sources, were taught to respect and revere older persons whom they called "aunt" and "uncle." It was customary for adult slaves to call each other "brother" and "sister." [19]

The implications of Gutman's massively documented study are extensive and require a total revision of the traditional picture of matriarchal families and unstructured sexual relationships. Gutman's data also demolish superficial "cycle of pathology" studies which say that the "problem" of the Black family—the "problem," to be precise, is not the Black family but the society that oppresses the Black family—is almost insoluble. For, as Professor Gutman said, "a vast difference exists in dealing with a problem rooted in 'three centuries of exploitation' and one caused by massive structural unemployment." [20]

5. The Black family collapsed after Emancipation. [21]

[22] In dealing with this myth, we have to notice first that it offers a theory of history and a theory of race. For we are asked to believe that the "fragile" roots of Black familyhood, nourished by nearness to ol' marsa and Scarlett O'Hara ("Lawdy, Miss Scarlett, I don't know nothin' 'bout birthin' no babies.") withered and almost died after the "mean" Northerners separated Blacks from the guiding model of White families and the guiding light of White morality. This, of course, is preposterous, for White morality *was* the problem; and once that obstacle was removed Blacks exploded in a post-Emancipation festival of family building. According to almost all witnesses, the roads of the South were clogged in 1865 with Black men and women searching for long-lost wives, husbands, children, brothers, and sisters. The in-gathering continued for several years and began in most communities with mass marriage ceremonies that legalized the slave vows. This was a voluntary process, for husbands and wives were free to renounce slave vows and search for new mates. Significantly, most freedmen, some of them 80 and 90 years old, decided to remain with their old mates, thereby giving irrefutable testimony on the meaning of their love. No one understood this better than Albion Tourgee, a North Carolina Reconstruction judge, who said: "Let the marriage bond be dissolved throughout the state of New York today, and it may be doubted if as large a proportion of the intelligent white citizens would choose again their old partners."

6. The Black family collapsed after the Great Migration to the North. [23]

[24] According to this myth, urbanization and the defiling lights of Chicago and Harlem destroyed the last vestiges of Black institutional life and doomed the Black family. The evidence does not support this view. The hard fact is that the Black family was an unusually strong institution for several decades after the Great Migration. According to Gutman and others, the overwhelming majority of Black households (85 percent in New York City in 1925) were headed by fathers and mothers until the 1930s. It has also been established that Black families were at least as stable as the households of Northern White ethnics.

7. The Black family is a product of White paternalism and government welfare. [25]

[26] This theory turns Black history inside out, like a glove, and

gives missionaries and government agencies credit for the heroic efforts of Black men and women. For it was internal giving, it was communal sharing the caring, that ensured the survival of Black America. From the very beginning of the Black American adventure, Black people, slaves and quasi-free people, assumed responsibility for one another and for the young, the weak, the halt and the blind. After Emancipation, the first Black schools and welfare institutions were founded not by White missionaries, as we have been told, but by Black men and women. Many, perhaps most, of the large number of Black orphans were taken in by Black families, and Black churches and lodges raised thousands of dollars for indigents. The most significant fact about this period is that the Freedmen's Bureau assisted only 0.5 percent of the four million freed Blacks. The Black tradition of self-help spilled over into the 20th century with the work of Black club women and Black churches and fraternal organizations. If Blacks are alive and reasonably well today, it is not because of missionaries and welfare agents—it is because of the extended Black family and house rent parties and church suppers and Black schools and Black churches.

8. **The Black family has always been a matriarchy characterized by strong and domineering women and weak and absent men.** [27]

This is a half-truth which hides and distorts and lies. For it is true that Black America has produced a long line of strong and beautiful Black women, and there is no need for anyone to apologize for it. Because of repeated and continuing attempts to destroy the economic foundations of Black manhood, these women played crucial and pioneering roles in the history of Black people and *the history of women*. But all this must be seen in proper perspective. For Black America has also produced a long line of extraordinary fathers, and Black fathers and mothers working together and loving and living together ensured the survival of Black people. Anyone who doubts this need only read the records (plantation records, Freedmen's Bureau records, census records) which tell us that the Black family was a whole in spirit and in fact until the beginning of the fifty-year Depression (except for World War II and the Korean War) in the 1930s. For some reason, it is not fashionable to celebrate that wholeness in popular plays and movies. Among the notable exceptions are *Sounder* and *Nothing But a Man*. Nor can we overlook the great scene in *A Raisin In The Sun,* when the allegedly matriarchal Mama Lena Younger remembers the strong Black man, now dead, who gave the family the Dream. [28]

9. **Black men cannot sustain stable relationships.** [29]

In simple and insulting terms, this myth asserts that Black men are no-good philanderers who were not made for monogamy. Although the factual lies of the present may appear to give some validity to some aspects of this myth, it is a perversion of the truth. What is so egregiously lacking in these assertions is a sense of social structure and a sense of the dynamics of oppression. For in every oppressed group, certain men (and women) destroy themselves—with drugs, with knives, with guns, with impotent rage—in vain attempts to destroy the loathsome images the oppressors have instilled within them. In other cases, in every oppressed group, certain men (and women) use alienating means, including sex, to affirm themselves and to make themselves real in their own eyes and in the eyes of others. These aberrations, inevitable in any situation of oppression, are expressions not of Black sexuality but of *oppressed* Black sexuality. And it should be borne in mind, in dealing with this myth, that although enforced unemployment and lives of harrowing insecurity have corrupted some men and reduced others to despair and macho futility, most Black fathers are still in their homes, and the Black center is still holding, despite poverty, despite drugs, *despite everything*. There is additional evidence which seems to indicate that middle-class Black fathers are oftentimes more family-oriented than middle-class White fathers. [30]

10. **The history of the Black family is a history of fussin' and fightin' by hard-hearted men and heartless women.** [31]

The images and tones of this myth are part of the national fantasy life. In movies, books and plays, in newspaper stories and TV documentaries, Blacks made in the image of this fantasy are always screeching at each other and playing the marital fool. Rarely if ever do they speak in civil and loving tones. Like archetypes, frozen in time, they seem to be destined to play prefabricated roles in portable and prefabricated Catfish Rows. [32]

"For the vast majority of Negroes," author Charles Keil wrote, "the battle of the sexes is no mere figure of speech. In the ghetto, men and women are considered to be separate and antagonistic species . . . ." [33]

Common sense, the Black birthrate and census figures contradict this idea, which would be funny if it did not carry so much weight in the myth of the Black love deficit. [34]

So persuasive is this myth, so intimidating are its constantly repeated themes, that even Blacks who know better, even Blacks [35] who were raised in the center of an overpowering love, are apologetic and say that there must be something wrong with us.

There is nothing wrong with us. And we must avoid the hyper-empiricist fallacy of constructing theories of Black biology and Black history on the basis of the economic dislocations of today. For when all is said and done the most significant social and sexual fact of our history is that we survived and that the overwhelming majority of Black men and women lived and loved in two-parent households until the 1930s and 1940s. There can be no understanding of the character of Black men and Black women without some understanding of this crucial and still undefined moment in their adventure together. For if, as the statistics say, the overwhelming majority of Black men and women were still living in double-headed households after 200 years of slavery and 80 years of segregation, if after all that time, after the hunger and the cotton and the lies and the blood, they were still together in their hearts and in their homes, then the true story of the Black family is the precise opposite of the myth, and Black men and women deserve credit for creating one of the great love stories of our era. [36]

Far from being ciphers, then, we are and always have been dreamers, witnesses, and *lovers*. The most persuasive evidence on this score is that we endured and created out of the miracle of our survival jazz and the blues and the cakewalk and *Little Sally Walker* and *For Once In My Life* and *Fine and Mellow* and *Satin Doll* and *When Malindy Sings* and *When Sue Wears Red*. [37]

[38]

When Susanna Jones wears red
A queen from some time-dead
Egyptian night
Walks once again.

Blow trumpets, Jesus!

And the beauty of Susanna Jones
in red
Burns in my heart a love-fire
sharp like pain.

Sweet silver trumpets,
*Jesus!**

These and other pieces of evidence, conventional and unconventional, tell us that we have been sold a false bill of goods in this [39] country and that we are greater, more loving and more giving than White media say. And to understand the trumpets and the love-fire of our experience, to understand how we got over and what we must do now to overcome, we must forget everything we think we know about Black women and Black men and go back to the rich soil of our tradition and *dig* there for the spreading roots of a love that slavery and segregation couldn't kill.

It is on this deep level, and in the context of personal family responsibilities, that the crisis of the Black family assumes its true meaning. For given the 300-year war against Black manhood and Black womanhood, and given the circumstances under which most Black fathers and mothers are forced to live, the mystery is not that some have fallen—the mystery is that so many still stand and love. [40]

Sweet silver trumpets,
Jesus!

VOCABULARY

Babylon	a place of excess and wickedness
ciphers	people of no importance
egregiously	notoriously
hyperempiricist	one who relies completely on sense data
impervious	incapable of being affected
indigents	poor people
pathology	deviation from health
philanderers	men who make love with no serious intent
psyche	a person's mental structure
synonymity	wording to express the same idea
vestiges	traces
voyeurism	deriving sexual pleasure from observing others

DESIGN AND MEANING

1. Look the word *myth* up in a college dictionary. Which meaning of the word is Bennett using in this article? Why compare and contrast myth with reality?
2. What three arguments does Bennett use against myth 1 in paragraph 4? Which one do you find strongest?
3. Explain the difference Bennett hints at between the Black and White attitudes toward illegitimacy in paragraph 8.

4. What are the two explanations for social ills given by Nathanson in paragraph 9? How is this point made again in the reply to myth 3?
5. Note three or more places where Bennett emphasizes the contrast between emotion and reason. Why does he emphasize this contrast?
6. You may have noticed that some of Bennett's ten myths overlap. Why do you think he chose to express ten? What other numbers of items do you often see in such a list?

SIMILARITY AND DIFFERENCE

What ideas do Lerone Bennett, Jr., and Deairich Hunter ("Ducks vs. Hard Rocks") share about the state of today's African-American male?

SHORT WRITING IDEA

Bennett uses several names and titles that may or may not be familiar to you. Research one of the following proper nouns and write briefly on its contribution to African-American culture: *Sounder, Raisin in the Sun,* W.E.B. DuBois, Catfish Row, *Nothing But a Man,* Langston Hughes.

LONGER WRITING IDEA

Copying Bennett's format, write an essay contrasting the myth versus the reality about a group of which you are a member.

PREREADING EXERCISE ("Men in Bondage on an Easter Morning")

> No man loveth his fetters, be they made of gold.
>
> —John Heywood, *Proverbs.* i. vii.

> Nor stony tower, nor walls of beaten brass,
> Nor airless dungeon, nor strong links of iron,
> Can be retentive to the strength of spirit.
>
> —Shakespeare, *The Tempest,* I. iii. 8

> Any person who claims to have deep feeling for other human beings should think a long, long time before he votes to have other men kept behind bars—caged.
>
> —Malcolm X, *Autobiography*

Write a paragraph explaining or responding to one of the quotations above.

Seymour Krim

Men in Bondage on an Easter Morning

A reporter, publicity writer, and teacher of writing, Krim (b. 1922) also writes essays which afford sardonic insights into American society. The following selection is taken from his collection *Shake It for the World, Smartass* (1971).

Ossining, N.Y.—God may be dead or hiding down in that neon-lit circus of the soul called Manhattan, but his traditional image was very much alive up here on Easter Sunday—both inside the walls of Sing Sing and out, both in the secure and in the disturbing sense. [1]

In this quiet town, the conservative Christian element went to church in the overcast late morning, then some saw "The Greatest Story Ever Told" at the Victoria Theater and topped it off with the $4.50 turkey dinner at Pastor's Steak House. Bright new bonnets were heaped on the checkroom counter; and the mothers watched carefully to see that giblet-and-gravy stains were efficiently sponged off eyecatching new dresses on their daughters and tight little three-button suits on their sons. [2]

Inside the flat grey prison compound, where the electric chair has been quiet these past two years, the mood of the day was almost exactly the same—except for the absence of the children. Downstairs in the visitor's room, after morning chapel and the noontime dinner of roast chicken and mashed potatoes, 40 cons in clean white shirts and sharply pressed trousers visited with wives and girlfriends across the tables that are divided by no screen. [3]

It was a time for reunion—mostly whispered, with hands doing the most expressive talking. [4]

Out on the ballfield, where the season starts in two weeks, four lone men with no dependents were loosening up on the bleak diamond. And in front of the messhall hundreds of prisoners sucked on cigarettes or played cards while waiting for *their* Easter movie to begin. [5]

They had seen a double-bill yesterday, "Operation Crossbow" and "Follow That Dream," but time hangs heavy for these 1800 long-termers and Paramount Pictures had sent up its 10-year-old [6] popularization of "The Ten Commandments" as an appropriate film for this particular day. At 1 P.M., more than 1000 of the men began to file into the chapel, now converted into an auditorium, and took hard wooden seats in front of a white screen with an American flag pinned over it.

[7] Paramount has made a neat $80 million out of its lush religious fairytale, which was the final life-work of the flamboyant Cecil B. DeMille, and the skilled business minds who earned that company a $6 million profit last year thought that this prison-locked Easter showing would be a wise move in the national reissue of the film. They were right. But they could never have anticipated why "The Ten Commandments" made such a sharp and disturbing impression on the men packed into the Sing Sing chapel yesterday afternoon.

[8] Although Mr. DeMille was apparently as much boy as he was man, and fashioned a shallow, brightly colored entertainment out of the enormous metaphysical riddles that surround the legend of Moses' confrontation with the God of the Old Testament, the men were gripped to silence by the pictures of the Israelites under the Egyptian whip.

[9] The reason for their intense silence was not hard to search for. Eighty percent of the men in that hall, a little over 800, were either Negro or Puerto Rican—they dominated the audience just as they dominate Sing Sing. And when the Jews in the film begged for a messiah, someone to deliver them from the impotence of their plight as slaves to the Egyptians, a Negro convict in the audience muttered, "Malcolm was our goddam messiah but he got shot down."

[10] There were wild cheers for the goodlooking women—some of them deep African or Ethiopian—who danced across the screen, and there were homosexually aware laughs when Moses (Charlton Heston) embraced Joshua (John Derek), but it was near to impossible to get a laugh out of the prisoners as they watched scene after scene of the degradation of Moses' people by the Egyptians.

[11] Suddenly, to an observer, all of the lyrics of Negro blues songs and spirituals that identify with "the children of Israel" became concrete as one watched the hunched men in the audience with their eyes riveted on the film. It was not far-fetched to imagine that they were watching a metaphor of their own situation in white America—one that has filled prisons across the country with a frustrated, often hopeless majority of darkskinned people that far outnumber their white counterparts and make U.S. prisons into black Harlems and Spanish Harlems that the average middleclass person never hears about.

[12] That, perhaps, is the most important news one can send out of Ossining at the end of a "traditional" Easter Sunday with all the so-called trimmings.

VOCABULARY

degradation	reduction to a low, hopeless condition; humiliation
determinism	the concept that environment and heredity control human destiny
flamboyant	flashy, showy
impotence	inability to act; state of being incapable
lush	luxurious
metaphor	an implied imaginative comparison of two unlike things by means of one trait they share
Ossining	town in New York where a famous state prison known as Sing Sing was located

DESIGN AND MEANING

1. Find five pairs of comparisons and contrasts in the essay. The main one is the comparison between the Jews of Israel and the prisoners in Sing Sing. What do the other contrasts contribute to the essay?
2. What expectations does the opening paragraph set up about what the tone and message of the essay will be?
3. What does Krim think of DeMille's movie *The Ten Commandments?* Point out specific words and phrases that led you to your answer. What are the connotations of those words and phrases in this context?
4. Krim's style benefits from masterful diction. List some examples of vivid descriptive writing that has sensory appeal. Be sure to look at the verbs as well as the adjectives, adverbs, and nouns.
5. Why is the one-sentence paragraph 4 left to stand by itself?
6. Focus on the words "traditional" (in quotation marks) and "so-called trimmings" in the conclusion. How do they contribute to the essay's unity and meaning?
7. What audience do you think Krim would like to reach with this essay?

SIMILARITY AND DIFFERENCE

Comparing Krim's essay with Hunter's "Ducks vs. Hard Rocks," would you say that one writer more than the other believes in individual free will over determinism, or would they probably agree on the subject of free will versus determinism?

SHORT WRITING IDEA

Observe a friend or relative watching a program on television. Record in as much detail as you can this person's responses to the program. Remember to include body language as well as facial expressions. Write a paragraph based on your observation.

LONG WRITING IDEA

Krim's essay is partly a description of the "haves" and the "have-nots" on Easter. Write an essay about another group of "haves" and "have-nots" that you are aware of. To make your contrasts clear, put these privileged and disadvantaged people into specific situations (celebrating a holiday, renting an apartment, choosing a college).

VOCABULARY CHECK

Complete the following sentences in any way that makes good sense.

1. The lush decor of the hotel lobby made him think of
2. Passing through Ossining, Marla said she felt
3. Marcia's metaphors are often
4. Edith felt impotent after
5. My flamboyant friend Fred wears
6. The degradation of bankruptcy forced

J. Baldwin

They Don't Make Them Like They Used To (Thank Goodness)

J. Baldwin says he has "no career," but is an industrial designer, teaches art and design, guides whitewater rafting trips, invents structures harmonious with the environment, and plays piano, autoharp, and saw. He is the technical editor of the periodical *Whole Earth Review* and is the editor of the 1986 *Essential Whole Earth Catalog,* both of which "give the readers access to tools and ideas that yuppies may have missed in their education but which are nonetheless essential."

Selective nostalgia seems to be the basis for claims that older cars were "better" than those sold today. Yas, Yas, remember the wonderful thick metal they used to use for fenders? We now realize that needlessly heavy metal made a wastefully heavy, fuel-hungry car. It added neither longevity nor safety. If it had, we'd see many more oldies on the road, and occupant crash-protection statistics would show a rise in deaths and injuries as older cars are phased out. But the studies show that the death rate in actual number and in deaths-per-mile-driven are both improving—despite the increasing number of lightweight cars. [1]

This is partly the result of better roads, but it is also the result of the modern automobile's far-superior brakes, roadholding, handling and general crash-worthiness. If you think your '53 Mercury was so great, I suggest you arrange to drive one or one of its porcine peers. Though the ambience may still be charming, you'll probably be horrified at the clumsy ineptitude on the road. If you try an older model of good repute, such as a 20-year-old Volvo, you may be surprised at how far even lowly cars have advanced since those worthy machines were sold new. [2]

What about longevity? Statistics show that modern cars are driven further than their predecessors before they're junked. 100,000 miles was once considered exceptional before overhaul time. Now it is common to see even pipsqueak foreign cars logging far more than that. But mechanical wear can be compensated for by repair or replacement. *Rust* is the real Grim Reaper because it [3] can't be fixed. Those fondly remembered thick fenders took a while to rust through, but eventually they did. Modern cars are made of thinner, but lighter, high-strength steels that are treated to resist corrosion far longer than previously. Many cars now are even galvanized.

[4] There are several other reasons why we don't see many of the older, supposedly better cars on the road today. One is that "The Road" has changed. Ford made 15 million Model Ts for use at a time when most roads were unpaved. Obviously the Tin Lizzie isn't appropriate anymore. Even in less developed countries where roads are still similar to 1920 U.S. roads, the T is not appropriate. A modern version of it might be, though—one that utilizes today's knowledge of metallurgy, chassis dynamics and safety.

[5] Another reason oldies aren't often seen is that tastes have changed. You could call it "driver education." Rolling living rooms that got 10 miles per gallon have given way to fuel-frugal cars that better obey the driver and hence celebrate, rather than deny, the act of hurtling. Newer models are more competent on country roads, too, in answer to demands of the many Americans now recreating in the boondocks instead of at slick, freeway-served resorts. As design has improved, even economy models that used to be insultingly crude and operationally rude have in most respects become superior to expensive models past.

[6] To be sure, the present sporty, roadable car has an image generated by advertising. So be it. The new cars *are* better in most ways for the average user. It's not just hype. If you object to ad-generated "demand," remember that manufacturers must encourage the Urge to Buy or they'd go out of business. Tooling up for a new model can cost billions. That has to be recouped, of course, but perhaps more important is that the *system* that brings cars has to be kept healthy so that cars can be afforded. Low sales mean higher unit prices. That's a capitalist fact of life, and it's also one reason cars don't last, say, 20 years. If they did, the market would soon be saturated. Economies of mass production would be lost as demand dropped.

[7] And what if you'd bought a 20-year car in 1972, the year before the "energy crisis"? Would you want to keep that gas pig until 1992? Some conditions change more often than in 20-year increments. You might also take a look at a twenty-year-old car you know. It's probably pretty beat up. Let's face it, cars and all other manufactured (or handmade) artifacts wear out. (*You* wear out.) Things have to be replaced sooner or later. Which brings this discussion to Planned Obsolescence—things deliberately designed to break or wear out "before their time." The bane of the eco-righteous.

[8] Planned obsolescence can't be reasonably examined until it is

separated from "fair wear and tear"—things deteriorating as expected. Many people don't realize that virtually all engineered artifacts have an expected lifespan consciously designed into them. Since anything inevitably wears out, *when* it does so must be decided. In critical cases such as aircraft, that point is chosen after careful analysis, so that parts can confidently and economically be replaced according to a predetermined schedule *before* they fail. With cars, where you can walk home, only parts critical to safety are designed so that failure is unlikely during the expected lifetime of the vehicle. To do otherwise would invite negligent-death lawsuits and public outcry. You hardly ever hear of total steering failure, for instance. But the designed life of noncritical parts is chosen according to other criteria, one of which could be said to be planned obsolescence.

[9] For example, the engine and drive system are, by custom, intended to last at least 100,000 miles. If they don't, the car's reputation would suffer. But the interior and other unguaranteed "soft trim" can be expected to reach tackydom well before that. For many users, that point will be reached at just about the same time the car is paid for and the buyer is most vulnerable to New Car Fever. Clever.

[10] It must also be said that cars are rarely sold at the currently-possible state-of-the-art. An annoying example is the rarely even optional ABS (non-skid) brake system. You would think that carmakers would gladly equip their wares with the best brakes available, or at least offer them as an option. The ideas of optional safety in an industry that kills so many people can certainly be questioned morally, but "safety doesn't sell" has long been considered a truism in the auto industry. In any case, it makes marketing sense to withhold improvements until an excessively frisky competitor forces your hand. Note, however, that when a significant improvement *does* make it to market, earlier models are obsoleted—truly and suddenly.

[11] When the changes and "improvements" are mere styling fads like fins or Opera Lamps, the obsolescence is in the mind of the buyer. In that case, we get what we deserve.

[12] To make things more clear, let's take a look at a vehicle of legendary reputation, the VW Beetle. It is ironic that most machines enjoying legendary status have been, even when new, basically awful. The Beetle was a remarkably poor design: singularly treacherous handling and a uniquely cramped interior for its size (other cars the same size are 40 percent bigger inside) combined with a valve-eating engine of weak, not particularly economical performance. Where did the good reputation come from? It came from three related sources (plus a little luck in having competition

that was even worse): *mechanical simplicity, comprehensibility,* and *fixability.* These salutary characteristics and the consequent mechanical reliability were augmented by a long production run that engendered a lively, knowledgeable subculture of used machines, used and reconditioned parts fitting most models, and a vast know-how among lay mechanics. The VW also possessed a strong character that made it a favorite of the funky 60s folk and others who eschewed the banal. Today's cars come from corporations run by unimaginative accountants instead of individualistic engineers. New cars are appliances. Boring, too.

New cars are also not particularly amenable to being serviced by ordinary people. The unfortunate complexity is mostly the result of the indisputable necessity of reducing emissions and conserving fuel. It is not generally recognized that the rest of the new cars' mechanism is often *simpler* than older models, and ritualistic maintenance procedures are much less frequent. Yes, turbos add complexity, but many folks apparently think it's worth it. [13]

This is not to say that cars with good performance cannot be built in a way that is easier to maintain than at present. It can certainly be done, and some companies are showing interest in the subject. The motives of companies that don't seem to care about owner maintenance can be understood, if not condoned, by asking yourself if you personally would give away large sums of money so that other people don't have to spend large sums of money. Most people just don't behave that way, and it isn't reasonable to expect a corporation to do differently. [14]

There's another aspect to this: you often hear do-it-yourself mechanics complain that certain parts of new cars can't be repaired, but must be replaced at annoying expense. This is because society has agreed that mechanics deserve a living wage. That wage makes it unreasonable to spend large amounts of expensive time fooling around with finicky repairs. Replacement is faster, and in the long run cheaper for you, despite the heart-stopping parts bill. It's cheaper for the average car owner, not the home mechanic. But the majority rules. [15]

In somewhat the same vein (hee hee), it can legitimately be claimed that modern suspension and steering joints without grease fittings don't last as long as the older designs with fittings. But the longer lifespan of the older parts was *potential*—true only if those fittings got the grease, and on time. Most didn't. For the average owner, the pre-greased parts are cheaper in the long run. For those who care for their own cars, "permanently" lubed parts are irritating and even insolent. It seems that most people prefer to drive it and forget it; the less maintenance the better. It's a delicious twist that makes it possible to assert that the no-maintenance machine [16] is the result of a growing distaste for technology. People like cars that don't make unseemly demands on people, but they pay for the privilege.

[17] One last point: In the wonderful, trouble-free past where things were made of steel and never wore out, the majority of vehicles (and everything else) were mediocre, just as it is now. The machines we revere in memory were exceptional in their own day, though that was not necessarily recognized at the time. It is possible and even probable that a few of today's models will be recognized as outstanding. Several Japanese models are in that category now.

[18] And remember that whenever you hear someone say, "I've just thought of a better way . . . ," obsolescence is creeping up on someone else's idea of nifty that has run its course. Surely the messier aspects of today's technology *deserve* obsoleting. Many of the objects we have learned to love are energy pigs or have some other obnoxious facet. Perhaps we are maddened by obsolescence because it reminds us of our own mortality.

VOCABULARY

ambience	the mood or character of an environment
amenable	agreeable, yielding
augment	increase
banal	stale, unoriginal
condone	pardon
eschew	avoid
facet	aspect, part
frugal	economical
galvanized	coated with zinc to prevent rust
increments	stages
insolent	insulting, arrogant
porcine	piglike
recoup	recover
salutary	beneficial
truism	an obviously true statement

DESIGN AND MEANING

1. What is the purpose of Baldwin's comparison of old and new cars? Do you find the essay persuasive—that is, does it fulfill its purpose?

2. What are some characteristics of the person Baldwin sees as the "average" American car owner?
3. Summarize Baldwin's main points about each of the following topics:

   safety

   longevity

   demand

   planned obsolescence

   service
4. After reading the essay, how would you define "selective nostalgia"?
5. Examine the opening of each body paragraph, which provides a bridge that indicates how this paragraph is related to the one before it. What are at least three techniques Baldwin uses to make these transitions?

SIMILARITY AND DIFFERENCE

What might Baldwin say to Williamson about his essay, "The Mudbacks" (Chapter 1)?

SHORT WRITING IDEA

In his conclusion, Baldwin says that "many of the objects we have learned to love are energy pigs or have some other obnoxious facet." Write a paragraph telling about some object that you have learned to love that has some "obnoxious facet." Suggestions: your old sweat pants, an unwanted gift, an antique personal computer, your little brother.

LONGER WRITING IDEA

Many times we feel nostalgic about old ways, customs, techniques, or things. Write an essay about something old that you feel nostalgic about and that has been replaced with something new. Be sure to tell whether the new thing is really an improvement or really a decline—or a mixture.

VOCABULARY CHECK

Put a form of one of the vocabulary words in each blank.

1. When Bob became engaged to Evelyn, the only words of praise his mother could muster were about sensible Evelyn's ______.
2. ______ those gutters before you put them up, Franklin.
3. Sal's irritation with Franklin was ______ : it multiplied with every odd quirk he displayed.
4. With her parents' help, Sally found her income plentifully ____.
5. Sal has always been rude to loved ones because her parents ______ such behavior.

poetry

Adrienne Rich

Living in Sin

Adrienne Rich (b. 1929), one of the most prestigious contemporary poets, has published five volumes of poetry. Many of her poems are widely anthologized.

She had thought the studio would keep itself;
no dust upon the furniture of love.
Half heresy, to wish the taps less vocal,
the panes relieved of grime. A plate of pears,
a piano with a Persian shawl, a cat [5]
stalking the picturesque amusing mouse
had risen at his urging.
Not that at five each separate stair would writhe
under the milkman's tramp; that morning light
so coldly would delineate the scraps [10]
of last night's cheese and three sepulchral bottles;
that on the kitchen shelf among the saucers
a pair of beetle-eyes would fix her own—
envoy from some village in the moldings . . .
Meanwhile, he, with a yawn, [15]
sounded a dozen notes upon the keyboard,
declared it out of tune, shrugged at the mirror,
rubbed at his beard, went out for cigarettes;
while she, jeered by the minor demons,
pulled back the sheets and made the bed and found [20]
a towel to dust the table-top,
and let the coffee-pot boil over on the stove.
By evening she was back in love again,
though not as wholly but throughout the night
she woke sometimes to feel the daylight coming [25]
like a relentless milkman up the stairs.

DESIGN AND MEANING

1. What two things are being contrasted in "Living in Sin"?
2. Which part does Rich give more space and description to? Why?
3. Where did the narrator get her image of what living together would be like?
4. What principle does Rich use to organize the details from line 8 to the end? What other principle could be used for such a description?
5. What associations does the final simile hold for you? How does this simile contrast with the way lovers traditionally feel about the coming of daylight?
6. How does the conclusion give unity to the poem?
7. What may the writer's purpose be in expressing this contrast?

SHORT WRITING IDEA

Copy the specific details in "Living in Sin." Then make a similar list of specific details that describe one everyday routine in your life: waking up, traveling to work, diapering the baby, coming home from school, or an activity along those lines.

LONGER WRITING IDEA

In Rich's poem, the woman expected one thing and got quite a different one. Write an essay in which you contrast an expectation you once had with the reality you found.

William Blake

The Garden of Love

William Blake (1757–1827), who was considered widely innovative, if not mad, in his day, was a professional engraver and illustrator whose poems received little attention. Today both his poetry and his illustrations are considered works of genius.

I went to the Garden of Love,
And saw what I never had seen:
A chapel was built in the midst,
Where I used to play on the green.

And the gates of this chapel were shut, [5]
And "Thou shalt not" writ over the door;
So I turned to the Garden of Love
That so many sweet flowers bore;

And I saw it was filled with graves,
And tomb-stones where flowers should be; [10]
And priests in black gowns were walking their rounds,
And binding with briars my joys & desires.

DESIGN AND MEANING

1. What contrast does "The Garden of Love" make?
2. What is the narrator's attitude toward organized religion? What details suggest this attitude? What detail most strongly reveals this attitude to you?
3. For the most part, the poem is written in simple, plain words—not the fancier words that many people consider more poetic. Do you think plain words can be appropriate in a poem? In this poem?
4. Find the patterns of sound in the poem. What do you think is the effect of the variations in the last two lines?
5. Find the pattern of punctuation in the poem. Does the poem use conventional sentence punctuation? How does the punctuation influence the way you would read the poem aloud?

SIMILARITY AND DIFFERENCE

Compare the ideas in "The Garden of Love" with the allegory of "The Other Side of the Hedge" at the end of this chapter. Do you think the writers of the two works basically agree or disagree?

SHORT WRITING IDEA

In Blake's poem, flowers are associated with life and love, and graves with death. Make a list of objects and sounds that you associate with life. Opposite that list, write a list of objects and sounds you associate with death. Your associations may be entirely personal: for instance, you may associate the sound of a train whistle with death even though no one else does.

LONGER WRITING IDEA

Write a poem or essay that makes a contrast between some place, person, or situation *then* and *now* in your life, and in which you reveal a strong preference for either *then* or *now*. Imply your preference, as Blake does in his poem, rather than stating it directly.

Edna St. Vincent Millay

The Spring and the Fall

Edna St. Vincent Millay (called "Vincent" by her family and close friends) lived from 1892 to 1950 and began winning awards for her writing at an early age. She won the 1923 Pulitzer Prize for her book *The Harp-Weaver and Other Poems*. Her abundant poetry reflects her wide travel, nontraditional lifestyle, social conscience, and introspective nature.

In the spring of the year, in the spring of the year,
I walked the road beside my dear.
The trees were black where the bark was wet.
I see them yet, in the spring of the year.
He broke me a bough of the blossoming peach [5]
That was out of the way and hard to reach.

In the fall of the year, in the fall of the year,
I walked the road beside my dear.
The rooks went up with a raucous trill.
I hear them still, in the fall of the year. [10]
He laughed at all I dared to praise,
And broke my heart, in little ways.

Year be springing or year be falling,
The bark will drip and the birds be calling.
There's much that's fine to see and hear [15]
In the spring of a year, in the fall of a year.
'Tis not love's going hurts my days,
But that it went in little ways.

DESIGN AND MEANING

1. What is the logic behind the division of stanzas in "The Spring and the Fall"? In other words, what is the topic of each stanza?
2. How is the change in the couple's relationship established? What incidents are significant?
3. What are the traditional associations with the seasons of spring and fall? How do they relate to the theme of this poem?

4. Why is the idea "broke my heart, in little ways" unusual? What do we ordinarily expect when people speak of broken hearts?
5. Can you speculate on what are some of the other "little ways" that the man broke the speaker's heart?

SIMILARITY AND DIFFERENCE

Relate the theme of this poem to the theme of Rich's "Living in Sin" in this chapter.

SHORT WRITING IDEA

Write a paragraph about something in your own life that "went in little ways": your innocence, your childhood, your love of learning, your bank account, your running shoes.

LONGER WRITING IDEA

Write an essay about a changed relationship in your life. Be sure to establish clearly the contrast between two periods of the relationship. The change you describe may be negative (as in the poem), positive, or just a significant shift.

Henry Reed

Naming of Parts

Since World War II, the British poet Henry Reed (b. 1914) has been writing for the BBC. "Naming of Parts" is the first section of a longer poem entitled "Lessons of the War."

Today we have naming of parts. Yesterday,
We had daily cleaning. And tomorrow morning,
We shall have what to do after firing. But today,
Today we have naming of parts. Japonica
Glistens like coral in all of the neighboring gardens, [5]
　　And today we have naming of parts.

This is the lower sling swivel. And this
Is the upper sling swivel, whose use you will see,
When you are given your slings. And this is the piling swivel,
Which in your case you have not got. The branches [10]
Hold in the gardens their silent, eloquent gestures,
　　Which in our case we have not got.

This is the safety-catch, which is always released
With an easy flick of the thumb. And please do not let me
See anyone using his finger. You can do it quite easy [15]
If you have any strength in your thumb. The blossoms
Are fragile and motionless, never letting anyone see
　　Any of them using their finger.

And this you can see is the bolt. The purpose of this
Is to open the breech, as you see. We can slide it [20]
Rapidly backwards and forwards: we call this
Easing the spring. And rapidly backwards and forwards
The early bees are assaulting and fumbling the flowers:
　　They call it easing the Spring.

They call it easing the Spring: it is perfectly easy [25]
If you have any strength in your thumb: like the bolt,
And the breech, and the cocking-piece, and the point of balance,
Which in our case we have not got; and the almond-blossom
Silent in all of the gardens and the bees going backwards and
　　forwards,
　　For today we have naming of parts. [30]

VOCABULARY

delineate	to explain point by point
dialect	a manner of speaking common only to people from, or living in, a specific area
eloquent	able to speak (or write) in an especially moving and effective way
envoy	a messenger from, or representative of, a higher authority
flunkie	a person who does small, boring, or meaningless tasks at the orders of someone else; a "go-fer" (also spelled "flunky," "flunkey")
heresy	a belief or action that contradicts the official or strongly held beliefs of a society or organization, especially a church
japonica	a shrub that flowers profusely in spring
relentless	untiring, unwavering, ceaseless, persistent
sepulchral	like a tomb; having a tomblike atmosphere
whence	from which; where something came from
writ	a legal document, usually ordering some specific action

DESIGN AND MEANING

1. There are two speakers in "Naming of Parts": a sergeant and a recruit. When, in each stanza, does the shift between speakers occur? What differences in style can you point out between the speakers? List specific words that indicate each speaker's diction.
2. Name the tensions the poem develops between the worlds of the two speakers in these areas:

   Psychological

   Physical (objects)

   Philosophical
3. Find phrases that are repeated in two different contexts within stanzas. Define the contrast between the phrase used in the first context and in the second.

4. How could you account for the difference between the concluding stanza and the other stanzas? Why does the last line give the poem unity?
5. Whom would you guess the writer would like as an audience for this poem? Why?
6. What sexual implications do you see in the word choice and imagery? What relationship does sex have to the meaning of the poem?

SIMILARITY AND DIFFERENCE

Unlike "The Garden of Love" and "The Spring and the Fall," "Naming of Parts" and "Living in Sin" do not have line divisions based on rhyme or traditional sentence structure. Can you find any logic to the line division in these last two poems?

SHORT WRITING IDEA

Write a paragraph or two describing a situation in which someone tried to explain something or teach something to you while your mind drifted off to completely different thoughts.

LONGER WRITING IDEA

Choose a word or phrase, and write an essay describing how it can have different meanings (even contrasting ones) in different contexts (for example, "Just a minute," "Excuse me," "I love you," "Here we are").

VOCABULARY CHECK

Indicate whether the italicized words in the following sentences are defined correctly or not by writing *true* or *false* beside each sentence.

_______ **1.** A *sepulchral* mood is a depressing one.

_______ **2.** To speak in *dialect* means to speak elegantly.

_______ **3.** A *flunky* is an amateur musician.

_______ **4.** A *writ* is an informal note.

_______ **5.** To *delineate* a problem helps to understand it.

_______ **6.** A person who is *eloquent* is always boring.

_______ **7.** A *relentless* pursuer is one who never gives up the chase.

_______ **8.** To speak *heresy* was dangerous in the Middle Ages.

_______ **9.** If you are an *envoy,* you carry messages.

_______ **10.** *Japonica* is a dessert made with heavy cream.

Short Story

E. M. Forster

The Other Side of the Hedge

Born in London and educated at Cambridge, Forster (1879–1970) was a member of the celebrated circle of intellectuals known as the Bloomsbury group. Although his reputation rests mainly upon his novels and critical works, he also produced several brilliant short stories which, like the following selection, involve the use of allegory.

My pedometer told me that I was twenty-five; and, though it is a shocking thing to stop walking, I was so tired that I sat down on a milestone to rest. People outstripped me, jeering as they did so, but I was too apathetic to feel resentful, and even when Miss Eliza Dimbleby, the great educationist, swept past, exhorting me to persevere, I only smiled and raised my hat. [1]

At first I thought I was going to be like my brother, whom I had had to leave by the roadside a year or two round the corner. He had wasted his breath on singing, and his strength on helping others. But I had travelled more wisely, and now it was only the monotony of the highway that oppressed me—dust under foot and brown crackling hedges on either side, ever since I could remember. [2]

And I had already dropped several things—indeed, the road behind was strewn with the things we all had dropped; and the white dust was settling down on them, so that already they looked no better than stones. My muscles were so weary that I could not even bear the weight of those things I still carried. I slid off the milestone into the road, and lay there prostrate, with my face to the great parched hedge, praying that I might give up. [3]

A little puff of air revived me. It seemed to come from the hedge; and, when I opened my eyes, there was a glint of light through the tangle of boughs and dead leaves. The hedge could not be as thick as usual. In my weak, morbid state, I longed to force my way in, [4] and see what was on the other side. No one was in sight, or I should not have dared to try. For we of the road do not admit in conversation that there is another side at all.

I yielded to the temptation, saying to myself that I would come back in a minute. The thorns scratched my face, and I had to use my arms as a shield, depending on my feet alone to push me forward. Halfway through I would have gone back, for in the passage all the things I was carrying were scraped off me, and my clothes were torn. But I was so wedged that return was impossible, and I had to wiggle blindly forward, expecting every moment that my strength would fail me, and that I should perish in the undergrowth. [5]

Suddenly cold water closed round my head, and I seemed sinking down for ever. I had fallen out of the hedge into a deep pool. I rose to the surface at last, crying for help, and I heard someone on the opposite bank laugh and say: "Another!" And then I was twitched out and laid panting on the dry ground. [6]

Even when the water was out of my eyes, I was still dazed, for I had never been in so large a space, nor seen such grass and sunshine. The blue sky was no longer a strip, and beneath it the earth had risen grandly into hills—clean, bare buttresses, with beech trees in their folds, and meadows and clear pools at their feet. But the hills were not high, and there was in the landscape a sense of human occupation—so that one might have called it a park, or garden, if the words did not imply a certain triviality and constraint. [7]

As soon as I got my breath, I turned to my rescuer and said: [8]

"Where does this place lead to?" [9]

"Nowhere, thank the Lord!" said he, and laughed. He was a man of fifty or sixty—just the kind of age we mistrust on the road—but there was no anxiety in his manner, and his voice was that of a boy of eighteen. [10]

"But it must lead somewhere!" I cried, too much surprised at his answer to thank him for saving my life. [11]

"He wants to know where it leads!" he shouted to some men on the hill side, and they laughed back, and waved their caps. [12]

I noticed then that the pool into which I had fallen was really a moat which bent round to the left and to the right, and that the hedge followed it continually. The hedge was green on this side—its roots showed through the clear water, and fish swam about in them—and it was wreathed over with dog-roses and Traveller's Joy. But it was a barrier, and in a moment I lost all pleasure in the grass, the sky, the trees, the happy men and women, and realized that the place was but a prison, for all its beauty and extent. [13]

We moved away from the boundary, and then followed a path almost parallel to it, across the meadows. I found it difficult walk- [14]

ing, for I was always trying to out-distance my companion, and there was no advantage in doing this if the place led nowhere. I had never kept step with anyone since I left my brother.

[15] I amused him by stopping suddenly and saying disconsolately, "This is perfectly terrible. One cannot advance: one cannot progress. Now we of the road——"

[16] "Yes. I know."

[17] "I was going to say, we advance continually."

[18] "I know."

[19] "We are always learning, expanding, developing. Why, even in my short life I have seen a great deal of advance—the Transvaal War, the Fiscal Question, Christian Science, Radium. Here for example—"

[20] I took out my pedometer, but it still marked twenty-five, not a degree more.

[21] "Oh, it's stopped! I meant to show you. It should have registered all the time I was walking with you. But it makes me only twenty-five."

[22] "Many things don't work in here," he said. "One day a man brought in a Lee-Metford, and that wouldn't work."

[23] "The laws of science are universal in their application. It must be the water in the moat that has injured the machinery. In normal conditions everything works. Science and the spirit of emulation—those are the forces that have made us what we are."

[24] I had to break off and acknowledge the pleasant greetings of people whom we passed. Some of them were singing, some talking, some engaged in gardening, hay-making, or other rudimentary industries. They all seemed happy; and I might have been happy too, if I could have forgotten that the place led nowhere.

[25] I was startled by a young man who came sprinting across our path, took a little fence in fine style, and went tearing over a ploughed field till he plunged into a lake, across which he began to swim. Here was true energy, and I exclaimed: "A cross-country race! Where are the others?"

[26] "There are no others," my companion replied; and, later on, when we passed some long grass from which came the voice of a girl singing exquisitely to herself, he said again: "There are no others." I was bewildered at the waste in production, and murmured to myself, "What does it all mean?"

[27] He said: "It means nothing but itself"—and he repeated the words slowly, as if I were a child.

[28] "I understand," I said quietly, "but I do not agree. Every achievement is worthless unless it is a link in the chain of development. And I must not trespass on your kindness any longer. I must get back somehow to the road, and have my pedometer mended."

"First, you must see the gates," he replied, "for we have gates, though we never use them." [29]

I yielded politely, and before long we reached the moat again, at a point where it was spanned by a bridge. Over the bridge was a big gate, as white as ivory, which was fitted into a gap in the boundary hedge. The gate opened outwards, and I exclaimed in amazement, for from it ran a road—just such a road as I had left—dusty under foot, with brown crackling hedges on either side as far as the eye could reach. [30]

"That's my road!" I cried. [31]

He shut the gate and said: "But not your part of the road. It is through this gate that humanity went out countless ages ago, when it was first seized with the desire to walk." [32]

I denied this, observing that the part of the road I myself had left was not more than two miles off. But with the obstinacy of his years he repeated: "It is the same road. This is the beginning, and though it seems to run straight away from us, it doubles so often, that it is never far from our boundary and sometimes touches it." He stooped down by the moat, and traced on its moist margin an absurd figure like a maze. As we walked back through the meadows, I tried to convince him of his mistake. [33]

"The road sometimes doubles, to be sure, but that is part of our discipline. Who can doubt that its general tendency is onward? To what goal we know not—it may be to some mountain where we shall touch the sky, it may be over precipices into the sea. But that it goes forward—who can doubt that? It is the thought of that that makes us strive to excel, each in his own way, and gives us an impetus which is lacking with you. Now that man who passed us—it's true that he ran well, and jumped well, and swam well; but we have men who can run better, and men who can jump better, and who can swim better. Specialization has produced results which would surprise you. Similarly, that girl——" [34]

Here I interrupted myself to exclaim: "Good gracious me! I could have sworn it was Miss Eliza Dimbleby over there, with her feet in the fountain!" [35]

He believed that it was. [36]

"Impossible! I left her on the road, and she is due to lecture this evening at Tunbridge Wells. Why, her train leaves Cannon Street in—of course my watch has stopped like everything else. She is the last person to be here." [37]

"People always are astonished at meeting each other. All kinds come through the hedge, and come at all times—when they are drawing ahead in the race, when they are lagging behind, when they are left for dead. I often stand near the boundary listening to the sounds of the road—you know what they are—and wonder if [38] anyone will turn aside. It is my great happiness to help someone out of the moat, as I helped you. For our country fills up slowly, though it was meant for all mankind."

"Mankind have other aims," I said gently, for I thought him well-meaning; "and I must join them." I bade him good evening, for the sun was declining, and I wished to be on the road by nightfall. To my alarm, he caught hold of me, crying: "You are not to go yet!" I tried to shake him off, for we had no interests in common, and his civility was becoming irksome to me. But for all my struggles the tiresome old man would not let go; and, as wrestling is not my speciality, I was obliged to follow him. [39]

It was true that I could have never found alone the place where I came in, and I hoped that, when I had seen the other sights about which he was worrying, he would take me back to it. But I was determined not to sleep in the country, for I mistrusted it, and the people too, for all their friendliness. Hungry though I was, I would not join them in their evening meals of milk and fruit, and, when they gave me flowers, I flung them away as soon as I could do so unobserved. Already they were lying down for the night like cattle—some out on the bare hillside, others in groups under the beeches. In the light of an orange sunset I hurried on with my unwelcome guide, dead tired, faint from want of food, but murmuring indomitably: "Give me life, with its struggles and victories, with its failures and hatreds, with its deep moral meaning and its unknown goal!" [40]

At last we came to a place where the encircling moat was spanned by another bridge, and where another gate interrupted the line of the boundary hedge. It was different from the first gate; for it was half transparent like horn, and opened inwards. But through it, in the waning light, I saw again just such a road as I had left—monotonous, dusty, with brown crackling hedges on either side, as far as the eye could reach. [41]

I was strangely disquieted at the sight, which seemed to deprive me of all self-control. A man was passing us, returning for the night to the hills, with a scythe over his shoulder and a can of some liquid in his hand. I forgot the destiny of our race. I forgot the road that lay before my eyes, and I sprang at him, wrenched the can out of his hand, and began to drink. [42]

It was nothing stronger than beer, but in my exhausted state it overcame me in a moment. As in a dream, I saw the old man shut the gate, and heard him say: "This is where your road ends, and through this gate humanity—all that is left of it—will come in to us." [43]

Though my senses were sinking into oblivion, they seemed to expand ere they reached it. They perceived the magic song of night- [44]

ingales, and the odour of invisible hay, and stars piercing the fading sky. The man whose beer I had stolen lowered me down gently to sleep off its effects, and, as he did so, I saw that he was my brother.

VOCABULARY

allegory	a story in which the literal happenings also have a set of symbolic meanings, usually expressing some truths or generalizations about human conduct or experience
buttresses	supports for something
civility	good manners, politeness
constraint	something that prevents people from doing something they might otherwise do; a hindrance
disquieted	uneasy, nervous, upset
emulation	deliberate use of someone else's life or behavior as an example or model
ere	before
exhorting	urging someone to do something
impetus	the spark or reason for doing something
irksome	unpleasant, bothersome
irony	an action or statement which expresses something other than, and especially the opposite of, its literal meaning
Lee-Metford	a British military rifle
milestone	a marker showing the distance from or to another place
morbid	deathlike
oblivion	complete forgetfulness; senselessness
obstinacy	great stubbornness
persevere	to continue despite hardships or failures
precipice	the edge of a cliff or other great height from which there is a long, sharp drop
prostrate	lying down or struck down by exhaustion, difficulties, or defeat
rudimentary	not yet developed
triviality	something unimportant

DESIGN AND MEANING

1. What judgments can you make about the story from the first sentence? From the first two paragraphs?

2. Name some situations inside the hedge that the narrator does not understand, does not like, or does not trust. Why does he have these reactions?
3. How would you summarize the basic contrasts between the two sides of the hedge? What specific details support your summary?
4. The story is an allegory. What truths about human experience does it attempt to reveal? Which side of the hedge do you think Forster prefers? How do you know?
5. Find examples of irony in the story.
6. Notice the use of coordinating conjunctions to begin sentences: for example, "But I had travelled" in paragraph 2 and "For we of the road" in paragraph 4. At other times, coordinating conjunctions are punctuated traditionally. Find examples of both in the story. Can you see a purpose for beginning some sentences with coordinating conjunctions?

SIMILARITY AND DIFFERENCE

Compare and contrast "The Other Side of the Hedge" with "Rope" in terms of the following items:

point of view

style

individuality of characters

SHORT WRITING IDEA

In a paragraph, describe a room you know fairly well. Through your specific details, imply your judgment about the room or the person or people who use it.

LONGER WRITING IDEA

Think of two possible views on one of these aspects of life: work, family, or sex. Write a paper that compares and contrasts two people who represent the two views.

VOCABULARY CHECK

Answer *true* or *false* for each statement. If you are not sure of the answer, first find the relevant word in the story and see if that helps. Use the list before the story only as a last resort.

_______ **1.** Whether or not to have children is a trivial decision.

_______ **2.** People try to emulate their heroes.

_______ **3.** Some folk tales are allegories.

_______ **4.** Many students flunk their courses owing to perseverance.

_______ **5.** The company of a person who is not civil can be irksome.

_______ **6.** A convincing argument against you should buttress your opinion.

_______ **7.** Loud insults and jeering are rudimentary behaviors.

_______ **8.** It's hard to feel comfortable in an atmosphere of constraint.

_______ **9.** An exhortation usually makes a person feel miserable.

_______ **10.** Obstinacy is a quality everyone desires in a sweetheart.

Katherine Anne Porter

Rope

Born in Texas, Porter (1894–1980) lived in Mexico and traveled extensively. Her one novel, *Ship of Fools*, received both the Pulitzer Prize and the National Book Award, but she is most admired for the perfection of her short stories, which focus on the intricacies of human relationships. "Rope" is from her collection *Flowering Judas and Other Stories* (1930).

On the third day after they moved to the country he came walking back from the village carrying a basket of groceries and a twenty-four-yard coil of rope. She came out to meet him, wiping her hands on her green smock. Her hair was tumbled, her nose was scarlet with sunburn; he told her that already she looked like a born country woman. His grey flannel shirt stuck to him, his heavy shoes were dusty. She assured him he looked like a rural character in a play. [1]

Had he brought the coffee? She had been waiting all day long for coffee. They had forgot it when they ordered at the store the first day. [2]

Gosh, no, he hadn't. Lord, now he'd have to go back. Yes, he would if it killed him. He thought, though, he had everything else. She reminded him it was only because he didn't drink coffee himself. If he did he would remember it quick enough. Suppose they ran out of cigarettes? Then she saw the rope. What was that for? Well, he thought it might do to hang clothes on, or something. Naturally she asked him if he thought they were going to run a laundry? They already had a fifty-foot line hanging right before his eyes. Why, hadn't he noticed it, really? It was a blot on the landscape to her. [3]

He thought there were a lot of things a rope might come in handy for. She wanted to know what, for instance. He thought a few seconds, but nothing occurred. They could wait and see, couldn't they? You need all sorts of strange odds and ends around a place in the country. She said, yes, that was so; but she thought just at that time when every penny counted, it seemed funny to buy more rope. That was all. She hadn't meant anything else. She hadn't just seen, not at first, why he felt it was necessary. [4]

Well, thunder, he had bought it because he wanted to, and that was all there was to it. She thought that was reason enough, and [5] couldn't understand why he hadn't said so, at first. Undoubtedly it would be useful, twenty-four yards of rope, there were hundreds of things, she couldn't think of any at the moment, but it would come in handy. Of course. As he had said, things always did in the country.

But she was a little disappointed about the coffee, and oh, look, look, look at the eggs! Oh, my, they're all running! What had he put on top of them? Hadn't he known eggs mustn't be squeezed? Squeezed, who had squeezed them, he wanted to know. What a silly thing to say. He had simply brought them along in the basket with the other things. If they got broke it was the grocer's fault. He should know better than to put heavy things on top of eggs. [6]

She believed it was the rope. That was the heaviest thing in the pack, she saw him plainly when he came in from the road, the rope was a big package on top of everything. He desired the whole wide world to witness that this was not a fact. He had carried the rope in one hand and the basket in the other, and what was the use of her having eyes if that was the best they could do for her? [7]

Well, anyhow, she could see one thing plain: no eggs for breakfast. They'd have to scramble them now, for supper. It was too damned bad. She had planned to have steak for supper. No ice, meat wouldn't keep. He wanted to know why she couldn't finish breaking the eggs in a bowl and set them in a cool place. [8]

Cool place! if he could find one for her, she'd be glad to set them there. Well, then, it seemed to him they might very well cook the meat at the same time they cooked the eggs and then warm up the meat for tomorrow. The idea simply choked her. Warmed-over meat, when they might as well have had it fresh. Second best and scraps and makeshifts, even to the meat! He rubbed her shoulder a little. It doesn't really matter so much, does it, darling? Sometimes when they were playful, he would rub her shoulders and she would arch and purr. This time she hissed and almost clawed. He was getting ready to say that they could surely manage somehow when she turned on him and said, if he told her they could manage somehow she would certainly slap his face. [9]

He swallowed the words red hot, his face burned. He picked up the rope and started to put it on the top shelf. She would not have it on the top shelf, the jars and tins belonged there; positively she would not have the top shelf cluttered up with a lot of rope. She had borne all the clutter she meant to bear in the flat in town, there was space here at least and she meant to keep things in order. [10]

Well, in that case, he wanted to know what the hammer and nails were doing up there? And why had she put them there when she knew very well he needed that hammer and those nails upstairs to fix the window sashes? She simply slowed down everything and [11] made double work on the place with her insane habit of changing things around and hiding them.

She was sure she begged his pardon, and if she had had any reason to believe he was going to fix the sashes this summer she would have left the hammer and nails right where he put them; in the middle of the bedroom floor where they could step on them in the dark. And now if he didn't clear the whole mess out of there she would throw them down the well. [12]

Oh, all right, all right—could he put them in the closet? Naturally not, there were brooms and mops and dustpans in the closet, and why couldn't he find a place for his rope outside her kitchen? Had he stopped to consider there were seven God-forsaken rooms in the house, and only one kitchen? [13]

He wanted to know what of it? And did she realize she was making a complete fool of herself? And what did she take him for, a three-year-old idiot? The whole trouble with her was she needed something weaker than she was to heckle and tyrannize over. He wished to God now they had a couple of children she could take it out on. Maybe he'd get some rest. [14]

Her faced changed at this, she reminded him he had forgot the coffee and had bought a worthless piece of rope. And when she thought of all the things they actually needed to make the place even decently fit to live in, well she could cry, that was all. She looked so forlorn, so lost and despairing he couldn't believe it was only a piece of rope that was causing all the racket. What *was* the matter, for God's sake? [15]

Oh, would he please hush and go away, and *stay* away, if he could, for five minutes? By all means, yes, he would. He'd stay away indefinitely if she wished. Lord, yes, there was nothing he'd like better than to clear out and never come back. She couldn't for the life of her see what was holding him, then. It was a swell time. Here she was, stuck, miles from a railroad, with a half-empty house on her hands, and not a penny in her pocket, and everything on earth to do; it seemed the God-sent moment for him to get out from under. She was surprised he hadn't stayed in town as it was until she had come out and done the work and got things straightened out. It was his usual trick. [16]

It appeared to him that this was going a little far. Just a touch out of bounds, if she didn't mind him saying so. Why the hell had he stayed in town the summer before? To do a half-dozen extra jobs to get the money he had sent her. That was it. She knew perfectly well they couldn't have done it otherwise. She had agreed with him at the time. And that was the only time so help him he had ever left her to do anything by herself. [17]

Oh, he could tell that to his great-grandmother. She had her [18] notion of what had kept him in town. Considerably more than a notion, if he wanted to know. So, she was going to bring all that up again, was she? Well, she could just think what she pleased. He was tired of explaining. It may have looked funny but he had simply got hooked in, and what could he do? It was impossible to believe that she was going to take it seriously. Yes, yes, she knew how it was with a man: if he was left by himself a minute, some woman was certain to kidnap him. And naturally he couldn't hurt her feelings by refusing!

Well, what was she raving about? Did she forget she had told him those two weeks alone in the country were the happiest she had known for four years? And how long had they been married when she said that? All right, shut up! If she thought that hadn't stuck in his craw. [19]

She hadn't meant she was happy because she was away from him. She meant she was happy getting the devilish house nice and ready for him. That was what she had meant, and now look! Bringing up something she had said a year ago simply to justify himself for forgetting her coffee and breaking the eggs and buying a wretched piece of rope they couldn't afford. She really thought it was time to drop the subject, and now she wanted only two things in the world. She wanted him to get that rope from underfoot, and go back to the village and get her coffee, and if he could remember it, he might bring a metal mitt for the skillets, and two more curtain rods, and if there were any rubber gloves in the village, her hands were simply raw, and a bottle of milk of magnesia from the drugstore. [20]

He looked out at the dark blue afternoon sweltering on the slopes, and mopped his forehead and sighed heavily and said, if only she could wait a minute for *anything*, he was going back. He had said so, hadn't he, the very instant they found he had overlooked it? [21]

Oh, yes, well . . . run along. She was going to wash windows. The country was so beautiful! She doubted they'd have a moment to enjoy it. He meant to go, but he could not until he had said that if she wasn't such a hopeless melancholiac she might see that this was only for a few days. Couldn't she remember anything pleasant about the other summers? Hadn't they ever had any fun? She hadn't time to talk about it, and now would he please not leave that rope lying around for her to trip on? He picked it up, somehow it had toppled off the table, and walked out with it under his arm. [22]

Was he going this minute? He certainly was. She thought so. Sometimes it seemed to her he had second sight about the precisely perfect moment to leave her ditched. She had meant to put the mattresses out to sun, if they put them out this minute they would [23] get at least three hours, he must have heard her say that morning she meant to put them out. So of course he would walk off and leave her to it. She supposed he thought the exercise would do her good.

[24] Well, he was merely going to get her coffee. A four-mile walk for two pounds of coffee was ridiculous, but he was perfectly willing to do it. The habit was making a wreck of her, but if she wanted to wreck herself there was nothing he could do about it. If he thought it was coffee that was making a wreck of her, she congratulated him: he must have a damned easy conscience.

[25] Conscience or no conscience, he didn't see why the mattresses couldn't very well wait until tomorrow. And anyhow, for God's sake, were they living *in* the house, or where they going to let the house ride them to death? She paled at this, her face grew livid about the mouth, she looked quite dangerous, and reminded him that housekeeping was no more her work than it was his: she had other work to do as well, and when did he think she was going to find time to do it at this rate?

[26] Was she going to start on that again? She knew as well as he did that his work brought in the regular money, hers was only occasional, if they depended on what *she* made—and she might as well get straight on this question once for all!

[27] This was positively not the point. The question was, when both of them were working on their own time, was there going to be a division of the housework, or wasn't there? She merely wanted to know, she had to make her plans. Why, he thought that was all arranged. It was understood that he was to help. Hadn't he always, in summers?

[28] Hadn't he, though? Oh, just hadn't he? And when, and where, and doing what? Lord, what an uproarious joke!

[29] It was such a very uproarious joke that her face turned slightly purple, and she screamed with laughter. She laughed so hard she had to sit down, and finally a rush of tears spurted from her eyes and poured down into the lifted corners of her mouth. He dashed towards her and dragged her up to her feet and tried to pour water on her head. The dipper hung by a string on a nail and he broke it loose. Then he tried to pump water with one hand while she struggled in the other. So he gave it up and shook her instead.

[30] She wrenched away, crying out for him to take his rope and go to hell, she had simply given him up: and ran. He heard her high-heeled bedroom slippers clattering and stumbling on the stairs.

[31] He went out around the house and into the lane; he suddenly realized he had a blister on his heel and his shirt felt as if it were on fire. Things broke so suddenly you didn't know where you were. She could work herself into a fury about simply nothing. She was terrible, damn it: not an ounce of reason. You might as well talk to

a sieve as that woman when she got going. Damned if he'd spend his life humoring her! Well, what to do now? He would take back the rope and exchange it for something else. Things accumulated, things were mountainous, you couldn't move them or sort them out or get rid of them. They just lay and rotted around. He'd take it back. Hell, why should he? He wanted it. What was it anyhow? A piece of rope. Imagine anybody caring more about a piece of rope than about a man's feelings. What earthly right had she to say a word about it? He remembered all the useless, meaningless things she bought for herself: Why? because I wanted it, that's why! He stopped and selected a large stone by the road. He would put the rope behind it. He would put it in the toolbox when he got back. He'd heard enough about it to last him a life-time.

When he came back she was leaning against the post box beside the road waiting. It was pretty late, the smell of broiled steak floated nose high in the cooling air. Her face was young and smooth and fresh-looking. Her unmanageable funny black hair was all on end. She waved to him from a distance, and he speeded up. She called out that supper was ready and waiting, was he starved? [32]

You bet he was starved. Here was the coffee. He waved it at her. She looked at his other hand. What was that he had there? [33]

Well, it was the rope again. He stopped short. He had meant to exchange it but forgot. She wanted to know why he should exchange it, if it was something he really wanted. Wasn't the air sweet now, and wasn't it fine to be here? [34]

She walked beside him with one hand hooked into his leather belt. She pulled and jostled him a little as he walked, and leaned against him. He put his arm clear around her and patted her stomach. They exchanged wary smiles. Coffee, coffee for the Ootsum-Wootsums! He felt as if he were bringing her a beautiful present. [35]

He was a love, she firmly believed, and if she had had her coffee in the morning, she wouldn't have behaved so funny . . . There was a whippoorwill still coming back, imagine, clear out of season, sitting in the crab-apple tree calling all by himself. Maybe his girl stood him up. Maybe she did. She hoped to hear him once more, she loved whippoorwills . . . He knew how she was, didn't he? [36]

Sure, he knew how she was. [37]

VOCABULARY

craw	a pouch in a bird's esophagus in which food is stored or digested
hyperbole	exaggeration

makeshift	a way of managing without the usual items or supplies
melancholiac	one who is always depressed
metaphor	an implied imaginative comparison of two unlike things by means of some trait they share
sarcasm	taunting, cutting remarks
simile	a metaphor expressed by using "like" or "as" (rather than implied)
smock	a covering open in the back like an apron but having sleeves
wary	cautious

DESIGN AND MEANING

1. Identify several elements of unusual punctuation in the story. Why do you think Porter punctuated the story so unconventionally? Would you prefer conventional punctuation? Try to rewrite a section using conventional punctuation.
2. Explain some of the games the couple plays—patterns of communication they fall into.
3. Among the conflicts between the man and the woman, which ones would you say are deeper and which more superficial? Could you name one main underlying conflict?
4. Both the man and the woman use hyperbole (exaggeration) and irony (saying the opposite of what they mean). Find some examples of each technique.
5. A "closed ending" is one that completely resolves the conflict of the story. An "open ending" offers an uncertain resolution. Is the ending of "Rope" open or closed? Why do you think so?
6. What do you think is the purpose of the story?

SIMILARITY AND DIFFERENCE

Copy by hand a paragraph from "The Other Side of the Hedge" and one from "Rope." Then list all the differences in writing style you can find. Can you find any similarities?

SHORT WRITING IDEA

For one day, listen closely to conversations you hear among your friends, your family, and people on television. Write a list of all the utterances that use irony or hyperbole.

LONGER WRITING IDEA

Think of two people you know who have clearly differing qualities. Jot down some of the characteristics of each. Then think of a situation that puts these people in conflict (for instance, in "Rope," one brings home a purchase that the other one thinks is unnecessary). Write a narration of what happens between the two people in the situation.

VOCABULARY CHECK

sarcasm
hyperbole
simile
metaphor

From the list of terms above, choose the appropriate word to identify each of the following figures of speech from Porter's story.

_______ **1.** "He looked like a rural character in a play."

_______ **2.** "Were they living *in* the house, or were they going to let the house ride them to death?"

_______ **3.** "Here she was stuck, . . . not a penny in her pocket and everything on earth to do."

_______ **4.** "He swallowed the words red hot, his face burned."

_______ **5.** "His shirt felt as if it were on fire."

_______ **6.** "Lord, now he'd have to go back. Yes, he would if it killed him."

_______ **7.** "This time she hissed and almost clawed."

_______ **8.** "Well, he thought it might do to hang clothes on, or something. Naturally she asked him if he thought they were going to run a laundry?"

Cause and Effect

WE LOOK FOR, and expect to find, cause-and-effect relationships in everything from growing tasty tomatoes to falling in love. If you planted tomatoes last summer and got a luscious crop, and you plant tomatoes this summer and get none, you're not likely just to shrug your shoulders and say, "Well, whaddaya' know, those tomatoes didn't grow this year," and go calmly about your business. No, you are much more likely to say, "Now how come those dumb tomatoes didn't make it?" and try to figure out the causes for their failure.

People who have good sense think about the effects, or consequences, of things too. For instance, if it hasn't rained in three weeks and you keep putting off hosing down the tomato patch, you have to consider the effects of your procrastination.

Most of us actually do go around every day blithely analyzing causes and effects as though everything made sense. Whether it does or not is debatable, but you can certainly learn to write a paper that makes life sound reasonable.

When you develop an essay by analyzing *causes,* you are explaining to your readers *why* something happened. If you go on to explore the *effects,* you are analyzing *what* happened—consequences. If your subject is being on probation and you write, "Why I Am on Probation," that's primarily a cause paper; if you write, "What Being on Probation Does to My Life," that's primarily an effect paper. You will probably want to content yourself with one or the other in a single essay, but you might tie into both if you should get turned loose without a word limit.

You may be able to fall back on chronological arrangement (according to time) if you can trace the causes from the earliest to the most recent. If you're explaining "Why my honeymoon was a disaster," you might track the cause back to the moment you decided to get married and then pinpoint several unfortunate decisions that followed, like this:

1. My first small mistake: I got engaged (cite details).
2. My next big blunder: I decided to have an elaborate wedding (cite details).
3. My final fatal error: I got smashed at the reception (cite details).

More likely, though, your organization will fall into some simple, logical pattern that has more to do with the importance of the causes or the effects than simply with the chronology. For example, the organization might progress from the least significant cause to the most critical, from a fairly obvious effect to the most subtle, from local to nationwide causes, or from the effects in your classroom to the effects in your university. The possibilities are endless. Simply present your ideas in the order you consider most clear and emphatic.

Some subjects are safer than others for cause and effect writing. "Why I Love Grammar" and "The Effects of My Divorce" are not risky because they are entirely personal. As long as your evidence sounds relevant and sincere, no one is going to argue with you. In this chapter, Jan Halvorsen describes the effects of losing her job, and since her subject is personal and her expression rings true, you aren't likely to question her conclusions. On the other hand, Harlan Ellison's statements about the mind-numbing effects of television are more likely to stir debate. (Of course, we think his reasoning is sound; otherwise we wouldn't have included the essay here.)

In the Writing Ideas sections, we encourage you to try a range of subjects. Be sure to outline your cause-and-effect reasoning carefully either before or after you write. An outline will let you see how your ideas fit together—that is, whether the thought of each paragraph follows logically and directly from the thought in the paragraph ahead of it. You should always make certain that your reasoning will bear close scrutiny.

essays

Susan J. Douglas

Flex Appeal, Buns of Steel, and the Body in Question

Born in 1950, Douglas teaches Media Studies at Hampshire College. Her scholarly work *Inventing American Broadcasting, 1899–1922* was published in 1987. "I want people to be as critical about what is shoved down their throats every day as possible," she says. Her insights can be found in *In These Times* and *The Village Voice.*

In the summer, the onslaught hits its peak. Everywhere we look, in the incessant get-back-in-shape TV ads and magazine articles, on billboards, in the catalogues that jam our mailboxes and in the endless diet soda and cereal ads, the perfectly smooth, toned buttocks and thighs of models and actresses accost the women of America. They jut out at us from high-cut bathing suits and exercise outfits, challenging us and humbling us, reminding all women that nothing in the world is more repulsive and shameful than "orange peel skin." They insist that the rest of us should feel only one thing when we put on a bathing suit: profound mortification. [1]

Sure, we're seeing more female biceps, and every few months the *New York Times* asserts that breasts are back "in." But still, it is the slim, dimple-free buttock and thigh that has become, in the '80s, the ultimate signifier of female fitness and beauty. Trim, smug models are positioned with their knees bent or their bodies curled so that their superhuman hindquarters are front and center. [2]

And not just in *Vogue* or *Cosmo,* either: even the *Village Voice,* in between the exposes on racism and government malfeasance, has ads for products such as the videotape called *Buns of Steel,* which promises that "Now you can have the buns you've always wanted." Why this part of the body, and why now? [3]

Emphasis on the thigh stems in part from the fitness craze of [4] the past 15 years, when many women discovered the physical and psychic benefits of exercise. The craze began as an oppositional, even radical reaction against the degradation of food by huge conglomerates, and the work routines and convenience technologies that encourage consumption and passivity. The organic health-food movement was, initially, at its core, anticapitalist. But one of capitalism's great strengths—perhaps its greatest—is its ability to co-opt and domesticate opposition, to transubstantiate criticism into a host of new, marketable products. And so it was with fitness.

Out on a limb: Corporations saw immediately that there was gold in them thar thighs. The key to huge profits was to emphasize beauty over health, sexuality over fitness, and to equate thin thighs with wealth and status. What had worked so well in the past was to set standards of beauty that are simultaneously unattainable and seemingly within reach if only the right product is purchased. [5]

Yet there is much more going on here than that old gambit. The flawless rump has become *the* female body part of the '80s because its cultivation and display fits in so well with the great myth of Reaganism: that superficial appearances can be equated with a person's deepest character strengths and weaknesses. [6]

Just listen to what Cher tells us in all those health spa ads: thin thighs and dimple-free buttocks are now instant, automatic evidence of female discipline, restraint and control. They are indicators of a woman's potential for success. Any woman, so the message goes, can achieve perfect thighs through concentrated effort, self-denial and deferred gratification, the basic tenets of the work ethic. [7]

Work-ethic workout: All she has to do is apply herself and, of course, be a discriminating, upscale consumer. "You don't get this far by accident," proclaims one sneaker ad displaying a tight, toned rump, "You've worked hard." Another magazine ad, this one for a spa that also foregrounds a machine-tooled hindquarter, intones, "When you work at it, it shows." Meaning, if you've been slacking off, that will show, too. [8]

It doesn't matter if you're healthy, exercise regularly and aren't overweight. If wearing one of the new, ultra-high-cut bathing suits would reveal too much roundness, a little fat (what the cosmetics industry calls "cellulite"), the offending woman can be dismissed as slothful and lacking moral fiber. No matter that the female hip area is naturally more fatty than the male's (a function of reproduction), or that most women's jobs require constant sitting, two factors that tend to work against developing buns of steel. [9]

A real woman, whatever her age, will get off her butt and, by overcoming her sloth, not just get in shape, but conquer genetics [10] and history. Her buns of steel will instantly identify her as someone who subscribes to the new yuppie work ethic, which insists that even in leisure hours, the truly tough, the truly deserving, never stop working. The sleek, smooth, tight butt is a badge, a medal asserting that anal compulsiveness is an unalloyed virtue.

Perfect thighs, in other words, are an achievement, a product, and one to be admired and envied. They signify that the woman has made something of herself, that she has character and class, that she is the master of her body and, thus, of her fate. If she has conquered her own adipose tissue, she can conquer anything. Narcissism equals liberation. [11]

She is a new woman, liberated and in control. She has made her buttocks less fatty, more muscular, more, well . . . like a man's. So here we have a variation on one of the media's most popular—and pernicious—distortions of feminism: that ambitious women want, or should want, to be just like men, especially those men committed to the most competitive, inhumane, macho aspects of patriarchy. The woman whose upper thigh best approximates a fat-free male hindquarter is the woman most entitled to enjoy the same privileges as men. [12]

These overworked thighs also suggest that women can compete with men while simultaneously increasing their own desirability. Thighs, rather than breasts, have become the focus in the '80s because presumably everyone, the flat-chested and the stacked, men and women, can work toward buns of steel. Women can develop the very same anatomical zones that men do, giving their muscles new definition, a definition that is meant to serve simultaneously as a warning and an enticement to men. Female buns of steel mark a woman as a desirable piece of ass, yet someone who can also kick ass when necessary. [13]

Kid stuff: What makes these thighs desirable is that, while they're fat-free, like men's, they are also the thighs of adolescent girls. The ideal rump—like Lisa Bonet's, recently displayed on the cover of *Rolling Stone*—bears none of the marks of age, responsibility, work or motherhood. And the crotch-splitting, cut-up-to-the-waistline, impossible-to-swim-in bathing suits featured in such publications as the *Sports Illustrated* "swimsuit issue" can never reveal that other marker of adulthood, pubic hair. So, beneath the guise of female fitness and empowerment lies an infantile ideal that helps keep women in their place. [14]

Aside from the impossible standards of perfection they impose, these buns of steel urge women to be all things to all people: to be ceaseless, competitive workaholics *and* sex objects, to be active workers in control of their bodies *and* passive ornaments for the [15] pleasure of men, to be hard-as-nails superwomen *and* vulnerable, unthreatening, teenaged beach bunnies. Straddling such contradictions, even on toned, fat-free, muscular legs is, in real life, impossible and preposterous.

And buns of steel are meant to separate the truly classy, deserving women from the rest of the lumpy female proletariat. Buns of steel, like a Pierre Cardin label, are a mark of well-earned exclusivity. Lumpy thighs have been cast as K-mart thighs, not the thighs of Rodeo Drive. [16]

A leg to stand on: So where do these buttocks and thighs leave the rest of us, the real women of America who sit at desks or stand at sinks, who are over 16 and don't have the time, money, personal trainer or surgical team to help us forge our own buns of steel? Even non-overweight women and women who should know better have been worked over so well that whenever we look at ourselves in the mirror or, worse, have to be seen in public in a bathing suit, all we can feel is disgust and shame. [17]

But it isn't just a shame of our bodies. Buns of steel have taught us to be ashamed of the way we live our day-to-day lives; of the fact that whatever we're doing, we aren't working hard enough; that we don't have that badge of entitlement; that we don't really have enough self-respect: that we aren't enough like men; and, worst of all, that we're adult females in a culture that still prefers, by and large, little girls. [18]

I'm tired of being told never to stop, and that some physical exertion, like pumping a Nautilus machine, is more valuable than other exertion, such as chasing a two-year-old. I'm tired of Cher's rump, Christie Brinkley's thighs and countless other starved, air-brushed, surgically enhanced hindquarters being shoved in my face. [19]

I'm tired of being told that if I just exercise a lot more and eat a lot less, I, too, can conquer biology, make my thighs less female and thus not be eyed with derision. I'm *real* tired of the Marquis-de-Sade, split-'em-in-two "bathing suits" foisted on us by the fashion industry. Most of all, I'm tired of the endless self-flagellation we women subject ourselves to because of the way this latest, unattainable physical ideal has been combined with the yuppie work ethic. [20]

It is time for women to reclaim the fitness movement from Kellogg's, Diet Pepsi, Biotherm and all the rest of the buttocks and thighs cartel. Buns of steel are not about fitness: they are about pretending that some anorexic, unnatural, corporate-constructed ideal is really a norm. Buns of steel are designed to humiliate women and, worse yet, to make us complicit in our own degradation. [21]

VOCABULARY

accost	confront, approach
adipose tissue	stored fat
anal compulsive	up-tight, overly organized
anorexic	deliberately, but usually unconsciously starving oneself
cartel	a combination of business interests
conglomerates	huge corporations made up of various companies
co-opt	take over
derision	scorn
entitlement	the right to do or have something
gambit	an opening strategy, often involving a subtle deception
malfeasance	misconduct, wrongdoing
Marquis de Sade	French nobleman noted for harsh cruelty
mortification	humiliation, shame
narcissism	love of oneself
onslaught	a great surge
patriarchy	government by males (from "patriarch" meaning "father")
pernicious	extremely destructive
proletariat	exploited working class
self-flagellation	self-punishment (literally, whipping oneself)
signifier	sign
slothful	lazy
tenets	doctrines, principles, rules
transubstantiate	transform
unalloyed	complete, pure

DESIGN AND MEANING

1. Douglas places her thesis at the end of paragraph 3. Why does she use a rhetorical question rather than a straightforward statement? Do you consider this an effective strategy?
2. Why, in paragraph 5, does she use the ungrammatical phrase, "there was gold in them thar thighs"?
3. Discuss the various meanings implicit in her phrase "machine-tooled hindquarters" in paragraph 8.
4. Does Douglas convince you that the need for "buns of steel" is a compulsion foisted upon women by corporate America through advertising? Or are men subject to these same pressures?

SIMILARITY AND DIFFERENCE

What similarities do you see between Douglas's analysis and King's "Getting 'Em Ready for Darrell" in Chapter 2 (Narration)?

SHORT WRITING IDEA

Douglas employs a number of synonyms for a woman's "hip area": *buns, buttocks, butt, rump, hindquarters,* and *ass*. Locate these words in her essay. Then, analyze and discuss the connotations that each word carries in its context.

LONGER WRITING IDEA

Locate several of the advertisements that Douglas refers to in her article. Analyze in detail their persuasive appeal to women in order to discover whether you agree or disagree with Douglas's argument. Photocopy each ad and turn in a copy with your paper.

PREREADING EXERCISE ("How It Feels to Be out of Work")

How do you feel about people who don't have jobs? Ask several of your friends or classmates to finish the following sentence with a word or a phrase: "Jobless people are ____________." Then write

Jan Halvorsen

How It Feels to Be out of Work

Fortunately, Jan Halvorsen was unemployed only four months. She is now assistant editor of the *Twin Cities Courier* in St. Paul, Minnesota. The following essay appeared as *Newsweek*'s "My Turn" feature in September of 1980.

Layoffs, unemployment and recession have always affected Walter Cronkite's tone of voice and the editorial page. And maybe they affected a neighborhood business or a friend's uncle. But these terms have always been just words, affecting someone else's world, like a passing ambulance. At least they were until a few weeks ago, when the ambulance came for me. [1]

Even as I sat staring blankly at my supervisor, hearing, "I've got bad news: we're going to have to let you go," it all still seemed no more applicable to my daily life than a "60 Minutes" exposé. I kept waiting for the alternative—"but you can come back after a couple of months," or "you could take a salary cut, a different position," or even, "April fool." But none of these came. This was final. There was no mistake and no alternative. [2]

You find yourself going back over it in your idle moments. There wasn't so much as a "Thank you" for the long nights working alone, the "Sure, no problem, I'll have it tomorrow," the "Let me know if I can help," the "I just went ahead and did it this weekend" and, especially, for the "You forgot to tell me it changed? Oh, that's all right, I'll just do it over. No big deal." [3]

No big deal. How it all echoes through your evenings and awakens you in the morning. The mornings are probably the worst—waking up with the habitual jar, for the first two weeks, thinking, "I'm late!" Late for what? The dull ache in your lower stomach reminds you: late for nothing. [4]

Depression: Again, you face the terms. "Loss of self-esteem and security, fear of the future, stress, depression." You wonder dully if eating a dozen chocolate-chip cookies, wearing a bathrobe until 4, combing your hair at 5, cleaning behind the stove (twice) and crying in an employment-agency parking lot qualify as symp- [5]

toms of stress or maybe loss of self-esteem. Fighting with your spouse/boyfriend? Aha—tension in personal relationships.

[6] The loss of a job is rejection, resulting in the same hurt feelings as if a friend had told you to "bug off." Only this "friend" filled up 40 to 60 (or more) hours of your week. Constant references to the staff as "family" only accentuate the feeling of desertion and deception. You picture yourself going home to your parents or spouse and being informed, "Your services as our daughter/my wife are no longer required. Pick up your baby pictures as you leave."

[7] Each new affirmation of unemployment renews the pain: the first trip to the employment agency, the first friend you tell, the first interview and, most dreaded of all, the first trip to the unemployment office.

[8] Standing in line at the unemployment office makes you feel very much the same as you did the first time you ever flunked a class or a test—as if you had a big red "F" for "Failure" printed across your forehead. I fantasize myself standing at the end of the line in a crisp and efficient blue suit, chin up, neat and straight as a corporate executive. As I move down the line I start to come unglued and a half hour later, when I finally reach the desk clerk, I am slouching and sallow in torn jeans, tennis shoes and a jacket from the Salvation Army, carrying my worldly belongings in a shopping bag and unable to speak.

[9] You do eventually become accustomed to being unemployed, in the way you might accept a bad limp. And you gradually quit beating yourself for not having been somehow indispensable—or for not having become an accountant. You tire of straining your memory for possible infractions. You recover some of the confidence that always told you how good you were at your job and accept what the supervisor said: "This doesn't reflect on your job performance; sales are down 30 per cent this month."

[10] But each time you recover that hallowed self-esteem, you renew a fight to maintain it. Each time you go to a job interview and give them your best and they hire someone else, you go another round with yourself and your self-esteem. Your unemployment seems to drag on beyond all justification. You start to glimpse a stranger in your rearview mirror. The stranger suddenly looks like a bum. You look at her with clinical curiosity. Hmmm. Obviously into the chronic stages. Definitely not employable.

[11] We unemployed share a social stigma similar to that of the rape victim. Whether consciously or subconsciously, much of the work-ethic-driven public feels that you've somehow "asked for it," secretly wanted to lose your job and "flirted" with unemployment through your attitude—probably dressed in a way to invite it (left the vest unbuttoned on your three-piece suit).

Satisfaction: But the worst of it isn't society's work-ethic morality; it's your own, which you never knew you had. You find out how much self-satisfaction was gained from even the most simple work-related task: a well-worded letter, a well-handled phone call—even a clean file. Being useful to yourself isn't enough. [12]

But then almost everyone has heard about the need to be a useful member of society. What you didn't know about was the loneliness. You've spent your life almost constantly surrounded by people, in classes, in dorms and at work. To suddenly find yourself with only your cat to talk to all day distorts your sense of reality. You begin to worry that flights of fancy might become one way. [13]

But you always were, and still are, stronger than that. You maintain balance and perspective, mainly through resorting frequently to sarcasm and irreverence. Although something going wrong in any aspect of your life now seems to push you into temporary despair much more easily than before, you have some very important things to hang on to—people who care, your sense of humor, your talents, your cat and your hopes. [14]

And beyond that, you've gained something—a little more knowledge and a lot more compassion. You've learned the value of the routine you scorned and the importance of the job you took for granted. But most of all, you've learned what a "7.6 per cent unemployment rate" really means. [15]

VOCABULARY

accentuate	to emphasize
affirmation	a positive declaration
chronic	having had an ailment for a long time
compassion	sorrow for the suffering and troubles of others
hallowed	honored as holy
infraction	the breaking of a rule
work ethic	the idea that work in itself is valuable and honorable

DESIGN AND MEANING

1. This essay investigates many effects of a single cause. What are the effects? What aspects of the state of being unemployed are emphasized?
2. Find at least five comparisons used. Are they effective?
3. What is the most important effect the writer discusses? Do you agree with its placement in the essay?

4. Why is the following sentence striking? "You begin to worry that flights of fancy might become one way" (paragraph 3).

SIMILARITY AND DIFFERENCE

What is the difference in tone between the opening of this essay and the opening of "Trouble on the Wind," the next selection in this chapter?

SHORT WRITING IDEA

Rewrite a few sentences of paragraph 5 in the essay using the first person ("I," "me," "my") instead of "you." Then rewrite a few sentences using the third person ("one"). Then justify the writer's use of the indefinite "you" in this essay.

LONGER WRITING IDEA

Explain the effects of any major change you have had in your life: a move, career shift, marriage or divorce, illness.

Harry Middleton

Trouble on the Wind

Middleton shares his discoveries about the fragility of our environment and the human impact on it. He writes passionately about the disappearing treasures of our wild country and the need to protect what remains. His work appears in magazines such as *Horticulture, Field & Stream, Sports Illustrated,* and *Southern Living.*

At 6,684 feet, the highest point east of the Mississippi River, the summit of Mount Mitchell has been a place of often violent extremes. In character, the mountain's summit is closer to regions of Canada or China than to North Carolina. Indeed, the higher reaches of Mount Mitchell are part of the band of boreal forest that survives atop the rugged spine of the Appalachian Mountains. Here amid the clouds, life is precarious at best, forever at the mercy of hard, unpredictable weather. The Appalachian high country is a merciless landscape, a paradox—at once exceptionally fragile and doggedly tenacious. [1]

It is a region of life and death. In such a harsh environment, death is common—a permanent resident. For as long as I can remember, there have always been dead trees, hosts of them, scattered about the summit of the mountain, ample evidence of the vagaries of life above 5,500 feet. [2]

Nothing struck me as unnatural or unusual about these dead and dying trees until the winter of 1983–84; as I studied the summit through powerful binoculars, suddenly there seemed so many of them. They passed before my eyes like piles of grizzled bones. The entire crest of the mountain looked like an immense grimy smudge against the cold, winter-blue sky. [3]

And the trees on top of Mount Mitchell went on dying, and the summit took on the aspect of a gray land through which some vile plague had passed. The thick forest of fir and spruce trees that had once thrived on the mountain looked as though they had been felled by some sudden and fierce killing wind. No matter the season or the weather, no matter that below the summit other mountains spread toward the north and south in undulations of blues and greens, the peak of Mount Mitchell remained a vexing place of leaden grays, a place of dead and dying trees. [4]

As early as 1983, Dr. Robert I. Bruck, a plant pathologist at [5]

North Carolina State University in Raleigh, noticed the dramatic changes taking place on Mount Mitchell and set about trying to determine the causes for the forest's decline. As I said, dead trees have marked the summit of Mount Mitchell for decades. For years, the common scientific explanation for this phenomenon had been the summit's severe winters and the appearance in the 1950's of insect pests among the firs and spruce, especially the woolly balsam aphid and microscopic nematodes. Imported into the country, the woolly aphid quickly made its way to the Appalachians and up into the boreal forest to feed on its favorite prey, Fraser firs. Nothing, as yet, has stopped this aphid assault; it seems as unremitting as the infamous chestnut tree blight. As serious as these environmental factors are, however, some scientists, including Dr. Bruck, believe there are other more pervasive and potentially dangerous reasons for the increasing stress and death among the trees atop Mount Mitchell. Among these, believes Dr. Bruck, is airborne pollution and acid rain.

[6] Dr. Bruck immediately began investigating the soil, air, and other vegetation on Mount Mitchell. Putting the blame for the destruction on this once healthy and beautiful forest solely on the woolly aphid simply didn't make sense. After all, the woolly aphid attacked mostly fir trees, and yet in places, the mountain's stands of red spruce were dying at an even faster rate than the firs.

[7] Bruck's findings are sobering and portray an atmosphere atop Mount Mitchell and elsewhere along the highest peaks of the Appalachians that is more chemically toxic than the worst smoggy days over downtown Knoxville, Nashville, Charlotte, perhaps even downtown Atlanta. This is surprising, as well as worrisome. After all, ozone, as a pollutant, is usually associated with smog, not with supposedly clear, clean, invigorating mountain air. Evidently, ruinous ozone now threatens not only our cities' health but that of our mountains too, even those so wild, so special that we have set them aside, supposedly preserved, protected from at least manmade harm.

[8] According to the Environmental Protection Agency, a concentration of 120 parts of ozone per billion parts of air at ground level for an hour a year is cause for some alarm. During one study on Mount Mitchell in 1986, Dr. Bruck measured ozone levels at or above this reading for 10 days out of a single month's worth of measurements. The eerie cloak of fog that so often envelops the mountain's summit, sometimes 8 out of every 10 days, Bruck discovered, is saturated with heavy, harmful doses of toxic compounds, heavy metals, and extremely acidic moisture. How sadly ironic, how shocking to learn that the air that fills our lungs atop the majestic

Mount Mitchell is potentially more harmful to our health than the smoggy air we thought we left behind in the cities.

[9] Dr. Bruck's work discloses a particularly vexing dilemma, the simultaneous onslaught of two catastrophes taking place atop Mount Mitchell, one natural (that is, the natural stresses of insects and environment) and one manmade, air pollution. Together, they are rapidly destroying the fir and spruce forests above 5,500 feet. Too, there are disturbing signs of stress beginning to appear in the trees, streams, and vegetation well below 5,500 feet. Clearly the effects of acid rain, once an ecological nightmare that everyone assumed only menaced the Northeast, Canada, and Europe, are now spreading throughout North America, especially to the south and southeast. In turn, acid rain leaches out of plants and trees, through their leaves, precious minerals like calcium, magnesium, and phosphorus.

[10] For trees, a constant exposure to acid rain results in slow strangulation. And along with higher concentrations of acidic moisture, soils on Mount Mitchell are also being exposed to increasing levels of toxic metals—cadmium, zinc, lead, mercury, and especially solubilized aluminum. Aluminum poisoning is particularly lethal to trees, freshwater lakes, and streams. To young seedlings it is deadly. Bruck's studies show that acid rain levels atop Mount Mitchell can be 80 to 100 times more acidic than what is considered average or normal acid rain, if there is such a thing. It is as if Mount Mitchell were dunked regularly in an ocean of uncut vinegar because it is so often wrapped in a nearly complete and suffocating blanket of tainted mists and fogs and rains that are heavy with airborne pollutants.

[11] Dr. Bruck and his colleagues are scientists, not soothsayers. They bring us neither bad news nor good but only facts, the hard facts that will have a great impact on the future of the natural South. The hard facts show that the high country of the Appalachians is under extreme stress, and some regions, such as Mount Mitchell, have already begun to die. Dr. Bruck does not claim to know or perfectly understand all the causes and consequences of this dramatic decline. Indeed, he remains hesitant even now to place the blame for the forest's ruin solely on acid rain. He believes, instead, that the problem may involve a host of interconnected causes, of which air pollution, as of now, is but one, though its heinous influences seem to be growing.

[12] I go to Mount Mitchell more often these days, sometimes reluctantly, the way one hesitates to visit a dying friend. I do not want to acknowledge what has happened to the mountain, what continues to happen. I do not like to think that the summit is dying, but I

must, we must, if we are to understand what is happening not only here atop Mount Mitchell but also in Southern mountains from the Ozarks to the Blue Ridge. Mount Mitchell is but an early tumor in what could be a vastly more devastating environmental melanoma if we choose to ignore it, make no effort to understand it, stop it. At stake is more and more of the natural South, that part of our remnant natural heritage that we have so wisely set aside not only for our own pleasure and enjoyment but also for all those to come after us. Mount Mitchell is but the first symptom of a potentially deadly disease that our generation must feel, suffer through, and understand, so that the next might have a chance to heal the scars, restore the land.

VOCABULARY

boreal	northern
grizzled	gray
heinous	devastatingly bad, ruinous, evil
leaches	(v.) dissolves out
melanoma	a malignant tumor
nematodes	threadlike worms
paradox	an apparent contradiction which proves to be true
solubilized	made soluble in water by some chemical agent
soothsayers	people who claim to predict events
tenacious	clinging firmly
undulations	appearing like waves
vagaries	things difficult to account for
vexing	troublesome, irritating

DESIGN AND MEANING

1. How does the title relate to the meaning of Middleton's essay?
2. How did Dr. Bruck go about investigating "the causes for the forest's decline" in paragraphs 5 and 6?
3. Middleton often employs *reiteration,* a restating in different words of the same idea, as in this example: ". . . the peak of Mount Mitchell remained a vexing *place of leaden grays, a place of dead and dying trees*" (found in paragraph 2, our italics). Find other sentences using deliberate repetition and explain what purpose this rhetorical strategy serves.
4. "Trouble on the Wind" was published in *Southern Living,* a mag-

azine in which Middleton's columns appear regularly. What details in the article show the writer's awareness of his particular audience?

SIMILARITY AND DIFFERENCE

Compare Middleton's objective causal analysis in "Trouble on the Wind" with Halvorsen's subjective analysis in "How it Feels to be Out of Work."

SHORT WRITING IDEA

The last sentence in paragraph 5 of Middleton's essay reads like this: "Among these, believes Dr. Bruck, is airborne pollution and acid rain." By rearranging the words, moving the modifiers, perhaps changing the verb from *is* to *are,* and adding the word *that* if needed, rewrite the sentence five different ways. Then decide which version you consider most effective and state why.

LONGER WRITING IDEA

Think of a pollution problem in your community or on your campus, like chemical fertilizer polluting the ground water in an agricultural area, garbage pollution in an urban area, or excessive use of throw-away plastic and paper products in the university food services. Then analyze the causes and try to propose some workable solutions.

PREREADING EXERCISE ("Books, TV, and the Imagination")

The following brief item appeared in Chicago's *In These Times* (Oct. 8–14, 1986):

> TUNE IN, TUNE OUT
>
> The Mexico City subway system has found the perfect use for music video: to keep mass transit passengers peaceful while they're waiting for the train. "We've noticed that people board the trains much more calmly than at other stations where there is no TV," said a subway official, after a pilot program installing TVs with nonstop video-clip programs. Tina Turner keeps the passengers occupied some of the time, and old-fashioned commercials such as those for Pepsi take up the slack. Just another reminder that the electronic commodity culture is international, along with its hypnotizing effects on viewers—at least when they're on a subway platform.

Why do you think television has a "hypnotizing effect"? Explain in a paragraph, using your own experience if you can.

Harlan Ellison

Books, TV, and the Imagination

Recognized as an outstanding, inventive science fiction writer, Ellison (b. 1934) is also a wry, sometimes cynical, critic of television. This selection is an excerpt from his introduction to *Strange Wine* (1978), a collection of short stories.

[1] Television, quite the opposite of books or even old-time radio that presented drama and comedy and talk shows (unlike Top Forty radio programming today, which is merely TV without moving parts), is systematically oriented toward stunning the use of individual imagination. It puts everything out there, *right there,* so you don't have to dream even a little bit. When they would broadcast a segment of, say, *Inner Sanctum* in the Forties, and you heard the creaking door of a haunted house, the mind was forced to *create the picture* of that haunted house—a terrifying place so detailed and terrifying that if Universal Studios wanted to build such an edifice for a TV movie, it would cost them millions of dollars and it *still* wouldn't be one one-millionth as frightening as the one your own imagination had cobbled up.

[2] A book is a participatory adventure. It involves a creative act at its inception and a creative act when its purpose is fulfilled. The writer dreams the dream and sets it down; the reader reinterprets the dream in personal terms, with personal vision, when he or she reads it. Each creates a world. The template is the book.

[3] At risk of repeating myself, and of once again cribbing from another writer's perfection of expression (in this case, my friend Dr. Isaac Asimov), here is a bit I wrote on this subject for an essay on the "craft" of writing teleplays:

[4] Unlike television, films, football games, the roller derby, wars in underdeveloped nations and Watergate hearings, which are spectator sports, a book requires the activation of its words by the eyes and the intellect of a reader. As Isaac Asimov said recently in an article postulating the perfect entertainment cassette, "A cassette as ordinarily viewed makes sound and casts light. That is its purpose, of course, but must sound and light obtrude on others who are not involved or interested? The ideal cassette would be visible and

audible only to the person using it . . . . We could imagine a cassette that is always in perfect adjustment; that starts automatically when you look at it; that stops automatically when you cease to look at it; that can play forward or backward, quickly or slowly, by skips or with repetitions, entirely at your pleasure . . . . Surely, that's the ultimate dream device—a cassette that may deal with any of an infinite number of subjects, fictional or non-fictional, that is self-contained, portable, non-energy-consuming, perfectly private and largely under the control of the will . . . . Must this remain only a dream? Can we expect to have such a cassette some day? . . . We not only have it now, we have had it for many centuries. The ideal I have described is the printed word, the book, the object you now hold—light, private, and manipulable at will . . . . Does it seem to you that the book, unlike the cassette I have been describing, does not produce sound and images? It certainly does . . . . You cannot read without hearing the words in your mind and seeing the images to which they give rise. In fact, they are *your* sounds and images, not those invented for you by others, and are therefore better . . . . The printed word presents minimum information, however. Everything but that minimum must be provided by the reader—the intonation of words, the expressions on faces, the actions, the scenery, the background, must all be drawn out of that long line of black-on-white symbols."

Quite clearly, if one but looks around to access the irrefutable evidence of reality, books strengthen the dreaming facility, and television numbs it. Atrophy soon follows. [5]

Oscar-winner Shelley Torgeson, who is the director of the spoken-word records I've cut, was also a mass media teacher at Harrison High School in Westchester. She told me some things that buttress my position: [6]

(1) A fifteen-year-old student summarily rejected the reading of books because it "wasn't real." Because it was your imagination, and your imagination isn't real. So Shelley asked her what was "real" and the student responded instantly, "Television." Because you could see it. Then, by pressing the conversation, Shelley discovered that though the student was in the tenth grade, when she read she didn't understand the words and was *making up* words and their meanings all through the text—far beyond the usual practice, in which we all indulge, of gleaning an *approximate* meaning of an unfamiliar word from its context. With television, she had no such problems. They didn't use words. It was real. Thus—and quite logically in a kind of Alice-down-the-rabbit-hole manner—the books *weren't* real, because she was making them up as she went along, not actually reading them. If you know what I mean. [7]

(2) An important school function was woefully under-attended [8]

one night, and the next day Shelley (suspecting the reason) confirmed that the absence of so many students was due to their being at home watching part two of the TV movie based on the Manson murder spree, *Helter Skelter.* Well, that *was* a bit of a special event in itself, and a terrifying program; but the interesting aspect of their watching the show emerged when a student responded to Shelley's comparison of watching something that "wasn't real" with a living event that "was real." The student contended it *was* real, he had seen it. No, Shelley insisted, it wasn't real, it was just a show. Hell no, the kid kept saying, it *was* real: he had *seen* it. Reasoning slowly and steadily, it took Shelley fifteen or twenty minutes to convince him (if she actually managed) that he had not seen a real thing, because he had not been in Los Angeles in August of 1969 when the murders had happened. Though he was seventeen years old, the student was incapable of perceiving, *unaided,* the difference between a dramatization and real life.

(3) In each classroom of another school at which Shelley taught, there was a TV set, mostly unused save for an occasional administrative announcement; the sets had been originally installed in conjunction with a Ford Foundation grant to be used for visual training. Now they're blank and silent. When Shelley had trouble controlling the class, getting them quiet, she would turn on the set and they would settle down. The screen contained nothing, just snow; but they grew as fascinated as cobras at a mongoose rally, and fell silent, watching nothing. Shelley says she could keep them that way for extended periods. [9]

Interestingly, as a footnote, when Shelley mentioned this device at lunch, a chemistry professor said he used something similar. When his students were unruly he would place a beaker of water on a Bunsen burner. When the water began to boil, the students grew silent and mesmerized, watching the water bubbling. [10]

And as a subfootnote, I'm reminded of a news story I read. A burglar broke into a suburban home in Detroit or some similar city (it's been a while since I read the item and unimportant details have blurred in my mind) and proceeded to terrorize and rob the housewife alone there with her seven-year-old son. As the attacker stripped the clothes off the woman at knife point, the child wandered into the room. The burglar told the child to go into the bedroom and watch television till he was told to come out. The child watched the tube for six straight hours, never once returning to the room where his mother had been raped repeatedly, tied and bound to a chair with tape over her mouth, and beaten mercilessly. The burglar had had free access to the entire home, had stripped it of all valuables, and had left unimpeded. The tape, incidentally, had been added when the burglar/rapist was done enjoying himself. All [11] through the assault the woman had been calling for help. But the child had been watching the set and didn't come out to see what was happening. For six hours.

[12 Another schoolteacher reminded me of a classroom experiment reported by the novelist Jerzy Kosinski, in which an instructor was set to speaking at one side of the front of a classroom, and a television monitor was set up on the other side of the room, showing the teacher speaking. The students had unobstructed vision of both. They watched the monitor. They watched what was real.

[13 Tom Snyder, late of the NBC *Tomorrow* show, was telling me that he receives letters from people apologizing for their having gone away on vacation or visiting with their grandchildren, or otherwise not having been at home so he could do his show—but now that they're back, and the set is on, he can start doing his show again. Their delusion is a strange reversal of the ones I've noted previously. For them, Snyder (and by extension other newscasters and actors) aren't there, aren't happening, unless *they* are watching. They think the actors can see into *their* living rooms, and they dress as if for company, they always make sure the room is clean, and in one case there is a report of an elderly woman who dresses for luncheon with "her friends" and sets up the table and prepares luncheon and then, at one o'clock, turns on the set for a soap opera. Those are her friends: she thinks they can see into her house, and she is one with them in their problems.

[1 To those of us who conceive of ourselves as rational and grounded in reality (yes, friends, even though I write fantasy, I live in the real world, my feet sunk to the ankles in pragmatism), all of this may seem like isolated, delusionary behavior. I assure you it isn't. A study group that rates high school populations recently advised one large school district that the "good behavior" of the kids in its classes was very likely something more than just normal quiet and good manners. They were *too* quiet, *too* tranquilized, and the study group called it "dangerous." I submit that the endless watching of TV by kids produces this blank, dead, unimaginative manner.

[1 It is widespread, and cannot possibly be countered by the minimal level of reading that currently exists in this country. Young people have been systematically bastardized in their ability to seek out quality material—books, films, food, lifestyles, life-goals, enriching relationships.

[1 Books cannot combat the spiderwebbing effect of television because kids simply cannot read. It is on a par with their inability to hear music that isn't rock. Turn the car radio dial from one end to another when you're riding with young people (up to the age of fifty) and you will perceive that they whip past classical music as if it were "white noise," simply static to their ears. The same goes for books. The printed word has no value to them and carries no possibility of knowledge or message that relates to *their* real world.

[17] If one chooses to say, as one idiot I faced on the *90 Minutes Live* talk show over the Canadian Broadcasting Corporation said, that people don't need to read, that people don't like books, that they want to be "entertained" (as if reading were something hideous, something other than *also* entertainment), then we come to an impasse. But if, like me, you believe that books preserve the past, illuminate the present, and point the way to the future . . . then you can understand why I seem to be upset at the ramifications of this epiphany I've had.

VOCABULARY

atrophy	wasting away
bastardized	made corrupt or inferior
buttress	to support or prop up
cobble up	to put together crudely
counter	to oppose or check
cribbing	petty theft; cheating by stealing ideas
delusion	a false belief or opinion
epiphany	a sudden, profound realization
facility	ready ability
glean	to collect or find
illuminate	to make clear; explain; elucidate
impasse	a difficulty without solution
inception	beginning
irrefutable	not to be disproved; absolutely true
manipulable	controllable, changeable
mesmerize	to hypnotize
minimal	smallest or least possible
mongoose	mammal noted for its ability to kill poisonous snakes
obtrude	to force oneself upon others unasked or unwanted
on a par	on an equal level
participatory	cooperative; taken part in by someone
postulate	to set up the basic principles of something
pragmatism	concern for practical results and everyday matters
ramification	effect, consequence, or outgrowth
stunning	making senseless or unconscious
summarily	hastily and arbitrarily
systemically	inherently, thoroughly
template	pattern
unimpeded	unhindered
unobstructed	unblocked

DESIGN AND MEANING

1. Summarize the major effects of watching television, according to Ellison.
2. What is the logic underlying Ellison's choice of examples of "spectator sports" in paragraph 4? What does he imply by labeling them this way?
3. Why is it important to strengthen instead of numb the "dreaming facility"?
4. What is the writer's basic method of supporting his claim that television has dehumanizing effects?
5. Defend the writer's use of sentence fragments.
6. Paragraph 15 makes extremely strong statements. To what extent do you agree with them?

SIMILARITY AND DIFFERENCE

What similarity of thesis do this essay and Barthes's "Toys" in Chapter 4 share?

SHORT WRITING IDEA

List the last five complete books you remember reading. How far back in time does your list extend? What makes you read—or not read?

LONGER WRITING IDEA

Live without watching any television for three days. Describe the effects of this change on your life.

VOCABULARY CHECK

Fill in each blank with either a word from the following list or a different form of one of them: delusion, irrefutable, inception, minimal, pragmatism, obtrude, atrophy, illuminate, stunning, ramification.

1. Cliff takes a ______ approach to life's problems, whereas Marla is idealistic.

2. Arlene tried not to ______ the dangers of climbing the mountain when she recruited the team.

3. Ben found the music of The B-52s too ______ to allow him to watch the stock market report.

4. If you don't use your mind, Clyde, it will undergo further ______.

5. Clyde's line of reasoning was faulty from its very ______ to its ridiculous conclusion.

6. The result of his argument was confusion rather than ______.

7. Clyde's mind is so muddled from alcohol abuse that he believed his statements were ______.

8. After watching television for ten hours straight, Clyde was ____ ____ for three days.

9. Some people prefer being ______ to facing the truth.

10. Marla would have an affair if she could avoid the ______.

Virginia Woolf

Shakespeare's Sister

Most admired for her brilliant stream-of-consciousness novels, Woolf (1882–1941) also worked as a publisher and wrote short stories, criticism, reviews, and volumes of lucid, imaginative essays. A feminist who felt sharply the loss of women's genius because of their prescribed role in society as nurturers of children and male egos, she accounts for the lesser achievements of her sex in *A Room of One's Own* (1929), from which the following excerpt is taken.

[1] It would have been impossible, completely and entirely, for any woman to have written the plays of Shakespeare in the age of Shakespeare. Let me imagine, since facts are so hard to come by, what would have happened had Shakespeare had a wonderfully gifted sister, called Judith, let us say. Shakespeare himself went, very probably—his mother was an heiress—to the grammar school, where he may have learnt Latin—Ovid, Virgil and Horace—and the elements of grammar and logic. He was, it is well known, a wild boy who poached rabbits, perhaps shot a deer, and had, rather sooner than he should have done, to marry a woman in the neighbourhood, who bore him a child rather quicker than was right. That escapade sent him to seek his fortune in London. He had, it seemed, a taste for the theatre; he began by holding horses at the stage door. Very soon he got work in the theatre, became a successful actor, and lived at the hub of the universe, meeting everybody, knowing everybody, practising his art on the boards, exercising his wits in the streets, and even getting access to the palace of the queen. Meanwhile his extraordinarily gifted sister, let us suppose, remained at home. She was as adventurous, as imaginative, as agog to see the world as he was. But she was not sent to school. She had no chance of learning grammar and logic, let alone of reading Horace and Virgil. She picked up a book now and then, one of her brother's perhaps, and read a few pages. But then her parents came in and told her to mend the stockings or mind the stew and not moon about with books and papers. They would have spoken sharply but kindly, for they were substantial people who knew the conditions of life for a woman and loved their daughter—indeed, more likely than not she was the apple of her father's eye. Perhaps she scribbled some pages up in an apple loft on the sly, but was careful

to hide them or set fire to them. Soon, however, before she was out of her teens, she was to be betrothed to the son of a neighbouring woolstapler. She cried out that marriage was hateful to her, and for that she was severely beaten by her father. Then he ceased to scold her. He begged her instead not to hurt him, not to shame him in this matter of her marriage. He would give her a chain of beads or a fine petticoat, he said; and there were tears in his eyes. How could she disobey him? How could she break his heart? The force of her own gift alone drove her to it. She made up a small parcel of her belongings, let herself down by a rope one summer's night and took the road to London. She was not seventeen. The birds that sang in the hedge were not more musical than she was. She had the quickest fancy, a gift like her brother's, for the tune of words. Like him, she had a taste for the theatre. She stood at the stage door; she wanted to act, she said. Men laughed in her face. The manager—a fat, loose-lipped man—guffawed. He bellowed something about poodles dancing and women acting—no woman, he said, could possibly be an actress. He hinted—you can imagine what. She could get no training in her craft. Could she even seek her dinner in a tavern or roam the streets at midnight? Yet her genius was for fiction and lusted to feed abundantly upon the lives of men and women and the study of their ways. At last—for she was very young, oddly like Shakespeare the poet in her face, with the same grey eyes and rounded brows—at last Nick Greene the actor-manager took pity on her; she found herself with child by that gentleman and so—who shall measure the heat and violence of the poet's heart when caught and tangled in a woman's body?—killed herself one winter's night and lies buried at some cross-roads where the omnibuses now stop outside the Elephant and Castle.

That, more or less, is how the story would run, I think, if a woman in Shakespeare's day had had Shakespeare's genius. [2]

VOCABULARY

agog	in a state of eager anticipation or excitement
betrothed	promised in marriage
Elephant and Castle	a typical name for an English tavern
escapade	a reckless adventure or prank
lusted	felt intense desire
moon about	to behave in an idle, dreamy, or abstracted way
poached	hunted illegally
substantial	having property; important

DESIGN AND MEANING

1. Why does Woolf emphasize that "facts are so hard to come by" in the first part of the selection?
2. What different causes does Woolf suggest for Shakespeare's sister's lack of success?
3. Woolf's thesis is incompletely stated. How would you state it?
4. Why did Judith's father choose the tactics he did to persuade her to marry?
5. The theater manager "hinted—you can imagine what." What? Why does Woolf not name it?

SIMILARITY AND DIFFERENCE

What conditions would be different for Shakespeare's sister today? What would be the same?

SHORT WRITING IDEA

Explain the irony of the statement "Nick Greene the actor-manager took pity on her."

LONGER WRITING IDEA

Write an essay about some situation or condition you have no (or little) control over which has affected the course of your life profoundly.

poetry

Edwin Arlington Robinson

Richard Cory

Edwin Arlington Robinson (1869–1935), born in Gardiner, Maine, enjoyed a privileged youth and spent two years at Harvard before the family lumber business collapsed, leaving him destitute. Thereafter, he struggled financially, even though he eventually published a number of volumes and won three Pulitzer Prizes. His most popular poems provide brief, dramatic glimpses of characters in a small New England village called "Tilbury Town."

Whenever Richard Cory went downtown,
We people on the pavement looked at him;
He was a gentleman from sole to crown,
Clean favored, and imperially slim.

And he was always quietly arrayed, [5]
And he was always human when he talked;
But still he fluttered pulses when he said,
"Good-morning," and he glittered when he walked.

And he was rich—yes, richer than a king—
And admirably schooled in every grace: [10]
In fine, we thought that he was everything
To make us wish that we were in his place.

So on we worked, and waited for the light,
And went without the meat, and cursed the bread;
And Richard Cory, one calm summer night, [15]
Went home and put a bullet through his head.

A. E. Housman

Loveliest of Trees

A. E. Housman (1859–1936), a British classical scholar, wrote superb poetry which reflects a fondness for the beauties of nature and a worldly cynicism toward life. "Loveliest of Trees" is dated 1896.

Loveliest of trees, the cherry now
Is hung with bloom along the bough,
And stands about the woodland ride
Wearing white for Eastertide.

Now, of my threescore years and ten, [5]
Twenty will not come again,
And take from seventy springs a score,
It only leaves me fifty more.

And since to look at things in bloom
Fifty springs are little room, [10]
About the woodlands I will go
To see the cherry hung with snow.

Edna St. Vincent Millay

You Will Be Sorry

Born in Rockland, Maine, Millay (1892–1950) wrote poetry and plays that gained her a reputation for vitality and strongly expressed emotion. She won the Pulitzer Prize in 1923 for poetry with *The Harp-Weaver and Other Poems*. She is known particularly for her sonnets, published in two separate editions.

Oh, oh, you will be sorry for that word!
Give back my book and take my kiss instead.
Was it my enemy or my friend I heard,
"What a big book for such a little head!"
Come, I will show you now my newest hat, [5]
And you may watch me purse my mouth and prink!
Oh, I shall love you still, and all of that.
I never again shall tell you what I think.
I shall be sweet and crafty, soft and sly;
You will not catch me reading any more: [10]
I shall be called a wife to pattern by;
And some day when you knock and push the door,
Some sane day, not too bright and not too stormy,
I shall be gone, and you may whistle for me.

VOCABULARY

arrayed — clothed
favored — appearing
in fine — in conclusion
prink — primp, fuss over one's appearance
ride — a road or path
score — twenty

DESIGN AND MEANING

1. From whose point of view is "Richard Cory" told? How can you tell?
2. What is the basic irony of "Richard Cory"? Irony is the contrast between expectation and actuality.

3. Why does Richard Cory kill himself?
4. Summarize the main point of "Loveliest of Trees."
5. In what two ways can you interpret the last line of Housman's poem?
6. To whom is Millay's poem addressed?
7. What is the "word" that angers the speaker?
8. What are the speaker's plans for getting even for the insult?
9. Do you think she has a legitimate reason for being outraged?

SIMILARITY AND DIFFERENCE

Compare the narrative point of view in "Richard Cory" and "You Will Be Sorry." Since both are first-person narratives, how do you account for the differences?

WRITING IDEA

Write an essay telling how you came to understand the reasons behind a friend's image or behavior.

Short Story

PREREADING EXERCISE ("The Use of Force")

We all sometimes find ourselves in conflict with authority: parents, teachers, police, and so on. Sometimes, too, we have our own authority questioned. Write a short essay about a time when you defied authority (successfully or not) or when someone else defied your authority (successfully or not). Questions to think about: What were your feelings at the time? Did they shift during the experience or stay the same? Looking back, how do you feel about the experience? What insights, if any, do you have about your behavior and the behavior of the other person or people involved?

Short Story

William Carlos Williams

The Use of Force

Williams (1883–1963), a major modern poet and short-story writer, was also a busy practicing pediatrician. "The Use of Force" is included in his collection entitled *Make Light of It* (1950).

They were new patients to me, all I had was the name, Olson. Please come down as soon as you can, my daughter is very sick. [1]

When I arrived I was met by the mother, a big startled looking woman, very clean and apologetic who merely said, is this the doctor? and let me in. In the back, she added. You must excuse us, doctor, we have her in the kitchen where it is warm. It is very damp here sometimes. [2]

The child was fully dressed and sitting on her father's lap near the kitchen table. He tried to get up, but I motioned for him not to bother, took off my overcoat and started to look things over. I could see that they were all very nervous, eyeing me up and down distrustfully. As often, in such cases, they weren't telling me more than they had to, it was up to me to tell them; that's why they were spending three dollars on me. [3]

The child was fairly eating me up with her cold, steady eyes, and no expression to her face whatever. She did not move and seemed, inwardly, quiet; an unusually attractive little thing, and as strong as a heifer in appearance. But her face was flushed, she was breathing rapidly, and I realized that she had a high fever. She had magnificent blonde hair, in profusion. One of those picture children often reproduced in advertising leaflets and the photogravure sections of the Sunday papers. [4]

She's had a fever for three days, began the father and we don't know what it comes from. My wife has given her things, you know, like people do, but it don't do no good. And there's been a lot of sickness around. So we tho't you'd better look her over and tell us what is the matter. [5]

As doctors often do I took a trial shot at it as a point of departure. Has she had a sore throat? [6]

Both parents answered me together, No . . . No, she says her throat don't hurt her. [7]

Does your throat hurt you? added the mother to the child. But the little girl's expression didn't change nor did she move her eyes from my face. [8]

Have you looked? [9]

I tried to, said the mother, but I couldn't see. [10]

As it happens we had been having a number of cases of diphtheria in the school to which this child went during that month and we were all, quite apparently, thinking of that, though no one had as yet spoken of the thing. [11]

Well, I said, suppose we take a look at the throat first. I smiled in my best professional manner and asking for the child's first name I said, come on, Mathilda, open your mouth and let's take a look at your throat. [12]

Nothing doing. [13]

Aw, come on, I coaxed, just open your mouth wide and let me take a look. Look, I said opening both hands wide. I haven't anything in my hands. Just open up and let me see. [14]

Such a nice man, put in the mother. Look how kind he is to you. Come on, do what he tells you to. He won't hurt you. [15]

At that I ground my teeth in disgust. If only they wouldn't use the word "hurt" I might be able to get somewhere. But I did not allow myself to be hurried or disturbed but speaking quietly and slowly I approached the child again. [16]

As I moved my chair a little nearer suddenly with one cat-like movement both her hands clawed instinctively for my eyes and she almost reached them too. In fact she knocked my glasses flying and they fell, though unbroken, several feet away from me on the kitchen floor. [17]

Both the mother and father almost turned themselves inside out in embarrassment and apology. You bad girl, said the mother, taking her and shaking her by one arm. Look what you've done. The nice man . . . [18]

For heaven's sake, I broke in. Don't call me a nice man to her. I'm here to look at her throat on the chance that she might have diphtheria and possibly die of it. But that's nothing to her. Look here, I said to the child, we're going to look at your throat. You're old enough to understand what I'm saying. Will you open it now by yourself or shall we have to open it for you? [19]

Not a move. Even her expression hadn't changed. Her breaths however were coming faster and faster. Then the battle began. I had to do it. I had to have a throat culture for her own protection. [20]

But I first told the parents that it was entirely up to them. I explained the danger but said that I would not insist on a throat examination so long as they would take the responsibility.

If you don't do what the doctor says you'll have to go to the hospital, the mother admonished her severely. [21]

Oh yeah? I had to smile to myself. After all, I had already fallen in love with the savage brat, the parents were contemptible to me. In the ensuing struggle they grew more and more abject, crushed, exhausted while she surely rose to magnificent heights of insane fury of effort bred of her terror of me. [22]

The father tried his best, and he was a big man but the fact that she was his daughter, his shame at her behavior and his dread of hurting her made him release her just at the critical moment several times when I had almost achieved success, till I wanted to kill him. But his dread also that she might have diphtheria made him tell me to go on, go on though he himself was almost fainting, while the mother moved back and forth behind us raising and lowering her hands in an agony of apprehension. [23]

Put her in front of you on your lap, I ordered, and hold both her wrists. [24]

But as soon as he did the child let out a scream. Don't, you're hurting me. Let go of my hands. Let them go I tell you. Then she shrieked terrifyingly, hysterically. Stop it! Stop it! You're killing me! [25]

Do you think she can stand it, doctor! said the mother. [26]

You get out, said the husband to his wife. Do you want her to die of diphtheria? [27]

Come on now, hold her, I said. [28]

Then I grasped the child's head with my left hand and tried to get the wooden tongue depressor between her teeth. She fought, with clenched teeth, desperately! But now I also had grown furious—at a child. I tried to hold myself down but I couldn't. I know how to expose a throat for inspection. And I did my best. When finally I got the wooden spatula behind the last teeth and just the point of it into the mouth cavity, she opened up for an instant but before I could see anything she came down again and gripping the wooden blade between her molars she reduced it to splinters before I could get it out again. [29]

Aren't you ashamed, the mother yelled at her. Aren't you ashamed to act like that in front of the doctor? [30]

Get me a smooth-handled spoon of some sort, I told the mother. We're going through with this. The child's mouth was already bleeding. Her tongue was cut and she was screaming in wild hysterical shrieks. Perhaps I should have desisted and come back in an hour or more. No doubt it would have been better. But I have seen at [31] least two children lying dead in bed of neglect in such cases, and feeling that I must get a diagnosis now or never I went at it again. But the worst of it was that I too had got beyond reason. I could have torn the child apart in my own fury and enjoyed it. It was a pleasure to attack her. My face was burning with it.

The damned little brat must be protected against her own idiocy, one says to one's self at such times. Others must be protected against her. It is social necessity. And all these things are true. But a blind fury, a feeling of adult shame, bred of a longing for muscular release are the operatives. One goes on to the end. [32]

In a final unreasoning assault I overpowered the child's neck and jaws. I forced the heavy silver spoon back of her teeth and down her throat till she gagged. And there it was—both tonsils covered with membrane. She had fought valiantly to keep me from knowing her secret. She had been hiding that sore throat for three days at least and lying to her parents in order to escape just such an outcome as this. [33]

Now truly she *was* furious. She had been on the defensive before but now she attacked. Tried to get off her father's lap and fly at me while tears of defeat blinded her eyes. [34]

VOCABULARY

abject	miserable; lacking self-respect
admonish	to warn or reprove
contemptible	deserving of scorn; worthless
desist	to stop
operatives	the elements at work
photogravure	a photomechanical reproduction of photographs, like those seen in the newspaper supplements
profusion	abundance

DESIGN AND MEANING

1. What do you find out about the family in the first page of the story? What details reveal things about them?
2. Why does the doctor say he has fallen in love with the child (paragraph 22)?
3. What are his motivations for the force he uses? What are the child's motivations?
4. Do the psychological dynamics of this incident apply to other situations?

5. Can you justify Williams's use of unconventional punctuation (fragments, comma splices, no quotation marks)?

SIMILARITY AND DIFFERENCE

Contrast the writing style of this story with that of "The Other Side of the Hedge" in Chapter 8. What differences in subject matter and theme can partly account for the difference?

SHORT WRITING IDEA

Write a paragraph explaining the significance of the title of the story.

LONGER WRITING IDEA

Describe a failure you once had and tell its causes or effects or both.

PREREADING EXERCISE ("Eveline")

How much have you been influenced by a religious upbringing? Can you think of a time when you were keen on doing something but your religious scruples kept you from it? Write a paragraph explaining the situation and then tell how you feel about it now.

James Joyce

Eveline

Born in "dear, dirty Dublin," Joyce (1882–1941) left what he considered a repressive Irish Catholic society and lived most of his life in Switzerland and France. Although he is acclaimed for his innovative stream-of-consciousness novels, Joyce's lucid short stories in *Dubliners* (1914), from which "Eveline" is taken, are some of the finest in the language.

She sat at the window watching the evening invade the avenue. Her head was leaned against the window curtains and in her nostrils was the odour of dusty cretonne. She was tired. [1]

Few people passed. The man out of the last house passed on his way home; she heard his footsteps clacking along the concrete pavement and afterwards crunching on the cinder path before the new red houses. One time there used to be a field there in which they used to play every evening with other people's children. Then a man from Belfast bought the field and built houses in it—not like their little brown houses but bright brick houses with shining roofs. The children of the avenue used to play together in that field—the Devines, the Waters, the Dunns, little Keogh the cripple, she and her brothers and sisters. Ernest, however, never played: he was too grown up. Her father used often to hunt them in out of the field with his blackthorn stick; but usually little Keogh used to keep *nix* and call out when he saw her father coming. Still they seemed to have been rather happy then. Her father was not so bad then; and besides, her mother was alive. That was a long time ago; she and her brothers and sisters were all grown up; her mother was dead. Tizzie Dunn was dead, too, and the Waters had gone back to England. Everything changes. Now she was going to go away like the others, to leave her home. [2]

Home! She looked round the room, reviewing all its familiar objects which she had dusted once a week for so many years, wondering where on earth all the dust came from. Perhaps she would never see again those familiar objects from which she had never dreamed of being divided. And yet during all those years she had never found out the name of the priest whose yellowing photograph hung on the wall above the broken harmonium beside the coloured print of the promises made to Blessed Margaret Mary Alacoque. He had been a school friend of her father. Whenever he showed the [3] photograph to a visitor her father used to pass it with a casual word:

"He is in Melbourne now." [4]

She had consented to go away, to leave her home. Was that wise? She tried to weigh each side of the question. In her home anyway she had shelter and food; she had those whom she had known all her life about her. Of course she had to work hard, both in the house and at business. What would they say of her in the Stores when they found out that she had run away with a fellow? Say she was a fool, perhaps; and her place would be filled up by advertisement. Miss Gaven would be glad. She had always had an edge on her, especially whenever there were people listening. [5]

"Miss Hill, don't you see these ladies are waiting?" [6]

"Look lively, Miss Hill, please." [7]

She would not cry many tears at leaving the Stores. [8]

But in her new home, in a distant unknown country, it would not be like that. Then she would be married—she, Eveline. People would treat her with respect then. She would not be treated as her mother had been. Even now, though she was over nineteen, she sometimes felt herself in danger of her father's violence. She knew it was that that had given her the palpitations. When they were growing up he had never gone for her, like he used to go for Harry and Ernest, because she was a girl; but latterly he had begun to threaten her and say what he would do to her only for her dead mother's sake. And now she had nobody to protect her. Ernest was dead and Harry, who was in the church decorating business, was nearly always down somewhere in the country. Besides, the invariable squabble for money on Saturday nights had begun to weary her unspeakably. She always gave her entire wages—seven shillings—and Harry always sent up what he could but the trouble was to get any money from her father. He said she used to squander the money, that she had no head, that he wasn't going to give her his hard-earned money to throw about the streets, and much more, for he was usually fairly bad on Saturday night. In the end he would give her the money and ask her had she any intention of buying Sunday's dinner. Then she had to rush out as quickly as she could and do her marketing, holding her black leather purse tightly in her hand as she elbowed her way through the crowds and returning home late under her load of provisions. She had hard work to keep the house together and to see that the two young children who had been left to her charge went to school regularly and got their meals regularly. It was hard work—a hard life—but now that she was about to leave it she did not find it a wholly undesirable life. [9]

She was about to explore another life with Frank. Frank was [10] very kind, manly, open-hearted. She was to go away with him by the night-boat to be his wife and to live with him in Buenos Ayres where he had a home waiting for her. How well she remembered the first time she had seen him; he was lodging in a house on the main road where she used to visit. It seemed a few weeks ago. He was standing at the gate, his peaked cap pushed back on his head and his hair tumbled forward over a face of bronze. Then they had come to know each other. He used to meet her outside the Stores every evening and see her home. He took her to see *The Bohemian Girl* and she felt elated as she sat in an unaccustomed part of the theatre with him. He was awfully fond of music and sang a little. People knew that they were courting and, when he sang about the lass that loves a sailor, she always felt pleasantly confused. He used to call her Poppens out of fun. First of all it had been an excitement for her to have a fellow and then she had begun to like him. He had tales of distant countries. He had started as a deck boy at a pound a month on a ship of the Allan Line going out to Canada. He told her the names of the ships he had been on and the names of the different services. He had sailed through the Straits of Magellan and he told her stories of the terrible Patagonians. He had fallen on his feet in Buenos Ayres, he said, and had come over to the old country just for a holiday. Of course, her father had found out the affair and had forbidden her to have anything to say to him.

"I know these sailor chaps," he said. [11]

One day he had quarrelled with Frank and after that she had to meet her lover secretly. [12]

The evening deepened in the avenue. The white of two letters in her lap grew indistinct. One was to Harry; the other was to her father. Ernest had been her favorite but she liked Harry too. Her father was becoming old lately, she noticed; he would miss her. Sometimes he could be very nice. Not long before, when she had been laid up for a day, he had read her out a ghost story and made toast for her at the fire. Another day, when their mother was alive, they had all gone for a picnic to the Hill of Howth. She remembered her father putting on her mother's bonnet to make the children laugh. [13]

Her time was running out but she continued to sit by the window, leaning her head against the window curtain, inhaling the odour of dusty cretonne. Down far in the avenue she could hear a street organ playing. She knew the air. Strange that it should come that very night to remind her of the promise to her mother, her promise to keep the house together as long as she could. She remembered the last night of her mother's illness; she was again in the close dark room at the other side of the hall and outside she [14] heard a melancholy air of Italy. The organ-player had been ordered to go away and given sixpence. She remembered her father strutting back into the sickroom saying:

"Damned Italians! coming over here!" [15]

As she mused the pitiful vision of her mother's life laid its spell on the very quick of her being—that life of commonplace sacrifices closing in final craziness. She trembled as she heard again her mother's voice saying constantly with foolish insistence: [16]

"Derevaun Seraun! Derevaun Seraun!"* [17]

She stood up in a sudden impulse of terror. Escape! She must escape! Frank would save her. He would give her life, perhaps love, too. But she wanted to live. Why should she be unhappy? She had a right to happiness. Frank would take her in his arms, fold her in his arms. He would save her. [18]

She stood among the swaying crowd in the station at the North Wall. He held her hand and she knew that he was speaking to her, saying something about the passage over and over again. The station was full of soldiers with brown baggages. Through the wide doors of the sheds she caught a glimpse of the black mass of the boat, lying in beside the quay wall, with illumined portholes. She answered nothing. She felt her cheek pale and cold and, out of a maze of distress, she prayed to God to direct her, to show her what was her duty. The boat blew a long mournful whistle into the mist. If she went, tomorrow she would be on the sea with Frank, steaming towards Buenos Ayres. Their passage had been booked. Could she still draw back after all he had done for her? Her distress awoke a nausea in her body and she kept moving her lips in silent fervent prayer. [19]

A bell clanged upon her heart. She felt him seize her hand: [20]

"Come!" [21]

All the seas of the world tumbled about her heart. He was drawing her into them: he would drown her. She gripped with both hands at the iron railing. [22]

"Come!" [23]

No! No! No! It was impossible. Her hands clutched the iron in frenzy. Amid the seas she sent a cry of anguish. [24]

"Eveline! Evvy!" [25]

He rushed beyond the barrier and called to her to follow. He was shouted at to go on but he still called to her. She set her white face to him, passive, like a helpless animal. Her eyes gave him no sign of love or farewell or recognition. [26]

* "The end of pleasure is pain!"

VOCABULARY

cretonne	a heavy, unglazed printed cotton or linen cloth
harmonium	a small kind of reed organ
quay	a dock for ships
quick	the living center

DESIGN AND MEANING

1. What details of Eveline's past are stated or implied? What details of her present life?
2. Eveline thinks that people will treat her with respect in Buenos Aires. Why? Is she right?
3. What causes her finally to refuse to go? Does anything earlier prepare you for her decision?
4. What are her feelings for Frank? In what sense is she "a helpless animal" as the boat leaves? Why does she give him "no sign of love or farewell or recognition"?
5. Some readers have claimed that Frank is not real, that he is just a creation of Eveline's imagination. Can you find any justification for this reading?

SHORT WRITING IDEA

Explain how one of the following items serves as a symbol—i.e., how it suggests a concept or a group of ideas broader than itself: the sea, Frank, Buenos Aires, the objects in Eveline's apartment, Eveline's mother, Eveline's father, dust.

LONGER WRITING IDEA

Explain the causes (or effects) of any drastic change of opinion, attitude, or behavior you have undergone in your life.

Argument and Persuasion

IF YOU SAY, "I had a big argument with my husband last night," no one is likely to think you presented a sound thesis, supported it with several reasonable points of evidence, rationally pointed out the flaws in his opposing points, and came to a well-phrased, emphatic conclusion. But in rhetorical terms, an argument is just that process; it need not be an ugly showdown, as it often is in everyday terms.

In writing, you have the advantage of letting your opponent interrupt you only when and where you like. First, you can introduce your own side in an interesting and straightforward way, and then you can give your support, usually in the form of cause-and-effect reasoning using examples, facts, and statistics, and the logical processes of induction, deduction, and analogy. Finally, just to show that you have thought both sides through, you can expose the major points of the opposition as illogical, ill-founded, untrue, or uninformed. On some occasions, you may need to concede a point gracefully, meanwhile explaining why you are nevertheless not swayed to the other side.

This plan follows the classical model of argumentation, and it still provides a sound writing strategy. In following it, you would make use of all the various modes of development we have discussed so far in this book. Writers also frequently vary the classical form, as you will see in the selections in this chapter.

Argumentation appeals to a reader's logical, reasoning side, but rationality is not always what governs the reader's opinions. A person's emotions often exercise a more powerful influence, and that is where *persuasion* comes in. A touching narrative, a moving example, a strongly connotative image—these are important elements in composition that can often convince where logic may fail.

Much of your persuasive success depends on your relationship to your audience. Think carefully about the people you are trying to reach in your essay. Who are they? Well, you really have to imagine them, using your experience of people and the world. If you plan to write a persuasive letter to your local newspaper, for example, you must think about the readers of that newspaper, what ideas they probably hold about your subject, and what they see as important and unimportant in life. The newspaper readers in our city, we imagine, are mostly middle- and upper-middle class employed persons who value security, family life, and upward mobility. Most are conservative and Republican and go to church.

Such an analysis is important to anyone trying to sway our citizenry. If you were writing a letter to the editor to convince this audience to walk, ride bicycles, carpool, or take busses to work instead of driving individual cars, you would need to be aware that most of your readers would quickly dismiss certain arguments as crackpot. Thus, you'd be wise not to mention that walking or biking back and forth from work would provide them with valuable time for meditation and for getting in touch with themselves (at least not in those terms). Instead, you would argue on the grounds of fewer traffic accidents, less exhaust fumes, and more revenue from increased bus ridership to improve service and lower the rates.

At no time should you suggest, in tone or content, that your readers are ignorant, unfeeling, or outmoded. People dig in their heels when someone challenges not only their ideas but their personal worth. If you really want to dissuade someone from an erroneous opinion, you must first figure out what is threatening to them about your viewpoint. You must soothe your readers' fears, reassure them, and decrease their anxieties until they are at least somewhat open to reason. The process of quieting their qualms involves two parts: first, sympathetically restate your readers' fears and give reassurance; and second, state a shared assumption or agreement as a starting point for your argument.

For example, let's say you decide you would rather enroll in a two-year community college program and become a court reporter than go to the university and become an accountant as your parents want you to. This decision, you are aware, is likely to upset your folks. Using fear-reducing tactics, you might begin your argument something like this: "I know you think that going to the university is a great opportunity, one that you never had, and I realize that you're right. But I also know that you want me to use my own good judgment and that what you want *most* is for me to be happy." How can they disagree?

In this chapter you will find persuasive arguments on a variety of subjects, from having faith in the human race to enticing someone into bed. Particularly notice in every selection the writer's choice of persuasive tactics.

essays

PREREADING EXERCISE (Are You Giving Your Child Too Much?)

Do you think that you were overindulged as a child? Why or why not?

essays

Benjamin Spock, M.D.

Are You Giving Your Kids Too Much?

Born in 1903, Spock is one of the few men ever to be blamed for the moral terpitude of an entire generation. Spock's books on child care have guided parents since 1946, the year in which *Baby and Child Care* was published. The author of more than eleven books on human care, Spock also protested American involvement in Vietnam, refusing to separate professional and personal concerns.

While traveling for various speaking engagements, I frequently stay overnight in the home of a family and am assigned to one of the children's bedrooms. In it, I often find so many playthings that there's almost no room—even on the bureau top—for my small toilet kit. And the closet is usually so tightly packed with clothes that I can barely squeeze in my jacket. [1]

I'm not complaining, only making a point. I think that the tendency to give children an overabundance of toys and clothes is quite common in American families, and I think that in far too many families not only do children come to take their parents' generosity for granted, but the effects of this can actually be somewhat harmful to children. [2]

Of course, I'm not only thinking of the material possessions children are given. Children can also be overindulged with too many privileges—for example, when parents send a child to an expensive summer camp that the parents can't really afford. [3]

Why do parents give their children too much, or give things they can't afford? I believe there are several reasons. [4]

One fairly common reason is that parents overindulge their children out of a sense of guilt. For instance, if a couple were unhappy about an unexpected pregnancy, they might feel guilty about these feelings long after the baby is born and try to compen- [5]

sate by showering the child with material possessions. Or parents who both hold down full-time jobs may feel guilty about the amount of time they spend away from their children and may attempt to compensate with gifts.

[6] Other parents overindulge because they want their children to have everything *they* had while growing up, along with those things the parents yearned for but didn't get. Still others are afraid to say no to their children's endless requests for toys for fear that their children will feel unloved or will be ridiculed if they don't have the same playthings their friends have.

[7] Overindulgence of a child also happens when parents are unable to stand up to their children's unreasonable demands. Such parents vacillate between saying no and giving in—but neither response seems satisfactory to them. If they refuse a request, they immediately feel a wave of remorse for having been so strict or ungenerous. If they give in, they feel regret and resentment over having been a pushover. This kind of vacillation not only impairs the parents' ability to set limits, it sours the parent-child relationship to some degree, robbing parents and their children of some of the happiness and mutual respect that should be present in healthy families.

[8] But overindulging children with material things does little to assuage parental guilt (since parents never feel that they've given enough), nor does it make children feel more loved (for what children really crave is parents' time and attention). Instead, the effects of overindulgence can be harmful. Children may, to some degree, become greedy, self-centered, ungrateful and insensitive to the needs and feelings of others, beginning with their parents. When children are given too much, it undermines their respect for their parents. In fact, the children begin to *sense* that a parent's unlimited generosity is not right. The paradoxical result may be that these children will push further, unconsciously hoping that, if they push *too* hard, they will force their parents into setting limits.

[9] Overindulged children also are not as challenged as children with fewer playthings to be more creative in their play. They have fewer opportunities to learn the value of money, and have less experience in learning to deal with a delay in gratification, if every requested object is given on demand.

[10] The real purpose of this discussion is not to tell parents how much or how little to give to their children. Rather, my intent is to help those parents who already sense that they might be overindulging their children but don't know how to stop.

[11] Parents who are fortunate enough not to have a problem with feelings of guilt don't need to respond crossly to their children when denying a specific request which is thought to be unreasonable. They can explain, *cheerfully,* that it's too expensive—except perhaps

as a birthday or holiday gift—or that the child will have to contribute to its purchase from an allowance or from the earnings of an outside job.

[12] It's the cheerfulness and lack of hesitation that impress upon the child that parents mean what they say. A cross response signals that the parents are in inner conflict. In fact, I'll make a rash statement that I believe is true, by and large: Children will abide by what their parents sincerely believe is right. They only begin arguing and pestering when they detect uncertainty or guilt, and sense that their parents can be pushed to give them what they want, if they just keep at it. But the truth is that a child *really* wants parents to be in control—even if it means saying no to a request—and to act with conviction in a kind and loving fashion.

[13] But, you may answer, I often *am* uncertain about whether to give in to many of my children's requests. That doesn't mean you can't change. First you should try to determine what makes you submissive or guilty. Then, even if you haven't uncovered the reason, you should begin to make firm decisions and practice responding to your children's requests in a prompt, definite manner.

[14] Once you turn over a new leaf, you can't expect to change completely right away. You are bound to vacillate at times. The key is to be satisfied with gradual improvement, expecting and accepting the occasional slips that come with any change. And even after you are handling these decisions in a firmer and more confident manner, you can't expect your children to respond immediately. For a while they'll keep on applying the old pressures that used to work so well. But they'll eventually come to respect your decisions once they learn that nagging and arguing no longer work. In the end, both you and your children will be happier for it.

DESIGN AND MEANING

1. Do you find the personal introduction effective?
2. What problem does Spock establish? What harm does overindulgence do to parents and children?
3. List reasons for overindulgence.
4. What solution does Spock propose for the problem of overindulgence?
5. How does Spock maintain a positive tone even when he is criticizing parents and children? If you are a parent, what is your emotional response to the essay?

SIMILARITY AND DIFFERENCE

Vidal refers to Spock in "Drugs" (this chapter) as "permissive Dr. Spock." Does Spock seem permissive to you in this essay? Do some research to see why Spock has a reputation for permissiveness.

SHORT WRITING IDEA

Define *inner conflict* and give an example from your own life. Is the conflict resolved? How? If not, will it ever be resolved?

LONGER WRITING IDEA

Spock's essay has a problem-solution structure, and it is directed toward parents. Write a problem-solution persuasive essay with a specific audience. For example, you might write for lecture hall professors explaining the problem of student absenteeism and suggesting a solution.

PREREADING EXERCISE ("Drugs")

Write a letter to the editor of your school or community newspaper in which you propose a solution or partial solution to a particular current "drug problem": alcohol, marijuana, cocaine, caffeine, heroin, Valium, or nicotine abuse. Be sure that you identify exactly which problem you are dealing with and why you believe your solution or partial solution would work.

Gore Vidal

Drugs

The author of numerous best-selling novels, successful plays, and distinguished essays, Vidal (b. 1925) is one of America's most versatile writers. The following piece was first published in *The New York Times,* September 26, 1970, and is included in *Homage to Daniel Shays: Collected Essays 1952–1972.*

It is possible to stop most drug addiction in the United States within a very short time. Simply make all drugs available and sell them at cost. Label each drug with a precise description of what effect—good and bad—the drug will have on the taker. This will require heroic honesty. Don't say that marijuana is addictive or dangerous when it is neither, as millions of people know—unlike "speed," which kills most unpleasantly, or heroin, which is addictive and difficult to kick. [1]

For the record, I have tried—once—almost every drug and liked none, disproving the popular Fu Manchu theory that a single whiff of opium will enslave the mind. Nevertheless many drugs are bad for certain people to take and they should be told why in a sensible way. [2]

Along with exhortation and warning, it might be good for our citizens to recall (or learn for the first time) that the United States was the creation of men who believed that each man has the right to do what he wants with his own life as long as he does not interfere with his neighbor's pursuit of happiness (that his neighbor's idea of happiness is persecuting others does confuse matters a bit). [3]

This is a startling notion to the current generation of Americans. They reflect a system of public education which has made the Bill of Rights, literally, unacceptable to a majority of high school graduates (see the annual Purdue reports) who now form the "silent majority"—a phrase which that underestimated wit Richard Nixon took from Homer who used it to describe the dead. [4]

Now one can hear the warning rumble begin: if everyone is allowed to take drugs everyone will and the GNP will decrease, the Commies will stop us from making everyone free, and we shall end up a race of Zombies, passively murmuring "groovie" to one another. Alarming thought. Yet it seems most unlikely that any reasonably [5] sane person will become a drug addict if he knows in advance what addiction is going to be like.

[6] Is everyone reasonably sane? No. Some people will always become drug addicts just as some people will always become alcoholics, and it is just too bad. Every man, however, has the power (and should have the legal right) to kill himself if he chooses. But since most men don't, they won't be mainliners either. Nevertheless, forbidding people things they like or think they might enjoy only makes them want those things all the more. This psychological insight is, for some mysterious reason, perennially denied our governors.

[7] It is a lucky thing for the American moralist that our country has always existed in a kind of time-vacuum: we have no public memory of anything that happened last Tuesday. No one in Washington today recalls what happened during the years alcohol was forbidden to the people by a Congress that thought it had a divine mission to stamp out Demon Rum—launching, in the process, the greatest crime wave in the country's history, causing thousands of deaths from bad alcohol, and creating a general (and persisting) contempt among the citizenry for laws of the United States.

[8] The same thing is happening today. But the government has learned nothing from past attempts at prohibition, not to mention repression.

[9] Last year when the supply of Mexican marijuana was slightly curtailed by the Feds, the pushers got the kids hooked on heroin and deaths increased dramatically, particularly in New York. Whose fault? Evil men like the Mafiosi? Permissive Dr. Spock? Wild-eyed Dr. Leary? No.

[10] The Government of the United States was responsible for those deaths. The bureaucratic machine has a vested interest in playing cops and robbers. Both the Bureau of Narcotics and the Mafia want strong laws against the sale and use of drugs because if drugs are sold at cost there would be no money in it for anyone.

[11] If there was no money in it for the Mafia, there would be no friendly playground pushers, and addicts would not commit crimes to pay for the next fix. Finally, if there was no money in it, the Bureau of Narcotics would wither away, something they are not about to do without a struggle.

[12] Will anything sensible be done? Of course not. The American people are as devoted to the idea of sin and its punishment as they are to making money—and fighting drugs is nearly as big a business as pushing them. Since the combination of sin and money is irresistible (particularly to the professional politician), the situation will only grow worse.

Clarence Page

The Trouble with Legalizing Drugs

Born in 1947 and living in Chicago, Page has written since 1984 for the editorial pages of the *Chicago Tribune,* from which this essay was taken. One of the few black men named to the editorial board of the newspaper, Page now has considerable influence on the hearts and minds of fellow Chicagoans. His ideas have also found their way into magazines like *The New Republic.*

If you can't win the game, change the rules. Such is the deliciously convenient reasoning that drives the rejuvenated movement to beat the drug problem by legalizing the very substances that lie at the center of the problem. Unfortunately, legalization sounds too good to be true and probably is. [1]

It sounds good because it's simple. It would immediately remove the immense profits drugs now pump into the criminal underworld, it would reduce the forbidden-fruit attraction drugs have for young people and it would take away the criminal stigma that prevents many addicts from seeking help. You even could tax the sale of now-illegal drugs and use the money to build more treatment centers, which are desperately needed. Addicts who want to quit face six-month waiting lists at overcrowded treatment centers. [2]

Deep thinkers of liberal and conservative stripes have long advocated lifting the prohibition on drugs, particularly ones, like marijuana, that are nonaddictive but still habit-forming. Last year the debate was stirred anew when Baltimore Mayor Kurt Schmoke, a former prosecutor, called for a serious national debate on the subject. [3]

Schmoke's advocacy was based on his experience. In spite of his stellar record as a drug prosecutor, he felt as though he was bailing out the ocean with a teaspoon. Prohibition of drugs is working no better than prohibition of liquor worked earlier this century, he told Congress. It increases crime without eliminating addiction. We're losing the game, so let's change the rules. [4]

He was not alone in his sentiments. "Prohibition is an attempted cure that makes matters worse—for both the addict and [5] the rest of us," wrote Nobel Prize-winning economist Milton Friedman in 1972, after President Nixon declared a "war" on drugs. "In drugs, as in other areas, persuasion and example are likely to be far more effective than the use of force to shape others in our image."

The simplicity of this prescription has proved irresistible to what seems to be a growing number of journalists, academics and writers of letters to editors. [6]

Unfortunately, the simple beauty of such logic has an ugly gaping hole: A guarantee that drug use and its accompanying social cost would decline. In fact, there is considerable evidence to suggest that with legalization drug use and its social costs actually would increase. Sharply. [7]

Advocates of legalization say such an increase would be temporary, at best. But how long is "temporary"? And how much of an increase are we willing to tolerate? [8]

Keeping drugs illegal may not eliminate them, but it almost surely reduces their use. If the time-worn comparison with the futile Prohibition era holds, an end to the prohibition against drugs would be followed by an upsurge in use that might just overwhelm the new drug-treatment facilities that revenue from drug taxes would provide. [9]

It may be amusing to consider the marketing possibilities of newly legalized and heavily taxed cocaine, or the transformation of campus pubs, fancy night clubs, singles bars and country club lounges into opium dens. But it is brutally sobering to consider an increase in wasted lives, broken families and cocaine-addicted babies. [10]

"Prof. James Q. Wilson tells us that during the years in which heroin could be legally prescribed by doctors in Britain, the number of addicts increased forty-fold," wrote drug czar William Bennett in the Sept. 19 *Wall Street Journal* in a rebuttal to an open letter economist Friedman had directed to him in an earlier issue. "And after the repeal of Prohibition—an analogy favored but misunderstood by legalization advocates—consumption of alcohol soared by 350 percent." [11]

Unfortunately, Bennett's approach—the center of President Bush's get-tough drug policy—also misses the boat. Drugs are a symptom of deeper ills in certain segments of our society, particularly the impoverished segments. You can call in all the troops you want and build more jails and drug boot camps, but as long as demand remains, the traffic will find ways to get through. And demand will remain as long as the social ills that feed it remain. [12]

Bennett has said in interviews that he doesn't want to attack the root causes until he can make the streets safe. Dream on. [13]

The heart of the drug problem, the part that causes Americans to cite drugs as the nation's biggest problem in opinion polls, is not the "casual user" Bennett has sworn to track down like some bureaucratic mountie. The real problem is the rise in fiercely addictive drugs with names like crack, crank and smack—the drugs that produce cocaine-addicted babies, devastate families and waste lives. [14]

Bennett is right to say the nation's drug problem is too multifaceted to be destroyed with a "magic bullet." But he is wrong to limit his targets. The proverbial quick fix that legalization would seem to provide is illusory. But so is the slow fix offered by further criminalization. [15]

VOCABULARY

curtail	to cut off
exhortation	strongly worded advice
illusory	unreal
perennial	continuing without interruption
rejuvenated	renewed to youth
repression	prevention by pressure or force
stellar	brilliant

DESIGN AND MEANING

1. What is the effect of the first sentence of the Vidal essay? How would you describe its tone?
2. In the Vidal essay, find an example of argument through *deductive reasoning* (deriving a conclusion by inferring from a general principle). Find an example of argument through *analogy* (inference that what is true of one thing will be true of another similar thing).
3. Does Vidal take up opposing arguments? If so, how does he deal with them?
4. What *premises* (basic assumptions) about human behavior does Vidal base his arguments on?
5. What points of agreement do Vidal and Page share?
6. What are the points of disagreement between Vidal and Page?
7. One of these essays was published in 1970, one in 1989. What differences between them are accounted for by time?

SIMILARITY AND DIFFERENCE

What premises do Vidal and Thomas Szasz ("Defining Mental Illness," Chapter 6) seem to share?

SHORT WRITING IDEA

Beginning with the premise "Dogs like to please their owners," write a paragraph that shows, through deductive reasoning, a good way to teach dogs to fetch.

LONGER WRITING IDEA

Write a letter to your school or job administrators arguing that they should change some rule or process that you believe creates more problems than it solves.

PREREADING EXERCISE ("The Bird and the Machine")

Machines can now do many of the things that people do—and do some of them better. Computers can think thousands of times faster and more accurately than people can. Write a paragraph explaining to your boss, your coworkers, or your family why your job (or one of your roles in life) can never be taken over by a machine.

Loren Eiseley

The Bird and the Machine

Respected equally as an anthropologist and as an author, Eiseley (1907–1977) writes both poetry and poetic prose. His scientific essays are illuminated by imaginative language and suffused with a love of nature. The following selection is an excerpt from *The Immense Journey* (1957).

I suppose their little bones have years ago been lost among the stones and winds of those high glacial pastures. I suppose their feathers blew eventually into the piles of tumbleweed beneath the straggling cattle fences and rotted there in the mountain snows, along with dead steers and all the other things that drift to an end in the corners of the wire. I do not quite know why I should be thinking of birds over the *New York Times* at breakfast, particularly the birds of my youth half a continent away. It is a funny thing what the brain will do with memories and how it will treasure them and finally bring them into odd juxtapositions with other things, as though it wanted to make a design, or get some meaning out of them, whether you want it or not, or even see it. [1]

It used to seem marvelous to me, but I read now that there are machines that can do these things in a small way, machines that can crawl about like animals, and that it may not be long now until they do more things—maybe even make themselves—I saw that piece in the *Times* just now. And then they will, maybe—well, who knows—but you read about it more and more with no one making any protest, and already they can add better than we and reach up and hear things through the dark and finger the guns over the night sky. [2]

This is the new world that I read about at breakfast. This is the world that confronts me in my biological books and journals, until there are times when I sit quietly in my chair and try to hear the little purr of the cogs in my head and the tubes flaring and dying as the messages go through them and the circuits snap shut or open. This is the great age, make no mistake about it; the robot has been born somewhat appropriately along with the atom bomb, and the brain they say now is just another type of more complicated feedback system. The engineers have its basic principles worked out; it's mechanical, you know; nothing to get superstitious about; [3]

and man can always improve on nature once he gets the idea. Well, he's got it all right and that's why, I guess, that I sit here in my chair, with the article crunched in my hand, remembering those two birds and the blue mountain sunlight. There is another magazine article on my desk that reads "Machines Are Getting Smarter Every Day." I don't deny it, but I'll still stick with the birds. It's life I believe in, not machines.

Maybe you don't believe there is any difference. A skeleton is all joints and pulleys, I'll admit. And when man was in his simpler stages of machine building in the eighteenth century, he quickly saw the resemblances. "What," wrote Hobbes, "is the heart but a spring, and the nerves but so many strings, and the joints but so many wheels, giving motion to the whole body?" Tinkering about in their shops it was inevitable in the end that men would see the world as a huge machine "subdivided into an infinite number of lesser machines." [4]

The idea took on with a vengeance. Little automatons toured the country—dolls controlled by clockwork. Clocks described as little worlds were taken on tours by their designers. They were made up of moving figures, shifting scenes and other remarkable devices. The life of the cell was unknown. Man, whether he was conceived as possessing a soul or not, moved and jerked about like these tiny puppets. A human being thought of himself in terms of his own tools and implements. He has been fashioned like the puppets he produced and was only a more clever model made by a greater designer. [5]

Then in the nineteenth century, the cell was discovered, and the single machine in its turn was found to be the product of millions of infinitesimal machines—the cell. Now, finally, the cell itself dissolves away into an abstract chemical machine—and that into some intangible, inexpressible flow of energy. The secret seems to lurk all about, the wheels get smaller and smaller, and they turn more rapidly, but when you try to seize it the life is gone—and so, by popular definition, some would say that life was never there in the first place. The wheels and the cogs are the secret and we can make them better in time—machines that run faster and more accurately than real mice to real cheese . . . . [6]

The cabin had not been occupied for years. We intended to clean it out and live in it, but there were holes in the roof and the birds had come in and were roosting in the rafters. You could depend on it in a place like this where everything blew away, and even a bird needed some place out of the weather and away from coyotes. A cabin going back to nature in a wild place draws them till they [7] come in, listening at the eaves, I imagine, pecking softly among the shingles till they find a hole and then suddenly the place is theirs and man is forgotten.

Sometimes of late years I find myself thinking the most beautiful sight in the world might be the birds taking over New York after the last man has run away to the hills. I will never live to see it, of course, but I know just how it will sound because I've lived up high and I know the sort of watch birds keep on us. I've listened to sparrows tapping tentatively on the outside of air conditioners when they thought no one was listening, and I know how other birds test the vibrations that come up to them through the television aerials. [8]

"Is he gone?" they ask, and the vibrations come up from below, "Not yet, not yet." [9]

Well, to come back, I got the door open softly and I had the spotlight all ready to turn on and blind whatever birds there were so they couldn't see to get out through the roof. I had a short piece of ladder to put against the far wall where there was a shelf on which I expected to make the biggest haul. I had all the information I needed just like any skilled assassin. I pushed the door open, the hinges squeaking only a little. A bird or two stirred—I could hear them—but nothing flew and there was a faint starlight through the holes in the roof. [10]

I padded across the floor, got the ladder up and the light ready, and slithered up the ladder till my head and arms were over the shelf. Everything was dark as pitch except for the starlight at the little place back of the shelf near the eaves. With the light to blind them, they'd never make it. I had them. I reached my arm carefully over in order to be ready to seize whatever was there and I put the flash on the edge of the shelf where it would stand by itself when I turned it on. That way I'd be able to use both hands. [11]

Everything worked perfectly except for one detail—I didn't know what kind of birds were there. I never thought about it at all, and it wouldn't have mattered if I had. My orders were to get something interesting. I snapped on the flash and sure enough there was a great beating and feathers flying, but instead of my having them, they, or rather he, had me. He had my hand, that is, and for a small hawk not much bigger than my fist he was doing all right. I heard him give one short metallic cry when the light went on and my hand descended on the bird beside him; after that he was busy with his claws and his beak was sunk in my thumb. In the struggle I knocked the lamp over on the shelf, and his mate got her sight back and whisked neatly through the hole in the roof and off among the stars outside. It all happened in fifteen seconds and you might think I would have fallen down the ladder, but no, I had a professional assassin's reputation to keep up, and the bird, of course, [12] made the mistake of thinking the hand was the enemy and not the eyes behind it. He chewed my thumb up pretty effectively and lacerated my hand with his claws, but in the end I got him, having two hands to work with.

[13] He was a sparrow hawk and a fine young male in the prime of life. I was sorry not to catch the pair of them, but as I dripped blood and folded his wings carefully, holding him by the back so that he couldn't strike again, I had to admit the two of them might have been more than I could have handled under the circumstances. The little fellow had saved his mate by diverting me, and that was that. He was born to it, and made no outcry now, resting in my hand hopelessly, but peering toward me in the shadows behind the lamp with a fierce, almost indifferent glance. He neither gave nor expected mercy and something out of the high air passed from him to me, stirring a faint embarrassment.

[14] I quit looking into that eye and managed to get my huge carcass with its fist full of prey back down the ladder. I put the bird in a box too small to allow him to injure himself by struggle and walked out to welcome the arriving trucks. It had been a long day, and camp still to make in the darkness. In the morning that bird would be just another episode. He would go back with the bones in the truck to a small cage in the city where he would spend the rest of his life. And a good thing, too. I sucked my aching thumb and spat out some blood. An assassin had to get used to these things. I had a professional reputation to keep up.

[15] In the morning, with the change that comes on suddenly in that high country, the mist that had hovered below us in the valley was gone. The sky was a deep blue, and one could see for miles over the high outcroppings of stone. I was up early and brought the box in which the little hawk was imprisoned out onto the grass where I was building a cage. A wind as cool as a mountain spring ran over the grass and stirred my hair. It was a fine day to be alive. I looked up and all around and at the hole in the cabin roof out of which the other hawk had fled. There was no sign of her anywhere that I could see.

[16] "Probably in the next county by now," I thought cynically, but before beginning work I decided I'd have a look at my last night's capture.

[17] Secretively, I looked again all around the camp and up and down and opened the box. I got him right out in my hand with his wings folded properly and I was careful not to startle him. He lay limp in my grasp and I could feel his heart pound under the feathers but he only looked beyond me and up.

[18] I saw him look that last look away beyond me into a sky so full

of light that I could not follow his gaze. The little breeze flowed over me again, and nearby a mountain aspen shook all its tiny leaves. I suppose I must have had an idea then of what I was going to do, but I never let it come up into consciousness. I just reached over and laid the hawk on the grass.

[19] He lay there a long minute without hope, unmoving, his eyes still fixed on that blue vault above him. It must have been that he was already so far away in heart that he never felt the release from my hand. He never even stood. He just lay with his breast against the grass.

[20] In the next second after that long minute he was gone. Like a flicker of light, he had vanished with my eyes full on him, but without actually seeing even a premonitory wing beat. He was gone straight into that towering emptiness of light and crystal that my eyes could scarcely bear to penetrate. For another long moment there was silence. I could not see him. The light was too intense. Then from far up somewhere a cry came ringing down.

[21] I was young then and had seen little of the world, but when I heard that cry my heart turned over. It was not the cry of the hawk I had captured; for, by shifting my position against the sun, I was now seeing further up. Straight out of the sun's eye, where she must have been soaring restlessly above us for untold hours, hurtled his mate. And from far up, ringing from peak to peak of the summits over us, came a cry of such unutterable and ecstatic joy that it sounds down across the years and tingles among the cups on my quiet breakfast table.

[22] I saw them both now. He was rising fast to meet her. They met in a great soaring gyre that turned to a whirling circle and a dance of wings. Once more, just once, their two voices, joined in a harsh wild medley of question and response, struck and echoed against the pinnacles of the valley. Then they were gone forever somewhere into those upper regions beyond the eyes of men.

[23] I am older now, and sleep less, and have seen most of what there is to see and am not very much impressed any more, I suppose, by anything. "What Next in the Attributes of Machines?" my morning headline runs. "It Might Be the Power to Reproduce Themselves."

[24] I lay the paper down and across my mind a phrase floats insinuatingly: "It does not seem that there is anything in the construction, constituents, or behavior of the human being which is essentially impossible for science to duplicate and synthesize. On the other hand . . ."

[25] All over the city the cogs in the hard, bright mechanisms have begun to turn. Figures move through computers, names are spelled

out, a thoughtful machine selects the fingerprints of a wanted criminal from an array of thousands. In the laboratory an electronic mouse runs swiftly through a maze toward the cheese it can neither taste nor enjoy. On the second run it does better than a living mouse.

[26] "On the other hand . . ." Ah, my mind takes up, on the other hand the machine does not bleed, ache, hang for hours in the empty sky in a torment of hope to learn the fate of another machine, nor does it cry out with joy nor dance in the air with the fierce passion of a bird. Far off, over a distance greater than space, that remote cry from the heart of heaven makes a faint buzzing among my breakfast dishes and passes on and away.

VOCABULARY

cavalcade	a procession
gyre	a circular or spiral motion
infinitesimal	extremely tiny
insinuating	slyly suggestive
juxtaposition	placement side by side or close together
marginal	on the border between being profitable and being unprofitable
premonitory	forewarning
reciprocal	done or given in return

DESIGN AND MEANING

1. Why do you think this selection would, strictly speaking, be considered persuasive rather than argumentative?
2. What does Eiseley mean by "the robot has been born somewhat appropriately along with the atom bomb"?
3. What effect does the repetition of "professional reputation to keep up" achieve?
4. The word choice "assassin" is obviously loaded with connotation. What other things in the narrative suggest the outcome before it is described?
5. What significance do you think Eiseley attaches to his statements about being "young" when the narrative happened and "older" now?

SIMILARITY AND DIFFERENCE

Compare and contrast Eiseley's and Morgan's attitudes toward humanity. (Morgan's essay follows.)

SHORT WRITING IDEA

In a paragraph, develop one argument *for* mechanization.

LONGER WRITING IDEA

Write a persuasive essay using a story from your life to argue the truth or falsity of some pithy saying: "Honesty is the best policy"; "Love is never having to say you're sorry"; "Unusual travel suggestions are dancing lessons from God" (Kurt Vonnegut, Jr.); "If you can't lick 'em, join 'em."

PREREADING EXERCISE ("The Pro-Rape Culture")

Which do you see as a bigger problem in society, racism or sexism? Which is a bigger problem in your own life?

Joan Morgan

The Pro-Rape Culture

This article is in response to a much-publicized 1989 gang rape and beating of a white woman by a group of black youths who attacked her as she was jogging in New York's Central Park at night. The reaction of people was varied, between those expressing an inability to understand how middle-class youth can be violent and those pointing to society's treatment of women and minorities as a root cause.

> Being an African-American youth in the U.S. today calls for living in a constant state of anger, paranoia and hostility against institutional racism, economic violence, massive unemployment, homelessness, deplorable living conditions and inferior education. [1]
>
> —Defense attorney Colin Moore in the *Amsterdam News*

Only the privileged few could take issue with Colin Moore's description of young black life. What's problematic is that he offered it as a rationale for the Central Park gang-rape. Moore's failure to address sexism as the most relevant of the "deplorable social conditions" contributing to this tragedy is no surprise. There is much less tolerance for racism than sexism in the black community. [2]

The need to see these kids as victims of deplorable social conditions is understandable—as people with a long history of social displacement as well as extended family ties, we're extremely reluctant to cast out our own, no matter how badly they fucked up. It's a tradition that sees the Shadrachs and the Teacakes as being as intrinsically valuable as the Reverend Jacksons, the Sulas as being as important as the Nells. We all have our roles. [3]

Even our more "progressive" brothers and, yes, sisters tend to see sexism as something that can be dealt with—later. These are the folks who will boycott *Mississippi Burning,* tongue-lash Alice Walker and Gloria Naylor, cringe at the mention of *Birth of a Nation,* and yet be able to see the humor in Run-D.M.C.'s *Tougher Than Leather* and drool over their own personal copy of Eddie Murphy's *Raw.* [4]

Okay, Joan, I can see what you're saying, but don't you think the opening scene when he's describing at length the blowjob this biddy gave him is hilarious?! . . . Uh, no. Nor do I find any humor in the fact that every woman in the film was portrayed as yet another juvenile wet-dream fantasy . . . . *But it was so funny!* . . . So are racist jokes—as long as you're not the butt of them. [5]

We live in a pro-rape culture (rape being defined as the "abusive or improper treatment, profanation, violation" of women). We are all victims of it. This case had much less to do with their blackness and her whiteness than it had to do with their maleness and her femaleness. This is not an issue of race, but of gender. Had I been in that park that night my blackness certainly would not have spared me. The only relevant thing about this woman's whiteness is that it and the media prevent us from ignoring this crime. And whether that's fair or not, it's become more difficult to stick our heads in the sand. [6]

This woman's decision to jog in a potentially dangerous area of the park was a naïve expression of "white female privilege" that led to a false sense of invulnerability. This was not a wise thing to do. [7]

Much has been said about this woman's display of white female privilege. Little has been said about the privilege of being male in this society or the false sense of entitlement that arises from it. This is a culture that measures human worth in terms of power. We need to look no further than our boy Boesky; being rich and white he thought he should be above the law. It is no wonder that so many men's, and yes, once again, women's, perceptions of manhood are so awry. Too often manhood is measured by the ability to exert power over others, particularly women. Being a man reduces to how much ass I can kick and how much ass I can get. [8]

This is why homeboy feels he has the right to stop a perfect stranger on the street and demand her name, address, telephone number, and pussy. That it's his right to call you "Bitch, Ugly Bitch, Dilly Hoe, Dyke" when you dare to ignore him. And if you choose to tell him, in no uncertain terms, that you don't owe him shit, it's the look in his eyes that warns you not to walk that way alone again. Sisters are very familiar with the concept of male privilege. [9]

Nor is male privilege limited to the working-class black/Latin/Italian boys on ghetto corners. Ask the white sexagenarian guy in the Brooks Brothers suit who rode the bus with me in Riverdale. [10]

You have such nice legs, you work? . . . You've got to be kidding. Okay, here we go. I'm a teacher, I said. . . . *Oh. I thought you worked like the other girls up here.* . . . This translates: maid. . . . *Don't go to work today, come home with me. You're too beautiful to work. I'll* [11] *make sure you never work again* . . . . This translates: prostitute. He only had the decency to flinch a little bit when I told him to drop dead.

There's the date you took home who thought you couldn't be serious when you said no, so he decided to fuck you anyway. There's being reintroduced to a close friend's rapist on the street. And the way you want to scream as your lover goes on and on about what a righteous and talented brother he is. There's the nausea you feel as he recognizes you, smiles, kisses you hello, and hands you his phone number. Tell her to call me, I'd love to speak to her. [12]

It's eight young men feeling their maleness late at night in Central Park. [13]

The picture that emerges is of good boys. It is not a picture of drugs, poverty or abusive homes. This is what I can't understand. [14]

Where did these kids come from? How could they have done this? The answer isn't so mysterious. They're susceptible children who receive messages from their environment. They watch the brothers verbally harass women on the street and get away with it. They listen to their favorite rappers wax macho and sexist. They watch television and movies in which "No" from a woman means at least "Maybe." And they live in a community that has been traditionally afraid to address the issues of sexism and rape. [15]

Until we actively acknowledge and commit ourselves to fighting sexism with the same fervor we bring to the fight against racism, our community can never fully trust itself. This is not an easy thing to do for people of a race systematically targeted for oppression. If sexists are truly of every hue and class, if we are as likely to meet them at the water cooler as we are in the alley, then safety is not something we can take for granted. We have yet another battle to fight. As a black woman, some of my battles against oppression are with black men. And they're ones I can't win until black men fight the battle within themselves. [16]

I still can't understand what a grown woman was doing running in that park at night by herself. She had to be crazy. [17]

Some who knew her have suggested that she was simply not the type to be hedged in by limitations or to accept being told that she could not do something because she was female. I can dig that. I know women like that. Sisters who refuse to internalize the filth, to turn themselves inside themselves. To hide their brownness in an effort not to be noticed. Women who still say FUCK YOU to those menacing bearers of uninvited commentary. Who still choose to walk down male-owned streets wearing miniskirts and flaunting [18] shapely, strong legs. Who dare to put bright red lipstick on full lips. Some of us fight because we've been doing it so long we've simply forgotten how not to.

[19] I guess we're crazy, too. We can be likened to the crazier brothers and sisters who refused 30 years ago to walk down southern streets yes ma'aming and no suhing. The ones who absolutely refused to step off the curb when white people chose to walk on the same side of the street. The ones who still opened up businesses and went to hate-filled white schools. Like them, we silently bear our scars, and we stand in the face of lynch mobs whose color, sometimes, is the same as our own.

VOCABULARY

fervor	intensity
sexagenarian	of the age between sixty and seventy years

DESIGN AND MEANING

1. Morgan organizes her arguments around four statements or points of view that she sees as faulty. List the four statements or points of view.
2. In paragraph 6, the author says, "This is not an issue of race, but of gender." What role *did* race play in the crime's aftermath?
3. How would you describe the tone of Morgan's essay? Give examples of words and phrases that support your description.
4. What general statement do the examples in paragraphs 9 through 11 support?
5. What similarities between racism and sexism are implied in paragraphs 16 through 18?

SIMILARITY AND DIFFERENCE

Point out the similarity in structure between this essay and "The Ten Biggest Myths About the Black Family" (Chapter 8). What are other similarities and differences?

SHORT WRITING IDEA

Sometimes a joke or remark offends you, but others around you think it acceptable or humorous. How do you deal with this uncomfortable situation? Give an example.

LONGER WRITING IDEA

Write a persuasive essay organized by counterargument: Take up common statements or points of view from the other side and provide refutation from your side.

Henry David Thoreau

from Civil Disobedience

Henry David Thoreau (1817–1862) has become, along with Emerson, a famous transcendentalist writer—one who reveres nature as the source of godliness. Thoreau, a Harvard graduate who made his living as a naturalist, a surveyor, and a pencil manufacturer, once complained that his hard-working yankee neighbors would rather see him cutting down a tree than sitting under one. In fact, he thought most of his contemporaries lived "lives of quiet desperation." After two years spent living alone in nature at Walden Pond outside his native Concord, Massachusetts, Thoreau published his best-known work, *Walden* (1854), a detailed account of his experiences in the woods. But his widest impact on the twentieth century stems from his essay advocating civil disobedience as a means of influencing governments to behave justly. Thoreau refused to pay his poll tax to protest congressional actions which he viewed as supporting slavery and thus as immoral. Mahatma Gandhi, Martin Luther King, Jr., and opponents of the Vietnam War were all influenced by Thoreau's philosophy. While in his mid-forties, he died of tuberculosis which worsened after he caught cold lying in the snow to count the rings of a tree trunk.

To speak practically and as a citizen, unlike those who call themselves no-government men, I ask for, not at once no government but *at once* a better government.[1] Let every man make known what kind of government would command his respect, and that will be one step toward obtaining it. [1]

After all, the practical reason why, when the power is once in the hands of the people, a majority are permitted, and for a long period continue, to rule is not because they are most likely to be in the right, nor because this seems fairest to the minority, but because they are physically the strongest. But a government in which the majority rule in all cases cannot be based on justice, even as far as men understand it. Can there not be a government in which majorities do not virtually decide right and wrong, but conscience?—in which majorities decide only those questions to which the rule of expediency is applicable? Must the citizen ever for a moment, or [2]

[1] Thoreau wrote "Civil Disobedience" during the time of the Mexican War (1846–1848), which New Englanders saw as a stratagem to aid the spread of Southern slavery. The essay was originally presented as a lecture at the Concord Lyceum on January 26, 1848, under the title "The Rights and Duties of the Individual in Relation to Government."

in the least degree, resign his conscience to the legislator? Why has every man a conscience, then? I think that we should be men first, and subjects afterward. It is not desirable to cultivate a respect for the law, so much as for the right. The only obligation which I have a right to assume is to do at any time what I think right. It is truly enough said that a corporation has no conscience; but a corporation of conscientious men is a corporation *with* a conscience. Law never made men a whit more just; and, by means of their respect for it, even the well-disposed are daily made the agents of injustice. A common and natural result of an undue respect for law is, that you may see a file of soldiers, colonel, captain, corporal, privates, powder-monkeys,[2] and all, marching in admirable order over hill and dale to the wars, against their wills, ay, against their common sense and consciences, which makes it very steep marching indeed, and produces a palpitation of the heart. They have no doubt that it is a damnable business in which they are concerned; they are all peaceably inclined. Now, what are they? Men at all? or small movable forts and magazines, at the service of some unscrupulous man in power? Visit the Navy-Yard,[3] and behold a marine, such a man as an American government can make, or such as it can make a man with its black arts,—a mere shadow and reminiscence of humanity, a man laid out alive and standing, and already, as one may say, buried under arms with funeral accompaniments, though it may be,—

> "Not a drum was heard, not a funeral note, [3]
> As his corse to the rampart we hurried;
> Not a soldier discharged his farewell shot
> O'er the grave where our hero we buried."[4]

[4] The mass of men serve the state thus, not as men mainly, but as machines, with their bodies. They are the standing army, and the militia, jailers, constables, *posse comitatus,*[5] etc. In most cases there is no free exercise whatever of the judgment or of the moral sense; but they put themselves on a level with wood and earth and stones; and wooden men can perhaps be manufactured that will serve the purpose as well. Such command no more respect than men of straw or a lump of dirt. They have the same sort of worth only as horses and dogs. Yet such as these even are commonly esteemed good citizens. Others—as most legislators, politicians, lawyers, ministers, and office-holders—serve the state chiefly with

[2] Boys who carried powder to cannon.

[3] Presumably the United States Navy Yard in Boston, Massachusetts.

[4] From "The Burial of Sir John Moore at Corunna" (1817), by Charles Wolfe (1791–1823), Irish poet.

[5] Citizens authorized to help keep the peace—a sheriff's "posse."

their heads; and, as they rarely make any moral distinctions, they are as likely to serve the devil, without *intending* it, as God. A very few—as heroes, patriots, martyrs, reformers in the great sense, and *men*—serve the state with their consciences also, and so necessarily resist it for the most part; and they are commonly treated as enemies by it. A wise man will only be useful as a man, and will not submit to be "clay," and "stop a hole to keep the wind away,"[6] but leave that office to his dust at least:—

> "I am too high-born to be propertied,
> To be a secondary at control,
> Or useful serving-man and instrument
> To any sovereign state throughout the world."[7]

[5]

[6] He who gives himself entirely to his fellow-men appears to them useless and selfish; but he who gives himself partially to them is pronounced a benefactor and philanthropist. . . .

[7] It is not a man's duty, as a matter of course, to devote himself to the eradication of any, even the most enormous, wrong; he may still properly have other concerns to engage him; but it is his duty, at least, to wash his hands of it, and, if he gives it no thought longer, not to give it practically his support. If I devote myself to other pursuits and contemplations, I must first see, at least, that I do not pursue them sitting upon another man's shoulders. I must get off him first, that he may pursue his contemplations too. See what gross inconsistency is tolerated. I have heard some of my townsmen say, "I should like to have them order me out to help put down an insurrection of the slaves, or to march to Mexico;—see if I would go"; and yet these very men have each, directly by their allegiance, and so indirectly, at least, by their money, furnished a substitute. The soldier is applauded who refuses to serve in an unjust war by those who do not refuse to sustain the unjust government which makes the war; is applauded by those whose own act and authority he disregards and sets at naught; as if the state were penitent to that degree that it hired one to scourge it while it sinned, but not to that degree that it left off sinning for a moment. Thus, under the name of Order and Civil Government, we are all made at last to pay homage to and support our own meanness. After the first blush of sin comes its indifference; and from immoral it becomes, as it were, *un*moral, and not quite unnecessary to that life which we have made.

[8] The broadest and most prevalent error requires the most dis-

[6] *Hamlet,* V. i. 237.
[7] *King John,* V. ii. 79–82.

interested virtue to sustain it. The slight reproach to which the virtue of patriotism is commonly liable, the noble are most likely to incur. Those who, while they disapprove of the character and measures of a government, yield to it their allegiance and support are undoubtedly its most conscientious supporters, and so frequently the most serious obstacles to reform. Some[8] are petitioning the State to dissolve the Union, to disregard the requisitions of the President.[9] Why do they not dissolve it themselves,—the union between themselves and the State,—and refuse to pay their quota into its treasury? Do not they stand in the same relation to the State that the State does to the Union? And have not the same reasons prevented the State from resisting the Union which have prevented them from resisting the State?

[9] How can a man be satisfied to entertain an opinion merely, and enjoy *it?* Is there any enjoyment in it, if his opinion is that he is aggrieved? If you are cheated out of a single dollar by your neighbor, you do not rest satisfied with knowing that you are cheated, or with saying that you are cheated, or even with petitioning him to pay you your due; but you take effectual steps at once to obtain the full amount, and see that you are never cheated again. Action from principle, the perception and performance of right, changes things and relations; it is essentially revolutionary, and does not consist wholly with anything which was. It not only divides States and churches, it divides families; ay, it divides the *individual,* separating the diabolical in him from the divine.

[10] Unjust laws exist: shall we be content to obey them, or shall we endeavor to amend them, and obey them until we have succeeded, or shall we transgress them at once? Men generally, under such a government as this, think that they ought to wait until they have persuaded the majority to alter them. They think that, if they should resist, the remedy would be worse than the evil. But it is the fault of the government itself that the remedy *is* worse than the evil. *It* makes it worse. Why is it not more apt to anticipate and provide for reform? Why does it not cherish its wise minority? Why does it cry and resist before it is hurt? Why does it not encourage its citizens to be on the alert to point out its faults, and *do* better than it would have them? Why does it always crucify Christ, and excommunicate Copernicus and Luther,[10] and pronounce Washington and Franklin rebels?

[8] Radical Massachusetts abolitionists.

[9] President James K. Polk's call for money and troops to fight Mexico.

[10] Nicolaus Copernicus, Polish astronomer (1473–1543) threatened with excommunication from the church for asserting that the earth was not the center of the universe. Martin Luther (1483–1546), German monk and a founder of Protestantism.

One would think, that a deliberate and practical denial of its authority was the only offence never contemplated by government; else, why has it not assigned its definite, its suitable and proportionate, penalty? If a man who has no property refuses but once to earn nine shillings[11] for the State, he is put in prison for a period unlimited by any law that I know, and determined only by the discretion of those who placed him there; but if he should steal ninety times nine shillings from the State, he is soon permitted to go at large again. [11]

If the injustice is part of the necessary friction of the machine of government, let it go, let it go: perchance it will wear smooth,—certainly the machine will wear out. If the injustice has a spring, or a pulley, or a rope, or a crank, exclusively for itself, then perhaps you may consider whether the remedy will not be worse than the evil; but if it is of such a nature that it requires you to be the agent of injustice to another, then, I say, break the law. Let your life be a counter-friction to stop the machine. What I have to do is to see, at any rate, that I do not lend myself to the wrong which I condemn. [12]

VOCABULARY

expediency	practicality
scourge	whip
transgress	break

DESIGN AND MEANING

1. What does Thoreau mean by, "I think that we should be men first, and subjects afterwards"? How does the description of soldiers, which follows, relate to this statement?
2. In paragraph 7 here, Thoreau argues that there is a similarity between direct and indirect wrongdoing and makes a distinction between immoral and *un*moral. Explain the similarity and the distinction.
3. In paragraph 9 here, an analogy is suggested by the story of the cheating neighbor. What situation are we supposed to compare this to?
4. Under what circumstances does Thoreau encourage us to break the law?

[11] I.e., tax money totaling 9 shillings (about $2) which Thoreau refused to pay.

SIMILARITY AND DIFFERENCE

What attitude toward the individual is shared by Thoreau and Hugh Drummond, writer of "Growing Your Own Revolution," in this chapter? (Drummond's essay follows.)

SHORT WRITING IDEA

Write a definition of "conscience" and give an illustrative example.

LONGER WRITING IDEA

Perhaps there is a law that you break because you consider it unjust—or a law that you consider unjust but that you follow anyway. Write an essay explaining what the law is, why you consider it unjust, and why you have chosen your line of action (or inaction).

Hugh Drummond

Growing Your Own Revolution

Hugh Drummond, a physician who thinks too many doctors care more about money than about their patients, advocates preventative medicine which should include breathing cleaner air, eating purer food, and living at a slower rate than most Americans presently do. "Valium," he says, "has replaced religion as the opiate of the masses." Dr. Drummond writes a regular column for *Mother Jones* magazine and has recently published a book called *Dr. Drummond's Spirited Guide to Health Care in a Dying Empire.*

> "And you," she said to Scott Nearing. "Do you think you could live in a planned society?" "I do," he said, gesturing with a sweep of his hand toward his garden. "I live in one now." [1]
>
> —*Horticulture,* November 1976

Some of the feedback we have received suggests that Mother's Healer has been too much of the social pathologist for your tastes. One wise-ass was overhead to mutter, "*Esquire* of the Left? With Drummond writing, it reads like a trade magazine for morticians." While this may be a trifle harsh, I have to agree that the columns lean to the lugubrious. [2]

On the other hand, the Left always suffered from the joylessness that comes from too closely scrutinizing human misery, and it takes the likes of Pablo Neruda and Mother Jones herself to put the sparkle back in revolutionary eyes. So this is going to be an up column about something you can all do this spring to bring good health and a taste of what life will be like when we join the rest of the world in some kind of anarcho-communistic ecological reunion. It has to do with gardening. [3]

I am going to ask all you urban types to be patient while I prove to you that growing your own food has so many implications for good health and good politics that not doing it is like . . . smoking. (But I promised not to nag this month.) As for all you rural types, you have to be patient, too, because I come to this rather late, having grown up in Brooklyn, where the only gardeners [4] were retired mafiosos who used suspiciously large amounts of bone meal under the escarole.

[5] But come to it I did, and it is only because I am so heavily involved in growing my own that I urge it on you.

[6] Back in April 1977 I told you about the cancer-producing, growth-reducing, mind-distorting chemicals that agribusiness uses to make our food piquant. Poisons are poured on and in everything you can buy from the air-conditioned shelves of your local supermarket. As our good government chooses not to protect us from this particular form of unnecessary death, the only sure way of avoiding it is to make your own food.

[7] Obviously, in doing so you should ignore all those helpful-hinters who advise you to add your very own poisons to the garden. A well-balanced and well-composted garden can tolerate the advances of any army of insects.

[8] It requires an effort, of course, but of the very best kind. In another column I told you that not all exercise is helpful in preventing cardiovascular disease. Short bursts of activity like push-ups are not as useful as prolonged periods of total body movement, which put a sustained but mild demand on cardiac output and pulse rate. The whole idea of a sweaty spasm of teeth-grinding agony followed by a reward of Scotch and soft steak is symptomatic of a decadent society terrified of its own courtship of death. Several hours of pulling up weeds, however, is the healthiest and most rational of exercises.

[9] Don't pull up all the weeds. One of the major pleasures of gardening is the discovery of the nutritional, gustatory and healing properties of a whole universe of garden-variety weeds. Many of these were originally cultivated as vegetables in Europe and began to grow wild in this country. Healthy edibles, such as purslane, lamb's-quarters and dandelion greens, are filled with vitamins and minerals and are a hell of a lot tastier than the iceberg lettuce you have to throttle with salad dressing in order to get some flavor out of it.

[10] Chinese physicians are currently in the process of compiling an exhaustive and sophisticated compendium of herbal remedies. Until that is available, we will have to struggle along with several centuries of pure empiricism about what some of these plants do. The reason, incidentally, that Western medicine has held them in such low repute is their empirical validation.

[11] For generation after generation, women passed on their observations about the effects on their children of things that grow in the wild. With a contempt for "old wives' tales," doctors are more inclined to trust a paragraph in the *Physician's Desk Reference* written by a pharmaceutical huckster than they are to accept a

backwoods woman's life-and-death knowledge about what a comfrey leaf will do for a purulent wound. Much of the persecution of witches in Europe was prompted by my medical progenitors, who were threatened by midwives and other noncredentialed practitioners whose effectiveness and femaleness were offensive to them.

[12] When I went off to medical school I was directed by my family to find out one thing: how is it that prunes work as a laxative? When we got to the part about the physiology of the bowel, I asked my professor: "How is it that prunes work?" He said, "They don't" and walked away. Later, when I reported this to my family, they looked at each other and shrugged. The old bubbah finally broke the silence. "For this we sent him to medical school?"

[13] Earlier I used the example of comfrey leaves because I had a personal experience with it. I had a sebaceous cyst on my back that periodically became abscessed. I would have to have it incised and drained and then be put on Declomycin, which is to antibiotics like the guns to Navarone. One day after the cyst started to swell again and before it was mature enough to be taken to a surgeon, I soaked it with some comfrey leaves from the garden. (I did it in an offhand sort of way, as if I were thinking about something else.) Within a few hours, the thing came to a head and drained spontaneously so thoroughly that it healed in a couple of days and has not recurred.

[14] Comfrey leaves, incidentally, contain a complete protein in higher concentration than even soybeans. They also contain large amounts of Vitamin B12, which non-vegetarian biologists used to call "the animal factor." Comfrey is, in short, one of those plants that could save the world given half a chance. And it will grow in your garden with just a bit of water.

[15] Another jewel of a weed I had personal experience with is jewelweed. It grows everywhere and has a short vine topped by a tiny yellow flower that looks like a trumpet with a scrotum. The stem exudes a fluid that is safer and more effective than cortisone on insect bites and poison ivy.

[16] With some reference books and a few square feet of earth, you can grow your own pharmacopoeia. And with legalization around the corner and the tobacco industry ready to get high on it, you might as well think about growing some recreational weeds as well.

[17] There is one note of anxiety to be sounded about urban gardening. It has to do with our old friend, lead, which contaminates both the soil and the air. In one metropolitan survey, five of 64 gardens had a soil-lead concentration of 2,000 parts per million or more. At that level a root vegetable, such as a turnip, would have a dry weight of 64 parts of lead per million (p.p.m.) of turnip, whereas 20 p.p.m. is the "acceptable" upper limit. These samples came from

gardens on demolition or landfill sites, which would have large amounts of lead, containing paints, battery casements or other toxic urban debris.

Happily, of those surveyed, 15 of the soil concentrations had a zero reading. These came from gardens in which the topsoil was imported from distant rural or suburban locations. [18]

Even with an acceptable soil concentration, we still need to worry about the effects of airborne lead, particularly on leafy vegetables. Lettuce grown near a highway has been found to have a dry-weight contamination of 20 to 40 parts per million. About half of this washes off rather easily, and considerably more will rinse off as lead acetate, if the leaves are soaked briefly in vinegar. [19]

The best assurance is to locate the garden more than 200 feet from a heavily trafficked route and upwind from it. With that location and a soil-lead check, you can at least be assured that your urban garden will not cause more problems than it solves, the usual characteristic of high-technology do-goodism. [20]

Several hours of working in the earth bring one to a different psychic space similar to a meditational one. You are cultivating the skin of the world, a thin, absolutely live crust over the planet's great dead rocky mass. It must vibrate with energy, and those of us who live in the city have been cut off from it. [21]

There is also a question of time. There is accumulating evidence that a major predictor of heart disease is what cardiologists Ray H. Rosenman and Meyer Friedman call Type-A behavior. It describes an orientation to life that involves a speeded-up sense of time, a quality of impatience and restlessness. It is as if one were wedged in the isthmus of an hourglass staring at the reservoir of sand above, unable to fix for a moment on each granule of life flying by. Speaking, moving, eating, love-making, every experience is thrust forward, propelled at some melancholy-mad, Parkinsonian gait. The whole fabric of Type-A life is a hasty, makeshift matter of becoming something that is never realized. There is no being, only having and discarding, until the heart stops from the exhaustion of constant anticipation. [22]

A garden is not compatible with Type-A behavior. It will not be hurried. It has an implacable tempo with subtle variations of rain and sun played out against an ancient, endless, changeless rhythm of the days. Getting in touch with that rhythm will add ten years to your life and a new vision of yourself. [23]

That vision is one in which a person's labor is authentic, enjoyable and unexploited. Gardening is an enterprise whose product has a use value rather than an exchange one. It has no role in a capitalist system, except a subversive one. It provides a vision of human [24] activity untouched by imperialism, classism, sexism, racism, ageism, careerism and all the other demented ways in which people have devastated themselves and their environment.

It is a vision of a planned system in which integrity is based on pluralism, and stability is based on change. And, finally, it is a vision of work that is cooperative and communal, rather than competitive and isolated. [25]

Throughout the country, community gardens are sprouting. They are nurtured by such organizations as the Rodale Press in Pennsylvania and the Institute of Local Self Reliance in Washington, D.C. There are even some government agencies prepared to support community gardens with seeds and technical assistance. [26]

The whole thing will make the corporations tremble. It is a model of how our revolution will come, as gently, relentlessly and inevitably as a spring rain. [27]

VOCABULARY

anarcho-communistic ecological reunion	a coming together (reunion) in a harmonious society without laws and restrictions (anarchy) in which the wealth would be equally shared (communistic) and the earth preserved (ecological)
cardiovascular	pertaining to the heart and blood vessels
compendium	a concise but complete collection
decadent	decayed, soft
demented	crazy
empiricism	experimental method; knowledge gained from observation and experiment
escarole	salad greens, endive
exhaustive	complete; leaving nothing out
gustatory	tasty
huckster	a person who sells or advertises in an aggressive, questionable way
implacable	relentless, not changeable
incised	cut into
inevitable	certain to happen
isthmus	a narrow strip of land connecting two larger bodies
lugubrious	excessively sad or mournful
Navarone	a German-occupied island in World War II, famous for installations of huge guns
noncredentialed	without entitlement or diplomas

Parkinsonian	suggesting the satirical economic laws of the British economist Parkinson; one of these laws states that work expands to fill the time allotted to it
pathologist	a doctor who deals with the conditions, processes, and results of disease
pharmaceutical	pertaining to drug dispensing
pharmacopoeia	a supply of drugs
piquant	savory, tasty
pluralism	the harmonious coexistence of differing groups within a nation or a society
progenitor	ancestor in a direct line
psychic	relating to the spirit or sense of self
purulent	discharging pus
relentless	unceasing, persistent, unremitting
scrutinize	to examine closely
sebaceous	containing a fatty or waxy substance

DESIGN AND MEANING

1. What are Drummond's main arguments in favor of urban gardening?
2. Find arguments supported by the following methods: statistics, example or illustration, cause-and-effect reasoning, specific detail.
3. When the writer tells of soaking his cyst with comfrey leaves, why does he say, "I did it in an offhand sort of way, as if I were thinking about something else"?
4. Why does he say that the spread of community gardening "will make the corporations tremble"?
5. What attitudes does Drummond seem to expect his audience to share?

SIMILARITY AND DIFFERENCE

Is Drummond's method of organization closest to Van Gelder's, Eiseley's, or Spock's?

SHORT WRITING IDEA

Write a paragraph giving an example of some type A behavior you've experienced or witnessed.

LONGER WRITING IDEA

Write an essay persuading others of the value of one of your favorite activities.

VOCABULARY CHECK

Complete each sentence in a reasonable way.

1. It's inevitable that this Chevy
2. Carla's progenitors believed
3. This lugubrious melody
4. Empiricism is a good method for studying
5. A television huckster sells things like
6. Scrutinize the label before you
7. Clyde's relentless criticism
8. Pluralism is preferable to
9. Marla's implacable neatness
10. An exhaustive book on childbirth would include

poetry

Wilfred Owen

Dulce et Decorum Est

Wilfred Owen (1893–1918), a promising British poet killed in action in World War I, wrote about the horrors of war with searing truthfulness and outrage.

Bent double, like old beggars under sacks,
Knock-kneed, coughing like hags, we cursed through sludge,
Till on the haunting flares we turned our backs
And towards our distant rest began to trudge.
Men marched asleep. Many had lost their boots [5]
But limped on, blood-shod. All went lame; all blind;
Drunk with fatigue; deaf even to the hoots
Of tired, outstripped Five-Nines that dropped behind.

Gas! Gas! Quick, boys!—An ecstasy of fumbling,
Fitting the clumsy helmets just in time; [10]
But someone still was yelling out and stumbling
And flound'ring like a man in fire or lime . . .
Dim, through the misty panes and thick green light,
As under a green sea, I saw him drowning.
In all my dreams, before my helpless sight, [15]
He plunges at me, guttering, choking, drowning.

If in some smothering dreams you too could pace
Behind the wagon that we flung him in,
And watch the white eyes writhing in his face,
His hanging face, like a devil's sick of sin; [20]
If you could hear, at every jolt, the blood
Come gargling from the froth-corrupted lungs,
Obscene as cancer, bitter as the cud
Of vile, incurable sores on innocent tongues,—
My friend, you would not tell with such high zest [25]
To children ardent for some desperate glory,
The old Lie: Dulce et decorum est
Pro patria mori.

John McCrae

In Flanders Fields

John McCrae (1872–1918), a Canadian, was a practicing physician as well as a successful poet. He died while on active duty as a medical officer in France during World War I. He is primarily remembered for this poem, "In Flanders Fields," which appeared first in *Punch* magazine in 1915.

In Flanders fields the poppies blow
Between the crosses, row on row
    That mark our place; and in the sky
    The larks still bravely singing, sly
Scarce heard amid the guns below. [5]

We are the Dead. Short days ago
We lived, felt dawn, saw sunset glow,
    Loved and were loved, and now we lie
        In Flanders fields.

Take up our quarrel with the foe: [10]
To you from failing hands we throw
    The torch; be yours to hold it high.
    If ye break faith with us who die
We shall not sleep, though poppies grow
        In Flanders fields. [15]

Andrew Marvell

To His Coy Mistress

Andrew Marvell (1621–1678), one of the major English poets of the seventeenth century, is admired today for his wit, his fresh images, and his perfect lyric form.

Had we but world enough, and time,
This coyness, lady, were no crime.
We would sit down and think which way
To walk, and pass our long love's day.
Thou by the Indian Ganges' side [5]
Should'st rubies find; I by the tide
Of Humber would complain. I would
Love you ten years before the Flood,
And you should, if you please, refuse
Till the conversion of the Jews. [10]
My vegetable love should grow
Vaster than empires, and more slow.
An hundred years should go to praise
Thine eyes, and on thy forehead gaze,
Two hundred to adore each breast, [15]
But thirty thousand to the rest.
An age at least to every part,
And the last age should show your heart.
For, lady, you deserve this state,
Nor would I love at lower rate. [20]
    But at my back I always hear
Time's winged chariot hurrying near;
And yonder all before us lie
Deserts of vast eternity.
Thy beauty shall no more be found, [25]
Nor in thy marble vault shall sound
My echoing song; then worms shall try
That long preserved virginity,
And your quaint honor turn to dust,
And into ashes all my lust. [30]
The grave's a fine and private place,
But none, I think, do there embrace.
    Now, therefore, while the youthful hue

Sits on thy skin like morning glew,
And while thy willing soul transpires [35]
At every pore with instant fires,
Now let us sport us while we may;
And now, like am'rous birds of prey,
Rather at once our time devour,
Than languish in his slow-chapped power, [40]
Let us roll all our strength, and all
Our sweetness, up into one ball;
And tear our pleasures with rough strife
Thorough the iron gates of life.
Thus, though we cannot make our sun [45]
Stand still, yet we will make him run.

VOCABULARY

amorous	full of love
ardent	passionate
complain	to sing sad songs
coy	shrinking from contact or familiarity; demure
cud	food brought up from the stomach by a grazing animal to be chewed again
Dulce et decorum est pro patria mori	a quotation from the Latin poet Horace, meaning "It is sweet and fitting to die for one's country."
Five-Nines	gas shells
glew	glow
guttering	flickering, about to go out
instant	urging, pressing
languish	to lose vigor and vitality
lime	calcium oxide, used to decompose bodies readily
quaint	skillfully done
shod	shoed
slow-chapped	slowly grinding, as though with jaws
sport	to have amorous or sexual play
thorough	through
vegetable	growing, flourishing

DESIGN AND MEANING

1. What is the basis of Owen's argument against Horace's lines?

2. Why is the word "lie" capitalized in line 27?
3. What method of persuasion does Owen rely on?
4. What basic reason for continuing the war is given in "In Flanders Fields"? To what human emotion does the argument appeal?
5. What might Owen say in reply to McCrae's poem?
6. "To His Coy Mistress" is structured like a syllogism: If . . . , but . . . , therefore . . . . Fill in the basic elements of the argument.
7. Why are the claims in the "If" section so exaggerated? What difference in tone would there be, for instance, if the lengths of time he refers to were more reasonable?
8. Explain the images in the last two lines.

SIMILARITY AND DIFFERENCE

What similar tactic do both "Dulce et Decorum Est" and "To His Coy Mistress" use in their persuasive attempts?

SHORT WRITING IDEA

Write a brief reply to Marvell from the lady.

LONGER WRITING IDEA

Write an essay persuading a reluctant family member, friend, or sweetheart to do something you want.

Short Story

Mary E. Wilkins Freeman

The Revolt of "Mother"

Born in rural New England, Freeman (1852–1930) was a frail child who loved books and turned to writing short stories in adulthood in order to help support her family. She captures in her work the struggles and frustrations of life in small New England towns during the period following the Civil War.

"Father!" [1]

"What is it?" [2]

"What are them men diggin' over there in the field for?" [3]

There was a sudden dropping and enlarging of the lower part of the old man's face, as if some heavy weight had settled therein; he shut his mouth tight, and went on harnessing the great bay mare. He hustled the collar on to her neck with a jerk. [4]

"Father!" [5]

The old man slapped the saddle upon the mare's back. [6]

"Look here, father, I want to know what them men are diggin' over in the field for, an' I'm goin' to know." [7]

"I wish you'd go into the house, mother, an' tend to your own affairs," the old man said then. He ran his words together, and his speech was almost as inarticulate as a growl. [8]

But the woman understood; it was her most native tongue. "I ain't goin' into the house till you tell me what them men are doin' over there in the field," she said. [9]

Then she stood waiting. She was a small woman, short and straight-waisted like a child in her brown cotton gown. Her forehead was mild and benevolent between the smooth curves of gray hair; there were meek downward lines about her nose and mouth; but her eyes, fixed upon the old man, looked as if the meekness had been the result of her own will, never of the will of another. [10]

They were in the barn, standing before the wide open doors. The spring air, full of the smell of growing grass and unseen blossoms, came in their faces. The deep yard in front was littered with [11] farm wagons and piles of wood; on the edges, close to the fence and the house, the grass was a vivid green, and there were some dandelions.

The old man glanced doggedly at his wife as he tightened the last buckles on the harness. She looked as immovable to him as one of the rocks in his pasture-land, bound to the earth with generations of blackberry vines. He slapped the reins over the horse, and started forth from the barn. [12]

"Father!" said she. [13]

The old man pulled up. "What is it?" [14]

"I want to know what them men are diggin' over there in that field for." [15]

"They're diggin' a cellar, I s'pose, if you've got to know." [16]

"A cellar for what?" [17]

"A barn." [18]

"A barn? You ain't goin' to build a barn over there where we was goin' to have a house, father?" [19]

The old man said not another word. He hurried the horse into the farm wagon, and clattered out of the yard, jouncing as sturdily on his seat as a boy. [20]

The woman stood a moment looking after him, then she went out of the barn across a corner of the yard to the house. The house, standing at right angles with the great barn and a long reach of sheds and out-buildings, was infinitesimal compared with them. It was scarcely as commodious for people as the little boxes under the barn eaves were for doves. [21]

A pretty girl's face, pink and delicate as a flower, was looking out of the house windows. She was watching three men who were digging over in the field which bounded the yard near the road line. She turned quietly when the woman entered. [22]

"What are they digging for, mother?" said she. "Did he tell you?" [23]

"They're diggin' for—a cellar for a new barn." [24]

"Oh, mother, he ain't going to build another barn?" [25]

"That's what he says." [26]

A boy stood before the kitchen glass combing his hair. He combed slowly and painstakingly, arranging his brown hair in a smooth hillock over his forehead. He did not seem to pay any attention to the conversation. [27]

"Sammy, did you know father was going to build a new barn?" asked the girl. [28]

The boy combed assiduously. [29]

"Sammy!" [30]

He turned, and showed a face like his father's under his smooth crest of hair. "Yes, I s'pose I did," he said, reluctantly. [31]

"How long have you known it?" asked his mother. [32]

" 'Bout three months, I guess." [33]

"Why didn't you tell of it?" [34]

"Didn't think 'twould do no good." [35]

"I don't see what father wants another barn for," said the girl, in her sweet, slow voice. She turned again to the window, and stared out at the digging men in the field. Her tender, sweet face was full of gentle distress. Her forehead was as bald and innocent as a baby's with the light hair strained back from it in a row of curl-papers. She was quite large, but her soft curves did not look as if they covered muscles. [36]

Her mother looked sternly at the boy. "Is he goin' to buy more cows?" [37]

The boy did not reply; he was tying his shoes. [38]

"Sammy, I want you to tell me if he's goin' to buy more cows." [39]

"I s'pose he is." [40]

"How many?" [41]

"Four, I guess." [42]

His mother said nothing more. She went into the pantry, and there was a clatter of dishes. The boy got his cap from a nail behind the door, took an old arithmetic from the shelf, and started for school. He was lightly built, but clumsy. He went out of the yard with a curious spring in the hips, that made his loose home-made jacket tilt up in the rear. [43]

The girl went to the sink and began to wash the dishes that were piled there. Her mother came promptly out of the pantry, and shoved her aside. "You wipe 'em," said she, "I'll wash. There's a good many this mornin'." [44]

The mother plunged her hand vigorously into the water, the girl wiped slowly and dreamily. "Mother," said she, "don't you think it's too bad father's going to build that new barn, much as we need a decent house to live in?" [45]

Her mother scrubbed a dish fiercely. "You ain't found out yet we're women-folks, Nanny Penn," said she. "You ain't seen enough of men-folks yet to. One of these days you'll find it out, an' then you'll know that we know only what men-folks think we do, so far as any use of it goes, an' how we'd ought to reckon men-folks in with Providence, an' not complain of what they do any more than we do of the weather." [46]

"I don't care; I don't believe George is anything like that, anyhow," said Nanny. Her delicate face flushed pink, her lips pouted softly, as if she were going to cry. [47]

"You wait an' see. I guess George Eastman ain't no better than other men. You hadn't ought to judge father though. He can't help it, 'cause he don't look at things jest the way we do. An' we've been [48] pretty comfortable here, after all. The roof don't leak—ain't never but once—that's one thing. Father's kept it shingled right up."

"I do wish we had a parlor." [49]

"I guess it won't hurt George Eastman any to come to see you in a nice clean kitchen. I guess a good many girls don't have as good a place as this. Nobody's ever heard me complain." [50]

"I ain't complaining either, mother." [51]

"Well, I don't think you'd better, a good father an' a good home as you've got. S'pose your father made you go out an' work for your livin'? Lots of girls have to that ain't no stronger an' better able than you be." [52]

Sarah Penn washed the frying-pan with a conclusive air. She scrubbed the outside of it as faithfully as the inside. She was a masterly keeper of her box of a house. Her one living-room never seemed to have in it any of the dust which the friction of life with inanimate matter produces. She swept, and there seemed to be no dirt to go before the broom; she cleaned, and one could see no difference. She was like an artist so perfect that he has apparently no art. To-day she got out a mixing bowl and a board, and rolled some pies, and there was no more flour upon her than upon her daughter who was doing finer work. Nanny was to be married in the fall and she was sewing on some white cambric and embroidery. She sewed industriously while her mother cooked; her soft milk-white hands and wrists showed whiter than her delicate work. [53]

"We must have the stove moved out in the shed before long," said Mrs. Penn. "Talk about not havin' things, it's been a real blessin' to be able to put a stove up in that shed in hot weather. Father did one good thing when he fixed the stove-pipe out there." [54]

Sarah Penn's face as she rolled her pies had that expression of meek vigor which might have characterized one of the New Testament saints. She was making mince-pies. Her husband, Adoniram Penn, liked them better than any other kind. She baked twice a week. Adoniram often liked a piece of pie between meals. She hurried this morning. It had been later than usual when she began, and she wanted to have a pie baked for dinner. However deep a resentment she might be forced to hold against her husband, she would never fail in sedulous attention to his wants. [55]

Nobility of character manifests itself at loop-holes when it is not provided with large doors. Sarah Penn's showed itself to-day in flaky dishes of pastry. So she made the pies faithfully, while across the table she could see, when she glanced up from her work, the sight that rankled in her patient and steadfast soul—the digging of the cellar of the new barn in the place where Adoniram forty years ago had promised her their new house should stand. [56]

The pies were done for dinner. Adoniram and Sammy were home a few minutes after twelve o'clock. The dinner was eaten with serious haste. There was never much conversation at the table in the Penn family. Adoniram asked a blessing, and they ate promptly, then rose up and went about their work. [57]

Sammy went back to school, taking soft sly lopes out of the yard like a rabbit. He wanted a game of marbles before school, and feared his father would give him some chores to do. Adoniram hastened to the door and called after him, but he was out of sight. [58]

"I don't see what you let him go for, mother," said he. "I wanted him to help me unload that wood." [59]

Adoniram went to work out in the yard unloading wood from the wagon. Sarah put away the dinner dishes, while Nanny took down her curl papers and changed her dress. She was going down to the store to buy some more embroidery and thread. [60]

When Nanny was gone, Mrs. Penn went to the door. "Father!" she called. [61]

"Well, what is it?" [62]

"I want to see you jest a minute, father." [63]

"I can't leave this wood nohow. I've got to git it unloaded an' go for a load of gravel afore two o'clock. Sammy had ought to helped me. You hadn't ought to let him go to school so early." [64]

"I want to see you jest a minute." [65]

"I tell ye I can't, nohow, mother." [66]

"Father, you come here." Sarah Penn stood in the door like a queen; she held her head as if it bore a crown; there was that patience which makes authority royal in her voice. Adoniram went. [67]

Mrs. Penn led the way into the kitchen and pointed to a chair. "Sit down father," she said; "I've got somethin' I want to say to you." [68]

He sat down heavily; his face was quite stolid, but he looked at her with restive eyes. "Well, what is it, mother?" [69]

"I want to know what you're buildin' that new barn for, father?" [70]

"I ain't got nothin' to say about it." [71]

"It can't be you think you need another barn?" [72]

"I tell ye I ain't got nothin' to say about it, mother; an' I ain't going to say nothin.' " [73]

"Be you goin' to buy more cows?" [74]

Adoniram did not reply; he shut his mouth tight. [75]

"I know you be, as well as I want to. Now, father, look here"—Sarah Penn had not sat down; she stood before her husband in the humble fashion of a Scripture woman—"I'm goin' to talk real plain to you; I never have sence I married you, but I'm goin' to now. I ain't never complained, an' I ain't goin' to complain now, but I'm goin' to talk plain. You see this room here, father; you look at it well. You see there ain't no carpet on the floor, an' you see the paper [76] is all dirty, an' droppin' off the wall. We ain't had no new paper on it for ten year, an' then I put it on myself an' it didn't cost but ninepence a roll. You see this room, father; it's all the one I've had to work in an' eat in an' sit in sence we was married. There ain't another woman in the whole town whose husband ain't got half the means you have but what's got better. It's all the room Nanny's got to have her company in; an' there ain't one of her mates but what's got better, an' their fathers not so able as hers is. It's all the room she'll have to be married in. What would you have thought, father, if we had had our weddin' in a room no better than this? I was married in my mother's parlor, with a carpet on the floor, an' stuffed furniture, an' a mahogany cardtable. An' this is all the room my daughter will have to be married in. Look here, father!"

Sarah Penn went across the room as though it were a tragic stage. She flung open a door and disclosed a tiny bedroom, only large enough for a bed and bureau, with a path between. "There, father," said she—"there's all the room I've had to sleep in forty year. All my children were born there—the two that died, an' the two that's livin'. I was sick with a fever there." [77]

She stepped to another door and opened it. It led into the small, ill-lighted pantry. "Here," said she, "is all the buttery I've got—every place I've got for my dishes, to set away my victuals in, an' to keep my milk-pans in. Father, I've been takin' care of the milk of six cows in this place, an' now you're goin' to build a new barn, an' keep more cows, an' give me more to do in it." [78]

She threw open another door. A narrow crooked flight of stairs wound upward from it. "There, father," said she. "I want you to look at the stairs that go up to them two unfinished chambers that are all the places our son an' daughter have had to sleep in all their lives. There ain't a prettier girl in town nor a more ladylike one than Nanny, an' that's the place she has to sleep in. It ain't so good as your horse's stall, it ain't so warm an' tight." [79]

Sarah Penn went back and stood before her husband. "Now, father," said she, "I want to know if you think you're doin' right an' accordin' to what you profess. Here, when we was married, forty year ago, you promised me faithful that we should have a new house built in that lot over in the field before the year was out. You said you had money enough, an' you wouldn't ask me to live in no such place as this. It is forty year now, an' you've been makin' more money, an' I've been savin' of it for you ever since, an' you ain't built no house yet. You've built sheds an' cow-houses an' one new barn, an' now you're going to build another. Father, I want to know if you think it's right. You're lodgin' your dumb beasts better than you are your own flesh and blood. I want to know if you think it's right." [80]

"I ain't got nothin' to say." [81]

"You can't say nothin' without ownin' it ain't right, father. An' there's another thing—I ain't complained; I've got along forty year, an' I s'pose I should forty more, if it wasn't for that—if we don't have another house, Nanny she can't live with us after she's married. She'll have to go somewhere else to live away from us, an' it don't seem as if I could have it so, noways, father. She wasn't ever strong. She's got considerable color, but there wasn't never any backbone to her. I've always took the heft of everything off her, an' she ain't fit to keep house an' do anything herself. She'll be all worn out inside a year. Think of her doin' all the washin' an' ironin' an' bakin' with them soft white hands an' arms, an' sweepin'! I can't have it so, noways, father." [82]

Mrs. Penn's face was burning; her mild eyes gleamed. She had pleaded her little cause like a Webster; she had ranged from severity to pathos; but her opponent employed that obstinate silence which makes eloquence futile with mocking echoes. Adoniram arose clumsily. [83]

"Father, ain't you got nothin' to say?" said Mrs. Penn. [84]

"I've got to go off after that load of gravel. I can't stand here talkin' all day." [85]

"Father, won't you think it over, an' have a house built there instead of a barn?" [86]

"I ain't got nothin' to say." [87]

Adoniram shuffled out. Mrs. Penn went into her bedroom. When she came out, her eyes were red. She had a roll of unbleached cotton cloth. She spread it on the kitchen table, and began cutting out some shirts for her husband. The men over in the field had a team to help them this afternoon; she could hear their halloos. She had a scanty pattern for the shirts; she had to plan and piece the sleeves. [88]

Nanny came home with her embroidery, and sat down with her needlework. She had taken down her curl-papers, and there was a soft roll of fair hair like an aureole over her forehead; her face was as delicately fine and clear as porcelain. Suddenly, she looked up, and the tender red flamed all over her face and neck. "Mother," said she. [89]

"What say?" [90]

"I've been thinking—I don't see how we're goin' to have any—wedding in this room. I'd be ashamed to have his folks come if we didn't have anybody else." [91]

"Mebbe we can have some new paper before then; I can put it on. I guess you won't have no call to be ashamed of your belongin's." [92]

"We might have the wedding in the new barn," said Nanny, with gentle pettishness. "Why, mother, what makes you look so?" [93]

Mrs. Penn had started, and was staring at her with a curious expression. She turned again to her work, and spread out a pattern carefully on the cloth. "Nothin'," said she. [94]

Presently Adoniram clattered out of the yard in his two-wheeled dump cart, standing as proudly upright as a Roman charioteer. Mrs. Penn opened the door and stood there a minute looking out; the halloos of the men sounded louder. [95]

It seemed to her all through the spring months that she heard nothing but the halloos and the noises of saws and hammers. The new barn grew fast. It was a fine edifice for this little village. Men came on pleasant Sundays, in their meeting suits and clean shirt bosoms, and stood around it admiringly. Mrs. Penn did not speak of it, and Adoniram did not mention it to her, although sometimes, upon a return from inspecting it, he bore himself with injured dignity. [96]

"It's a strange thing how your mother feels about the new barn," he said, confidentially, to Sammy one day. [97]

Sammy only grunted after an odd fashion for a boy; he had learned it from his father. [98]

The barn was all completed ready for use by the third week in July. Adoniram had planned to move his stock in on Wednesday; on Tuesday he received a letter which changed his plans. He came in with it early in the morning. "Sammy's been to the post-office," said he, "an' I've got a letter from Hiram." Hiram was Mrs. Penn's brother, who lived in Vermont. [99]

"Well," said Mrs. Penn, "what does he say about the folks?" [100]

"I guess they're all right. He says he thinks if I come up country right off there's a chance to buy jest the kind of a horse I want." He stared reflectively out of the window at the new barn. [101]

Mrs. Penn was making pies. She went on clapping the rollingpin into the crust, although she was very pale, and her heart beat loudly. [102]

"I dun' know but what I'd better go," said Adoniram. "I hate to go off jest now, right in the midst of hayin', but the ten-acre lot's cut, an' I guess Rufus an' the others can git along without me three or four days. I can't get a horse around here to suit me, nohow, an' I've got to have another for all that wood-haulin' in the fall. I told Hiram to watch out, an' if he got wind of a good horse to let me know. I guess I'd better go." [103]

"I'll get out your clean shirt an' collar," said Mrs. Penn calmly. [104]

She laid out Adoniram's Sunday suit and his clean clothes on the bed in the little bedroom. She got his shaving-water and razor ready. At last she buttoned on his collar and fastened his black cravat. [105]

Adoniram never wore his collar and cravat except on extra occasions. He held his head high, with a rasped dignity. When he was all ready, with his coat and hat brushed, and a lunch of pie and cheese in a paper bag, he hesitated on the threshold of the door. He looked at his wife, and his manner was definitely apologetic. "*If* them cows come to-day, Sammy can drive 'em into the new barn," said he; "an' when they bring the hay up, they can pitch it in there." [106]

"Well," replied Mrs. Penn. [107]

Adoniram set his shaven face ahead and started. When he had cleared the door-step, he turned and looked back with a kind of nervous solemnity. "I shall be back by Saturday if nothin' happens," said he. [108]

"Do be careful, father," returned his wife. [109]

She stood in the door with Nanny at her elbow and watched him out of sight. Her eyes had a strange, doubtful expression in them; her peaceful forehead was contracted. She went in, and about her baking again. Nanny sat sewing. Her wedding-day was drawing nearer, and she was getting pale and thin with her steady sewing. Her mother kept glancing at her. [110]

"Have you got that pain in your side this mornin'?" she asked. [111]

"A little." [112]

Mrs. Penn's face, as she worked, changed, her perplexed forehead smoothed, her eyes were steady, her lips firmly set. She formed a maxim for herself, although incoherently with her unlettered thoughts. "Unsolicited opportunities are the guide-posts of the Lord to the new roads of life," she repeated in effect, and she made up her mind to her course of action. [113]

"S'posing' I *had* wrote to Hiram," she muttered once, when she was in the pantry—"s'posin' I had wrote, an' asked him if he knew of any horse? But I didn't an' father's goin' wa'nt none of my doing. It looks like a providence." Her voice rang out quite loud at the last. [114]

"What you talkin' about, mother?" called Nanny. [115]

"Nothin'." [116]

Mrs. Penn hurried her baking; at eleven o'clock it was all done. The load of hay from the west field came slowly down the cart track, and drew up at the new barn. Mrs. Penn ran out. "Stop!" she screamed, "stop!" [117]

The men stopped and looked; Sammy upreared from the top of the load, and stared at his mother. [118]

"Stop!" she cried out again. "Don't put the hay in that barn; put it in the old one." [119]

"Why, he said to put it in here," returned one of the haymakers, wonderingly. He was a young man, a neighbor's son, whom Adoniram hired by the year to help on the farm. [120]

"Don't you put the hay in the new barn; there's room enough in the old one, ain't there?" said Mrs. Penn. [121]

"Room enough," returned the hired man, in his thick, rustic tones. "Didn't need the new barn, nohow, far as room's concerned. Well, I s'pose he changed his mind." He took hold of the horses' bridles. [122]

Mrs. Penn went back to the house. Soon the kitchen windows were darkened, and a fragrance like warm honey came into the room. [123]

Nanny laid down her work. "I thought father wanted them to put the hay into the new barn?" she said, wonderingly. [124]

"It's all right," replied her mother. [125]

Sammy slid down from the load of hay, and came in to see if dinner was ready. [126]

"I ain't going to get a regular dinner to-day, as long as father's gone," said his mother. "I've let the fire go out. You can have some bread an' milk an' pie. I thought we could get along." She set out some bowls of milk, some bread, and a pie on the kitchen table. "You'd better eat your dinner now," said she. "You might jest as well get through with it. I want you to help me afterwards." [127]

Nanny and Sammy stared at each other. There was something strange in their mother's manner. Mrs. Penn did not eat anything herself. She went into the pantry, and they heard her moving dishes while they ate. Presently she came out with a pile of plates. She got the clothes-basket out of the shed, and packed them in it. Nanny and Sammy watched. She brought out cups and saucers, and put them in with the plates. [128]

"What you goin' to do, mother?" inquired Nanny, in a timid voice. A sense of something unusual made her tremble, as if it were a ghost. Sammy rolled his eyes over his pie. [129]

"You'll see what I'm goin' to do," replied Mrs. Penn. "If you're through, Nanny, I want you to go upstairs an' pack up your things; an' I want you, Sammy, to help me take down the bed in the bedroom." [130]

"Oh, mother, what for?" gasped Nanny. [131]

"You'll see." [132]

During the next few hours a feat was performed by this simple, pious New England mother which was equal in its way to Wolfe's storming of the Heights of Abraham. It took no more genius and audacity or bravery for Wolfe to cheer his wondering soldiers up those steep precipices, under the sleeping eyes of the enemy, than for Sarah Penn, at the head of her children, to move all their little household goods into the new barn while her husband was away. [133]

Nanny and Sammy followed their mother's instructions without a murmur; indeed, they were overawed. There is a certain uncanny [134] and superhuman quality about all such purely original undertakings as their mother's was to them. Nanny went back and forth with her light load, and Sammy tugged with sober energy.

At five o'clock in the afternoon the little house in which the Penns had lived for forty years had emptied itself into the new barn. [135]

Every builder builds somewhat for unknown purposes, and is in a measure a prophet. The architect of Adoniram Penn's barn, while he designed it for the comfort of four-footed animals, had planned better than he knew for the comfort of humans. Sarah Penn saw at a glance its possibilities. Those great box-stalls, with quilts hung before them, would make better bedrooms than the one she had occupied for forty years, and there was a tight carriage-room. The harness-room, with its chimney and shelves, would make a kitchen of her dreams. The great middle space would make a parlor, by-and-by, fit for a palace. Up-stairs there was as much room as down. With partitions and windows, what a house would there be! Sarah looked at the row of stanchions before the alotted space for cows, and reflected that she would have her front entry there. [136]

At six o'clock the stove was up in harness room, the kettle was boiling, and the table was set for tea. It looked almost as homelike as the abandoned house across the yard had ever done. The young hired man milked, and Sarah directed him calmly to bring the milk to the new barn. He came gaping, dropping little blots of foam from the brimming pails on the grass. Before the next morning he had spread the story of Adoniram Penn's wife moving into the new barn all over the little village. Men assembled in the store and talked it over, women with shawls over their heads scuttled into each other's houses before their work was done. Any deviation from the ordinary course of life in this quiet town was enough to stop all progress in it. Everybody paused to look at the staid, independent figure on the side track. There was a difference of opinion with regard to her. Some held her to be insane; some of a lawless and rebellious spirit. [137]

Friday the minister went to see her. It was in the forenoon, and she was at the barn door shelling peas for dinner. She looked up and returned his salutation with dignity, then she went on with her work. She did not invite him in. The saintly expression on her face remained fixed, but there was an angry flush over it. [138]

The minister stood awkwardly before her, and talked. She handled the peas as if they were bullets. At last she looked up, and her eyes showed the spirit that her meek front had covered for a lifetime. [139]

"There ain't no use talkin', Mr. Hersey," said she. "I've thought it all over an' over, an' I believe I'm doin' what's right. I've made it [140] the subject of prayer, an' it's betwixt me an' the Lord an' Adoniram. There ain't no call for nobody else to worry about it."

[141] "Well, of course, if you have brought it to the Lord in prayer, and feel satisfied that you are doing right, Mrs. Penn," said the minister, helplessly. His thin gray-bearded face was pathetic. He was a sickly man; his youthful confidence had cooled; he had to scourge himself up to some of his pastoral duties as relentlessly as a Catholic ascetic, and then he was prostrated by the smart.

[142] "I think it's right jest as much as I think it was right for our forefathers to come over here from the old country 'cause they didn't have what belonged to 'em," said Mrs. Penn. She arose. The barn threshold might have been Plymouth Rock from her bearing. "I don't doubt you mean well, Mr. Hersey," said she, "but there are things people hadn't ought to interfere with. I've been a member of the church for over forty years. I've got my own mind an' my own feet, an' I'm goin' to think my own thoughts an' go my own way, an' nobody but the Lord is goin' to dictate to me unless I've a mind to have him. Won't you come in an' set down? How is Mis' Hersey?"

[143] "She is well, I thank you," replied the minister. He added some more perplexed apologetic remarks; then he retreated.

[144] He could expound the intricacies of every character study in the Scriptures, he was competent to grasp the Pilgrim Fathers and all historical innovators, but Sarah Penn was beyond him. He could deal with primal cases, but parallel ones worsted him. But, after all, although it was aside from his province, he wondered more how Adoniram Penn would deal with his wife than how the Lord would. Everybody shared the wonder. When Adoniram's four new cows arrived, Sarah ordered three to be put in the old barn, the other in the house shed where the cooking-stove had stood. That added to the excitement. It was whispered that all four cows were domiciled in the house.

[145] Towards sunset on Saturday, when Adoniram was expected home, there was a knot of men in the road near the new barn. The hired man had milked, but he still hung around the premises. Sarah Penn had supper all ready. There were brown-bread and baked beans and a custard pie; it was the supper that Adoniram loved on a Saturday night. She had on a clean calico, and she bore herself imperturbably. Nanny and Sammy kept close at her heels. Their eyes were large, and Nanny was full of nervous tremors. Still there was to them more pleasant excitement than anything else. An inborn confidence in their mother over their father asserted itself.

[146] Sammy looked out of the harness-room window. "There he is," he announced, in an awed whisper. He and Nanny peeped around the casing. Mrs. Penn kept on about her work. The children watched

Adoniram leave the new horse standing in the drive while he went to the house door. It was fastened. Then he went around to the shed. That door was seldom locked, even when the family was away. The thought how her father would be confronted by the cow flashed upon Nanny. There was a hysterical sob in her throat. Adoniram emerged from the shed and stood looking about in a dazed fashion. His lips moved, he was saying something, but they could not hear what it was. The hired man was peeping around the corner of the old barn, but nobody saw him.

Adoniram took the new horse by the bridle and led him across the yard to the new barn. Nanny and Sammy slunk close to their mother. The barn doors rolled back, and there stood Adoniram, with the long mild face of the great Canadian farm horse looking over his shoulder. [147]

Nanny kept behind her mother, but Sammy stepped suddenly forward, and stood in front of her. [148]

Adoniram stared at the group. "What on airth you all down here for?" said he. "What's the matter over to the house?" [149]

"We've come here to live, father," said Sammy. His shrill voice quavered out bravely. [150]

"What"—Adoniram sniffed—"what is it smells like cookin'?" said he. He stepped forward and looked in the open door of the harness-room. Then he turned to his wife. His old bristling face was pale and frightened. "What on airth does this mean, mother?" he gasped. [151]

"You come in here, father," said Sarah. She led the way into the harness-room and shut the door. "Now, father," said she, "you needn't be scared. I ain't crazy. There ain't nothin' to be upset over. But we've come here to live, an' we're goin' to live here. We've got jest as good a right here as new horses an' cows. The house wasn't fit for us to live in any longer, an' I made up my mind I wa'nt goin' to stay there. I've done my duty by you forty year, an' I'm goin' to do it now; but I'm goin' to live here. You've got to put in some windows and partitions; an' you'll have to buy some furniture." [152]

"Why, mother!" the old man gasped. [153]

"You'd better take your coat off an' get washed—there's the wash basin—an' then we'll have supper." [154]

"Why, mother!" [155]

Sammy went past the window, leading the new horse to the old barn. The old man saw him, and shook his head speechlessly. He tried to take off his coat, but his arms seemed to lack the power. His wife helped him. She poured some water into the basin, and put in a piece of soap. She got the comb and brush, and smoothed his thin gray hair after he had washed. Then she put the beans, hot bread, and tea on the table. Sammy came in, and the family [156] drew up. Adoniram sat looking dazedly at his plate, and they waited.

"Ain't you goin' to ask a blessin', father?" said Sarah. [157]

And the old man bent his head and mumbled. [158]

All through the meal he stopped eating at intervals and stared furtively at his wife; but he ate well. The home food tasted good to him, and his old frame was too sturdily healthy to be affected by his mind. But after supper he went out, and sat down on the step of the smaller door at the right of the barn, through which he had meant his Jerseys to pass in stately file, but which Sarah designed for her front house door, and he leaned his head on his hands. [159]

After the supper dishes were cleared away and the milkpans washed, Sarah went out to him. The twilight was deepening. There was a clear green glow in the sky. Before them stretched the smooth level of field; in the distance was a cluster of hay-stacks like the huts of a village; the air was very cool and calm and sweet. The landscape might have been an ideal one of peace. [160]

Sarah bent over and touched her husband on one of his thin, sinewy shoulders. "Father!" [161]

The old man's shoulders heaved: he was weeping. [162]

"Why, don't do so, father," said Sarah. [163]

"I'll—put up the—partitions, an'—everything you—want, mother." [164]

Sarah put her apron up to her face; she was overcome by her own triumph. [165]

Adoniram was like a fortress whose walls had no active resistance, and went down the instant the right besieging tools were used. "Why, mother," he said, hoarsely, "I hadn't no idea you was so set on't as all this comes to." [166]

VOCABULARY

audacity	boldness
commodious	comfortably spacious
domicile	to provide with a home
furtive	stealthy
incoherent	lacking orderly continuity
infinitesimal	immeasurably small
maxim	a general truth briefly stated
sedulous	conscientious, diligent
stanchions	upright posts
unsolicited	not asked for

DESIGN AND MEANING

1. How early is the male-female conflict in the story introduced? What are some of the details that continue the conflict throughout?
2. Why is there a difference between what Sarah says to Nanny and what she says to Adoniram? What does the difference show about the family power structure?
3. When Sarah first confronts Adoniram fully about the barn, she uses both persuasive and argumentative techniques. To what emotions in him does she try to appeal? What reasoning does she attempt to use? Why do her efforts fail?
4. How do the opinions of the townspeople about Sarah's move to the barn seem to differ from the author's? How do you know?
5. Why does Sarah win the last confrontation, even though she has no new arguments?
6. The story itself serves as an argument. What for?

SIMILARITY AND DIFFERENCE

Contrast the relationships of the couple in "Rope" (Chapter 8) with the couple in this story. Are there any similarities?

SHORT WRITING IDEA

Rewrite one of Sarah's argumentative speeches in standard English.

LONGER WRITING IDEA

Write an essay about a personal or political situation in which you think actions spoke louder than words.

THE READER'S RESOURCES

The Uses and Abuses of Language

YOUR OWN USE OF LANGUAGE, both spoken and written, will affect your success in life—in your personal relationships as well as in your career. But the way other people use language will just as surely affect your life in more subtle, sometimes sinister, ways.

You need to develop a critical eye: examine thoughtfully everything you read. You must learn to recognize slanted writing so that you will not be taken in by it. Most persuasive writing is slanted to some degree, of course. A writer will present only one side of a two-sided issue and subtly appeal to your emotions in order to win you over. This technique is not necessarily dishonest, but if you are not aware of the connotations (emotional appeals) of words, you may be swayed by arguments that are factually weak or even in error. The first two essays in this chapter present differing viewpoints on an emotionally charged issue: welfare payments. By examining the facts and the language of each essay, you may be able to determine which argument is more valid. Or you may discover that since both writers present convincing cases, the issue is not one that can be easily resolved.

The next four essays examine various ways in which language can be used to manipulate behavior, control thinking, and reinforce stereotypes. J. C. Mathes reports on how poorly written memos contributed to the disaster at Three Mile Island nuclear plant. Fred M. Hechinger in the next selection warns of the deception which can result from euphemisms (words intended to avoid offending but often used to conceal meaning, like calling the neutron bomb a "radiation enhancement device," calling a lie a "counterfactual proposition," or calling medical malpractice a "therapeutic misadventure"). Christopher Hitchens shows the damage that an often-used but ill-defined term can cause, and Ellen Goodman warns us of the power of warlike language.

The two versions of the Twenty-Third Psalm included here vividly illustrate the difference between clear, simple language and meaningless, bureauractic jargon (like using "semantic and quantitative symbolizations" to mean "words and numbers"). The e.e. cummings poem satirizes the emotion-laden clichés of a call to patriotism, while Mark Twain's story "The War Prayer" exposes the ugly realities concealed beneath the glorious rhetoric of a call to arms. Martin Luther King's famous "I Have a Dream" speech shows how glorious rhetoric can be put to honorable purposes.

essays

Dick Gregory

Not Poor, Just Broke

Famous as a comedian, lecturer, and political activist, Gregory (b. 1932) has published five books of satirical nonfiction. The following excerpt is taken from his autobiography, entitled *Nigger* (1964).

Like a lot of Negro kids, we never would have made it without our Momma. When there was no fatback to go with the beans, no socks to go with the shoes, no hope to go with tomorrow, she'd smile and say: "We ain't poor, we're just broke." Poor is a state of mind you never grow out of, but being broke is just a temporary condition. She always had a big smile, even when her legs and feet swelled from high blood pressure and she collapsed across the table with sugar diabetes. You have to smile twenty-four hours a day, Momma would say. If you walk through life showing the aggravation you've gone through, people will feel sorry for you, and they'll never respect you. She taught us that man has two ways out in life—laughing or crying. There's more hope in laughing. A man can fall down the stairs and lie there in such pain and horror that his own wife will collapse and faint at the sight. But if he can just hold back his pain for a minute she might be able to collect herself and call the doctor. It might mean the difference between his living to laugh again or dying there on the spot. [1]

So you laugh, so you smile. Once a month the big gray relief truck would pull up in front of our house and Momma would flash that big smile and stretch out her hands. "Who else you know in this neighborhood gets this kind of service?" And we could all feel proud when the neighbors, folks who weren't on relief, folks who had Daddies in their houses, would come by the back porch for some of those hundred pounds of potatoes, for some sugar and flour and salty fish. We'd stand out there on the back porch and hand out the food like we were in charge of helping poor people, and then we'd take the food they brought us in return. [2]

And Momma came home one hot summer day and found we'd been evicted, thrown out into the streetcar zone with all our orange-crate chairs and secondhand lamps. She flashed that big smile and dried our tears and bought some penny Kool-Aid. We stood out there and sold drinks to thirsty people coming off the streetcar, and we thought nobody knew we were kicked out—figured they thought we *wanted* to be there. And Momma went off to talk the landlord into letting us back in on credit. [3]

But I wonder about my Momma sometimes, and all the other Negro mothers who got up at 6 A.M. to go to the white man's house with sacks over their shoes because it was so wet and cold. I wonder how they made it. They worked very hard for the man, they made his breakfast and they scrubbed his floors and they diapered his babies. They didn't have too much time for us. [4]

I wonder about my Momma, who walked out of a white woman's clean house at midnight and came back to her own where the lights had been out for three months, and the pipes were frozen and the wind came in through the cracks. She'd have to make deals with the rats: leave some food out for them so they wouldn't gnaw on the doors or bite the babies. The roaches, they were just like part of the family. [5]

I wonder how she felt telling those white kids she took care of to brush their teeth after they ate, to wash their hands after they peed. She could never tell her own kids because there wasn't soap or water back home. [6]

I wonder how my Momma felt when we came home from school with a list of vitamins and pills and cod liver oil the school nurse said we had to have. Momma would cry all night, and then go out and spend most of the rent money for pills. A week later, the white man would come for his eighteen dollars rent and Momma would plead with him to wait until tomorrow. She had lost her pocketbook. The relief check was coming. The white folks had some money for her. Tomorrow. I'd be hiding in the coal closet because there was only supposed to be two kids in the flat, and I could hear the rent man curse my Momma and call her a liar. And when he finally went away, Momma put the sacks on her shoes and went off to the rich white folk's house to dress the rich white kids so their mother could take them to a special baby doctor. [7]

Momma had to take us to Homer G. Phillips, the free hospital, the city hospital for Negroes. We'd stand on line and wait for hours, smiling and Uncle Tomming every time a doctor or a nurse passed by. We'd feel good when one of them smiled back and didn't look at us as though we were dirty and had no right coming down there. All the doctors and nurses at Homer G. Phillips were Negro, too. [8]

I remember one time when a doctor in white walked up and [9] said: "What's wrong with him?" as if he didn't believe that anything was.

[10] Momma looked at me and looked at him and shook her head. "I sure don't know, Doctor, but he cried all night long. Held his stomach."

[11] "Bring him in and get his damned clothes off."

[12] I was so mad the way he was talking to my Momma that I bit down too hard on the thermometer. It broke in my mouth. The doctor slapped me across the face.

[13] "Both of you go stand in the back of the line and wait your turn."

[14] My Momma had to say: "I'm sorry, Doctor," and go to the back of the line. She had five other kids at home and she never knew when she'd have to bring another down to the City Hospital.

[15] And those rich white folks Momma was so proud of. She'd sit around with the other women and they'd talk about how good their white folks were. They'd lie about how rich they were, what nice parties they gave, what good clothes they wore. And how they were going to be remembered in their white folks' wills. The next morning the white lady would say: "We're going on vacation for two months, Lucille, we won't be needing you until we get back." Damn. Two-month vacation without pay.

[16] I wonder how my Momma stayed so good and beautiful in her soul when she worked seven days a week on swollen legs and feet, how she kept teaching us to smile and laugh when the house was dark and cold and she never knew when one of her hungry kids was going to ask about Daddy.

[17] I wonder how she kept from teaching us hate when the social worker came around. She was a nasty bitch with a pinched face who said: "We have reason to suspect you are working, Miss Gregory, and you can be sure I'm going to check on you. We don't stand for welfare cheaters."

[18] Momma, a welfare cheater. A criminal who couldn't stand to see her kids go hungry, or grow up in slums and end up mugging people in dark corners. I guess the system didn't want her to get off relief, the way it kept sending social workers around to be sure Momma wasn't trying to make things better.

[19] I remember how that social worker would poke around the house, wrinkling her nose at the coal dust on the chilly linoleum floor, shaking her head at the bugs crawling over the dirty dishes in the sink. My Momma would have to stand there and make like she was too lazy to keep her own house clean. She could never let on that she spent all day cleaning another woman's house for two dollars and carfare. She would have to follow that nasty bitch around those drafty three rooms, keeping her fingers crossed that

the telephone hidden in the closet wouldn't ring. Welfare cases weren't supposed to have telephones.

But Momma figured that some day the Gregory kids were going to get off North Taylor Street and into a world where they would have to compete with kids who grew up with telephones in their houses. She didn't want us to be at a disadvantage. She couldn't explain that to the social worker. And she couldn't explain that while she was out spoon-feeding somebody else's kids, she was worrying about her own kids, that she could rest her mind by picking up the telephone and calling us—to find out if we had bread for our baloney or baloney for our bread, to see if any of us had gotten run over by the streetcar while we played in the gutter, to make sure the house hadn't burnt down from the papers and magazines we stuffed in the stove when the coal ran out. [20]

But sometimes when she called there would be no answer. Home was a place to be only when all other places were closed. [21]

Bernard Sloan

Aunt Charlotte's Reward

Bernard Sloan, an advertising executive, has contributed several essays to *Newsweek*'s "My Turn" column on diverse topics and has recently published a book called *The Best Friend You'll Ever Have.* The following "My Turn" essay appeared in *Newsweek* in September of 1980.

My wife's Aunt Charlotte lives in Brooklyn. A tiny, soft-spoken woman of 74, she could easily pass for 60 with her relatively unlined face and undyed brown hair that is just beginning to break out in gray flecks. Only her diminished hearing gives her age away, and the cautious steps she takes in her orthopedic shoes. Her mind and her vision are sharper than those of many 40-year-olds. A shy woman, Charlotte never married. When she telephones us she says, "It's only me." [1]

In 1923, when she was 17, Charlotte went to work for the telephone company, eventually attaining the position of customer-service representative, a role she performed with pride, skill and dedication for nearly a half century. She responded with patience and courtesy to every customer, even to those whose complaints were voiced in somewhat questionable language. Charlotte, who would commit hari-kiri before permitting an unladylike word to slip through her lips, never displayed a hint of anger or disapproval, although she confided to us that some of her clients should have their mouths washed out with soap. The days she was out sick could be counted on her fingers; it took a transit strike to make Charlotte late. [2]

As a reward for her dedication, the U.S. Government forced Charlotte to retire. She was given a luncheon, a subscription to a retirement magazine, free home-telephone service and a pension and sent home. Two women in their 20s replaced her. Since the government made it difficult for them to be fired no matter what their attitude or degree of competence, neither felt compelled to duplicate Charlotte's conscientiousness. Or productivity, as we say today. [3]

Distress Call: Several months afterward the telephone company sent out a distress call for retired workers. Temporary help was needed in the Upper West Side of Manhattan to handle the surge of problems arising from the minority groups in the area, [4] many of whom either did not know English or were baffled by the complexities of maintaining telephone service—problems the new employees displayed no interest in solving. Giving up her social-security checks, Charlotte set off each day to a part of the city considered dangerous for the young and fit, let alone a woman of Charlotte's age. Before long she had added an extensive Spanish vocabulary to her store of black English and was being presented with gifts by her clients. Unable to change old habits, she arrived early, stayed late and quickly worked herself out of a job.

The government was not finished with Charlotte. Now it was the city's turn to take a whack at her. It moved welfare families by the score into her neighborhood, many into her building, which was like moving the fox into the hen yard. For many of these families consist of a mother and unsupervised children—children who often stand 6 feet tall and carry knives or worse. Soon mailboxes were found ripped open, social-security checks stolen. The once neat hallways are now filled with beer cans, soft-drink and liquor bottles and the smell of marijuana. Groups of youths, radios blaring, congregate on the front steps late into the night, making obscene remarks and giggling as people pass. There are purse snatchings and muggings in the once quiet neighborhood. An elderly couple were found tied to their bed, beaten and robbed. Charlotte has stopped going out at night. When she ventures out during the day she conceals cash in various places on her person, leaving a carefully calculated amount in her purse to placate an attacker. Visiting Charlotte requires driving past miles of burnt-out apartment buildings; fires are set either by landlords for the insurance or by welfare tenants for the hardship money. (Everyone has been given an equal opportunity to profit by the system.) Although Charlotte remains outwardly cheerful, she knows she will have to do something soon. But what? [5]

The neighbors who drive her to the market (the nearby one has been boarded up since the blackout riot) are moving to New Jersey. Others have fled to upstate New York and Florida. It is easier for couples to move to new areas. The widowed have moved in with their children. We have suggested that Charlotte move near us, but that would mean tripling her rent and being a stranger in a new community, as well as being dependent on us. Charlotte is not comfortable imposing on people. [6]

Mistake: She found something that would have answered her needs beautifully. In a group of buildings clustered around a senior center, there were apartments with safety features designed for seniors, including buzzers to summon aid; meals were available in the center. Unfortunately, the government limited it to people with little or no money, and Charlotte had made the mistake of saving [7] hers. There are other such places to which she might be admitted if she moved away from the city, leaving her entire life behind. But if welfare people don't have to move, she wonders, why should she?

When she decided to call on different government agencies for guidance, she learned that not one of the myriad programs for the aging she had heard about over the years, and which her taxes helped support, was for her. They were reserved for the penniless. [8]

The other day she visited a sick woman in her building, a woman on welfare for whom the city provided a homemaker, a nurse and a cab to and from free medical attention. If Charlotte were ill, she would have to fend for herself. No government department would rush to her rescue. [9]

Perhaps the time has come to reconsider which of our citizens are entitled to first claim on our resources. In our haste to better the lives of the lowest economic level of our society we have betrayed another, far larger and more deserving group. People who have worked hard, paid their taxes, contributed to the country. Shouldn't their needs be met first? Their housing, their neighborhoods, their security? [10]

If a choice must be made, shouldn't first choice be given Aunt Charlotte? She has earned it. [11]

Or doesn't that count anymore? [12]

DISCUSSION IDEAS

Compare and contrast the tone of "Not Poor, Just Broke" and "Aunt Charlotte's Reward." How do the tones of the selections help or hinder their arguments? Does either essay omit or gloss over significant points the opposition might bring up? Which writer would you rather have as a nephew or son? Why?

J. C. Mathes

Technical Communication: The Persuasive Purpose

On March 28, 1979, a nuclear power reactor at Three Mile Island, Pennsylvania, overheated and partially melted down, releasing radioactive water and gas in a twelve-day crisis. The full aftereffects of the nuclear plant accident are still not known. The firm of Babcock and Wilcox, referred to in the following excerpt, was the designer and builder of Three Mile Island and many more of the nation's nuclear power plants. Within an article about persuasive technical writing, author J. C. Mathes emphasizes that poorly planned technical writing was at least one cause of the disastrous failure of Three Mile Island's cooling system.

A professional who concentrates on the transfer of information rather than exercises judgment to write a persuasive report, either implicitly or explicitly, could well fail to fulfill his or her professional responsibility. The Presidential Commission investigating the accident at Three Mile Island uncovered a serious failure in technical communication. Memoranda within Babcock and Wilcox during the year prior to the accident had warned that a premature shut-off of emergency cooling pumps could lead to serious problems. The Manager of the Plant Integration Department at Babcock and Wilcox testified about one important memo that informed him that action had not yet been taken although earlier memos "suggest the possibility of uncovering the core if present HPI [high pressure injection] policy is continued." He said, concerning this important memo, that "I recall glancing over it very quickly and keying on the two specific questions. I do not recall reading it very carefully at that time . . . . I remember thinking that they were rather routine questions . . . . I then, just that quickly, disposed of this piece of paper crossing my desk." [1]

Had the manager responded to this memo, the accident at Three Mile Island might well have been prevented. His failure to respond in part seems attributable to the informational rhetoric of the memo. The subject line, "Operator Interruption of High Pressure Injection," is descriptive rather than an imperative to action; it also is the same subject line of the two previous memos on the problem. The memo proceeds to discuss the recombinations to change oper- [2]

ating procedures in the two previous memos, suggests further evaluation to determine the side effects of the recommended changes, and states that Nuclear Service has not yet notified operating plants. It closes with the "request that Integration resolve the issue of how the HPI system should be used. We are available for help as needed." The manager did not respond to this request; as he testified, he instead keyed "on the two specific questions" and thought they were "rather routine."

[3] Rather than end with the request, the memo should have been designed from the outset with the writer's judgment dominant, with the request becoming a persuasive report to change the organization's present operating procedures or resolve the expressed concerns. It instead essentially fails to distinguish between previous recommendations and current questions and requests, and at most seems to expect further investigation and analysis. A busy manager, however, might well quickly dispose of such a memo that in structure and tone seems explanatory and informational—almost a status report—rather than persuasive in structure and tone.

[4] The hearing also identified weaknesses in the communication process within Babcock and Wilcox as well as in the rhetoric of specific memos. The casualness of distribution lists was queried by the commissioners, and the lack of feedback loops was stressed. In sum, the hearing disclosed that both writers and the communication process within Babcock and Wilcox were not oriented to the persuasive function of technical communication, which emphasizes that the writer must design his or her reports to make certain that those who receive the reports take the necessary and appropriate actions.

Fred M. Hechinger

In the End Was the Euphemism

Hechinger, who serves on the editorial board of *The New York Times,* reports in the following selection on the efforts of English teachers to eliminate "doublespeak"—George Orwell's term for deceptive euphemisms, double-talk, and gobbledygook. His article first appeared in the *Saturday Review/World,* March 9, 1974, and was reprinted in *Language and Public Policy* (1974).

It was George Orwell's grim prediction that by 1984 the official language of Newspeak would persuade the populace that "ignorance is strength" and "war is peace." To assure a continuous revision of history, Orwell wrote in 1949, the "day-to-day falsification of the past, carried out by the Ministry of Truth, is as necessary to the stability of the regime as the work of repression and espionage carried out by the Ministry of Love." [1]

With ten years left until the target date of Orwell's political-science horror fiction, some observers of the American language scene are afraid that the horror was not entirely fictitious and that the United States is ahead of schedule on its way to Newspeak. Since they consider this more than a matter of semantics, they have begun to organize a linguistic counteroffensive. [2]

The rebels are part of a normally unobtrusive organization, the National Council of Teachers of English (NCTE). An alarmed group within the council has formed the Committee on Public Doublespeak, which intends not only to bemoan the pollution of the language but also to mobilize a purification drive, with the classroom as the basic decontamination unit. [3]

Examples of Doublespeak—the sometimes unwitting but more often deliberate misuse of words to cover up, rather than explain, reality—are easy to find almost everywhere. Government bureaus, for instance, have been instructed to eliminate the word *poverty* from official documents, replacing it with *low-income,* a term not nearly as alarming as *poverty.* For similar reasons, the unpleasantness of *slums* or *ghettos* has long given way to *inner city.* Instead of *prisons,* there are now only *correctional facilities.* [4]

U.S. State Department employees are not *fired* but *selected out,* [5] a term that sounds like an award for excellence. Other government types tend to be *terminated.*

[6] In each instance, the aim is to make things appear better than they are or, in the case of *correctional facilities,* actually to seem what they decidedly are not. If all this were only a matter of semantics and style, there would be little cause for concern. Unfortunately, the truth is that the linguistic cosmetics are often used to create the impression that nasty problems have already been solved or were not really too nasty in the first place. The result: smug lack of concern. Inaction. A comfortable rest on political—or even pedagogical—laurels.

[7] Some of the new committee's members have cited such post-Watergate Doublespeak as calling *inoperative* something that the President had said earlier but later turned out not to have been true. Others have aimed their fire at even more troublesome semantics, such as the explanation by American bombers—after having struck the enemy first—that the maneuver was a *protective reaction strike.*

[8] When "the other side" sends its troops into neutral territory, it is characterized as *aggression* or *invasion;* when "our side" does the same, it is an *incursion* to protect the lives of American soldiers. When a Watergate witness admits, under pressure, that he ought not to have done what he did, he describes the action, not as *wrong,* but as *inappropriate* and then only in *the particular time frame.*

[9] Although the immediate suspicion is that the new committee may be excessively political in its own right—a number of the members probably fall into the category that Spiro Agnew, himself a master of Newspeak, called *radiclibs*—there is clearly much room for semantic recycling in totally non-political areas. For example, public utilities and other commercial interests tend to announce new procedures that result in higher rates or less service with the explanation that they are doing so *for your convenience.*

[10] When an airline tells you that there will be *a change of equipment* in Chicago, it means nothing less than that you have to get off the plane and onto another one, if and when it is available. When a recorded voice over the telephone informs you that your call will be *answered sequentially,* it means simply that you had better wait your turn, buster.

[11] Schoolchildren might examine—for classroom analysis is the committee's ultimate goal—the meaning of *free gifts* offered by savings banks in return for new deposits. Strictly speaking, if a gift is not free, it is not a gift. The bank's gifts, however, are not really free: If the deposit is withdrawn before a minimum period, the gift, or an equivalent amount of money, is taken back. The free gift thus turns out to have been a conditional gift all along.

Walker Gibson, until recently NCTE president and professor of English at the University of Massachusetts, whose brainchild the Doublespeak group is believed to have been, feels that official statements and commercial advertising ought to be read as critically as Shakespeare. [12]

Professor Gibson said his antennae first sent out an alarm when, quite a number of years ago, the War Department renamed itself the Department of Defense. The use of euphemisms subsequently became one of his scholarly interests. "Watergate itself is a spectacular example of euphemism," Professor Gibson said. He added that educators might have been slow to do battle against Doublespeak because "they are themselves so blatantly guilty of their own gobbledygook." He seemed encouraged, however, by a special factor of timing: English departments, he pointed out, are in a state of depression and they may welcome the opportunity to get into a broader field of activity and impact. [13]

PREREADING EXERCISE ("Wanton Acts of Usage")

Write one- or two-sentence definitions of the following words:

communism

dictator

terrorism

democracy

love

Trade papers with three or four other students. Then write a paragraph that tells the biggest difference you saw between one of another person's definitions and your own.

Christopher Hitchens

Wanton Acts of Usage

Christopher Hitchens is an astute journalist who summarizes his special interests this way: "I don't like to see people fooled or fooling themselves. I write against deception, especially self-deception." Hitchens currently holds positions with *The Nation*, *Harper's*, and *The New Statesman*, and his greatest pleasure is writing for *Grand Street*, a literary and political quarterly published in New York. Besides analyzing the farcical and fishy side of current events, Hitchens studies and writes about ancient and modern Greece.

Terrell E. Arnold is a consultant to the State Department on terrorism and executive director of the Institute on Terrorism and Subnational Conflict. In 1983 and 1984, he was principal deputy director of the State Department's Office for Counter Terrorism and Emergency Planning. He is the co-editor, with Neil C. Livingston, of *Fighting Back: Winning the War Against Terrorism*. He's also a very nice guy. On April 28 I spent an hour debating with him on C-SPAN, the cable TV network, before an audience of high school students. I asked him plainly, perhaps half a dozen times, whether he could do the elementary service of defining his terms. Could he offer a definition of "terrorism" that was not: [1]

- Tautological or vacuous ("the use of violence for political ends," as Constantine Menges, late of the National Security Council, once put it) in a way that would cover any state, party, movement, or system not explicitly committed to pacifism: [2]
- A cliché ("an attack on innocent men, women, and children") of the kind that all warring states and parties have always used to attack all other warring states and parties; or
- A synonym for "swarthy opponent of United States foreign policy."

My reason for asking so insistently was that the Reagan Administration has yet to define terrorism; the numerous institutes and think tanks which are paid to study it have yet to define terrorism; and the mass media which headline it have yet to define terrorism. I wasn't just looking for a debating point. I really—since this is an issue that might take us to war—wanted to know. Finally, [3]

Terrell E. Arnold, who is as I say a nice guy, decided to answer my question. He said:

> Can I provide a universally acceptable definition of terrorism? I fear I have to say I cannot. [4]

That was honest. So, in a clumsier way, was CIA director William J. Casey, in the opening essay of *Hydra of Carnage: International Linkages of Terrorism—The Witnesses Speak,* edited by Uri Ra'anan, Robert L. Pfaltzgraff, Jr., Richard H. Shultz, Ernest Halperin, and Igor Lukes. Kicking off this volume, which seems to represent the distilled counterterrorist scholarship of the Fletcher School of Law and Diplomacy at Tufts University, Casey begins, promisingly: [5]

> In confronting the challenge of international terrorism, the first step is to call things by their proper names, to see clearly and say plainly who the terrorists are, what goals they seek, and which governments support them. [6]

Yes, yes. Who, what, and which? Let's have it. Next sentence: "What the terrorist does is kill, maim, kidnap, and torture." [7]

In other words, and if we are to believe the director of the CIA, the terrorist is nothing new, and nothing different. Can that be right? [8]

. . . The Rand Corporation, which has made rather a good thing out of "terrorism" consultancy, has produced a masterwork, *Trends in International Terrorism, 1982 and 1983*. The introduction to this pamphlet inquires, as well it might: [9]

> What do we mean by terrorism? The term, unfortunately, has no precise or widely accepted definition. The problem of definition is compounded by the fact that *terrorism* has become a fad word that is applied to all sorts of violence. [10]

Six scholars labored to produce this report for Rand, and they were obviously not about to let this piece of throat-clearing get in the way of their grants, trips, and fellowships. For the rest of the study, the word "terrorism" is used without qualification to mean whatever they want it to mean: [11]

> In Rand's continuing research on this subject, *terrorism* is defined by the nature of the act, not by the identity of the perpetrators or the nature of the cause. Terrorism is violence, or the threat of violence, calculated to create an atmosphere of fear and alarm. All terrorist acts are crimes. [12]

A connoisseur might savor that last grace note, given that the Rand study also states, "In Nicaragua, international terrorist vio- [13]

lence during 1982–1983 consisted only of four hijackings involving Nicaraguans seizing planes in which to flee the country." Aside from the obvious omissions, what is "international" about a Nicaraguan using force to leave Nicaragua?

My initial question is a simple one. How can a word with no meaning and no definition, borrowed inexpertly from the second-rate imitators of Burke and his polemic against the French Revolution of 1789—when "Terror" meant "big government"—have become the political and media buzzword of the eighties? How can it have become a course credit at colleges, an engine of pelf in the think tanks, and a subject in its own right in the press, on television, and at the movies? [14]

Some people have noticed the obvious fact that the word carries a conservative freight. It is almost always used to describe revolutionary or subversive action, though there is no reason in any of the above "definitions" why this should be. And I think one could also add that it's taken on a faint but unmistakable racist undertone (or overtone) in much the same way as the word "mugger" once did. There's always the suspicion, to put it no higher, that the politician or journalist who goes on and on about "terrorism" has not got the South African police in mind, any more than the "law and order" big mouth means business about the Mafia. [15]

In a defensive reaction to this hypocritical and ideological emphasis, many liberals have taken simply to inverting the word, or to changing the subject. Typically, a sympathizer of the Palestinians will say that it is Ariel Sharon who is "the real terrorist"; a Republican Irishman, that it is the British occupier who fills the bill; and so on. Still others will point suavely to the "root cause" of unassuaged grievance. This is all right as far as it goes, which is not very far. You don't draw the sting from a brainless propaganda word merely by turning it around. The word "terrorist" is not—like "communist" and "fascist"—being abused; it is itself an abuse. It disguises reality and impoverishes language and makes a banality out of the discussion of war and revolution and politics. It's the perfect instrument for the cheapening of public opinion and for the intimidation of dissent . . . . [16]

This is a bit of a disgrace to language as well as to politics. English contains rather a number of words, each of them individually expressive, with which to describe violence and to suggest the speaker's attitude toward it. Any literate person could duplicate, expand, or contest the following set of examples: [17]

1. One who fights a foreign occupation of his country without putting on a uniform: guerrilla or *guerrillero;* partisan; (occasionally) freedom fighter. [18]

2. One who extorts favors and taxes on his own behalf while affecting to be a guerrilla: bandit; brigand; pirate.
3. One who wages war on a democratic government, hoping to make it less democratic: nihilist; (some versions) fascist, anarchist, Stalinist.
4. One who gives his pregnant fiancée a suitcase containing a bomb as she boards a crowded airliner: psychopath; murderer.
5. One who cuts the throat of an unarmed civilian prisoner while he lies in a shallow grave and buries him still living after inviting an American photographer to record the scene: *contra.*
6. One who makes a living by inspiring fear and temporary obedience in the weak and vulnerable: goon; thug; kidnapper; blackmailer; hijacker; hoodlum.
7. One who directs weapons of conventional warfare principally at civilian objectives: war criminal.
8. One who believes himself licensed to kill by virtue of membership in a religious or mystical fraternity: fanatic; (traditionally) assassin.

Only the fifth of these examples is mischievously propagandistic, and I include it both as a true incident and as a joke about the prevailing self-righteousness. Meanwhile, we have not even begun to parse the words, "tyrant," "despot," "dictator," "absolutist," and "megalomaniac." "Terrorist," however, is a convenience word, a junk word, designed to obliterate distinctions. It must be this that recommends it so much to governments with something to hide, to the practitioners of instant journalism, and to shady "consultants." [19]

Stupidity here makes an easy bedfellow, as always, with racism, and with the offensive habit of referring to "the Arabs." All Arab states and all Arab parties and communities recognize the PLO as the representative of the Palestinians. Define the PLO as "terrorist" and what have you done? You've flattened the picture of the Middle East, for one thing. All Arabs are, *ex hypothesi,* terrorists or terrorist sympathizers. And what can't you do with terrorism? *Compromise* with it, that's what you can't do. *Anybody* knows that, for gosh sakes. So—no need to compromise with the Arabs, who have to keep apologizing for living in the Middle East too. This idiot syllogism is a joke only if you haven't seen the *Congressional Record* for May and June, and read the contributions of our legislators to the Saudi arms "debate." Like bootleggers smashed on their own hooch, the "anti-terrorism" types were debauched by their own propaganda. [20]

You can see the same process at work if you turn the pages of the report issued by the Long commission, set up by the Defense Department to find out "what went wrong" with the Marine expe- [21]

dition to Beirut. This document is a pitiful thing from whichever political or literary standpoint it is approached. It reeks of self-pity and self-deception. We learn that "it was anticipated that the [marines] would be perceived by the various factions as evenhanded and neutral." Anticipated by whom? And which factions?

[22] Later, according to the commission, the "environment could no longer be characterized as peaceful. The image of the [marines], in the eyes of the factional militias, had become pro-Israel, pro-Phalange, and anti-Muslim." When would the "environment" of Beirut have been "characterized as peaceful"? Again, which factional militias? And were the militias right or wrong about the tendency of American allegiance, or was it, as the report says, an "image" problem? There would be no glue with which to hold this tenth-rate explanation together if the report did not use the words "terrorism" and "terrorist" 178 times. So that's all right then. We know our enemy.

[23] The terrorist is always, and by definition, the Other. Call your enemy communist or fascist and, whatever your intentions, you will one day meet someone who proudly claims to be a communist or fascist. Define your foe as authoritarian or totalitarian, and, however ill-crafted your analysis, you are bound to find a target that amplifies the definition. But "terrorist" is hardly more useful than a term of abuse, and probably less so.

[24] One way of putting this simple point is to take the "anti-terrorist" argument at its strongest. Random violence is one thing, say the well-funded experts, but it gets really serious when it's "state-sponsored" terrorism. The two words that are supposed to intensify the effect of the third actually have the effect, if we pause for thought, of diminishing it. It is terrifying to be held at gunpoint by a person who has *no demands*. A moment of *terror* is the moment when the irrational intrudes—when the man with the gun is hearing voices or wants his girlfriend back or has a theory about the Middle Pyramid. But if the gunman is a proxy for Syria or Iran or Bangladesh or Chile (the fourth being the only government mentioned here that has ever detonated a lethal bomb on American soil), then it isn't, strictly speaking, the irrational that we face. It may be an apparently irreconcilable quarrel or an apparently unappeasable grievance, but it is, finally, political. And propaganda terms, whether vulgar or ingenious, have always aimed at making political problems seem one-sided.

[25] Why should they not? That is the propagandist's job. What is frightening and depressing is that a pseudoscientific propaganda word like "terrorist" has come to have such a hypnotic effect on public debate in the United States. A word which originated with the most benighted opponents of the French Revolution; a word

which is a commonplace in the handouts of the Red Army in Afghanistan and the South African army in Namibia; a word which was in everyday use during the decline of the British, French, Portuguese, and Belgian empires. Should we not be wary of a term with which rulers fool themselves and by which history is abolished and language debased? Don't we fool and console ourselves enough as it is?

Ellen Goodman

We Do Not Need More Talk of War

Born in 1941, Ellen Goodman is a nationally syndicated columnist who writes about the changing mores in our society. She was educated at Radcliffe and wrote for *Newsweek* and several newspapers before becoming syndicated. She won a Pulitzer Prize in 1980 for commentary. She writes two columns a week which appear either on the editorial pages or in the women's sections of newspapers.

War-talk again. This time it's the war on drugs, inanimate chemicals that have acquired the human characteristics of an insidious enemy. Fighting words fill the air like bugle sounds. [1]

The president calls for an "assault on every front." A Democratic critic, Joe Biden, says we need "another D-Day, not another Vietnam." A Republican supporter, Bob Dole, says: "It's a war on drugs, not a war on the American taxpayer." [2]

The great massing of the metaphors has begun anew. We hear about attacks and weapons, front lines and battle plans. Even the media "mobilizes" its "arsenal" of war rhetoric to fill headlines and leads. [3]

We leap to this language. Nothing but war seems to have the same power to mobilize people in some communal effort against a perceived enemy, a named threat. Only a declaration of war stirs the juices enough to call us to sacrifice, to get civilians to join up. [4]

The power of the military image is so enormous in our minds that even pacifists are trapped by its vocabulary. [5]

Martin Luther King, Jr., used to talk of the army of nonviolence, Gandhi of his soldiers. Religious leaders talk about holy crusades as if the model had been a moral mission, not a bloody mess. [6]

To the American ear, surely to the veteran-president, the war on drugs is meant to conjure up that good war, World War II. A war we were forced into by tyranny, a war we won while remaining good guys. [7]

But if the martial sounds of the past week sounded false, it was not just a matter of linguistics. War is just the wrong metaphor for the drug problems of this country and hemisphere. [8]

War simplifies the complex. It draws sides. War demands a [9] human enemy, people that in time become dehumanized. War has only one set of responses to a myriad number of situations: violence. It has only one approved pattern of behavior: power. Once begun it can only respond with more.

[10] And, of course, war, especially a "just war," demands sacrifice, even of our liberties. The one end it can see or accept without humiliation is total victory—zero tolerance—or abject surrender.

[11] Where imagery leads, policy follows. And the way we label things inevitably has an effect on how we behave.

[12] So the military cast to this declared war on drugs easily becomes a disastrous way of thinking and planning. A variation of the old oxymoron of Military Intelligence. A one-dimensional fight.

[13] This is the likely outcome of this military strategy, not only because an overwhelming proportion of the money goes to making prisoners of war. Not only because "ultimate victory," a Victory Over Drugs Day, is an impossible goal. But because this war, like most, offers the least to the poor.

[14] It emphasizes enemies and not allies, combatants and not civilians, aggression and not protection, destruction over building.

[15] The creatures of the drug culture have taken over great hunks of the inner cities. If there were a military term to describe this reality, it would be called an "insurgency."

[16] We don't know how to solve the many problems that collect under the label "drugs." We do know something about the vulnerability of the poor and hopeless who join this insurgency. We know that hope, a sense of life's possibilities, is the best protection.

[17] What is needed is less of an assault mentality and more of a healing one. But metaphor makes the mind-set, and so it appears that, once again, it's off to war we go.

[18] Too bad that this time we didn't skip the war and go directly to the Marshall Plan.

VOCABULARY

banality	meaningless pursuit
cliché	an overused, trite expression
connoisseur	an expert
debauched	corrupted
explicitly	clearly and definitely
ideological	politically slanted
ingenious	clever, resourceful
Marshall Plan	American aid to war-torn Europe after World War II
insurgency	a takeover through armed revolt
pelf	riches, booty

Phalange	Christian sect in power in Lebanon
savor	enjoy
swarthy	dark-skinned
unappeasable	not relievable or satisfiable
unassuaged	not made milder

DISCUSSION AND WRITING IDEAS

1. Taking to heart the advice about memos in Mathes's article, write a persuasive memorandum to one of your professors (present or past) whose methods could be improved. Identify a concrete action that you would like the professor to take and be sure that he or she would not be able to skip over or misconstrue your suggestion.
2. Make up euphemisms for some of the realities of college life: exam, criticism, fail, cheat, flunk out, roommate problems, procrastinate, cram, skip.
3. Discuss why Hitchens finds the lack of a definition of "terrorism" so frightening. Are there words you and your friends use that are similarity lacking exact definition? Write a list of possible definitions for such a word.
4. Ellen Goodman writes, "Metaphor makes the mindset" in paragraph 17, and "The way we label things inevitably has an effect on how we behave" in paragraph 11. Give another case in which these statements apply.

poetry

e e cummings

next to of course god america i

e e cummings (1894–1962), an innovative poet who used little punctuation and few capital letters, often presented a satirical view of American attitudes in deliberately fractured syntax and imaginative typographical arrangements.

"next to of course god america i
love you land of the pilgrims' and so forth oh
say can you see by the dawn's early my
country 'tis of centuries come and go
and are no more what of it we should worry [5]
in every language even deafanddumb
thy sons acclaim your glorious name by gorry
by jingo by gee by gosh by gum
why talk of beauty what could be more beauti-
iful than these heroic happy dead [10]
who rushed like lions to the roaring slaughter
they did not stop to think they died instead
then shall the voice of liberty be mute?"

He spoke. And drank rapidly a glass of water

The Bible (King James Version)

The Twenty-Third Psalm

The Lord is my shepherd; I shall not want.
He maketh me to lie down in green pastures, he leadeth me beside the still waters.
He restoreth my soul; he leadeth me in the paths of righteousness for his name's sake.
Yea, though I walk through the valley of the shadow of death, I will fear no evil: for thou art with me; thy rod and thy staff they comfort me.
Thou preparest a table before me in the presence of mine enemies; thou anointest my head with oil; my cup runneth over. [5]
Surely goodness and mercy shall follow me all the days of my life: and I will dwell in the house of the Lord forever.

Alan J. Simpson and Robert A. Baker

The Twenty-Third Psalm

Alan J. Simpson (b. 1912), British by birth but an American citizen since 1954, is a noted historian, now president of Vassar.

Robert Allen Baker (b. 1921) a respected research scientist and educator, presently heads the Department of Psychology of the University of Kentucky. The following revised version of the Twenty-Third Psalm, which Simpson and Baker wrote, first appeared in *Washington University Magazine* in 1961.

The Lord is my external-internal integrative mechanism,
  I shall not be deprived of gratification for my viscerogenic hungers or my need-dispositions.
He motivates me to orient myself towards a non-social object with affective significance,
  He positions me in a non-decisional situation.
He maximizes my adjustment. [5]
  Although I entertain masochistic and self-destructive id impulses,
  I will maintain contact with reality for my superego is dominant.
His analysis and tranquilizers, they comfort me.
  He assists in the resolution of my internal conflicts despite my Oedipal problem and psychopathic compulsions.
He promotes my in-group identification.
  My personality is totally integrated. [10]
Surely my prestige and status shall be enhanced as a direct function of time
  And I shall remain sociologically, psychologically and economically secure forever.

DISCUSSION IDEAS

In what ways does e e cummings make the patriotic formulas of the speaker sound ridiculous?

Using Simpson and Baker's poem for inspiration, make up jargon versions of William Blake's poem "The Garden of Love" (Chapter 8) and A. E. Houseman's "Loveliest of Trees" (Chapter 9). These poems, like the King James version of the Twenty-Third Psalm, are eloquent in their simplicity.

Short Story

Mark Twain

The War Prayer

Known and loved the world over as a novelist and humorist, Twain (1835–1910) also had a dark side and wrote quantities of pessimistic diatribes on political and social matters. The incisive satire which follows conveys Twain's loathing for the kind of knee-jerk patriotism that made possible the Spanish-American War, which was the impetus for the story. "The War Prayer" was first published in *Harper's* in 1916, six years after Twain's death.

It was a time of great and exalting excitement. The country was up in arms, the war was on, in every breast burned the holy fire of patriotism: the drums were beating, the bands playing, the toy pistols popping, the bunched firecrackers hissing and spluttering; on every hand and far down the receding and fading spread of roofs and balconies a fluttering wilderness of flags flashed in the sun; daily the young volunteers marched down the wide avenue gay and fine in their new uniforms, the proud fathers and mothers and sisters and sweethearts cheering them with voices choked with happy emotion as they swung by; nightly the packed mass meeting listened, panting, to patriot oratory which stirred the deepest deeps of their hearts and which they interrupted at briefest intervals with cyclones of applause, the tears running down their cheeks the while; in the churches the pastors preached devotion to flag and country and invoked the God of Battles, beseeching His aid in our good cause in out-pouring of fervid eloquence which moved every listener. It was indeed a glad and gracious time, and the half-dozen rash spirits that ventured to disapprove of the war and cast a doubt upon its righteousness straightway got such a stern and angry warning that for their personal safety's sake they quickly shrank out of sight and offended no more in that way. [1]

Sunday morning came—next day the battalions would leave for the front: the church was filled; the volunteers were there, their young faces alight with martial dreams—visions of the stern advance, the gathering momentum, the rushing charge, the flashing [2] sabers, the flight of the foe, the tumult, the enveloping smoke, the fierce pursuit, the surrender!—then home from the war, bronzed heroes, welcomed, adored, submerged in golden seas of glory! With the volunteers sat their dear ones, proud, happy, and envied by the neighbors and friends who had no sons and brothers to send forth to the field of honor, there to win for the flag or, failing, die the noblest of noble deaths. The service proceeded; a war chapter from the Old Testament was read; the first prayer was said; it was followed by an organ burst that shook the building, and with one impulse the house rose, with glowing invocation—

> "God the all-terrible! Thou who ordainest,
> Thunder thy clarion and lightning thy sword!"

Then came the "long" prayer. None could remember the like of it for passionate pleading and moving and beautiful language. The burden of its supplication was that an ever-merciful and benignant Father of us all would watch over our noble young soldiers and aid, comfort, and encourage them in their patriotic work; bless them, shield them in the day of battle and the hour of peril, bear them in His mighty hand, make them strong and confident, invincible in the bloody onset: help them to crush the foe, grant to them and to their flag and country imperishable honor and glory—

[3] An aged stranger entered and moved with slow and noiseless step up the main aisle, his eyes fixed upon the minister, his long body clothed in a robe that reached to his feet, his head bare, his white hair descending in a frothy cataract to his shoulders, his seamy face unnaturally pale, pale even to ghastliness. With all eyes following him and wondering, he made his silent way; without pausing, he ascended to the preacher's side and stood there, waiting. With shut lids the preacher, unconscious of his presence, continued his moving prayer, and at last finished it with the words, uttered in fervent appeal, "Bless our arms, grant us the victory, O Lord our God, Father and Protector of our land and flag!"

[4] The stranger touched his arm, motioned him to step aside—which the startled minister did—and took his place. During some moments he surveyed the spellbound audience with solemn eyes in which burned an uncanny light; then in a deep voice he said:

[5] "I come from the Throne—bearing a message from Almighty God!" The words smote the house with a shock; if the stranger perceived it he gave no attention. "He has heard the prayer of His servant your shepherd and will grant it if such shall be your desire after I, His messenger, shall have explained to you its import—that is to say, its full import. For it is like unto many of the prayers of men, in that it asks for more than he who utters it is aware of—except he pause and think.

"God's servant and yours has prayed his prayer. Has he paused and taken thought? Is it one prayer? No, it is two—one uttered, the other not. Both have reached the ear of Him Who heareth all supplications, the spoken and the unspoken. Ponder this—keep it in mind. If you would beseech a blessing upon yourself, beware! lest without intent you invoke a curse upon a neighbor at the same time. If you pray for the blessing of rain upon your crop which needs it, by that act you are possibly praying for a curse upon some neighbor's crop which may not need rain and can be injured by it. [6]

"You have heard your servant's prayer—the uttered part of it. I am commissioned of God to put into words the other part of it—that part which the pastor, and also you in your hearts, fervently prayed silently. And ignorantly and unthinkingly? God grant that it was so! You heard these words: 'Grant us the victory, O Lord our God!' That is sufficient. The *whole* of the uttered prayer is compact into these pregnant words. Elaborations were not necessary. When you have prayed for victory you have prayed for many unmentioned results which follow victory—*must* follow it, cannot help but follow it. Upon the listening spirit of God the Father fell also the unspoken part of the prayer. He commandeth me to put it into words. Listen! [7]

"O Lord our Father, our young patriots, idols of our hearts, go forth to battle—be Thou near them! With them, in spirit, we also go forth from the sweet peace of our beloved firesides to smite the foe. O Lord our God, help us to tear their soldiers to bloody shreds with our shells; help us to cover their smiling fields with the pale forms of their patriot dead; help us to drown the thunder of guns with the shrieks of their wounded, writhing in pain; help us to lay waste their humble homes with a hurricane of fire; help us to wring the hearts of their unoffending widows with unavailing grief; help us to turn them out roofless with their little children to wander unfriended the wastes of their desolated land in rags and hunger and thirst, sports of the sun flames of summer and the icy winds of winter, broken in spirit, worn with travail, imploring Thee for the refuge of the grave and denied it—for our sakes who adore Thee, Lord, blast their hopes, blight their lives, protract their bitter pilgrimage, make heavy their steps, water their way with their tears, stain the white snow with the blood of their wounded feet! We ask it, in the spirit of love, of Him Who is the Source of Love, and Who is the ever-faithful refuge and friend of all that are sore beset and seek His aid with humble and contrite hearts. Amen. [8]

(*After a pause*) "Ye have prayed it; if ye still desire it, speak! The messenger of the Most High waits." [9]

It was believed afterward that the man was a lunatic, because there was no sense in what he said. [10]

DISCUSSION IDEAS

What contradictions between patriotism and Christianity does Twain see? What are the similarities and differences between the rhetoric of Christianity and the rhetoric of patriotism? What does the closing sentence of the story add to its theme?

PREREADING EXERCISE ("I Have a Dream")

You have grown up hearing about "the American dream." Consider exactly what that phrase means to you.

Write a paragraph in which you explain—using specific details—what you think the American dream is.

Then, in a second paragraph tell whether you think you will achieve the dream in your lifetime. Conclude by telling how you expect to make the dream a reality—or else tell why you think the dream is not a possibility for you.

Speech

Martin Luther King, Jr.

I Have a Dream

Marin Luther King, Jr. (1929–1968), was the brave and eloquent leader of the 1960s nonviolent movement to achieve civil rights for black people. The son of a Baptist minister, he also became a minister, holding degrees from Morehouse College, Grozer Theological Seminary, and Boston University. Dr. King became famous through his advocacy of civil disobedience as a means of ending the segregation of blacks in the south. He organized economic boycotts of segregated business establishments and led sit-ins at segregated lunch counters and waiting rooms. Frequently harassed, arrested, and jailed by southern law enforcement officers and reviled by FBI head J. Edgar Hoover, Dr. King was admired by right-minded people around the world. In 1964 he was awarded the Nobel Peace Prize; in 1968 he was assassinated in Memphis, Tennessee. His birthday is now a national holiday. The speech reprinted here was delivered at the huge Civil Rights demonstration in Washington, D.C., in 1963 and drew thunderous applause from the quarter of a million people assembled there.

Five score years ago, a great American, in whose symbolic shadow we stand, signed the Emancipation Proclamation. This momentous decree came as a great beacon light of hope to millions of Negro slaves who had been seared in the flames of withering injustice. It came as a joyous daybreak to end the long night of captivity. [1]

But one hundred years later, we must face the tragic fact that the Negro is still not free. One hundred years later, the life of the Negro is still sadly crippled by the manacles of segregation and the chains of discrimination. One hundred years later, the Negro lives on a lonely island of poverty in the midst of a vast ocean of material prosperity. One hundred years later, the Negro is still languishing in the corners of American society and finds himself an exile in his own land. So we have come here today to dramatize an appalling condition. [2]

In a sense we have come to our nation's capital to cash a check. [3]

When the architects of our republic wrote the magnificent words of the Constitution and the Declaration of Independence, they were signing a promissory note to which every American was to fall heir. This note was a promise that all men would be guaranteed the unalienable rights of life, liberty, and the pursuit of happiness.

[4] It is obvious today that America has defaulted on this promissory note insofar as her citizens of color are concerned. Instead of honoring this sacred obligation, America has given the Negro people a bad check; a check which has come back marked "insufficient funds." But we refuse to believe that the bank of justice is bankrupt. We refuse to believe that there are insufficient funds in the great vaults of opportunity of this nation. So we have come to cash this check—a check that will give us upon demand the riches of freedom and the security of justice. We have also come to this hallowed spot to remind America of the fierce urgency of *now*. This is no time to engage in the luxury of cooling off or to take the tranquilizing drugs of gradualism. *Now* is the time to make real the promises of Democracy. *Now* is the time to rise from the dark and desolate valley of segregation to the sunlit path of racial justice. *Now* is the time to open the doors of opportunity to all of God's children. *Now* is the time to lift our nation from the quicksands of racial injustice to the solid rock of brotherhood.

[5] It would be fatal for the nation to overlook the urgency of the movement and to underestimate the determination of the Negro. This sweltering summer of the Negro's legitimate discontent will not pass until there is an invigorating autumn of freedom and equality. 1963 is not an end, but a beginning. Those who hope that the Negro needed to blow off steam and will now be content will have a rude awakening if the nation returns to business as usual. There will be neither rest nor tranquillity in America until the Negro is granted his citizenship rights. The whirlwinds of revolt will continue to shake the foundations of our nation until the bright day of justice emerges.

[6] But there is something that I must say to my people who stand on the warm threshold which leads into the palace of justice. In the process of gaining our rightful place we must not be guilty of wrongful deeds. Let us not seek to satisfy our thirst for freedom by drinking from the cup of bitterness and hatred. We must forever conduct our struggle on the high plane of dignity and discipline. We must not allow our creative protest to degenerate into physical violence. Again and again we must rise to the majestic heights of meeting physical force with soul force. The marvelous new militancy which has engulfed the Negro community must not lead us to a distrust of all white people, for many of our white brothers, as evidenced by their presence here today, have come to realize that their destiny

is tied up with our destiny and their freedom is inextricably bound to our freedom. We cannot walk alone.

And as we walk, we must make the pledge that we shall march ahead. We cannot turn back. There are those who are asking the devotees of civil rights, "When will you be satisfied?" We can never be satisfied as long as the Negro is the victim of the unspeakable horrors of police brutality. We can never be satisfied as long as our bodies, heavy with the fatigue of travel, cannot gain lodging in the motels of the highways and the hotels of the cities. We cannot be satisfied as long as the Negro's basic mobility is from a smaller ghetto to a larger one. We can never be satisfied as long as a Negro in Mississippi cannot vote and a Negro in New York believes he has nothing for which to vote. No, no, we are not satisfied, and we will not be satisfied until justice rolls down like waters and righteousness like a mighty stream. [7]

I am not unmindful that some of you have come here out of great trials and tribulations. Some of you have come fresh from narrow jail cells. Some of you have come from areas where your quest for freedom left you battered by the storms of persecution and staggered by the winds of police brutality. You have been the veterans of creative suffering. Continue to work with the faith that unearned suffering is redemptive. [8]

Go back to Mississippi, go back to Alabama, go back to South Carolina, go back to Georgia, go back to Louisiana, go back to the slums and ghettos of our northern cities, knowing that somehow this situation can and will be changed. Let us not wallow in the valley of despair. [9]

I say to you today, my friends, that in spite of the difficulties and frustrations of the moment I still have a dream. It is a dream deeply rooted in the American dream. [10]

I have a dream that one day this nation will rise up and live out the true meaning of its creed: "We hold these truths to be self-evident; that all men are created equal." [11]

I have a dream that one day on the red hills of Georgia the sons of former slaves and the sons of former slaveowners will be able to sit down together at the table of brotherhood. [12]

I have a dream that one day even the state of Mississippi, a desert state sweltering with the heat of injustice and oppression, will be transformed into an oasis of freedom and justice. [13]

I have a dream that my four little children will one day live in a nation where they will not be judged by the color of their skin but by the content of their character. [14]

I have a dream today. [15]

I have a dream that one day the state of Alabama, whose gov- [16]

ernor's lips are presently dripping with the words of interposition and nullification, will be transformed into a situation where little black boys and black girls will be able to join hands with little white boys and white girls and walk together as sisters and brothers.

I have a dream today. [17]

I have a dream that one day every valley shall be exalted, every hill and mountain shall be made low, the rough places will be made plain, and the crooked places will be made straight, and the glory of the Lord shall be revealed, and all flesh shall see it together. [18]

This is our hope. This is the faith with which I return to the South. With this faith we will be able to hew out of the mountain of despair a stone of hope. With this faith we will be able to transform the jangling discords of our nation into a beautiful symphony of brotherhood. With this faith we will be able to work together, to pray together, to struggle together, to go to jail together, to stand up for freedom together, knowing that we will be free one day. [19]

This will be the day when all of God's children will be able to sing with new meaning [20]

[21]

My country, 'tis of thee,
Sweet land of liberty,
Of thee I sing:
Land where my fathers died,
Land of the pilgrims' pride,
From every mountain-side
Let freedom ring.

And if America is to be a great nation this must become true. So let freedom ring from the prodigious hilltops of New Hampshire. Let freedom ring from the mighty mountains of New York. Let freedom ring from the heightening Alleghenies of Pennsylvania! [22]

Let freedom ring from the snowcapped Rockies of Colorado! [23]

Let freedom ring from the curvaceous peaks of California! [24]

But not only that, let freedom ring from Stone Mountain of Georgia! [25]

Let freedom ring from Lookout Mountain of Tennessee! [26]

Let freedom ring from every hill and molehill of Mississippi. From every mountainside, let freedom ring. [27]

When we let freedom ring, when we let it ring from every village and every hamlet, from every state and every city, we will be able to speed up that day when all of God's children, black men and white men, Jews and Gentiles, Protestants and Catholics, will be able to join hands and sing in the words of the old Negro spiritual, "Free at last! free at last! thank God almighty, we are free at last!" [28]

DISCUSSION IDEAS

1. What audience is Dr. King trying to persuade in this speech? How can you tell? What is his main point?
2. Why does he begin with the somewhat archaic "Five score years ago" instead of saying simply "One hundred years ago"?
3. Underline or highlight with a marker all of the examples of deliberate repetition you can find. Explain how this repetition functions to increase the effectiveness of Dr. King's appeal.
4. In paragraph 2, he observes that "the life of the Negro is still sadly crippled by the manacles of segregation and the chains of discrimination." He could have said the same thing this way: "The life of the Negro is still sadly curtailed by segregation and discrimination." What does he achieve through his choice of the words "crippled," "manacles," and "chains"?
5. Explain why the metaphor of "to cash a check" is effective in paragraph 4.
6. Several times Dr. King uses extremely short sentences: "We cannot walk alone" (end of paragraph 6), "We cannot turn back" (paragraph 7), "I have a dream today" (paragraphs 15 and 17). Can you explain why he chose to make these sentences so short?
7. Point out three transitional devices used in this speech.
8. If you did not know of Dr. King's Christian ministry, would you guess that he was a preacher from reading his speech? What strong biblical influences can you detect there?

Kurt Vonnegut

What I'd Say if They Asked Me

Vonnegut was born in Indianapolis in 1922. Ahead of his time stylistically, he became popular with readers long before critics noticed him. Notable works include *The Sirens of Titan* (1959), *Slaughterhouse Five* (1969), and *Breakfast of Champions* (1973). He mixes fantasy, science fiction, and realism, emphasizing the pressing moral concerns of humans and aliens alike.

I am here to serve the people of the United States of America—all of them, in all ways which are lawful. [1]

I will not now speak of my humbleness. It has been said with some truth, I suppose, that almost anyone can grow up to be President. I have to add, "But surely not an humble child." The Presidency is simultaneously a pinnacle of power and of vanity, and God help us all. [2]

An aspect of my vanity, which seems to have found favor with a majority of those who chose to vote, is my belief that, with the help of the fourth branch of government mentioned in our Constitution, "We the people," I can do a lot to help the United States of America become the United States of America—at last, at last. [3]

The echo of Martin Luther King in my words is intentional when I say, "At last, at last." [4]

It will do us no harm today, as it has surely done no harm to other nations I need not name, to acknowledge a past soiled with atrocities, including, in our case, slavery and genocide, and the treatment of women of whatever race under law as though they were not citizens but property. Let us celebrate how far we have come from such bad old days in so short a time, and measure how far we have yet to go. [5]

What better measurement might we use for progress made and progress yet to come than the health and happiness and wisdom and safety of all our people? And make no mistake about it: This nation is the most astonishing and admirable experiment in pluralistic democracy in history. Because of our wealth, the fairness of our Bill of Rights and the openness of our long borders, every conceivable sort of human being is now an American. [6]

We are the world. [7]

There is much in the recent past I would undo, if I could, especially our overwhelming national debt, whose undoing will be slow and painful. I will try to find out what good things, if any, we bought with all that money, borrowed mostly from foreigners. I will report back to you, whose children and grandchildren must pay it back with interest. I will be surprised, as I am sure most of you will be, too, if I find many purchases our descendants might thank us for. [8]

With your encouragement, and with the cooperation of your elected representatives, I will attempt, after listening to the best-informed advisers I can find, to give future generations reasons to think well of us after all. There you have it, the principal mission of my administration: to create and bequeath to the future a decent habitat for all, free of poisons, free of hunger, free of ignorance, free of hate. [9]

Too much, too much? [10]

Ah, but a man's reach should exceed his grasp, [11]
Or what's a heaven for?

Those are the words of Robert Browning, of course. I can put it a lot less elegantly, if you like: [12]

Company's coming! Let's clean up this mess. [13]

Many of the poisons in the water and the air and the topsoil are new. One which can sicken our spirit is ancient, and only since World War II has this country begun to fight it with any seriousness: the idea that females and persons of color are second-class citizens. That poison would love to make a great big comeback, to take its lethal place alongside nerve gas and radioactive wastes and PCBs and crack, and DDT and Agent Orange and the AIDS virus, and on and on. [14]

Not while I'm President. In the words of Patrick Henry: [15]

If this *be treason, make the most of it.*

Am I proposing a redistribution of wealth? You bet, since the wealth is being redistributed in any case, and often most crazily, and against the national interest. Am I proposing that we tax and spend and spend? Yes, I am. Virtually every transaction is being skimmed already, and some private persons have done this at such confiscatory rates as to become as rich as smaller sovereign nations in a few years' time. And they spend and spend. On what? On what? [16]

Ah, me. [17]

Am I proposing an enormous public works program? How else might we describe our military-industrial complex, so mistrusted by that great Republican, General of the Armies Dwight David Eisenhower, when he himself became our President? With your [18] encouragement I want to take much of the money now going into that public works program, and invest it instead in the arts of peace, the noblest of which are public health and education.

Who says otherwise? And why? [19]

Company's coming. [20]

I thank you for your attention. [21]

DISCUSSION IDEAS

1. How does the opening line of Vonnegut's address reflect on other U.S. Presidents?
2. In paragraph 3, Vonnegut makes a seemingly redundant remark: "I can do a lot to help the United States of America become the United States of America—at last, at last." How do you explicate this statement?
3. What effect would it have on an audience to make the first direct reference to Martin Luther King, Jr., and his speech?
4. What effort does Vonnegut make to win the goodwill of his audience?
5. Explain the references to other famous people in the speech. Why do you think Vonnegut chose these specific people?
6. How does Vonnegut predict the criticisms of his detractors and defend against them?
7. Note several similarities between Martin Luther King, Jr.'s, speech and Kurt Vonnegut's in the areas of style, content, and structure.
8. King's speech was written in 1963, Vonnegut's in 1988. What differences are explained by the gap in time?

advertisements for analysis

You can love it without getting your heart broken.

All over the country, people are breaking up with their cars in record numbers. It's in the paper every day. Just check the used-car section.

You could avoid this kind of heartbreak with a little foresight and a trip to your local Saab dealer.

There, you might fall in love with a Saab like the 900 Turbo Convertible pictured here. You could do it with an easy conscience, because unlike most convertibles, ours is a Saab as well.

It wouldn't elate you in the spring, then let you down in the gloom of winter. Like all Saabs, it features front-wheel drive for great traction in any weather. Plus heated front seats and a double-insulated top for comfort, heated glass rear window for visibility and reinforced windshield pillars for safety.

You could drive it all year long and not realize it's a convertible until you dropped the top.

The Saab 900 Turbo Convertible is just one of the ways Saab dealers help keep people from buying the wrong cars–cars that offer fun without practicality or practicality without fun or status at prices that sting long after the honeymoon is over.

Don't buy the wrong car. Don't fall in love with a car you can't live with. Instead, make a date to test drive a Saab.

Your Saab dealer will be more than happy to set you up.

SAAB

The most intelligent cars ever built.

Saabs are intelligently priced from $16,995 to $32,095. 900 Turbo Convertible shown here: $32,095. MSRP, not including taxes, license, freight, dealer charges or options. Prices subject to change. ©1989 Saab-Scania of America, Inc.

To unlock your body's potential, we proudly offer Soloflex. Twenty-four traditional iron pumping exercises, each correct in form and balance. All on a simple machine that fits in a corner of your home.

For a free Soloflex brochure, call anytime **1-800-453-8501.** VHS Video Brochure™ available upon request.

For a 24″ x 33″ poster of this ad, send a check or money-order for $12.00 (includes postage and handling) to: Soloflex, Inc., Hawthorn Farm Industrial Park, Hillsboro, OR 97124-6494 Credit cards, call **1-800-547-8802.**

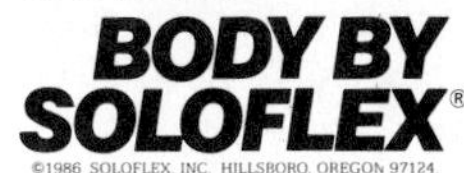

©1986 SOLOFLEX, INC. HILLSBORO, OREGON 97124

IDEAS FOR DISCUSSION AND WRITING

From what comparison does the Saab ad draw its humor? List some ways in which the comparison is extended. From your experience, is the comparison apt—that is, *are* there similarities between choosing a car and choosing a spouse? To what pitfalls of romance does the ad refer? Do you find the advertisement effective?

How many ways can you find in which the Soloflex ad embodies the idea of simplicity? Why would the advertiser desire to extol this quality? Why is the model's face obscured by his undershirt? Is he taking the undershirt off or putting it on? Is the targeted audience males, females, or both? Why do you think this specific lighting was chosen? Do you find the advertisement effective? Do you consider it an unwarranted use of sexuality or a pleasant distraction?

Find a magazine advertisement that strikes you as interesting or effective. Show it to friends and classmates for discussion. Write an essay that analyzes the advertisement's techniques.

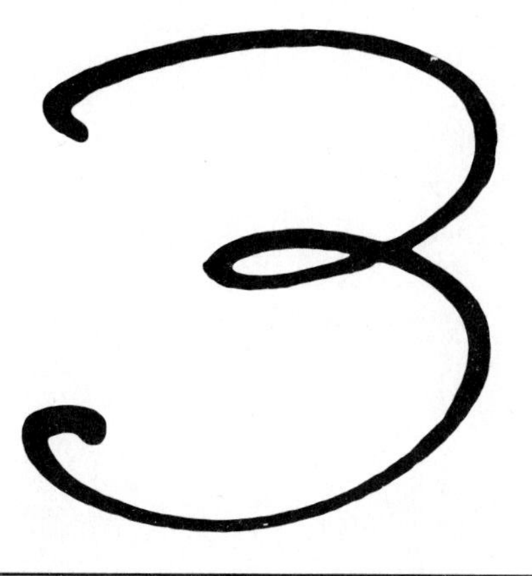

AN APPENDIX ON USING RESOURCES

Using Sources

AT SOME TIME, you will either want to use, or be required to use, other people's writing to support the ideas in a paper of your own. But your days of sitting down to copy the encyclopedia's entry on Brazil and calling that a research paper are decidedly over. This chapter will introduce you to some of the skills you need in order to use sources in your writing.

SUMMARIZING

One crucial art is the ability to summarize another person's written ideas. Making an accurate short account of the writer's main points is much more difficult than it sounds. To demonstrate, we are reprinting a review of the popular television series *thirtysomething* and following it with five 100-word summaries. Four of them show some of the most grievous pitfalls of summarizing, and one is fine. Read the selection and make your own judgments; our discussion of each summary will follow.

essays

Dan Wakefield

Celebrating "the Small Moments of Personal Discovery"

Born in Indianapolis in 1932, Wakefield makes his bread and butter writing for and about television. He created the NBC series *James at 15. Returning: A Spiritual Journey* is his latest book from Doubleday. He worked as a reporter before turning to network television. His reviews appear in *TV Guide*.

Their friends were surprised and concerned when Elliot and Nancy went to see a marriage counselor. So was I. After all, they were a warm, appealing couple who'd been married 12 years, had two children and seemed to be doing fine. That just shows how little we may know about people we like and to whom we feel close—the way I've come to feel about Elliot, Nancy and their friends on *thirtysomething*, the ABC series (airing Tuesdays at 10 P.M. [ET]) whose quality and intelligence put me in mind of the superb television dramas like *Upstairs, Downstairs* and *Brideshead Revisited* that I'd begun to think only the British could produce. [1]

Watching *thirtysomething* every week gives me the satisfied sensation of reading a good novel. It reminds me, in fact, of my favorite definition of a novel, given by one of my college English professors: a story of "how it was with a group of people." [2]

The group of people in this weekly drama are bright, attractive, college-educated friends who are all "thirtysomething." Nancy (Patricia Wettig) is a full-time housewife and mother whose husband (Timothy Busfield) is a partner in an advertising agency he started with his best friend Michael (Ken Olin). Michael and his wife, Hope (Mel Harris), and their new baby daughter are the center of the group of friends who come to their house for beer and pizza and basketball games on TV, Scrabble and coffee and gossip, advice and [3] comfort and bagels with cream cheese that may be hurled across the room for friendly emphasis. Michael's cousin Melissa (Melanie Mayron), is a free-lance, free-spirited photographer. Hope's best friend, Ellyn (Polly Draper), works as an administrator at City Hall, while long-haired Gary (Peter Horton) might be more likely to be mistaken for a '60s-style dropout than what he really is—a professor specializing in the epic. The scene is Philadelphia, but it could just as well be almost any American city that has seasons but no Southern accents.

What I see and am fascinated and moved by in the show are not the momentous dramas of life but the small moments of personal discovery, the daily details and nuance of relationships. I was rooting for reconciliation the night Nancy greeted Elliot after work with a bottle of champagne and a sexy outfit featuring a miniskirt and boots. It looked as if they'd finally make love later that night until in the midst of a passionate embrace he stopped rubbing his hand on her thigh and asked if she didn't shave her legs any more. I cringed as Nancy got up and left the room. [4]

In a subsequent episode, when Elliot and Nancy were separated, they unexpectedly made love with more passion than they had in years, and in the confusion that followed he told her not to pretend to understand it "because you don't" and it was obvious he didn't, either. The people in this drama do not come up with easy answers but often raise deeper, more complex questions. [5]

They also have fun. They laugh a lot, with and at one another, and tease and play. Sometimes they have fantasies, which we see—like Melissa acting as her own psychiatrist when she was jealous of Ellyn, who she thought was competing for the same man; or Elliot after his separation envisioning Nancy on her first date roaring off with a leather-clad stud on a motorcycle. [6]

Anger as well as joy, arising from real-life conflict among the characters, is made more dramatic by being underplayed. In the best holiday drama of recent memory, Michael and Hope clashed over their respective Jewish and Christian backgrounds. She wanted to have a tree for their daughter's first Christmas, and assured Michael they could also observe Hanukkah. As they dressed to go out to dinner, Michael answered her assurances by saying, "I don't see you polishing any menorahs, Hope." They finished dressing in silence as we watched the scene play out, absorbing the impact of the impasse. In a later epiphany, Michael brought home a tree to find Hope holding the baby and waiting for him in the glow of the menorah candles. No words were necessary, and none were spoken. [7]

We could almost "see" Michael growing up in the episode in which his father died. It was up to Michael to make a decision on [8] whether to close down his father's ailing clothing business. His younger brother was of no help at all, and instead added another, emotional dimension to the dilemma. Michael made the hard decision to shut down the business, and not only emerged as a more mature man, but drew closer to the brother.

The story that *thirtysomething* tells employs the themes of our greatest literature, whatever the outer social and cultural trappings of the characters: the frailty and honor of our aspirations, nourishment of friendship, complexity of love. [9]

Summary A

The television series *thirtysomething* invites us to share the lives of a group of friends in Philadelphia. The extraordinary script gives life to the characters, all intelligent, affluent people over thirty years of age. Two of the men, Elliot and Michael, own an ad agency together. Elliot's wife, Nancy, is a full-time housewife, and Michael's wife, Hope, has a newborn child. Melissa, a photographer, is single and footloose. Ellyn, another character, is a city official in Philadelphia. Gary is a literature professor. Elliot and Nancy's marital problems are frequently the focus of the well-written script, bringing up deeper questions of love and commitment. The difficulties of single life are depicted, too.

Summary B

The television series *thirtysomething* invites us to share the lives of a group of friends in Philadelphia. These characters are smart, affluent college graduates over thirty. The well-written script does a good job of dealing with both trivial and deep issues. My favorite was the episode in which we see one argument from the points of view of each of the four characters involved. The viewer becomes intensely involved with the characters in this series. For example, Hope is an inspiring example of a woman who combines family and career. The underlying themes of hope, friendship, and love are expressed with intelligence in *thirtysomething*.

Summary C

The television series *thirtysomething* is as satisfying as good literature. The high-quality, intellectual script lets us in on the lives of a group of smart, educated, over-thirty professionals. The show is best at laying bare the telling details of everyday life and love. Several episodes show characters not only dealing with amusing, frustrating, sad, or angry situations but grappling with the complicated questions these situations bring up: Can passion last? How deep are religious differences? In what form does one honor a parent? Such questions go beyond the specific conditions of the characters in *thirtysomething* and take up universal themes.

Summary D

The television series *thirtysomething* brings us into the lives of a group of friends—all bright, attractive, and college educated. These over-thirty people portray not only the major dilemmas of life, but also the smaller events of personal discovery, the everyday details and nuance of relationships. Sometimes, just as in our own lives, the characters themselves don't quite understand what happens to them. The script doesn't come up with easy answers but instead makes us think of deeper, more complicated questions. The tales of *thirtysomething* encompass the great themes of literature: aspiration, friendship, and love.

Summary E

The television series *thirtysomething* is truly awesome. It really gets down with a group of hip yuppies out in Philly. These dudes have lives that we can really get into—like not just the big stuff, but the everyday stuff that sometimes blows you away, you know? Relationships and all, how either being married or being single can be such a drag, how not digging the same religion is a bummer, and how having a parent croak really turns your head around. You get to know these people like they were your own gang. It's almost like getting into a good heavy read. Catch it next Tuesday, man!

EVALUATION OF THE SUMMARIES

Summary A concentrates on introducing the characters in *thirtysomething*. Because it goes into so much detail about them, there is little space left for anything else. Thus, the main point of Wakefield's review gets short shrift in this summary. It suffers from incompleteness.

Summary B does accurately reflect Wakefield's main point. However, the summary writer has added information and opinions of her own. She writes about her own favorite episode and gives her own example of becoming involved with a character. This blend of source material and personal opinion could be fine in a researched essay (see the sample paper in this chapter), but a plain summary should include only the material found in the source.

Summary C is the best one. It reproduces the thesis of Wakefield's essay and covers the main supporting points, leaving out most specific details. It also reflects the tone and, roughly, the order of the original piece. Notice, too, that it includes the comparison of the series to literature, which seems important to Wakefield since he makes the comparison both at the beginning and end of his review.

Summary D also fulfills the requirements of a good summary, but it has one glaring and egregious flaw: it plagiarizes. Several phrases are taken directly from the review with no quotation marks to indicate that they are quoted, like "details and nuance of relationships" and "deeper, more complicated questions." Other phrases are far too close to the original for comfort, like "bright, attractive, and college-educated" and "smaller events of personal discovery." This summary writer is guilty of dishonesty. Keep the idea of fairness in mind: if *you* had written the review and someone else had written this summary, would you feel that your phraseology had been stolen?

Summary E shows a humorous example of a fault that is not always this obvious. It is written in a completely different tone and style from the original. Though the style in a summary might justifiably be simpler than the source's, it should not shift drastically or perceptibly. In a way, you change the meaning when you change the style this much, violating the rules of summary writing.

PARAPHRASES

We cannot overemphasize that you must *paraphrase* when you use sources: you must summarize the writer's ideas in your own words and carefully avoid letting the original phraseology slip in, even unconsciously. The duty often requires thought, but you can paraphrase gracefully. For example, summarizer C writes, "the telling details of everyday life and love" as a paraphrase of "the daily details and nuance of relationships." And even a paraphrase must be acknowledged within your own writing, since you still owe the idea, though not the exact words, to another writer.

DIRECT QUOTATIONS

Although you should paraphrase your source most of the time, in special circumstances you may want to quote directly. When your source is written in an irresistibly authoritative or apt way, you may copy the phrasing exactly and use quotation marks around it. For example, you might want to quote Wakefield directly like this:

One reviewer summarizes the themes of *thirtysomething* as "the

> frailty and honor of our aspirations, nourishment of friendship, complexity of love."

But you'd never directly quote like this:

> Wakefield describes what happens "in a subsequent episode, when Elliot and Nancy were separated."

You could easily rephrase that yourself.

WORKING YOUR SOURCE IN SMOOTHLY

Whether you paraphrase or quote directly, you need to show in your prose that you are using material from a source. Quotation marks and parenthetical information after the source material give your reader clues, but it is helpful and correct to introduce such material with a bit of explanation, like, "Dan Wakefield, a *TV Guide* reviewer, observes that . . ." This way, your readers know that Wakefield is not just your next door neighbor, but some kind of an authority. After you explain your source the first time, you can use shorter options for introducing it in the essay: "As Wakefield notes . . . ," "According to one reviewer. . .," or "*TV Guide* observes that . . ."

Many times, you can make most of a sentence your own paraphrase and quote only the telling phrase or key ideas of your source, like this:

> Wakefield asserts that *thirtysomething* is far above the level of ordinary TV fare, saying that it "employs the themes of our greatest literature."

When you integrate a quotation into your own sentence, you have to make sure the grammar matches up. Do not accidentally write:

> Wakefield thinks that the show is "anger as well as joy, arising from real-life conflict."

A smoother verson would read:

> Wakefield thinks that the show portrays "anger as well as joy, arising from real-life conflict."

When you must omit something from a quotation, put in ellipses—three spaced periods used like this:

> Wakefield writes that *thirtysomething* calls to mind "the superb television dramas . . . that I'd begun to think only the British could produce."

DOCUMENTING YOUR SOURCES

You must give your readers enough information so that they themselves could look up the sources you used. You do this by following one of many documentation systems; your teacher, editor, or boss will usually choose one system for you to use and give you examples.

The sample paper we are reproducing here uses the MLA system, which includes two parts: (1) a list of sources with complete publishing information at the end of the paper, and (2) the name of the author and a specific page number in parentheses after each quotation or paraphrase. A sentence in an essay using the Wakefield article might look like this:

> A *TV Guide* reviewer asserts that *thirtysomething* fits his "favorite definition of a novel" (Wakefield 524).

At the end of the essay, if the writer were using the book in your hands, the following entry would appear in an alphabetized list of sources:

> Wakefield, Dan. "Celebrating 'The Small Moments of Discovery.' " *The Writer's Resource*. 3rd ed. Eds. Susan Day and Elizabeth McMahan. New York: McGraw-Hill, 1990. 524–526.

WRITING FROM SOURCES

To give you some practice in writing from sources, we are including another view of *thirtysomething*. This one is not as glowing as Wakefield's. Your job is to write a comparison of the two reviews (see Chapter 8). If you have seen the television series, you may add your own opinion as well. Be sure to document your sources within your essay and list both of them at the end. Look at the sample student essay in this chapter for guidance.

James Hynes

And They Called It Yuppie Love . . .

Living and watching in Iowa City, Hynes is a thinking-man's couch potato whose critiques and reviews of television almost make network television worth watching. His work can be found in *Mother Jones* and *In These Times*. The article we reprint here prompted a marriage proposal from a woman he did not know. Wait until she reads his novel *The Wild Colonial Boy* (Atheneum, 1990).

I don't want to bore you with my problems, but what is a socialist television critic of a certain age to do about *thirtysomething,* ABC's Tuesday night hit? [1]

On the one hand, the temptation is to jerk one's knee, well, rather violently: it's about *yuppies,* for chrissakes; two of the male leads are *advertising men;* the two single woman characters are neurotic as the day is long and only ever talk about the lack of good men; plots hinge on such crises as getting a sitter or whether one should buy one's apartment or rent it; the show's idea of an ethical issue is whether you should hire your friend's ad agency or not; the theme song is vapid, New Age, Windham Hill elevator music . . . my God, I've been possessed by Sam Kinison . . . these people are brain-dead, narcissistic, pathologically self-indulgent and self-pitying *ass-holes.* [2]

They should all choke on their nouvelle cuisine! They should lose limbs in horrible Cuisinart accidents! The brakes should fail on their BMWs and send them shrieking into bridge abutments! *Thirtysomething,* my ass!! THEY SHOULD CALL THIS SHOW *YUPPIESCUM*!!! [3]

The Good Part: Ahem. As I was saying. The problem with this approach is that, on the other hand, *thirtysomething* is, well, *good,* okay? It's stylish, handsomely filmed, extremely well-acted, and, in the sharpness of its wit and the depth of its characterizations, one of the best written shows on primetime television. Not to mention that for those of us who are white and college educated and, okay, over 30, there isn't another show on television that so regularly provides the shock of recognition. [4]

Well, as we socialist TV critics say, I reckon what we got here [5] is a dialectic. But what's unusual about this particular dialectic is not that there are two camps in the debate over *thirtysomething,* not that those who like it, love it, and that those who don't like it, hate it with a passion—although that's certainly often the case. Rather, what's fascinating about *thirtysomething* is that these two mutually exclusive positions are very often held by one person, often at the *same time.* Which changes the debate considerably. So, instead of arguing about whether the show is bad or not (it clearly isn't), the question then becomes, why is a television show this good so goddamn annoying?

What's annoying about *thirtysomething* is pretty obvious, even to its fans. At its worst, the show can be insufferably glib and facile when it aims to be breezy and witty; its characters are often guilty of the worst sort of Neil Simon one-liners, setting each other up for punchlines like characters from *Plaza Suite.* The worst offenders are admen Elliot and Michael, who don't sound like admen so much as they sound the way admen would like us to think they talk. [6]

Designer Culture: And much of the humor depends excessively on a knowledge of yuppie iconography: in the first 15 minutes of one episode, the characters managed to refer to Georgia O'Keeffe, the bestselling novel *Presumed Innocent,* and four movies (*The Philadelphia Story, The Way We Were, The Parent Trap,* and *Now Voyager*). The joke here lies in the simple mention of the names: these yuppie icons don't allude to anything, really. It's just name dropping with movies and books and artists reduced to fetishized commodities. [7]

Then there are the fantasy sequences: hip college professor Gary takes on his tenure committee as Sir Gawain, single photographer Melissa psychoanalyzes herself in double-exposure, Elliot imagines estranged wife Nancy on a date with another man. This stuff was mildly adventurous when *Moonlighting* started doing it (and both shows stole it from Woody Allen, who's been doing it since *Play It Again, Sam*), but by now it's de rigueur for yuppie television, as commonplace as male hugging on sitcoms. (And puh-lease, no more Hitchcock pastiches: leave *North by Northwest* alone!) [8]

More important, though, is the lack of social or political context for these yuppie lives. The show is set in Philadelphia, but it could be anywhere. You see the offices and homes of these people, but nothing else, apart from the usual up-market hangouts: expensive restaurants, movie theaters, video stores. [9]

Dirty Something: Nobody's ever caught in traffic, nobody has to step over junkies in doorways, none of the women ever worry about rape. Evidently nobody on this show gets a morning paper, nobody reads magazines or books (*Presumed Innocent* notwithstanding), nobody listens to *All Things Considered.* And despite being [10] set in the hometown of Bill Cosby—a city with a black mayor that still feels the aftershocks of the MOVE bombing—there is not one black person on *thirtysomething. Hill Street Blues'* imaginary city had more urban verisimilitude than *thirtysomething*'s Philadelphia.

[11] If this were all there was to *thirtysomething,* I could jerk my knee in good conscience and be done with it. The problem is that *thirtysomething* is really two shows, and only one is the sub-Woody Allen comedy of yuppie manners. The other show is an often painfully accurate depiction of modern romance (at least for those of us who are white, college educated, etc.).

[12] Like Allen, *thirtysomething* wants to have it both ways: it wants to be Ingmar Bergman half the time. And unlike Allen, who generally vents his comic and serious urges into different films, *thirtysomething* is often schizophrenic, alternating between *Manhattan* and *Scenes from a Marriage.*

[13] Like no other show on television, *thirtysomething*'s representation of the dodgy relations between men and women can make you squirm. While the rest of the show often comes across like a particularly obnoxious Grape-Nuts ad, the depiction of romantic relationships, both inside and outside of marriage, is a relentless downer, a harrowing series of petty cruelties, bitter arguments, willful misunderstandings, and breathtaking mistakes arising out of egotism, vanity and lust.

[14] When *thirtysomething* is firing on all cylinders—and avoids ending on a note of *St. Elsewhere* sentimentality—it can be almost as clear-eyed and bullshit-free about modern romance as, well, a Bergman film. The show's only been on one season, but already Nancy and Elliot's marriage has blown apart, Melissa has worn her heart on her sleeve for anyone to break, Gary has callously hurt Melissa and at least two other women (by my count). Even Hope and Michael, the show's centerpiece couple, occasionally make the Kramdens look like a happy couple ("One of these days, Hope . . . Bang! Zoom! Right to the moon!").

[15] **Love in the Ruins:** Although some of this comes across as schematic (Gary as overgrown adolescent who won't commit, Melissa as aging ingenue who wants a baby), there's a lot of real pain and confusion reflected here, if the response to the show is any indication. And it is here that the show uses its hip modernism to greatest effect: on the best episode of the first season, a bitter argument between Nancy and Elliot is shown, *Rashomon*-style, from the point of view of the four main characters, each version speaking volumes about the relationships between men and women.

[16] While ignoring the cultural and political legacy of the '60s, the show manages to depict the equivocal aftermath of the sexual revolution with something approaching accuracy. At the risk of sound-

ing like Phil Donahue, this may be the worst time in years to be either single or married, and what's most amazing about *thirtysomething* is that, upon occasion, it comes very close—or as close as prime-time television dares—to saying that relations between men and women are fundamentally hopeless.

[17] This is a pretty unconventional way to sell automobiles and breakfast cereal, and as far as it goes, it's first-rate television, showing without sentiment and without conscious dissembling the way some of us live now. The problem is that even where the show is strongest and most evocative, it is blind-sided by its own lack of context.

[18] For all the harrowing realism of *thirtysomething*'s romantic disappointments, these relationships exist in a social vacuum every bit as complete as that of, say, *Father Knows Best*. Sure, Michael's job affects his home life, but mostly on a "Daddy's tired" level, and the fact that Ellyn's lover is also her boss—which would be a hot potato in real life—is dealt with only in passing, while the show concentrates instead on their mutual reluctance to commit.

[19] In other words, the difficulty between men and women in the '80s is depicted as being purely sexual, as if feminism never existed, as if there were no cultural or economic or political aspect to it. Patriarchy is not at issue anymore, evidently, while the lack of good men is.

[20] In the end, the reason *thirtysomething* annoys as it entertains is that it raises one of the great cultural questions of the late 20th century without attempting an answer, without even being aware, perhaps, that the question is being raised. To wit, why is it that this generation of white, middle-class, baby boom Americans—the best-fed, best-educated, healthiest and wealthiest generation in *history*—is also the *whiniest*? Why aren't they happy with their fabulous jobs and gadgets and lovers? From Woody Allen to Jay McInerny, this most narcissistic of generations is obsessed with its own comfortable misery.

[21] Yet with such exceptions as Walker Percy and Robert Stone, few artists in this skillful outpouring of *New Yorker* ennui have bothered to suggest a reason for this unhappiness, and *thirtysomething* is no exception. Which is a shame, because in its two halves (didn't I say something about a dialectic?)—the comedy of yuppie manners and the tragicomedy of yuppie romance—the show contains the seeds of an answer: the reification of personal relationships in a commodity culture, the fetishization of personal happiness in a world of atomized communities . . .

[22] Something's wrong with the way we live now and everybody knows it, but nobody wants to go the extra distance and say *what* it is. In the end, *thirtysomething* is simply a more cynical and world-

weary *Father Knows Best,* vastly more sophisticated, but a fantasy of the purely personal nevertheless. And at least *Father Knows Best* had the advantage of *knowing* it was a fantasy.

VOCABULARY

All Things Considered	a program on public radio stations examining current events
de rigueur	required by fashion
dialectic	weighing of contradictory facts to resolve the differences
dissembling	faking
ennui	boredom
equivocal	uncertain
evocative	suggestive
fetishized	endowed with magical (or sexual) powers
icon	a sacred image or symbol
iconography	the study of interrelated symbols
ingenue	an actress playing the role of a young woman
Ingmar Bergman	admired Swedish director of serious films
narcissistic	full of self-love
pastiche	an art work imitating the style of another artist
patriarchy	male-controlled culture
veification	objectification
verisimilitude	having the appearance of reality

SAMPLE STUDENT ESSAY

In your writing for this course and others, you may be inspired to refer to other print sources within a piece that is basically your own. The following student essay gives you an idea how to handle these references.

Laurie Dahlberg

That's *Not* Entertainment

In that "sweltering summer of the Negro's legitimate discontent" of 1963, Dr. Martin Luther King delivered his historic speech "I Have A Dream" to a massive, spellbound audience in Washington, D.C. (King 511). Brilliantly delivering those eloquent and passionate words, King demanded for Black Americans all the freedom and dignity promised to them by the Constitution—rights that had been blocked by whites for a century (510). That I knew nothing of eloquent Negroes and stifled freedoms in 1963 can be excused by the fact that I was a five-year-old white suburban girl, but truth be told, the culture had already taught me some fundamentals about Blacks.

My parents tell this anecdote about something that I said one day that summer of '63—one of those innocent, stupid things that kids say, which are regarded as "cute." Fearing the encroaching presence of Blacks in the city, my father had set up our family in one of the nice new suburbs outside Chicago, and one afternoon we were driving back to the city to visit my grandmother. It seems we had pulled up to a toll booth alongside a lot of other cars, and on this hot summery day, we all had our windows open. A nice convertible, top down, pulled up next to us, waiting for the toll. There were a couple of black men in that car. "Oh, look, Mommy," I squealed, leaning out the window and pointing. "There's Amos and Andy!" The men laughed good-naturedly, and my parents smiled nervously, threw a handful of change at the tollgate, and sped on ahead. With the safety of a quarter-mile between us and the convertible, they started laughing uproariously.

The moral of this story would be lost on anyone who does not remember the *Amos and Andy Show,* so let me fill you in. *Amos and Andy* was an old radio show which featured the exploits of two characters who were supposed to be Negroes, but really, they were just white guys who talked like this: "Why, Andy, I is suhprised at you! What you thinkin' you be standin' in?" "Oh, I don' know, Amos, but I sho' hopes it be Shi-NOLA!" The popularity of Amos and Andy precipitated the show's move to television in the late fifties; at that point, they had to find real blacks to play the characters.

People like my parents—people whom Black historian Lerone Bennett refers to as "the guiding light of White morality" (331)—

saw nothing questionable in the content of *Amos and Andy*. On the contrary, they would have told you it was providing Negroes with a marvelous opportunity to break into show business. But there was so much more to it than that. The image of the eyes-a-poppin', stupid yet crafty, scared-of-his-own-shadow Negro characterized by Amos and Andy provided me with my first representation of Blacks, a representation I thoughtlessly applied to Black strangers at the toll booth, much to my parents' thoughtless amusement. This was precisely the way White America wanted it. If we whites had to look at Blacks at all, let them be inane and sassy, but above all, let them be ineffectual clowns who nourished the national myths of the Black experience (Bennett 327–335).

There are still those people who would argue that *Amos and Andy* was intended as entertainment, not to be taken seriously, and that anyone who would find this program offensive—along with the scores of other degrading representations of Blacks in books, films, popular art—just doesn't have a sense of humor. But apart from the questionable amusement value of these images, they were most effective as educational tools, teaching people of all colors to believe that these images represented the real, immutable character of Blacks. Such "entertainment," as innocuous as it seems on the surface, is nothing more than spoon-fed racism, part and parcel of the "manacles of segregation and the chains of discrimination" that Dr. King decried in 1963 (510). So the next time you hear an ethnic joke, consider that chains are forged with cheap laughs.

Works Cited

Bennett, Lerone, Jr. "The Ten Biggest Myths About the Black Family." The Writer's Resource, 3rd ed. Eds. Susan Day and Elizabeth McMahan. New York: McGraw, 1990. 327–335.

King, Martin Luther, Jr. "I Have a Dream." The Writer's Resource. 3rd ed. Eds. Susan Day and Elizabeth McMahan. New York: McGraw, 1990. 510–513.

SUGGESTIONS FOR WRITING FROM SOURCES

You can get more practice in writing from sources by using the works in this book. You can criticize an editorial or political speech using Hechinger's article in Chapter 11 as a source on euphemism and Vonnegut's and Thompson's pieces in Chapter 5 as sources on style and clarity. You can even choose an essay you heartily disagree with and voice your disagreement in a critical paper: paraphrases and quotations from the disputed essay would need documentation. Finally, like the author of the sample essay here, you may be inspired to write an essay that integrates information from two or more selections from this book—an essay on the socialization of children, for example.

Acknowledgments

Sherwood Anderson, "The Untold Lie," from *Winesburg, Ohio* by Sherwood Anderson. Copyright 1919 by B. W. Huebsch. Copyright renewed 1947 by Eleanor Copenhaver Anderson. Reprinted by permission of Viking Penguin, a division of Penguin Books USA, Inc.

Peter Andrews, "The Hating Game." Copyright © 1980 by *Saturday Review.* All rights reserved. Reprinted by permission.

W. H. Auden, "The Unknown Citizen." Copyright 1940 and renewed 1968 by W. H. Auden. Reprinted from *W. H. Auden: Collected Poems* edited by Edward Mendelson, by permission of Random House, Inc. And reprinted by permission of Faber and Faber Ltd. from *Collected Poems* by W. H. Auden.

James Baldwin, "They Don't Make Them Like They Used To (Thank Goodness)" in *Whole Earth Review,* Winter 1985. Reprinted by permission of the author.

Roland Barthes, "Toys" from *Mythologies* by Roland Barthes. Selected and translated from the French by Annette Lavers (first published in French by du Seuil in 1957). Copyright © 1972 by Jonathan Cape, Ltd. Reprinted by permission of Hill and Wang, a division of Farrar, Straus and Giroux, Inc.; the Estate of Roland Barthes; and Jonathan Cape, Ltd.

Sharon Begley, "The Stuff That Dreams Are Made Of," from *Newsweek,* August 14, 1989, © 1989, Newsweek, Inc. All rights reserved. Reprinted by permission.

Robert Benchley, "Why I Am Pale" from *Chips Off the Old Benchley* by Robert Benchley. Copyright 1949 by Gertrude D. Benchley. Reprinted by permission of Harper & Row, Publishers, Inc.

Lerone Bennett, Jr., "The 10 Biggest Myths about the Black Family" in *Ebony,* November 1989. Reprinted by permission of *Ebony* Magazine and Lerone Bennett, Jr., © 1989 Johnson Publishing Company, Inc.

Mary Kay Blakely, "I Do, I Do, I Do . . ." Copyright 1988 by Mary Kay Blakely. Originally appeared in *Ms.* Magazine, December 1988.

Paul Blumberg, "Snarling Cars." Reprinted by permission of *The New Republic,* copyright © 1983, The New Republic, Inc.

Dwight Bolinger and Donald Sears, excerpt from *Aspects of Language* by Dwight Bolinger and Donald Sears, copyright © 1968 by Harcourt Brace Jovanovich, Inc., reprinted by permission of the publisher.

Marisa Bowe, "Black to Basics" in *In These Times,* November 25-December 8, 1978. Reprinted by permission.

Katharine Brush, "Birthday Party." Copyright 1946 by Katharine Brush. Originally published in *The New Yorker.* Reprinted by permission of Thomas S. Brush.

Anton Chekov, "The Darling" from *The Portable Chekhov,* edited and translated by Avrahm Yarmolinsky. Copyright 1947, © 1968 by The Viking Press, Inc. Copyright renewed, © 1975 by Avrahm Yarmolinsky. Reprinted by permission of Viking Penguin, Inc.

Walter Van Tilburg Clark, "The Portable Phonograph" from *The Watchful Gods and Other Stories* by Walter Van Tilburg Clark. Copyright © 1950 by Walker Van Tilburg Clark. Reprinted by permission of International Creative Management, Inc.

Countee Cullen, "Incident," reprinted by permission of GRM Associates, Inc., Agent of the Estate of Ida M. Cullen, from the book *On These I Stand: An Anthology of the Best Poems of Countee Cullen* by Countee Cullen. Copyright 1925 by Harper & Brothers, copyright renewed 1953 by Ida M. Cullen.

E. E. Cummings, "next to of course god america i" is reprinted from *Is 5,* poems by E. E. Cummings, edited by George James Firmage, by permission of Liveright Publishing Corporation. Copyright © 1985 by E. E. Cummings Trust. Copyright 1926 by Horace Liveright. Copyright © 1954 by E. E. Cummings. Copyright © 1985 by George James Firmage.

Laurie Dahlberg, "That's *Not* Entertainment," unpublished student essay. Reprinted by permission.

David Denby, "Walk on the Mild Side" in *Premier* Magazine, October 1989. Reprinted by permission.

Emily Dickinson, "Much Madness Is Divinest Sense." Reprinted by permission of the publishers and the Trustees of Amherst College from *The Poems of Emily Dickinson,* Thomas H. Johnson, ed., Cambridge, Mass.: The Belknap Press of Harvard University Press, copyright 1951, © 1955, 1979, 1983 by the President and Fellows of Harvard College.

Joan Didion, "In Bed" from *The White Album* by Joan Didion. Copyright © 1968, 1979, 1989 by Joan Didion. Reprinted by permission of Farrar, Straus and Giroux, Inc.

Susan J. Douglas, "Flex Appeal, Buns of Steel, and the Body in Question" in *In These Times,* September 7-13, 1988. Reprinted by permission.

Hugh Drummond, "Growing Your Own Revolution" in *Mother Jones,* 1987. Reprinted by permission of *Mother Jones* magazine.

Wayne W. Dyer, "Immobilization," excerpt from *Your Erroneous Zones* by Wayne W. Dyer. Copyright © 1976 by Wayne W. Dyer. Reprinted by permission of Harper & Row, Publishers, Inc.

John E. Eichenlaub, "How to Fight Cold-Proneness," from the book, *A Minnesota Doctor's Home Remedies for Common and Uncommon Ailments* by John E. Eichenlaub, M.D. © 1981. Used by permission of the publishers, Prentice-Hall, Inc., Englewood Cliffs, N.J.

Loren Eiseley, "The Bird and the Machine." Copyright © 1955 by Loren Eiseley. Reprinted from *The Immense Journey* by Loren Eiseley, by permission of Random House, Inc.

Harlan Ellison, "Books, TV, and the Human Imagination" by Harlan Ellison (excerpted from the introduction to the author's short story collection *Strange Wine*), copyright © 1978 by Harlan Ellison. Reprinted by arrangement with, and permission of, the author and the author's agent, Richard Curtis Associates, Inc., New York. All rights reserved.

Lawrence Ferlinghetti, "The World Is a Beautiful Place," from *A Coney Island of the Mind.* Copyright © 1958 by Lawrence Ferlinghetti. Reprinted by permission of New Directions Publishing Corporation.

E. M. Forster, "The Other Side of the Hedge," from *The Collected Tales* of E. M. Forster. Published 1947 by Alfred A. Knopf, Inc. Reprinted by permission of the publisher; King's College, Cambridge; and The Society of Authors as the literary representatives of the E. M. Forster Estate.

John Hope Franklin, "The Psychological Situation of Slavery," from *From Slavery to Freedom,* 4th edition, by John Hope Franklin. Copyright © 1974 by Alfred A. Knopf, Inc. Reprinted by permission of the publisher.

Robert Frost, "Departmental" and "Out, Out," from *The Poetry of Robert Frost* edited by Edward Connery Lathem. Copyright 1916, © 1969 by Holt, Rinehart and Winston. Copyright 1936, 1944, by Robert Frost. Copyright © 1964 by Lesley Frost Ballantine. Reprinted by permission of Henry Holt and Company, Inc.

Ellen Goodman, "We Do Not Need More Talk of War" as it appeared in *The Pantagraph,* September 1989. © 1989, The Boston Globe Newspaper Co./Washington Post Writers Group. Reprinted with permission.

Michael Greene and Beverly Rainbolt, "He Doesn't Hit Me, But . . ." in *Woman,* July 1989. Reprinted with special permission of North America Syndicate.

Dick Gregory, "Not Poor, Just Broke," from *Nigger: An Autobiography* by Dick Gregory, with Robert Lipsyte. Copyright © 1964 by Dick Gregory Enterprises, Inc. Reprinted by permission of the publisher, Dutton, an imprint of New American Library, a division of Penguin Books USA, Inc.

Robert Guillain, "I Thought My Last Hour Had Come . . . ," from *I Saw Tokyo Burning.* Reprinted by permission of Doubleday, a division of Bantam, Doubleday, Dell Publishing Group, Inc.

Jan Halvorsen, "How It Feels to Be out of Work" in *Newsweek* 1980.

Fred Hechinger, "In the End Was the Euphemism." Copyright © 1974 by *Saturday Review.* Reprinted by permission.

Christopher Hitchens, "Wanton Acts of Usage." Copyright © 1986 by *Harper's Magazine.* All rights reserved. Reprinted from the September issue by special permission.

Roy Hoffman, "How to Say Thank You." Copyright © 1982 by Roy Hoffman. Originally printed in *Esquire,* September 1982. Reprinted by permission of Melanie Jackson Agency.

A. E. Housman, from "A Shropshire Lad"—Authorized Edition—from *The Collected Poems of A. E. Housman.* Copyright 1939, 1940, © 1965 by Holt, Rinehart and Winston. Copyright © 1967, 1968 by Robert E. Symons. Reprinted by permission of Henry Holt and Company, Inc.

Jane Howard, "Arethra Has the Best Man," excerpt from *Families* by Jane Howard. Copyright © 1978 by Jane Howard. Reprinted by permission of Simon & Schuster, Inc.

Langston Hughes, "Salvation," from *The Big Sea* by Langston Hughes. Copyright © 1940 by Langston Hughes. Renewal copyright © 1968 by Arna Bontemps and George Houston Bass. Reprinted by permission of Hill and Wang, a division of Farrar, Straus and Giroux, Inc.

Deairich Hunter, "Ducks vs. Hard Rocks" in *Newsweek* 1980. Reprinted by permission of the author.

Kaatje Hurlbut, "Eve in Darkness," in *Mademoiselle,* December 1957. Copyright © 1957 by Kaatje Hurlbut. Reprinted by permission of McIntosh and Otis, Inc.

James Hynes, "And They Called It Yuppie Love . . . ," in *In These Times,* June 22-July 5, 1988. Reprinted by permission.

Randall Jarrell, "The Death of the Ball Turret Gunner," from *The Complete Poems* by Randall Jarrell. Copyright © 1945, 1972 by Mrs. Randall Jarrell. Reprinted by permission of Farrar, Straus and Giroux, Inc.

James Joyce, "Eveline," from *Dubliners* by James Joyce. Copyright 1916 by B. W. Huebsch. Definitive text copyright © 1967 by the Estate of James Joyce. Reprinted by permission of Viking Penguin, a division of Penguin Books USA, Inc.

Larry L. King, "Getting 'Em Ready for Darrell," from *The Old Man and Lesser Mortals* by Larry L. King. Copyright © 1979 by Larry L. King. Reprinted by permission of Viking Penguin, a division of Penguin Books USA, Inc.

Martin Luther King, Jr., "I Have a Dream" speech. Copyright © 1963 by Martin Luther King, Jr. Reprinted by permission of Joan Daves.

Seymour Krim, "Men in Bondage on an Easter Morning," excerpt from *Shake It for the World, Smartass* by Seymour Krim, copyright © 1970 by Seymour Krim. Used by permission of Doubleday, a division of Bantam, Doubleday, Dell Publishing Group, Inc.

D. H. Lawrence, "Baby Running Barefoot," from *The Complete Poems of D. H. Lawrence,* collected and edited by Vivian de Sola Pinto and F. Warren Roberts. Copyright © 1964, 1971 by Angelo Ravagli and C. M. Weekley, Executors of The Estate of Frieda Lawrence Ravagli. Reprinted by permission of Viking Penguin, a division of Penguin Books USA, Inc.

F. L. Lucas, "Brevity" from "On the Fascination of Style" in *Holiday* magazine, March 1960. Lucas has written on the same subject in his book *Style,* published by Macmillan Publishing Co., Inc.

J. C. Mathes, "Technical Communication: The Persuasive Purpose" in *English in Texas,* Summer 1980. Copyright © 1980. Reprinted by permission of the author.

Harry Middleton, "Trouble on the Wind" in *Southern Living.* Copyright Southern Living, Inc., September 1989. Reprinted with permission.

Edna St. Vincent Millay, "Oh, Oh, You Will Be Sorry for that Word!" and "The Spring and the Fall" by Edna St. Vincent Millay. Copyright 1923, 1951 by Edna St. Vincent Millay and Norma Millay Ellis. Reprinted by permission of Elizabeth Barnett, Literary Executor.

Jonathan Miller, "Your Reflex System," excerpt from *The Body in Question* by Jonathan Miller. Copyright © 1978 by Jonathan Miller. Reprinted by permission of Random House, Inc., and Jonathan Cape Ltd.

Joan Morgan, "The Pro-Rape Culture" as it appeared in *The Village Voice,* May 9, 1989. Copyright © 1989 by Joan Morgan. Reprinted by permission of the author.

Ann Nietzke, "Doin' Somebody Wrong." Copyright © 1975 *Human Behavior* magazine. Reprinted by permission.

Tillie Olsen, "I Stand Here Ironing," excerpted from the book *Tell Me a Riddle* by Tillie Olsen. Copyright © 1956, 1957, 1960, 1961 by Tillie Olsen. Reprinted by permission of Delacorte Press/Seymour Lawrence.

George Orwell, "A Hanging" from *Shooting an Elephant and Other Essays* by George Orwell, copyright 1950 by Sonia Brownell Orwell and renewed 1978 by Sonia Pitt-Rivers, reprinted by permission of Harcourt Brace Jovanovich, Inc., the estate of the late Sonia Brownell Orwell, and Secker & Warburg.

Wilfred Owen, "Dulce et Decorum Est" from *Collected Poems of Wilfred Owen.* Copyright © 1963 by Chatto & Windus Ltd. Reprinted by permission of New Directions Publishing Corporation and Chatto and Windus Ltd.

Clarence Page, "The Trouble with Legalizing Drugs" in *Chicago Tribune,* Sunday, September 24, 1989. Reprinted by permission: Tribune Media Services.

Dorothy Parker, "Résumé," from *The Portable Dorothy Parker.* Copyright 1926, renewed © 1954 by Dorothy Parker. Reprinted by permission of Viking Penguin, a division of Penguin Books USA, Inc.

Katherine Anne Porter, "Rope," from *Flowering Judas and Other Stories,* copyright 1930 and renewed 1958 by Katherine Anne Porter, reprinted by permission of Harcourt Brace Jovanovich, Inc.

Andrew Potok, "Dash and Me," in *Life* Magazine, July 1988. © Time Warner Inc.

Ezra Pound, "In a Station of the Metro," from *Personae*. Copyright 1926 by Ezra Pound. Reprinted by permission of New Directions Publishing Corporation.

Henry Reed, "Naming of Parts," from *A Map of Verona* by Henry Reed. Reprinted by permission of John Tydeman, BBC Radio and Drama.

Adrienne Rich, "Living in Sin" is reprinted from *Poems, Selected and New, 1950-1974,* by Adrienne Rich, with the permission of W. W. Norton & Company, Inc. Copyright © 1975, 1973, 1971, 1969, 1966 by W. W. Norton & Company, Inc. Copyright © 1967, 1963, 1962, 1961, 1960, 1959, 1958, 1957, 1956, 1955, 1954, 1953, 1952, 1951, by Adrienne Rich.

Saab ad as it appeared in *Newsweek,* June 12, 1988. Reprinted by permission of Saab-Scania of America, Inc.

Richard Selzer, "An Absence of Windows," from *Confessions of a Knife* by Richard Selzer. Copyright © 1979 by David Goldman and Janet Selzer, Trustees. By permission of William Morrow & Co.

Anne Sexton, "You All Know the Story of the Other Woman," from *Love Poems* by Anne Sexton. Copyright 1967, 1968, 1969 by Anne Sexton. Reprinted by permission of Houghton Mifflin Co.

Karl Shapiro, "Auto Wreck," from *Collected Poems 1940-1978* by Karl Shapiro. © 1978 by Karl Shapiro, c/o Wieser & Wieser, Inc., 118 East 25th St., New York, NY 10010.

Laurence Sheehan, "Fighting Bugs Organically." Originally appeared in *Harper's Magazine*. Reprinted by permission of Lawrence Sheehan.

Earl Shorris, "How 114 Washing Machines Came to the Crow Reservation," from *Death of the Great Spirit* by Earl Shorris. Copyright © 1971 by Earl Shorris. Reprinted by permission of Simon & Schuster, Inc.

Alan J. Simpson and Robert Allen Baker, Jr., "The Twenty-Third Psalm," from *A Stress Analysis of a Strapless Evening Gown*. Reprinted by generous permission of Robert A. Baker.

Bernard Sloan, "Aunt Charlotte's Reward." Copyright 1980 by Newsweek, Inc. All rights reserved. Reprinted by permission.

"Body by Soloflex" ad as it appeared in *Newsweek,* July 18, 1983. Reprinted by permission of 53rd Street Advertising.

Benjamin Spock, "Are You Giving Your Kids Too Much?" Copyright © 1988 by Benjamin Spock, M.D. Originally appeared in *Redbook* November 1988. Reprinted by permission.

Betty Lee Sung, "Bicultural Conflict," from *The Adjustment Experience of Chinese Immigrant Children* by Betty Lee Sung, Professor and Chair, Department of Asian Studies, City College, New York. Copyright © 1987 by Betty Lee Sung. Reprinted by permission of the author.

Judy Syfers, "Why I Want a Wife." Reprinted by permission of the author. Originally appeared in *Ms.,* December 1971.

Thomas Szasz, "Our Despotic Laws Destroy the Right to Self Control" in *Psychology Today,* December 1974. Reprinted with permission from *Psychology Today* Magazine. Copyright © 1974 (PT Partners, L.P.).

Hernando Tellez "Just Lather, That's All" in *Great Spanish Short Stories* edited by Angel Flores, translated by Donald Yeats. Dell, 1962.

Dylan Thomas, "Do Not Go Gentle into That Good Night" from *Poems of Dylan Thomas.* Copyright 1952 by Dylan Thomas. Reprinted by permission of New Directions Publishing Corporation and David Higham Associates Ltd.

Edward T. Thompson, "How to Write Clearly." Copyright International Paper Co. Reprinted by permission.

James Thurber, "Generalization," copyright © 1953 James Thurber. Copyright © 1981 Helen Thurber and Rosemary A. Thurber. From *Thurber Country,* published by Simon & Schuster, Inc. "Which Which," copyright © 1931, 1959 James Thurber. From *The Owl in the Attic,* published by Harper & Row, Publishers, Inc.

Tom Tiede, "Another Copter's Comin' In, Cap'n." Reprinted by permission of Newspaper Enterprise Association.

"Tune In, Tune Out," in *In These Times,* October 8-14, 1986. Reprinted by permission.

Mark Twain, "Boyhood Remembered," from *Mark Twain's Autobiography.* Copyright 1924 by Clara Gabrilowitsch. Copyright renewed 1952 by Clara Clemens Samossoud. "The Lowest Animal," from *Mark Twain Letters from the Earth,* edited by Bernard De Voto. Copyright © 1962 by The Mark Twain Company. "The War Prayer," from *Europe and Elsewhere* by Mark Twain. Copyright 1923, 1951 by The Mark Twain Company. Reprinted by permission of Harper & Row, Publishers, Inc.

Gore Vidal, "Drugs," from *Homage to Daniel Shays* by Gore Vidal. Copyright © 1972 by Gore Vidal. Reprinted by permission of Random House, Inc.

Judith Viorst, "Friends, Good Friends—and Such Good Friends." Copyright © 1977 by Judith Viorst. Reprinted by permission of Lescher & Lescher, Ltd.

Kurt Vonnegut, Jr., "How to Write with Style." Copyright International Paper Company. Reprinted by permission. "What I'd Say if They Asked Me," in *The Nation,* July 16, 1988. Reprinted by permission of The Nation Company, Inc.

William Carlos Williams, "The Use of Force," from *The Farmer's Daughters.* Copyright 1938 by William Carlos Williams. Reprinted by permission of New Directions Publishing Corporation.

Dan Wakefield, "Celebrating 'The Small Moments of Personal Discovery.' " Reprinted with permission from *TV Guide®* Magazine. Copyright © 1988 by News America Publications, Inc., Radnor, Pennsylvania.

Dereck Williamson, "Wall Covering," from *The Complete Book of Pitfalls: A Victim's Guide to Repairs, Maintenance, and Repairing the Maintenance* by Dereck Williamson. Copyright 1971 by Dereck Williamson. Reprinted by permission of the author. "The Mudbacks," copyright © 1971 by *Saturday Review.* All rights reserved. Reprinted by permission.

Virginia Woolf, "Shakespeare's Sister," excerpt from *A Room of One's Own* by Virginia Woolf, copyright 1929 by Harcourt Brace Jovanovich, Inc., and renewed 1957 by Leonard Woolf, reprinted by permission of the publisher, the Executors of the Virginia Woolf Estate, and The Hogarth Press.

INDEX OF AUTHORS AND TITLES